January 2014

The Reverend
Buford W. Braswell

BISHOPS,
BOURBONS,
and BIG MULES

BISHOPS, BOURBONS, *and* BIG MULES

A History of the Episcopal Church in Alabama

J. Barry Vaughn

THE UNIVERSITY OF ALABAMA PRESS
Tuscaloosa

Typeface: Garamond

Cover image: "Gifts of Grace," St. Paul's Episcopal Church, Lowndesboro, Alabama.
From the series Alabama Churches in Watercolor, © Bob Moody. Courtesy of the
artist. www.moodypaints.com
Author photograph: © Michael Mixon, Hanging Around Hoover, Inc.
Cover design: Erin Bradley Dangar / Dangar Design

Interior figures 1-7 and 9-11 are courtesy of the Birmingham Public Library Archives

∞

The paper on which this book is printed meets the minimum requirements of
American National Standard for Information Sciences—Permanence of Paper for
Printed Library Materials, ANSI Z39.48-1984.

Library of Congress Cataloging-in-Publication Data

Vaughn, J. Barry, 1955–
    Bishops, Bourbons, and big mules : a history of the Episcopal Church in Alabama /
J. Barry Vaughn.
        pages cm. — (Religion and American culture)
    Includes bibliographical references and index.
    ISBN 978-0-8173-1811-6 (trade cloth : alk. paper) — ISBN 978-0-8173-8721-1
(e book) 1. Episcopal Church—Alabama—History. 2. Alabama—Church history.
3. Episcopal Church—Influence. I. Title.
    BX5917.A2V38 2013
    283'.761—dc23

                                                            2013015884

To my mother,
Vera Roper Vaughn,
my first and best teacher,
and to the memory of my father,
Henry Clay Vaughn

Contents

Photographs follow page 100.

Acknowledgments

The Episcopal Diocese of Alabama celebrated its 175th anniversary in 2005. Its history touches on a number of important topics in national, regional, and denominational history. Remarkably, however, only one historian has told its story, and that was over a century ago. Walter Whitaker, rector of Christ Church, Tuscaloosa, did an excellent job in his *History of the Protestant Episcopal Church in Alabama, 1763–1891*. Whitaker also published a good biography of Alabama's second bishop, titled *Richard Hooker Wilmer, Second Bishop of Alabama: A Biography*. However, Whitaker failed to document his sources. Prior to the twentieth century, it was not unusual for amateur historians (and even some professional historians) to do this, but it is a major nuisance for those of us who follow in their footsteps. Nevertheless, his work is useful and was updated by Thomas McAdory Owen and Marie Bankhead Owen, who added some material pertaining to the early twentieth century. I seek to update further the history of the Episcopal Church in Alabama, a story worth telling not only for its own sake but also for the light it sheds on the history of the state and on the Episcopal Church USA of which it is a part. The faults and failings of this book are mine alone; for its strengths and virtues I owe innumerable debts to others. The number is legion of those whose help, often intangible, was nonetheless so essential that no words of gratitude could ever be adequate.

I am grateful to the scholars who have made contributions to the history of the Episcopal Church in Alabama. Chief among these is Barbara Brandon Schnorrenberg. She has written histories of Grace Episcopal Church and St. Andrew's Episcopal Church (both in Birmingham) as well as several articles and papers chronicling women and African Americans in Alabama. Dr. Schnorrenberg graciously and generously shared her research with me and immeasurably enriched my study of the history of the Episcopal Church in Alabama. Also, Jonathan Bass of Samford University contributed to our understanding of the Episcopal Church's response to the civil rights movement in *Blessed Are the Peacemakers*, his study of the eight white religious leaders who wrote to Martin Luther King Jr., urging him to postpone his Birmingham campaign in 1963.

Thanks, also, to all the faithful folks who maintain parish archives and especially to those who have written parish histories. I am grateful to these chroniclers of Alabama's parishes for telling stories that would otherwise be forgotten. Especially helpful to me were Ronald Caldwell's history of St. Luke's, Jacksonville, and St. Luke's, Cahaba; Frances Roberts's *Sesquicentennial History of Church of the Nativity, Episcopal, 1843–1993*; Lynn Willoughby's history of Ascension, Montgomery, *The Church of the Ascension: A Resurrection Story*; and Henry Walker's *Let Us Keep the Feast*, a history of Christ Episcopal Church in Tuscaloosa.

The best of the parish histories is *From the Day of Small Things*, a history of Trinity, Mobile, by its retired rector, S. Albert Kennington. Father Kennington not only wrote a superb history of his parish, he also served for many years as historiographer of the Diocese of the Central Gulf Coast. Albert quickly responded to my numerous e-mails asking for information about Alabama's second diocese. He and Kit Caffey, who succeeded Albert as historiographer, were invaluable resources for the history of the Central Gulf Coast.

Dr. Thomas Oey of the People's Republic of China, a Baptist church historian, graciously shared his research into the early Episcopal missionaries to China and the remarkable connections between the Diocese of Alabama and China. Stephen McNair, who at the time of this writing is working on his PhD at the University of Edinburgh, helpfully shared his research and insights with me, especially with regard to the architecture of some of Alabama's earliest Episcopal churches.

William Yon is a vast repository of information about more recent history in the Diocese of Alabama (as well as being a wonderful person and fine priest). I'm grateful for the questions he answered and for the use of his unpublished autobiography, *No Trumpets, No Drums*. Many other individuals were kind and helpful in sharing their memories and answering questions. Anne and Joe Knight of Selma have been staunch friends for years, and Anne was indispensable in helping me find documents at St. Paul's, Selma, and articles from the *Selma Times-Journal*, which her father, Roswell Falkenberry, edited. Patrick Cather has an excellent collection of Alabamiana, including some items related to the Episcopal Church that can be found nowhere else. I am grateful to him for letting me browse through his library and for much else. Attorney Charles Hart of Gadsden was a fellow member of the Diocese of Alabama's Taskforce on Slavery and Racial Reconciliation and brought to my attention some useful and important facts about Holy

Comforter, Gadsden. My college friend Frank McPhillips, whose father, Julian McPhillips, was rector of St. Luke's, Mountain Brook, during the civil rights era, shared his parents' unpublished autobiography (*The Drummer's Beat: Our Life and Times*), the sermon his father preached a week after the "Bloody Sunday" march in Selma, and the research he did for his senior thesis on the church and the civil rights movement. My colleague Brandt Montgomery wrote a very fine MDiv thesis about Bishop Charles Colcock Jones Carpenter and the civil rights movement that I found helpful. I must also thank Vernon Jones, Lee Martin, Mary Adelia McLeod, Camille Morgan, and Yvonne Willie. I am also grateful to all my colleagues who made room for me to plug in my laptop and work in a corner of their church offices and let me rummage in the dusty closets that contained their old vestry minutes and other church records.

Douglas Carpenter, a retired priest in the Diocese of Alabama and the son of Alabama's sixth bishop, Charles Colcock Jones Carpenter, allowed me to look at some of Bishop Carpenter's papers that are not in the diocesan archives. While I am critical of the role that Bishop Carpenter played in the civil rights movement, I believe that Doug's father served the diocese to the best of his ability and left behind a great legacy of service and achievement.

This book began in 1995 when I was rector of St. Stephen's in Eutaw, Alabama, and also teaching at the University of Alabama. One of my students, blessed with an entrepreneurial streak, published *Our Church*, a collection of photographs he had taken of all the churches in the Diocese of Alabama,[1] and I wrote a short essay on the history of the Episcopal Church in Alabama as an introduction to it. After several years serving parishes in other states, I returned to Alabama in 2005; then work began in earnest.

Writing this book has made me acutely aware that the librarians and archivists who preserve the history of the South in general and Alabama in particular do indispensable work and receive far too little recognition. I must say a special word of thanks to the staff of the Linn-Henley Research Library at the Birmingham Public Library, an unparalleled resource for studying southern history; the Alabama Department of Archives and History; the W. S. Hoole Special Collections Library at the University of Alabama; the Archives of the Episcopal Church at the Seminary of the Southwest in Austin, Texas; Samford University's Special Collections (where, in a gracious ecumenical spirit, they maintain not only the parish records of their own denomination [Baptist] but also those of Roman Catholics, United Methodists, Presbyterians, Jews, and Episcopalians); and the Southern History Collection at the University of North Carolina–Chapel Hill. The University of the South at Sewanee, Tennessee, has had a special relationship with the Episcopal Church in Alabama since Alabama's first bishop, Nicholas Hamner Cobbs, participated in its founding. Sewanee's Jessie Ball duPont Library is a wonderful resource for all things Anglican, especially relating to the Episcopal Church in the South. I am grateful for its helpful staff and its handy location.

Several fellow historians went above and beyond in rendering assistance. My friend and parishioner Tennant McWilliams, a retired professor of history at the University of Alabama–Birmingham, critiqued the entire manuscript and gave generously of his time and wise counsel. Leah Rawls Atkins read an early draft of the first chapter, critiqued it, and encouraged me. Thomas Merrill, another friend and parishioner and an excellent genealogist and amateur historian, helped me track down information about some of Alabama's priests and bishops.

While writing this book I served as rector of St. Alban's Episcopal Church in Birmingham's Bluff Park neighborhood. My parishioners heard far more than they cared to about this book and learned to stop asking, "When will it be finished?" They gave me the time and freedom I needed to complete this history and also made a place for me in their hearts. I am deeply grateful to them.

The Birmingham Public Library's Department of Archives and Manuscripts maintains the archives of the Diocese of Alabama, and my deepest thanks go to its director, James Baggett, and his staff. For many years, the archives of the diocese have been on deposit there, and this is an especially happy arrangement. I know of no other diocese (including some far larger and wealthier ones) whose historically important documents are as well maintained and well cataloged as the Diocese of Alabama. Furthermore, this work is all done without any financial compensation from the diocese. The staff maintains the papers of the bishops of Alabama from Cobbs to Stough, as well as official diocesan documents and innumerable items related to the parishes and institutions of the diocese. They have undertaken the Herculean task of creating a database of all the baptism, confirmation, marriage, and death records of the parishes and making the database available online; they are making good progress toward realizing this goal. Without the work they do, the stuff of history (letters, journals, newspapers, official documents, and so on) would either be deteriorating in a closet somewhere or would long ago have been tossed out with the garbage. Very few Episcopalians in Alabama are aware of this remarkable resource, but the diocese should give "most hearty thanks" for Jim's and his staff's work. Jim is also one of my best friends, and I am grateful for his stewardship of the diocesan archives and even more for his friendship. This book would not have been possible without his support and advice.

I also thank Dan Waterman and his staff at the University of Alabama Press who patiently helped me turn my manuscript into a book. Special thanks to my wonderful staff at Christ Church, Las Vegas, who helped me prepare the index.

My deepest and warmest gratitude goes to the people who loved me and believed in me and taught me life's most important lessons. Among these are my uncle, the late Cecil M. Roper, professor at Southwestern Baptist Theological

Seminary for thirty years; Gordon Kaufman of Harvard and George Lindbeck of Yale, who taught me to think theologically; and B. R. White, former principal of Regent's Park College, Oxford, who helped me become a church historian.

Sadly, the Reverend Professor Peter J. Gomes, Pusey Minister in Harvard University's Memorial Church, died while I was writing this book. I shook Peter's hand at the door of Memorial Church on Freshman Sunday in 1974, and we were friends for the next thirty-seven years. Peter taught the first church history class I ever took and indirectly had a lot to do with the writing of this book and with much else that is good in my life. He generously gave me a C for the essay I wrote for his seminar on New England history, but I would like to think that this book might have persuaded him to revise and upgrade his opinion of my abilities as a historian.

Above all I must thank my mother, Vera Roper Vaughn, a teacher and principal for forty years, who was my first and best teacher; and my father, the late Henry Clay Vaughn. To them I dedicate this book.

BISHOPS, BOURBONS, *and* BIG MULES

Introduction

When most people hear the words *religion* and *Alabama,* they rarely think first of the Book of Common Prayer and mitred bishops. They are more likely to conjure up images of fire-and-brimstone preaching, tent revivals, and converts being immersed in river water. For example, when an Israeli concert pianist with whom I studied while an undergraduate at Harvard came to give a concert in Birmingham, she mentioned to a friend in New York that she was going to visit a former student who was now a minister in Alabama. "How did that happen?" her friend exclaimed.

Although clergy of the Church of England began to establish parishes in the South soon after the founding of Jamestown in 1607 and dominated the southern religious landscape until the Revolutionary War, scholars of southern religion have long accepted that the First and Second Great Awakenings (especially the latter) transformed the South and made evangelicalism the dominant influence in southern religion. Judging by the number of Baptist and Methodist churches (not to mention the kind of preaching one hears via radio and television), this appears to be correct. And yet Episcopalians served as governors of Alabama for twenty years of the twentieth century, and four of the twenty-eight governors Alabamians elected between 1900 and 2000 were Episcopalians.[1] Although the number of Episcopalians in Alabama has usually been below 1 percent, about 10 percent of Alabama's governors, legislators, congressmen, and other significant leaders have been members of the Episcopal Church. Despite their small numbers, Episcopalians have always been overrepresented at the upper levels of social, cultural, economic, and political leadership in Alabama. Although it does not dominate popular culture, the Episcopal Church wields an extraordinary amount of influence in the Heart of Dixie.

Clergy of the Church of England served the spiritual needs of the garrison at Fort Charlotte in Mobile between 1763 and 1780, but the history of the Episcopal Church in Alabama really begins in 1828, when Christ Church, Tuscaloosa, and Christ Church, Mobile, were organized within a few weeks of each other.[2] Two years later, Thomas Brownell, the bishop of Connecticut, presided at the organizing convention of the Diocese of Alabama, which took place at Christ Church, Mobile, in January. When Bishop Brownell came to Mobile, there were three Episcopal churches in Alabama: Christ Church, Mobile; Christ Church, Tuscaloosa; and St. Paul's, Greensboro. However, the delegates to the first few conventions of the Diocese of Alabama included George W. Owen, a mayor of Mobile who represented the Alabama Territory in Congress; Samuel H. Garrow, another mayor of Mobile and member of Alabama's first constitutional convention; Abner Lipscomb, a future secretary of state of the Republic of Texas; and John Gayle, governor of Alabama from 1831 to 1835.[3]

Alabama's most powerful citizens have long been more likely to occupy the pews of the Episcopal Church than those of other denominations. In his biography of Nicholas Hamner Cobbs, Alabama's first Episcopal bishop, author Greenough White wrote: "the Episcopal was the slaveholders' church . . . it was in fact the church of a class." According to historian Charles Reagan Wilson, "While the Baptists and Methodists were numerically dominating the Southern religious picture, the Presbyterians managed to hold their own in terms of influence because their ministers were well educated and their congregations tended to include prominent societal leaders. Similarly, the Episcopal church was the church of the planter class, concentrated in Virginia, coastal South Carolina, and the Mississippi delta."[4]

The title of this book is also its thesis: Bishops govern the Episcopal Church, but Bourbons and "Big Mules" have also dominated its history in Alabama. "Bourbon" was a name given to the planters after the Civil War. Just as France's royal house, the Bourbons, survived the revolution of 1789 and returned to power following the defeat of Napoleon, so the planters of the South survived the Civil War and following Reconstruction returned to power in the 1870s. In 1934 Governor Bibb Graves dubbed Alabama's industrial barons the "Big Mules." Like the planters, they, too, tended to worship in Episcopal churches. For example, several members of the Elyton Land Company that launched Birmingham were Episcopalians, and the Noble family members who founded Anniston were also Episcopalians. Most Alabama Episcopalians have been wealthy and powerful people (for example, the planters, their heirs, and the industrialists); and a disproportionate number of Alabama's wealthy and powerful people have been Episcopalians.[5]

Alabama's earliest Episcopal churches were heavily concentrated in the Black Belt, the wide swath of rich, black soil that runs from northeast to southwest across the middle of the state that was the heartland of plantation culture. When Alabama's Episcopalians elected their first bishop in 1844, seven of Alabama's eight Episcopal churches were in this region, and the lone exception, Christ Church, Mobile, was in a city whose economy was dependent on the plantations.

In being the church of the powerful and affluent, the Episcopal Church in Alabama is a microcosm of the Episcopal Church USA. Kit and Frederica Konolige put it well at the conclusion of their sociological study of the Episcopal Church, *The Power of Their Glory*: "[The Episcopal Church] was . . . the cause of great opportunity in the United States, the foundation of public service, of a massive tradition of private support of irreplaceable public institutions, the root of much that was best in political thought and practice. . . . To a large degree, the Episcopal Church produced, like it or not, America."[6] Could one say that the Episcopal Church also produced Alabama? Not quite. The Episcopal Church in Alabama has been the church of an extraordinary number of Alabama's leaders, but it has not produced the institutions (e.g., colleges, universities, hospitals, and such) that have shaped life in Alabama. The Episcopal Church's failure to produce an "institutional legacy" in Alabama is a topic to which I shall return in the conclusion.

Nevertheless, Episcopalians have played large and heroic roles in the history of Alabama. Emma Jones, a member of Mobile's Christ Church, was one of the first two women who served as missionaries for the Episcopal Church in China. Another well-known Alabamian affiliated with the Episcopal Church was William Lowndes Yancey, a member of the vestry both at St. Luke's, Cahaba, and St. John's, Montgomery, who played a critical role in fomenting secession. Scottish immigrant Kate Cumming of St. John's, Mobile, nursed wounded soldiers within earshot of Union artillery. Hilary Herbert, of St. Thomas, Greenville, served as Grover Cleveland's secretary of the navy. Zelda Sayre Fitzgerald was baptized at Holy Comforter, Montgomery, and, with her husband, F. Scott Fitzgerald, practically defined the Jazz Age. St. Mary's, Jasper, claims the flamboyant actress Tallulah Bankhead, who was the daughter of the speaker of the US House of Representatives and the niece of a US senator. In the aftermath of the 1963 bombing of Sixteenth Street Baptist Church in Birmingham, a member of St. Luke's, Mountain Brook, attorney Charles Morgan, told the Young Men's Business Association that Birmingham was "dead."

The parish clergy and bishops of the Episcopal Church in Alabama have often led the Episcopal Church at the national level. Henry C. Lay, who virtually refounded Nativity Church, Huntsville, was a prisoner of war during the Civil War and served as the first bishop of Arkansas and later bishop of Easton (Maryland).

Theodore Roosevelt admired Edgar Gardner Murphy, the rector of St. John's, Montgomery, for his expertise on the problem of child labor. Selma native John Gardner Murray was rector of Church of the Advent, Birmingham, bishop of Maryland, and was the first elected Presiding Bishop of the Episcopal Church. Mary Adelia McLeod, ordained in Alabama (as were her husband and later her son), was elected bishop of Vermont in 1993 and was the first woman to lead a diocese in the Episcopal Church. The bishops of the Episcopal Church in Alabama have opposed secession, ordered their clergy not to pray for the president of the United States, been forced from power because of their high-handed ways, worked with leaders of other churches and the American Civil Liberties Union to seek justice for poor black men accused of sexually assaulting white women, and built housing for low-income elderly people. Three have been candidates for Presiding Bishop of the Episcopal Church (though none have yet been elected to that office).[7]

Too often church history means a history of the clergy. Sometimes it also means a history of the ideas and institutions of the Christian church and its denominations. Surely church history should also be a history of all those who call themselves Christians, the vast majority of whom are not ordained. Wherever possible I have tried to include the stories of lay Episcopalians. They are the ones who, for better or worse, have exercised the greatest influence on Alabama's history. However, the material with which I have worked has imposed certain constraints. Because bishops govern the Episcopal Church, most of the material in the archives of the Episcopal Church in Alabama is related to its bishops. Where possible I have also consulted the records of individual parishes, but vestries are charged with overseeing the finances and physical plants of the parishes, not with worship, theology, and mission. Most vestry minutes are the tedious records of paying bills and raising money.

The story of the Episcopal Church in Alabama is a story of a diocese that covered an entire state until it divided in 1970. It is the story of parishes large and small, and their struggles to survive and be faithful. It is the story of bishops, priests, and deacons, but it is no less the story of its lay leaders who have always greatly outnumbered the ordained leaders and whose commitment to the faith has often outshone the clergy. This book is the story of the men and women of the Episcopal Church in Alabama and of the church they built and the institutions they launched. It is the story of how they shaped Alabama's history and how that history shaped them. In many ways, the story of the Episcopal Church in Alabama *is* the story of Alabama.

I
How Anglicanism Came to America

Long before there was an Episcopal Church, the Church of England established itself in English settlements on the east coast of the North American continent. It has been said that Great Britain acquired its empire in a fit of absent-mindedness; one could say the same about the Anglican Communion.[1] The cross followed the flag, and wherever English colonists sought riches or adventure, the Church of England came along to minister to their spiritual needs. Thus a global empire spawned a global church. In eighteenth-century Boston, New York, Philadelphia, and Charleston, members of the Church of England worshiped in impressive churches and could count governors, legislators, and wealthy merchants among their number. Although never as numerous as the more evangelical churches, Anglicans in the larger towns along North America's east coast had respectably large congregations. From elegant wine glass pulpits, clergy educated at Oxford or Cambridge rehearsed the stories of the Bible and exhorted the faithful comfortably seated in their rented box pews to do their Christian duty.

The Church of England in America

There was no British "plantation" or colony in the land that became Alabama, but when Great Britain's victory in the Seven Years' War forced France to cede Mobile in 1763, British troops arrived and France's Fort Condé became Britain's

Fort Charlotte, named after George III's queen. In 1768–69, the British civil list included an annual salary of £100 for a minister in Mobile. The minister, Samuel Hart, stayed for only a year, leaving because "he had no church building, parsonage, nor hope of promotion to chaplainship of the fort, and found it impossible to support his family." Hart preached "a lengthy and quite dogmatic sermon" to the Indians and "was utterly unable to impart any idea of his subject matter to his hearer." Finally, the native chief cut him short and said, "Beloved man, I will always think well of this friend of ours, God Almighty, of whom you tell me so much; and so let us drink his health." The British authorities may have addressed some of Hart's concerns, because his successor, William Gordon, seems to have had both a house and a church, although they were probably burned during the Spanish assault on Mobile in 1780.[2]

In 1750 the 289 Anglican churches in the thirteen colonies that became the United States were second in number only to the 465 Congregational churches. Almost half of the Anglican churches were in Virginia and Maryland (ninety parishes in Virginia and fifty in Maryland). Anglicanism even penetrated the Puritan stronghold of Massachusetts in 1686, when King's Chapel was founded in Boston.[3] Quaker William Penn's "holy experiment" in Pennsylvania tolerated all Protestants and even welcomed Jews, but his sons, Thomas, Richard, and John, converted to Anglicanism (although they maintained their father's principle of toleration). On the eve of the American Revolution, there were twenty-two Anglican churches in Pennsylvania, including Philadelphia's prestigious Christ Church (1695). The Church of England became the established church in New York in 1693, and four years later Trinity Church was organized in lower Manhattan and given a large grant of land. Trinity's real estate holdings made it the wealthiest congregation of any denomination in the United States and also enabled it to support the extension of Anglicanism throughout the New York area. Thus New York became "the launching stage for the spread of Anglicanism into Connecticut, New Jersey, and the developing area up the Hudson River."[4] Anglicanism also flourished in Charleston and the surrounding tidewater region of South Carolina. The Anglicans in Charleston helped organize churches in nearby Savannah and Augusta, and although Anglicanism was never as strong in Georgia as in South Carolina, John Wesley served as a missionary in Savannah in 1736.

In the years leading up to the American Revolution, the Church of England was growing, but it was not keeping pace with the growth of the population. One-fourth of all Americans were Anglican in 1700, but only one-sixth were Anglican by 1750 and one-ninth in 1775. The Church of England was mostly confined to the eastern seaboard and was not moving westward into the interior; nor was it converting newly arrived immigrants. However, on the eve of the American

Revolution, the Church of England was beginning to make great strides. "In the fifteen years after 1760 no less than 100 new churches were built, whereas for the longer forty-year period 1720–1760, a relatively smaller number of parishes, 130, were constructed."[5]

A major obstacle to the growth and health of Anglicanism in North America was the Church of England's failure to provide episcopal leadership. American Anglicans were some three thousand miles from the Bishop of London, who (from 1688) had authority over the Anglican parishes in North America. Ordination and even confirmation required a difficult and dangerous sea voyage of several weeks. There was precedent for the creation of new dioceses: Henry VIII had created six dioceses after breaking from Rome. So why did the Church of England lack the will and the vision to provide episcopal oversight for Britain's colonies? There were many obstacles. First, English bishops administered vast dioceses, as well as serving in the House of Lords. Recasting themselves in the role of missionaries was an imaginative leap they simply could not make. But more importantly, the American colonists (including some Anglicans) were not eager to welcome yet another official of the Crown to oversee affairs in the colonies, and New England's Puritans were hostile to the idea. To Jonathan Mayhew (1720–1766), minister of Boston's Old West Church, bishops were not only "unscriptural," they were "a pernicious set of men, both to church and state." In lieu of establishing a diocese in America, the Bishop of London sent agents known as "commissaries" to represent him; these commissaries frequently served as rectors of large and influential churches, but their presence may have done more harm than good to the Anglican cause. Because they were priests, not bishops, they could perform only the most unpopular functions of the bishop they represented—enforcing discipline and doctrine—and were unable to ordain, confirm, or provide the kind of strategic planning that American Anglicans needed.[6]

Some of America's most important leaders were members of the Church of England. More signers of the Declaration of Independence belonged to the Church of England than to any other religious group. Patrick Henry, Thomas Jefferson, Alexander Hamilton, and George Washington were raised as Anglicans, as were many other staunch patriots. At various times Benjamin Franklin, Betsy Ross, and Francis Hopkinson attended Philadelphia's Christ Church. Nevertheless, the American Revolution caused havoc among members of the Church of England in America, because as part of their ordination, Anglican clergy swore loyalty to the Crown and fidelity to the Book of Common Prayer, which included prayers for George III as "supreme governor" of the Church of England. The overwhelming majority of Anglican laypeople favored American independence, but more than half of America's Anglican clergy remained loyal to the Crown.[7]

The Organization of the Protestant Episcopal Church in the USA

With the end of the American War of Independence and the establishment of the United States, Anglicanism was profoundly weakened. It had lost not only many of its clergy and some of its lay leaders, it had also lost its favored position as the established church in several of the colonies. The members of what had been the Church of England faced several challenges: they had to secure episcopal leadership; they had to redefine themselves, because in most states they were no longer the "church by law established" but just one denomination among many; and finally, they had to rebuild their membership because of the losses they had suffered during the war.

The first task—securing episcopal leadership—was in some ways the least complicated, although it caused a crisis that threatened to divide the American church even before it was organized. In 1783 the clergy of Connecticut chose Samuel Seabury to be their bishop and sent him to England to seek consecration from bishops of the Church of England. However, the English bishops were bound by law to require new bishops to swear loyalty to the Crown, something that Seabury could not do. Thus Seabury turned to the bishops of Scotland who did not demand that he swear allegiance to the Crown, and he was duly consecrated in Aberdeen on November 14, 1784.

The organizing convention of the Episcopal Church met in Philadelphia in 1785. The next two American bishops—William White, rector of Christ Church, Philadelphia, and Samuel Provoost of Trinity Church, New York—sought and received consecration from English bishops, after Parliament changed the law that required bishops to swear loyalty to the Crown. However, White and Provoost regarded Seabury with suspicion and distrust for two reasons: First, they had been patriots, but Seabury had been a loyalist. Second, Seabury's theological views were decidedly "high church"; White and Provoost represented the "low" or evangelical side of the church. If the two groups had not found a way to work out their differences, the American church might have been fatally weakened.

Delegates to the 1789 General Convention hammered out a compromise that brought the two sides together and also gave the new church a name—the Protestant Episcopal Church in the United States of America (PECUSA).[8] Seabury favored the English model of ecclesiastical polity in which bishops wield enormous power, but White and Provoost favored a more democratic model in which laypeople would be involved in church governance. The compromise created an ecclesiastical polity that resembled the civil polity in many ways. The new church would have a bicameral structure: an upper house of bishops alone and a lower house composed of priests, deacons, and laymen. The bishops of the Episcopal Church would have the dignity of English bishops but not their enormous power.

Like the US president, bishops of the Episcopal Church are constrained by checks and balances. They can articulate a vision, set priorities, and establish goals, but laypeople are involved at almost every level of decision making.

At the 1789 General Convention, the Episcopal Church made great strides. It had episcopal leadership, a workable polity, and a name. However, it had not yet established an identity that would enable it to compete in the religious marketplace of the new republic. The Church of England was the "church by law established" in England, but what did it become when it was transplanted to a new republic that had rejected the monarch who was the church's "supreme governor" and implicitly rejected the bishops who sat in the House of Lords as "lords spiritual"?

The Hobartian Synthesis and the Evangelical Alternative

The vision that ultimately prevailed was that of John Henry Hobart (1775–1830), who became assistant bishop of New York in 1811 and diocesan bishop in 1816. Hobart reinvented the Episcopal Church as a latter-day incarnation of the apostolic church. "From the parochial American perspective Episcopalians might be a weak minority, with odd and peculiar views, but in actuality, Hobart insisted, they uniquely represented the catholic and apostolic faith." For Hobart, the fact that the bishops of the Episcopal Church possessed an authority they had inherited from the apostles both differentiated them from other Reformed churches and also united them to the Church of England whose bishops possessed the same authority. However, the Episcopal Church was different from the Church of England in being less burdened by irrelevant and unnecessary "trappings," such as cathedrals, deaneries, canons, and so on. The theological position Hobart articulated emphasized baptismal regeneration, apostolic succession, and sacramental grace.[9]

Hobart drew a sharp a line between church and state. His ideal was the pre-Constantinian church—that is, the Christian church before Constantine's conversion and patronage began a long and uneasy relationship between church and state. The fact that religious toleration was enshrined in the US Constitution and that the US government did not officially give any religion a favored position made the pre-Constantinian church an obvious model for Hobart. Furthermore, the young American republic was bound to receive favorably Hobart's rejection of an alliance between the hierarchies of the church and state. Hobart's vision of the Episcopal Church as the one, true successor of the apostolic church made him reluctant to make common cause with other Christian bodies. For example, Hobart opposed Episcopalian participation in the American Bible Society and instead formed the Bible and Common Prayer Book Society as an alternative. In

Hobart's time, however, reform was in the air and the evangelical churches were the great engines of reform. Thus the Episcopal Church was largely a bystander as Methodists, Baptists, and others tried and often succeeded in ameliorating the conditions of prisoners, the sick in body and mind, the poor, and above all, slaves. Hobart's vision goes a long way toward explaining why the slavery issue did not divide the Episcopal Church.[10]

Although Hobart's vision prevailed, it was not the only way of understanding the Episcopal Church. Evangelicals had a different vision of the Episcopal Church. Leading evangelicals included William Meade (1789–1862), who became the third bishop of Virginia in 1842, and Charles Pettit McIlvaine (1799–1873), who became the second bishop of Ohio in 1832. Its intellectual leader was William H. Wilmer, a faculty member at Virginia Theological Seminary and father of the second bishop of Alabama, Richard Hooker Wilmer. The main differences between the evangelical and high church wings of the PECUSA in the early nineteenth century were more about emphasis than substance. Both used the Book of Common Prayer, although many evangelicals pleaded for more flexibility in using the Prayer Book while high churchmen insisted on rubrical precision. (Rubrics are instructions for performing liturgical acts, e.g., "Here the minister lays his hand upon the bread and wine." They were usually printed in red because rubric is derived from the Latin *rubrica,* meaning red.) Both parties accepted episcopal polity but some evangelicals regarded episcopacy (government of the church by bishops) as only one form of polity among many while high churchmen viewed it as a divine institution. Probably the most substantial differences between evangelical and high church Episcopalians in the early nineteenth century concerned their respective attitudes toward baptism and conversion. The evangelicals believed that baptism was "a *badge* of Christian profession; a *symbol* of regeneration; *a covenanting* and *sealing* act; and an *evidence* to the identity of the church . . . from generation to generation."[11] However, the evangelicals, regarding scriptural truth as more important than church order, were among the few prophetic voices in the Episcopal Church in the early nineteenth century. The few members who spoke out against slavery were mostly evangelicals. Among them were laymen William Jay and John Jay and the Reverends Alexander Crummell (an African American), Evan Johnson, John P. Lundy, and Thomas Atkins.

Theology was not the only factor that shaped the identity of the Episcopal Church. Culture and geography were also important, and colonial America's religious culture differed from region to region. A communitarian impulse was deeply embedded in the culture of New England puritanism. Soon after their arrival in the early seventeenth century, the Puritans began to establish schools and colleges. The Puritan ethic encouraged the formation of strong families, and there was rough parity between the numbers of men and women in New England. Unlike the New England Puritans, the Anglicans in Virginia had not emigrated from England expecting to bring their families, put down roots, and stay permanently. The culture of the Chesapeake Bay area (primarily Virginia and Maryland) did not encourage the establishment of schools, colleges, churches, and other institutions. Because of a preponderance of young, unmarried men, the environment of the Chesapeake Bay tended to be more violent, alcohol abuse was common, and there were fewer stable families. These cultural differences may help account for the fact that Puritan New England produced more educational institutions than Anglican Virginia, and that America's evangelical churches have created more of the institutions (colleges, hospitals, and so on) that have woven more of America's cultural and institutional fabric.[12]

Evangelizing the New Country

At the beginning of the nineteenth century, the Episcopal Church had to grapple with the overwhelming question of how to transmit the Christian faith in its Anglican form to a new republic already spreading westward to fill a vast continent. In 1821 the PECUSA formed the Domestic and Foreign Missionary Society (DFMS), and then radically reorganized it in 1835. Even though it was slow to begin evangelizing the American frontier, the Episcopal Church did not make the Church of England's mistake and fail to provide episcopal leadership for its far-flung parishes. Thus in 1835, Jackson Kemper was consecrated to serve as the first missionary bishop of the Episcopal Church and given responsibility for the northwestern frontier. West Point graduate Leonidas Polk followed Kemper in 1838, although Polk was charged with serving the southwestern frontier.[13]

As the Episcopal Church spread south and west in the years following 1789, it was challenged by rationalism on one side and by the enthusiasm of the Second Great Awakening on the other. America's first great wave of religious enthusiasm had been the Great Awakening in the mid-eighteenth century, but the Second Great Awakening was arguably more important. The Second Great Awakening was an outbreak of religious fervor that began simultaneously at Cane Ridge, Kentucky, and in New Haven and other Connecticut towns in the 1790s. Not only did the Second Great Awakening help launch the expansion of America's two largest denominations—Baptists and Methodists—it is also credited with producing the abolitionist movement and the Mormons. Furthermore, the religious impulse that we know as "revivalism" also came out of the Awakening. The Awakening spread south and west during the early nineteenth century, the same years in which Alabama's Episcopal diocese was beginning to grow. David Brown, a DFMS missionary in Florence and Tuscumbia from 1841 to 1846, described his station as "stony ground at best" because it had "been frequently swept over by storm[s] of fanaticism, raised and impelled by the united powers of all the sects. . . . The people generally here seem to have no notion of religion but as occasionally or periodically producing a *mass-meeting*, and bringing together some 'celebrated orators' to tickle their ears and excite their passions. And when excited they are said to 'get religion,' and are fully licensed to say to all others, we are holier than you and so they pass through the arena of scoffing fanaticism into the cavernous vortex of scoffing infidelity; and by the sop of their native piety and fear of God, their last state is very far worse than the first." Brown concluded that "the sober and solemn services of the church are ill-adapted to the taste of this country." Just a few years later (1854) Richard Cobbs, son of Alabama's first bishop, wrote that "this whole region of country has been peculiarly under the influences of the 'Revival System,' and nowhere are its deadening effects more clearly manifested. The natural consequence has been, that the minds of the people are not at all disposed to like the sober and solemn forms of the Church which are so little calculated to minister to mere physical excitement." In Marion in 1848, William A. Stickney noted, "three years ago the whole land was aroused by these excitement meetings which now it is very difficult for them to get up any kind of an excitement, though they waste steam enough to have carried a ten times greater power a few years ago."[14]

Even though there was a significant evangelical component in the Episcopal Church in the early nineteenth century, the Episcopal Church received little, if any, benefit from the Awakening, while the Baptists and Methodists grew at a rapid pace. As John Boles wrote, "Distrusted, depressed, and perhaps a little disdainful, the once ascendant church saw its position drop precipitously. Its fate mirrored the growing domination of the popularly supported churches: Baptist, Methodist, and Presbyterian." Evangelicalism became practically synonymous with the South. It is undoubtedly true that evangelical churches and their members were and are numerically dominant in the South, and that the religious images linked to the South in popular culture, such as tent meetings, revivals, river baptisms, and so on, are associated with evangelicalism. Episcopalians, however, have always been an important and influential subculture. Although never as numerous as evangelicals, Episcopalians have wielded influence vastly out of proportion to their numbers, as mentioned earlier. Richard Rankin argues that North Carolina Episcopalians "displayed such an obvious measure of political, economic, social, and educational preeminence that it must be apparent that they formed a genteel elite." Rankin partly bases his claim on a study that estimates that "nearly 60 percent of all great planters [in North Carolina], those who owned more than seventy slaves, were attached to the Episcopal church." This is consistent with Harriet E. Amos Doss's estimate that almost 61 percent of Mobile's civic leaders were members of the Episcopal Church. The Episcopal Church appealed to the economic, social, and cultural elite because it represented a via media between the aridness of rationalism and the emotional excesses of evangelicalism. Gentlemen could become Episcopalians without giving up "'worldly amusements' such as dueling, gaming, theatergoing, and public balls," and ladies did not need to renounce the "code of fashion" to be members of the Episcopal Church. In Alabama, as in the rest of the South, at least three of the four churches at every intersection tended to be evangelical, but Episcopalians occupied many, if not most, of the plantation houses.[15]

When the Diocese of Alabama was organized in 1830 it became a part of a church whose tradition linked it with the apostles but which was also an heir of the Reformation. It had withstood the chastening fire of the Revolutionary War and had adapted to the new reality of the American republic. The Diocese of Alabama was on the leading edge of the Episcopal Church as it began its westward march across the continent.

2

"No gentleman would choose any but the Episcopalian way"

From the Beginning to the 1850s

In 1846 eminent British geologist Sir Charles Lyell, whose work was a precursor to Darwin's *On the Origin of Species*, visited Alabama. While in Tuscaloosa, Lyell attended Christ Episcopal Church and heard a sermon by Nicholas Hamner Cobbs, the first bishop of the Diocese of Alabama, who had been elected only two years earlier. Lyell also had occasion to chat with a priest of the diocese: "A few days later, when I was on my way, in a steamer, to Mobile, I conversed with an Episcopal clergyman, a high churchman, whose profession I had recognised by the strictness of his costume. . . . He seemed to know the names of almost every bishop and dignitary of the English Church, their incomes and shades of opinion, and regretted that Archbishop Whately had taken such low ground with regard to apostolic succession . . . he was convinced that as the wealthiest class are so often Episcopalians, his church is a gainer in worldly advantages as well as spiritual influence, by being wholly unconnected with the State." When Lyell visited Alabama, the Episcopal Diocese of Alabama was only sixteen years old and the church in which he heard Bishop Cobbs preach was only slightly older. Lyell did not record his opinion of the bishop's sermon, but he was impressed with the fact that unlike English churches, there was no "clerk"—that is, a layman hired to assist the priest by reading the lessons and responding at the appropriate points in the service with the parts of the liturgy designated for laypeople. "It often struck me as an advantage in the United States, that the responses are never read by an illiterate man, as happens not uncommonly in our country parishes, and the congregation joins in the service more earnestly when the part which properly belongs to them does not devolve on a regular functionary."[1]

Life on the Alabama Frontier

Religion flourished in old Alabama. When British temperance activist and author James Buckingham visited Alabama, he was amazed that a town as small as Montgomery had six churches—Episcopalian, Presbyterian, Baptist, Methodist, Unitarian, and Roman Catholic—and that all seemed to be well attended. The admission of Alabama into the Union in 1819 seems to have been a catalyst for the major religious groups to create judicatories. Comprised of 125 churches and representing some five thousand Baptists, the Alabama Baptist Convention met for the first time in 1823. Although the Alabama Methodist Conference would not come into existence until 1832 (two years after the Episcopal Diocese of Alabama was formed), Methodists were already numerous and well organized by 1830. In 1813 a Methodist camp meeting was organized at Fort Easley, and by 1832, white and black Methodists in Alabama numbered about eleven thousand. With its roots deep in Alabama's Spanish and French past, the Roman Catholic Church, geographically limited to the area near the Gulf Coast and numerous only there, established Mobile as a separate diocese in 1829 under the leadership of Bishop Michael Portier. Only the Presbyterian Church was slower to organize and had more sluggish growth than the Episcopal Church.[2]

Writing to the Episcopal Church's publication *The Spirit of Missions* in 1838, "a gentleman of Lafayette, Chambers County," described the Alabamians he knew as "comparatively moral and religious. Scenes of bloodshed are rare; a large proportion of the community are professing Christians." But he went on to say that "religion . . . is mixed with some grossness, and ignorance, and party contention, and political feuds . . . and is especially apt to be so in an unsettled, prosperous, emigrant community." Hungarian visitors Francis and Theresa Pulszky were surprised to find public buildings so often used for religious services. In Mobile they attended a public meeting to honor their fellow countryman, nationalist leader Lajos Kossuth. The meeting took place in a large public hall known as the "Circus" that was sometimes used for religious services. The Pulszkys noted that it was one of the "peculiarities" of America that "places of worship are often thrown open for lectures and profane music, and that concert-rooms and lecture-halls are used for worship."[3]

From the very beginning, hospitality has been a hallmark of Alabama and its people. Lyell found Alabamians interested in and eager to assist his hunt for fossils. The people he encountered were "hospitable and obliging to a stranger" and "each planter seemed to vie with another in his anxiety to give me information in regard to the precise spots where organic remains had been discovered." In 1838 another Alabama visitor, the teacher and naturalist Philip Henry Gosse, praised the "generous, almost boundless hospitality, in the southern planter." One reason for the abundance of hospitality may have been the scarcity of amenities for travelers. Except in Mobile, travelers could not expect comfortable lodgings. Lyell was disconcerted by the practice of sharing a bed with another traveler: "I could have dispensed cheerfully with milk, butter, and other such luxuries; but I felt much the want of a private bed-room. Very soon, however, I came to regard it as no small privilege to be allowed to have even a bed to myself." Even "wealthy and respectable planters," wrote Gosse, lived in homes that were built "of rough and unhewn logs, and to an English taste are destitute of comfort to a surprising degree." However, Gosse also found other houses "much superior . . . regularly clapboarded, and ceiled, and two, or even three stories high, including the ground-floor," which contained "comforts and elegancies in them which would do no dishonour to an English gentleman."[4]

Nearly all travelers praised Mobile for its relative sophistication and often compared it favorably with New Orleans and the older, more settled metropolitan areas along America's east coast. Buckingham was impressed by Mobile's "four daily newspapers . . . two morning and two evening" and its "weekly literary gazette." He also found that the newspapers were "all conducted with more than average talent." According to the Pulszkys, Mobile's gardens were "filled with roses, orange and lemon trees, and magnificent magnolias." They found "the air full of fragrance." "The main streets are long and broad," wrote Scottish author Alexander Mackay, "well shaded by trees, and admirably paved." In Huntsville in 1818, Anne Newport Royall noted the presence of "260 houses, principally built of brick . . . a bank, a court house and a market house." Huntsville's residents, she observed, came "mostly from Georgia and the Carolinas—though there are a few from almost every part of the world;—and the town displays much activity. The citizens are gay, polite, and hospitable, and live in great splendor."[5]

Most travelers also commented on Alabama's natural beauty and extraordinary fertility. Mackay claimed that Alabama "produces cotton and Indian corn in abundance" and added, "Alabama is not surpassed, in point of fertility, by any of the sister States of the Confederation." Anne Newport Royall wrote glowingly of the "astonishingly large" cotton fields in the Tennessee Valley near Huntsville. "Fancy is inadequate to conceive a prospect more grand! . . . To a stranger, coming suddenly amongst these fields, it has the appearance of magic. He is lost in wonder, and nothing but the evidence of his senses can persuade him it is reality."[6]

In the shadow of the numerous churches, gracious hospitality, and physical beauty was another Alabama in which alcohol abuse was common and violence abounded. James Buckingham observed "grog-shops of the common order . . . at every corner of almost every street." "Hardly a night passes," he wrote, "without a riot or a fight, or without furnishing an occasion for a duel or a murder at some subsequent time." Lyell also noted frequent episodes of public drunkenness. Not only did he find his innkeeper drunk early in the morning, but while in Washington, DC, Lyell also witnessed a congressman from Alabama "the worse for liquor, on his legs in the House."[7]

The use and abuse of alcohol goes a long way toward explaining the "quarrelsomeness" and "recklessness of human life" that Gosse observed. "The terrible bowie-knife," he asserted, "is ever ready to be drawn, and it is drawn and used too, on the slightest provocation. Deeds are fought with this horrible weapon, in which the combatants are almost chopped to pieces; or with the no less fatal, but less shocking rifle, perhaps within pistol-distance." While traveling downriver to Mobile, Leonidas Polk, the Episcopal Church's missionary bishop of the southwest, was deeply disturbed when he saw corpses floating on the river. Polk attributed this to "the shocking indifference to the value of human life, and the rights of the dead. . . . Men are knocked overboard, and . . . boats . . . [are] blown up, by which many lives are every year lost, producing frequently nothing more than a fleeting show of sympathy, or an idle remark. I have, on more than one occasion, seen the bodies of the dead floating unnoticed among the drifting timber. . . . These things ought not to be. They betray a depravity dishonorable to us as a people."[8]

Slavery, however, was the topic about which all early nineteenth-century visitors to Alabama were curious. Almost unanimously, they condemned it, but their opinions differed on how great an evil it was and how it might be done away with. Lyell praised the churches for their outreach to slaves but recognized that evangelizing the captive Africans undermined the institution of slavery. "It is no small gain that he should simply become a member of the same church with his master, and should be taught that the white and coloured man are equal before God, a doctrine calculated to raise him in his own opinion, and in that of the dominant race." Lyell witnessed no "mal-treatment of slaves in this State" but believed that the widespread drunkenness he observed meant, "the power [slave owners] exercise must often be fearfully abused." In the churches, Buckingham was distressed to see the "negroes and coloured people . . . in the gallery, where alone they are permitted to sit in this country" and reflected on the "melancholy consideration" that they were "excluded . . . from all the benefits of intellectual cultivation, since, throughout the South, it is unlawful to teach a slave even to read!"[9]

The Pulszkys found southerners to be defensive about slavery. At a dinner party in Montgomery, their hostess raised the topic of slavery "in the very first moment of our acquaintance." This was a pattern they found repeatedly in their travels. "As they feel how much horror slavery inspires in Europeans, they wish at once to explain their position." Gosse believed that slavery "helps to brutalize the character, by familiarizing the mind with the infliction of human suffering," but he was reluctant to be too explicit about the evils he had witnessed because "there is a very stern jealousy of a stranger's interference on these points." "What will be the end of American slavery?" he asked. He then presciently speculated that it was "a huge deadly serpent, which is kept down by incessant vigilance, and by the strain of every nerve and muscle." Prophetically, Gosse concluded: "some day or other, it will burst the weight that binds it, and take a fearful retribution."[10]

Alabama's First Episcopal Churches and their Members

Long before Alabama had a bishop and even before the diocese was organized, the Episcopal Church began to take root and grow. Parishes sprang up in the prosperous planter communities of the Black Belt and Tennessee Valley regions of Alabama, as well as sophisticated Mobile. Without any apparent coordination, Alabama's first two Episcopal churches were organized only weeks apart in early 1828. Robert Davis, a representative of the Episcopal Church's Domestic and Foreign Missionary Society (DFMS), presided at a meeting to launch Christ Church, Tuscaloosa, on January 7, 1828. Scarcely more than a month later, on February 26, a group of Mobile's civic leaders organized Christ Episcopal Church in that city.[11]

Historian William E. Dodd's comment aptly characterizes the early leaders of the Episcopal churches in Alabama: "It is still said in the South that, although there may be other roads to the Celestial City, no gentleman would choose any but the Episcopalian way." From the very beginning, Alabama's Episcopal churches attracted a disproportionate share of the state's economic, political, and cultural leaders. The founders of Christ Church, Tuscaloosa, included James M. Davenport, a physician; Tuscaloosa's postmaster William Gould, a former member of the US consular staff in France; Henry Minor, a member of the convention that drafted Alabama's first constitution and successful candidate for the Alabama Supreme Court in 1823; Armand Pfister, a merchant and respected music teacher; and Thomas Bolling, proprietor of the Indian Queen Hotel. Another leading member of Christ Church, Tuscaloosa, was merchant Joel White, who served as a director of the state bank both in Tuscaloosa and Montgomery.[12]

The founders of Christ Church, Mobile, were even more prestigious than the founders of Christ Church, Tuscaloosa. They included Samuel H. Garrow, a former mayor of Mobile and a member of the convention to draft Alabama's first constitution, and Henry Hitchcock, who had been secretary of the Alabama Territory, served on the constitutional convention, and would become chief justice of the Alabama Supreme Court in 1836. George W. Owen, a member of the Mobile church's vestry, served as mayor of Mobile in the 1830s, was elected speaker of the

Alabama House of Representatives in 1820, and served in the US Congress from 1823 to 1829. Another member of Christ Church, Mobile, was Abner Lipscomb, who apprenticed in the law office of John C. Calhoun, was a member of the legislature, an associate justice of the Alabama Supreme Court, and eventually rose to become secretary of state for the Republic of Texas.[13]

Greensboro, only forty miles from Tuscaloosa and on the same side of the Black Warrior River, was an obvious place to launch a new Episcopal church, so Albert Muller, the rector of Christ Church, Tuscaloosa, organized St. Paul's there in 1830. Muller's vestry, however, was reluctant to share him with Greensboro and urged him to focus only on his Tuscaloosa responsibilities. However, John Gayle, governor of Alabama from 1831 to 1835, represented St. Paul's at several Diocesan Conventions, including the organizing convention in 1830.[14]

St. Luke's Episcopal Church in Cahaba (Alabama's capital from statehood until 1826) was organized in 1839. Historian Ronald J. Caldwell estimates that by 1860, 20 percent of the citizens of Cahaba belonged to St. Luke's and that Cahaba's Episcopalians owned "43 percent of the town's real estate and personal property." The leading member of St. Luke's, Cahaba, was Edward M. Perine, a wealthy merchant from New York whose real estate holdings (according to the census of 1860) amounted to $164,580. Perine and his wife owned real estate and personal property valued at $278,000. Another of St. Luke's prestigious members (and members of the vestry) was John Starke Hunter (1793–1866), a lawyer and South Carolina native who was elected to both houses of Alabama's legislature.[15]

Representing St. Luke's at the annual convention of the Diocese of Alabama when it was recognized as a parish was William Lowndes Yancey (1814–1863), whose impact on the course of history in Alabama (and the United States) can hardly be overstated, as will be shown. Elected to Congress in 1844, Yancey served only one term and became convinced that the South would eventually secede from the Union. In 1860 Yancey was a principal architect of the "Alabama Platform," which proposed opening all states to slavery and establishing a federal slave code. Yancey's platform was calculated to split the Democratic Party, and it succeeded. When delegates to the 1860 Democratic convention in Charleston rejected it, Yancey led the Alabama delegation when it walked out of the convention. With the Democrats hopelessly divided, the way was clear for Lincoln's victory, and secession became all but inevitable. In the same year, Yancey called for a convention that would debate secession. Yancey's fierce advocacy of Southern independence and his efforts to achieve it caused one historian to suggest that "without Yancey's brilliant oratory, and indefatigable labors there would have been no secession, no Southern Confederacy." That may overstate the case, but clearly Yancey played a key role in the events that led to secession and war.[16]

Episcopalians in Montgomery, Selma, and Huntsville also played important roles in early nineteenth-century Alabama. St. John's, Montgomery, which joined the diocese in 1834 and is located near the capitol building and state offices, has played many roles in Alabama's history. The Confederate president, Jefferson Davis, and his wife, Varina, worshiped there, as did other Confederate government officials. Members of St. John's included Nimrod Benson, a member of the legislature in the 1820s and mayor of Montgomery in the 1830s, and Charles T. Pollard, one of Alabama's railroad pioneers. Selma's St. Paul's parish was founded in 1838. Its leaders included Albert Gallatin Mabry, a graduate of the University of Pennsylvania and a founder of the Alabama Medical Association who was instrumental in founding Alabama's first hospital for the insane. Huntsville's Church of the Nativity was admitted to the diocese in 1843, although it was more or less dormant until 1847. John Withers Clay, editor of the *Huntsville Democrat,* served on Nativity's vestry and was the son of a governor and a brother of a US senator.[17]

Although the Episcopal Church in early nineteenth-century Alabama attracted the wealthy, powerful, and socially prominent, it did not grow nearly as rapidly as the Methodist and Baptist churches. Many of Alabama's most prominent citizens were Episcopalians, but middle-class and poorer Alabamians did not join the Episcopal Church in large numbers. One barrier that kept out people of modest means was the practice of selling or renting pews. Until the late nineteenth century underwriting the parish budget by the sale or rental of pews was common in the Episcopal Church (although it did happen in some other denominations as well); nevertheless, it served to push the poor to one side—literally. Christ Church, Mobile, authorized a committee to determine how much rent to charge for its pews and to rent them "to such persons as they may deem most for the interest of the church." They acknowledged, however, that some room should be made available for persons without the means to pay pew rent and instructed the committee to set aside "sufficient room for the use of strangers, and poor persons . . . and also to have benches for the colored persons." Christ Church's system had at least three tiers: those well-to-do enough to rent pews, "strangers" and the poor, and "colored persons." In practice, however, the system was even more stratified. Pew rent varied depending on the location of the pew, so the affluence and status of a family worshiping at Christ Church would be obvious just by observing where they sat. In 1837 Christ Church rented eighty-four pews for a total of $7,995. Christ Church, Tuscaloosa, sold its pews at public auction for $100 per pew. (On average, that was about the same rate that Christ Church, Mobile, received in rent per pew.) An exception to the pew rental system (at least for a while) was Trinity Church, Mobile. The Ladies' Missionary Sewing Society of Christ Church underwrote the salary of the Reverend B. M. Miller of Norfolk, Virginia—and thereby facilitated his 1845 organization of the congregation that became Trinity Church, Mobile's second Episcopal church—on the condition that the new church would be founded "upon the free pew system, thus affording an open way to the Altars of our beloved Zion." However, in 1867 financial pressures forced Trinity to rent most of its pews. Mobile's third Episcopal church, St. John's, also began as a "free church" (i.e., its pews were free) and remained so.[18]

Finding "An Episcopal Head"

No sooner had the Diocese of Alabama been organized, however, than it sought to merge with the dioceses of Mississippi and Louisiana to form a Southwestern Diocese. The General Convention authorized this experiment to proceed, but the Southwestern Diocese proved impractical, and in 1835 the canon providing for a Southwestern Diocese was repealed. The Diocese of Alabama was reconstituted at the 1836 convention in Mobile. The reason given for the short-lived experiment of merging Alabama, Mississippi, and Louisiana into a single diocese was to facilitate the election of a bishop for these three dioceses. The only attempt at electing a bishop for this vast and unwieldy diocese was unsuccessful. At its first (and last) convention, held in New Orleans on March 4 and 5, 1835, the Diocese of the Southwest elected the Reverend Francis L. Hawks, rector of St. Thomas Church, New York, to be its bishop. However, Hawks declined the honor of becoming bishop of Alabama, Mississippi, and Louisiana.[19]

In 1843 the Committee on the State of the Church identified "the want of an Episcopal head" as an obstacle to the growth of the Episcopal Church in Alabama. The span of fourteen years between the organization of the diocese and the election of the first bishop seems long but was not unusual. The dioceses of Tennessee, Florida, Georgia, and Mississippi took anywhere from five to twenty-three years to elect bishops. Part of the problem was finding priests willing to serve as frontier bishops. After Hawkes's 1835 refusal, the next attempt to elect a bishop for Alabama came in 1842, and again the man chosen was unwilling to accept the position. So Alabama was prepared (with the help of Mississippi and Louisiana) to elect a bishop in 1835, and there was a hiatus of only seven years before it felt ready to hold its next episcopal election. However, the long delay before electing a bishop seems odd. The reason usually given for Alabama's failure to elect a bishop earlier is that the diocese did not have enough money, but this is not convincing. Christ Church, Mobile, had sufficient financial resources to pay its minister $2,000 per year in 1828 and to authorize the construction of a church at a cost of at least $12,000. By March of 1830, Episcopalians in Tuscaloosa had constructed a church, and their minister was helping to organize congregations in Greensboro and Demopolis. And at the first meeting of the Diocese of Alabama following the unfortunate Diocese of the Southwest experiment, there were at least three Episcopal church buildings in the state. The lay leaders of the Episcopal Church in Alabama included some of the state's wealthiest and most influential citizens. Alabama's Episcopalians did not lack the money to pay a bishop; they lacked the will to elect one.

One strategy for funding a bishop's salary that had been used successfully elsewhere in the PECUSA was for a bishop to function both as rector of a parish and as diocesan bishop. America's first bishop, Samuel Seabury, was both bishop of Connecticut and rector of St. James' Church, New Haven, from 1785 to 1796. New York's first bishop, Samuel Provoost, was simultaneously bishop of New York and rector of Trinity Church in lower Manhattan from 1787 to 1800. And the man more responsible than any other for the organization of the PECUSA, William White, was bishop of Pennsylvania, as well as rector of Philadelphia's Christ Church from 1787 until his death in 1836. Alabama's first bishop, Nicholas Hamner Cobbs, first rejected then later accepted a similar arrangement. Cobbs served as rector of Christ Church, Tuscaloosa, and later as rector of St. John's, Montgomery. One suspects that at least part of the reason for the delay in electing a bishop (in Alabama and elsewhere) was that (in spite of the Committee on the State of the Church's plea for "an Episcopal head," bishops were seen (either consciously or unconsciously) as somewhat peripheral. The Church of England's failure to install a resident bishop in North America and the deliberate decision by the organizers of the Episcopal Church to weaken the office of bishop created an ethos in the Episcopal Church that can best be described as "episcopal polity but congregational praxis."[20]

A Bishop for Alabama

Delegates to the 1842 convention chose Martin Parks, the chaplain at West Point, to serve as bishop of Alabama, but he refused the position. The following year they elected James T. Johnston, who also declined. Finally, delegates to the 1844 Diocesan Convention at St. Paul's, Greensboro, elected the Diocese of Alabama's first bishop: Nicholas Hamner Cobbs. A Virginia native, Cobbs was serving as the rector of St. Paul's Church in Cincinnati, and was then consecrated at Christ Church, Philadelphia, on October 20, 1844. Cobbs had no apparent connection to Alabama, but his Virginia roots may help explain how he came to be elected Alabama's first bishop. The Diocese of Virginia was a veritable nursery of bishops. Parks and Johnston, the priests who had declined election, were also Virginians. Furthermore, two of Alabama's provisional bishops, Leonidas Polk and James Hervey Otey, had strong Virginia connections. Polk had been the assistant rector at Richmond's Monumental Church, and Otey had grown up near Cobbs in Virginia. It is also possible that John Withers Clay, a member of the vestry at Nativity, Huntsville, had known Cobbs while he was a student at the University of Virginia. One additional reason for Cobbs's election may have been that his moderately high church theological position was a good fit for the theological climate that had already been established in the Diocese of Alabama.[21]

Regardless of the reason for electing Cobbs, Alabama's Episcopalians chose well. Cobbs proved to be deeply pious, conscientious, and industrious to a fault. Born February 5, 1795, near Lynchburg, Cobbs's father was a Presbyterian and his mother was an Episcopalian. Greenough White, Cobbs's biographer, reports that Cobbs's mother was so determined that her son would be baptized by a priest of the church that she traveled sixty miles on horseback to the nearest clergyman. This has the ring of hagiography rather than biography, because such a journey would have taken four or five days. However, it does point to the deep imprint his mother's loyalty to the Episcopal Church must have had on Cobbs.[22] White also tells us the more believable facts that Cobbs read Hooker's *Ecclesiastical Polity* and taught himself to read Hebrew. Although he had attended an Episcopal service only once, his mother drilled him in the catechism. Even though his experience of the Episcopal Church was slight, he felt called to its ordained ministry and applied for Holy Orders. At the 1824 convention of the Diocese of Virginia, Cobbs was confirmed, received communion for the first time, and was ordained deacon.[23]

Cobbs was a schoolteacher at the time of his ordination to the diaconate and continued to derive most of his income from teaching for several years thereafter. However, after ordination he took charge of two churches in Russell parish—St. Stephen's and Trinity—and helped restore them to vitality. Apparently, Cobbs quickly distinguished himself; in 1829 he became a trustee of General Theological Seminary, and he preached the convention sermon at the 1830 convention of the Diocese of Virginia. Cobbs served for one year as chaplain of the University of Virginia and afterward returned to Russell parish. In 1839 Cobbs was called to serve the Episcopal Church in Bristol parish (Petersburg). In 1841 he was discussed as a possible missionary bishop of Texas, and he was also in the running to become the suffragan bishop of Virginia (a suffragan bishop assists a diocesan bishop yet does not have the right of succession). In 1843 New York's Hobart College conferred the degree of Doctor of Divinity on Cobbs, and in the same year he was called to St. Paul's Church in Cincinnati. Then, less than a year after moving to Cincinnati, Nicholas Hamner Cobbs became the first bishop of Alabama.[24]

The Spiritual Care of African Americans

Care of African Americans, both slave and free, was a major theme of Cobbs's episcopate. When Cobbs delivered his first annual report to the diocese, he noted that during a pastoral visit to Mobile he had "preached to a small congregation of

Colored people." Cobbs also committed himself and the diocese to reaching out to Alabama's African Americans. Slaves were a part of the Episcopal Church in Alabama from the very beginning, although this prompts the question of whether their participation in the Episcopal Church was coerced or voluntary. Although their presence was not voluntary, the opportunity to hear the stories of scripture, sing psalms and hymns, and receive the sacraments of the church may also have given a measure of comfort and hope to enslaved African Americans. Historian Blake Touchstone observes, "Slaves accepted Christianity and made it an essential part of their culture. It gave meaning and purpose to those in bondage, buttressing both individual and communal identities."[25]

Committed though he was to the spiritual care of African Americans, Cobbs grew up in a culture that took slavery for granted, and he seems to have had no moral qualms about the "peculiar institution." His biographer notes that when Cobbs was called to St. Paul's in Cincinnati, Ohio, a free state, he freed his slaves rather than selling them. His former slaves followed the future bishop to Ohio; more than likely they were motivated to follow Cobbs less out of a sense of loyalty than because a free state offered emancipated slaves more opportunities, freedoms, and legal protection. The slave censuses for 1850 and 1860, however, show that when Cobbs moved to Alabama he once again acquired slaves; but Alabama's first bishop professed a sincere commitment to the spiritual welfare of African Americans, both free and slave. In his very first address to the Diocesan Convention, Cobbs stated his hope "that 'ere long, we shall see multitudes of the African race coming to the Ordinances of the Church." He was convinced that slaves would respond positively to the repetitive nature of the Anglican liturgy and to its "call and response" format. Cobbs believed that "the services of the Church are eminently suited to the wants and circumstances of the colored people. They embody the elementary instruction specially needed by that class of people, and they seem by constant repetition to fasten truth upon the memory and conscience: and besides the benefit of its devotional teaching, the Liturgy furnishes in its chants and responses something that is peculiarly in harmony with the genius, and taste and habits of the African race."[26] The bishop's annual reports make frequent mention of services he conducted for "colored people." Ironically, however, Cobbs helped institutionalize the Diocese of Alabama's "separate but equal" treatment of African Americans by requiring parochial reports to record white and "colored" baptisms, confirmations, weddings, and burials in separate columns. When Cobbs began his episcopate he stated that it was his "purpose to pay special attention to the Slave population in the Diocese," a remark that also seems to indicate an enlightened attitude. He also constantly urged his clergy to see to the spiritual needs of blacks and routinely praised both priests and laypeople who ministered to blacks. However, in "Naaman and the Hebrew Maid" (one of his few published sermons), Cobbs's attitude seems to be aptly characterized as noblesse oblige. Cobbs wrote, "the peace, comfort and happiness of a whole family depend on the tempers and deportment of domestics and dependents." Thus, he reasoned, "let us be careful to value the respect, the prayer and benedictions of the poor and the dependents."[27]

For the most part, Alabama's Episcopal clergy seem to have heeded their bishop's godly admonition regarding the spiritual care of African Americans. They routinely baptized and buried slaves and sometimes officiated at slave weddings, although these had no standing in law. Both before and after Cobbs's election Alabama's clergy were constantly urged to provide religious instruction for slaves. In 1842 the Committee on the State of the Church stated that they "were gratified to observe . . . that the colored population have received some attention from our clergy, and they would earnestly recommend to this Convention the importance of devising some efficient means for their religious instruction. In the mean time they hope that the clergy will continue their individual exertions for this purpose, and avail themselves of such opportunities as may offer to preach the gospel to them."[28] But there is reason to believe that slave owners used the sacraments and rites of the church as a means of social control. As war clouds gathered, the number of slaves being baptized increased dramatically. In the 1850s Francis Hanson's diary records several occasions when slave owners had him baptize large numbers of their slaves. On a single Sunday in August 1854, Francis Hanson visited three plantations and baptized a total of 106 "negro children." While he was bishop, Nicholas Hamner Cobbs baptized 1,500 slaves. Historian Henry Walker suggests that as war drew close, slave owners had their slaves baptized, hoping that this would make them more docile in the event of civil war followed by a Northern victory and emancipation.[29]

Cobbs not only urged his clergy to care for slaves, he also urged slave owners to care for them and praised those who did so. Bishop Cobbs spoke approvingly of slave owners, in most cases women, who drilled their slaves in the catechism. In his address to the Diocesan Convention in 1846, the bishop reported that he had visited the Faunsdale Plantation and observed Louisa Harrison "giving regular instruction to her servants [slaves] by reading the services of the Church, and by steadily catechising the children. . . . It was impossible to hear their prompt answers, and to listen to their excellent singing and chanting, without the liveliest sensibility." In 1847 the minister at Union Parish, Uniontown, similarly recorded that the

ladies of the congregation . . . are still zealously engaged in Catechising the colored children. On each Sabbath, it is the custom of such ladies as are engaged in this good work, to assemble around them all children on the

plantations, who are old enough to receive instruction. Bishop Ives' Catechism is chiefly used, and when the classes are sufficiently advanced, they are
then taught the Catechism of the Church. To prevent tediousness, singing
is intermingled with the instruction—it never fails to produce the desired
effect. From time to time, I attend the recitations, and often has my heart
been cheered by hearing the Hymns and Chants of the Church by the different classes.

These references to clergy and slave owners instructing or catechizing slaves could
be multiplied many times. The constant emphasis on instructing and catechizing
slaves strongly suggests the idea that religious instruction was an instrument of
social control.

The most significant outreach to blacks occurred at the Faunsdale Plantation
in Marengo County. Louisa Harrison, widow of planter Thomas Harrison, catechized her slaves weekly on Sunday afternoons. Bishop Cobbs often praised her efforts at religious education among her "servants": "In this interesting Parish there
is manifested on the part of the Ladies an increasing interest in the catechitical
[sic] instruction of their servants. It is truly delightful to the heart of a Christian to be present at the examination of one of these classes of colored children,
to hear their prompt answers and their delightful singing."[30] William Stickney,
one of the first men Bishop Cobbs ordained, spent almost his entire career as a
priest at St. Michael's, the chapel for the Faunsdale Plantation, and in 1863 Bishop
Wilmer designated Stickney "Missionary to the Negroes." In 1864 Stickney married Louisa Harrison, who became not only his wife but, in a sense, also his fellow
minister among the African Americans of the Black Belt.

Alongside slaves, but in far smaller numbers, Alabama's earliest Episcopalians
also included "free persons of color." A notable parishioner of Christ Church, Tuscaloosa, was Solomon Perteet, a free black man who had accumulated remarkable
wealth. Although most black Episcopalians were slaves, Perteet was an exception—
but by no means the only free black Episcopalian in Alabama. In 1854, Bishop
Cobbs confirmed seven free black men and women at Trinity Church, Mobile.
These seven became the nucleus of Good Shepherd, Mobile, Alabama's first black
Episcopal Church. In his first address to the Diocesan Convention, Cobbs mentioned that during a visitation to Mobile he had "preached to a small congregation
of Colored people." One wonders if some of these might have been among the
seven he confirmed nine years later, but there is no way to know. Founding Good
Shepherd was a courageous and perhaps even a subversive act. Leah Rawls Atkins
writes, "free blacks . . . were looked upon with distrust by whites, who considered
them a dangerous example in a slave society." Indeed, it was illegal for free blacks

to form a church. Only in urban Mobile, with its large population of free blacks, could a black Episcopal Church have been established in the 1850s.[31]

The Role of Women

Although barred from ordained ministry and elected office, women played many roles in the early history of the Diocese of Alabama. The women of Alabama's first Episcopal churches sometimes raised substantial amounts of money for vital parish needs. At Christ Church, Mobile, the most affluent parish in the diocese, women provided the following items for the church: pew cushions, a mahogany "Communion-table," two chairs for the chancel, a surplice for the rector, and cushions for the pulpit and reading desk. It would be difficult to determine how much these items cost, but it must have been substantial. In his parochial report for 1847, John Linebaugh implies that St. Paul's, Selma, would not have survived without a contribution of $125 by the "Ladies sewing society." Still, Episcopal laywomen did not focus exclusively on building and beautifying their own parishes. They were at least as concerned about outreach beyond the parish. For example, in 1857 George Stickney, the rector of the Church of the Good Shepherd, Mobile, noted that two women's organizations, the Christ Church Sewing Society and the Little Girls' Sewing Society, had raised a total of $726.75 for his parish and that a further $270 had been raised by "a Committee of Ladies." In the very first parochial report for Christ Church, Tuscaloosa, its rector records that the women of the parish had organized a "society for the promotion of Christian knowledge and piety." Another women's group gave material and financial help to missionaries in Greece. In 1845 the women of Christ Church, Mobile, undertook their most ambitious outreach project. They raised the money to underwrite a "City Missionary, who should preach the gospel . . . to all who might feel disposed to attend upon his services, as well as to pay particular attention to the spiritual wants of the colored population, and to visit the poor, sick, and distressed, without regard to denominational distinctions, so far as enabled to do so."[32]

In addition to fund-raisers for outreach, the women of the Diocese of Alabama also produced one of the most important foreign missionaries that the DFMS sent abroad in the nineteenth century. Emma Jones of Christ Church, Mobile, accompanied William Jones Boone, missionary bishop of China, to Shanghai in 1844. Jones and fellow missionary Mary J. Morse cofounded a mission school in 1846 that may have first served both boys and girls, but in 1856, Jones wrote a letter to *The Spirit of Missions* referring to it only as a girls' school. After Jones left China, the girls' school was renamed the Emma G. Jones School, but Shanghai's Bishop Samuel Schereshewsky merged it into St. Mary's Hall. Under its latter name, it became one of Shanghai's leading girls' schools for a century, until it was incorporated into the system of state schools in 1952. Jones wrote that her motivation in founding a girls' school was "to collect the female children of China, and instruct them in that blessed Gospel which has elevated their sex wherever it has been promulged [*sic*]." Ill health forced Jones to leave China in 1856, but she returned only to leave permanently in 1861 because of the US Civil War. She died in 1879.[33]

It is likely that Francis Hanson, the rector of Trinity, Demopolis, from 1843 to 1873,[34] inspired Jones to serve as a missionary to China. Hanson and Henry Lockwood were two of the first Episcopal missionaries to go to China. In 1835 they traveled to Shanghai, but their ministry there was not a success. They were not allowed to stay in China and went instead to Jakarta (then Batavia in the Netherlands East Indies). However, Hanson not only seems to have inspired Jones, he also was probably the reason for Bishop William Jones Boone's visit to Christ Church, Mobile, in 1843. Christ Church gave Bishop Boone $400 for the Chinese mission, and "one gentleman of the parish" gave an additional $350 "for the first year's education of [a] Chinese youth." The youth was probably Huang Guangcai, a Chinese convert to the Christian faith, who accompanied Bishop Boone on his visit to Mobile.[35]

Another woman, Mary Anne Cruse, a member of Nativity, Huntsville, wrote two books—*The Little Episcopalian; or, The Child Taught by the Prayer Book* (1854) and *Bessie Melville; or, Prayer Book Instructions Carried Out into Life* (1858)—that were widely read among Episcopalians, and a third book—*Cameron Hall, a Story of the Civil War* (1867), a fictionalized account of her experiences during the Civil War. The first was dedicated to her priest with these words: "To the Rev. Henry C. Lay, her Rector, this little work is affectionately inscribed, and if, in its simple pages she has been enabled faithfully to set forth the teachings of the church, she acknowledges that it is principally to his instruction and guidance that she owes her knowledge of them."[36]

Alabama's Earliest Episcopalian Clergy

It seems safe to say that the early leaders of the Diocese of Alabama were powerful and wealthy, but it is more difficult to generalize about the clergy. Writing in *The Spirit of Missions* in 1838, "a gentleman of Lafayette" stated that an "Episcopal minister" who was "permanently settled" would be able to effect "lasting good" if he possessed "learning, gravity, and piety." The great majority of them were indeed grave and pious, but beyond that it is difficult to generalize. Their educational accomplishments were widely varied; some had impressive degrees from old, well-established colleges, and many had also trained at the Episcopalian seminaries in New York or Alexandria, Virginia. Bishop Cobbs had neither a university nor a seminary degree, although he served for a time as chaplain to the University of Virginia and was awarded a DD by New York's Hobart College. Henry C. Lay of Nativity, Huntsville, was educated at the University of Virginia and the Virginia Theological Seminary. General Theological Seminary graduates included William Stickney, Nathaniel Knapp, and possibly J. Avery Shepherd. They came primarily from the upper South but many also came from states farther north, and a surprising number of Alabama's earliest clergy were from New England. Norman Pinney, who succeeded Henry Shaw at Christ Church, Mobile, was from Connecticut, and both Caleb Ives, one of the most energetic and successful DFMS missionaries in Alabama, and the longtime rector of Christ Church, Mobile, Samuel S. Lewis, were natives of Vermont. Henry N. Pierce, rector of St. John's, Mobile, from 1857 to 1868, and then bishop of Arkansas, hailed from Rhode Island. Nathaniel P. Knapp, who succeeded Samuel S. Lewis, was a New Yorker. John H. Linebaugh, who helped organize churches at Eutaw, Cahaba, and Selma, was from Kentucky and came to the ministry after a career as a lawyer. He subsequently left the ministry and worked as a journalist during the Civil War. His life ended tragically when he fell from a steamboat and drowned while traveling from Montgomery to Selma.[37]

One of Alabama's most important early clergymen was Henry C. Lay, rector of Huntsville's Church of the Nativity from 1847 to 1859. Journalist and lawyer John Withers Clay had known Lay when both were students at the University of Virginia, and Clay recruited his college friend for Nativity: "I shall not rest perfectly satisfied," Clay wrote to his friend, "until we get you into this diocese. What are the prospective chances for our success?" Lay became Cobbs's protégé and close personal friend. Indeed, they were so close that the bishop wrote, "No father can love a Son more than I love you." When the General Convention appointed Lay to be missionary bishop of the southwest in 1859 we can be certain that Cobbs must have lobbied heavily for him.[38]

Many of the Episcopal clergy who served the Diocese of Alabama in the early nineteenth century received support from the Episcopal Church's Domestic and Foreign Missionary Society. In 1829 the DFMS heard the first reports of "missionaries, most of whom are now labouring with highly encouraging prospects, [who] have been sent . . . to Tuscaloosa in Alabama." Not long before Christ Church, Mobile, was organized, Henry Shaw became the pastor of Mobile's Protestant "union" church. Robert Davis presided at the meeting to organize Christ Church, Tuscaloosa, but afterward he may have left the ministry. According to Jackson Kemper, missionary bishop of the northwest, who visited Tuscaloosa in 1838, Davis "preached once or twice after he came here, as an Episcopal clergyman—then studied law, but continued his habits of intoxication, & died suddenly." During Bishop Brownell's 1830 visit to Mobile he "visited the grave of the lamented Judd, the Missionary of the Society for Tuscaloosa." Judd had served as first rector of Tuscaloosa's Christ Church. After the organization of the diocese in 1830 many more DFMS missionaries came to Alabama and helped organize Episcopal churches in Tuscaloosa, Huntsville, Jacksonville, Florence, and elsewhere.[39]

The DFMS also provided provisional episcopal leadership to Alabama by at least partially underwriting the expenses of Alabama's four provisional bishops: Thomas C. Brownell, bishop of Connecticut; James Hervey Otey, bishop of Tennessee; Jackson Kemper, missionary bishop of the Northwest (later the first bishop of Wisconsin); and Leonidas L. Polk, missionary bishop of the Southwest (later the first bishop of Louisiana). Brownell, Otey, Kemper, and Polk were men of heroic faith. They traveled thousands of miles to administer confirmations, ordain clergy, preside at diocesan meetings, mediate disputes between vestries and clergy, or simply to encourage isolated congregations and priests. Polk's experience illustrates the point. In 1839 his report to the DFMS noted that he had traveled about five thousand miles in five months. During that time he "preached forty-four sermons, performed fourteen baptisms, forty-one confirmations, laid the corner stone of one church, and consecrated another."[40]

In spite of the challenge of being a frontier bishop, Cobbs set an ambitious example of hard work for his clergy, as we can see in Henry C. Lay's account of Cobbs's pastoral visitation to points in the Tennessee Valley: "At Florence 2 persons were confirmed, but the good time was in Tuscumbia, where Mr. Cobbs members numbering 17, were increased by the addition of fifteen confirmed: We were at work in good earnest for four or five days, preaching in the most pointed way we could, visiting and talking all day long, and rejoicing with exceeding joy as one poor sinner after another agreed to give up, and dedicate himself to the Lord. . . . In the band were the old & the young, men & women, a Presbyterian, a Campbellite, and two Roman Catholics." We know few details about the daily routines of Alabama's first bishop and his clergy, but Henry C. Lay's letters give us some ideas of how hard they worked. "This North Alabama work is an Egyptian sort of business," wrote Lay to a friend in 1854, "make brick—make brick—why don't you make brick? While the straw is very scarce." Lay, like Cobbs, was prone to overwork, and the bishop had to caution Lay against doing too much. Not long after Lay came to Huntsville, Cobbs wrote and admonished him against preaching three times a Sunday during Lent. "Twice a day is enough for any man, however robust he may be. Even that number with our service is equal to four sermons a day. Your life is too valuable to be wantonly thrown away."[41]

In areas such as the Black Belt, where the distance between towns was relatively short, clergy might have had to serve two or three churches at a time. An example was Francis Hanson who ministered to churches in Demopolis, Gallion, and other towns. Hanson regularly conducted two services every Sunday: "On Easter Sunday I preached and administered the Holy communion [*sic*] in St. Andrews church in the morning. . . . In the afternoon I preached, and administered the Holy Communion in Trinity Church, Demopolis. The same sermon in both places. . . . Sunday May the first, preached in the morning in St. Andrews and in the afternoon in Trinity church, Demopolis."

Even when the distance from one town to the next *was* fairly short, though, the clergy's task was made even more onerous by the state of transportation in early nineteenth-century Alabama. When Cobbs became bishop in 1844 the principal means of transportation was the river, and the only rail line ran from Montgomery to the Georgia border. In spite of the primitive state of transportation, Bishop Cobbs resolved to visit every Episcopalian household in Alabama.[42] J. H. Ticknor, a DFMS missionary at Livingston, wrote in 1855 that his closest parishioners were ten miles away and that it took him "four hours and a half driving 2 horses in a light buggy [to go] ten miles" on a good day, but that "a few days later the buggy could not have been pulled through the road." Under the circumstances, Ticknor wrote, it was an accomplishment just "to keep the church alive."[43] On his way to church on Sunday morning, W. A. Harris, missionary at Florence, faced an obstacle he could not surmount when "the ferryman refused to take me across the Tennessee . . . on account of the quantity of ice in the river."[44] When traveling longer distances the clergy had to rely on the notoriously dangerous steamboats that plied the Alabama and Tombigbee Rivers. According to Scottish traveler Alexander Mackay, steamboats had an "ominous name to European ears" because they "so often prove fatal to their passengers."[45] One of Alabama's priests complained to Sir Charles Lyell that when the clergy had to "travel through these woods in summer" they had to "endure the bites of countless musquitos [*sic*], fleas, and bugs."[46]

Another challenge was the daily reality of sickness and death, especially in wild and unsettled places such as the Alabama frontier. Sometimes the missionaries feared for their lives. In 1836, Thomas A. Cook, a DFMS missionary at Florence, Alabama, wrote of "a rupture" that was "about to commence with the Creek Indians, who lie across my path," but was confident that God would protect him "from all danger."[47] Cook was wise to fear trouble from the Creeks. The attempt to remove the Creeks from eastern Alabama precipitated a brief war that forced Governor Clay to call out the militia.[48] At other times the missionaries or their families fell prey to sicknesses common on the frontier. Writing from Selma in 1846, John H. Linebaugh informed the DFMS that though he was "sick in bed most of the time, and all the time feeble" he managed to preach eleven times. However, the greater sacrifice was borne by his family. Linebaugh wrote that his youngest child died "from congestion of the Brain on the 13th of August. He was a son and in 12th month of his age. He died in the county of Tuscaloosa, at the residence of my wifes Mother, and was buried by the Bishop."[49] Bishop Cobbs lost a daughter in 1852; he described her as the "light & the pride & the joy of a Father's heart."[50]

Money was also a concern for some of the clergy. In a letter to the convention of the Diocese of Alabama in 1837, Caleb S. Ives defended his decision to leave parochial ministry to teach school. Ives took up teaching "to liquidate a debt, which I, under indigent circumstances incurred in educating myself for the ministry of the church."[51] Bishop Cobbs had to remind the diocese in his annual addresses both in 1849 and 1858 that one of the difficulties "in the way of building up the Church" was "the inadequate support of the Clergy." Not only was the compensation meager, but clergy were not always "punctually and fully paid."[52]

There was also little job security for Alabama's earliest Episcopal clergy, especially in the years between 1830 and 1844 when Alabama's provisional bishops were seldom available to mediate conflicts between parish clergy and their vestries. Clergy in Alabama's earliest Episcopal churches had one-year contracts that were voted on by the vestry at the annual meeting, which in most parishes took place on Easter Monday (which was also the day on which vestry members stood for election). The tenuousness of clergy employment is demonstrated by the history of Christ Church, Tuscaloosa, which had eleven rectors in its first thirteen years.[53] Christ Church, Mobile, was considerably more stable; between 1830 and 1854 the average tenure of its rectors was more than seven years.

Quite often clergy that left one parish went to another parish in the diocese. The Committee on the State of the Church regarded the "frequent removal of ministers from one parish to another one of the Diocese" as "deleterious to the best interests of the Church."[54] Samuel Lewis and Nathaniel Knapp illustrate the problem. Both had been rectors of Christ Church, Tuscaloosa, before going to Christ Church, Mobile. Knapp began at St. Peter's, Lowndes County, in 1838, and moved to Christ Church, Tuscaloosa, and then to St. John's, Montgomery, in 1843. Then in 1848 he went to Christ Church, Mobile, first as Samuel Lewis's assistant and later as the rector.

The Episcopal Church and Other Denominations

Because they were not numerous, the people and clergy of the Episcopal Church had to develop relationships with other denominations, and they encountered both warm hospitality and deep suspicion from members of other churches. Some churches freely extended their hospitality to Episcopalians and their clergy. For example, in his 1830 visit to Selma, Connecticut bishop Thomas C. Brownell wrote that "the Clergyman of the Presbyterian Church immediately called on us, and invited us to officiate in the House of worship there." Similarly, in Montgomery he preached in the Methodist church, although he noted "a large portion of the population of the village found a stronger attraction at the Theatre." In Florence, Thomas Cook noted he had met "with greater kindness from other denominations than . . . ever . . . before" and that there was a high degree of friendship and cooperation between the Episcopal Church and other denominations. Cook alluded to the belief common among evangelicals that the Episcopal Church was doctrinally suspect, but said that other denominations had started "to look upon our Church as Orthodox and Christian" and that they had begun to believe that "our doctrines are so much like the Bible." Cook's successor in Florence, W. A. Harris, wrote that he had "preached in the Campbellite and Methodist meeting houses, to very good and attentive congregations."

Prior to erecting its own building, St. John's, Montgomery, met primarily in the local Baptist church but also sometimes in either the Universalist or Presbyterian churches. Francis Hanson notes several times in his diary that he preached in churches of other denominations, and in one place notes that the bishop not only preached in a Presbyterian church but also administered the rite of confirmation there. Sometimes even the Diocesan Convention had to be held in churches of other denominations. In Mobile in 1836, Greensboro in 1837, and Selma in 1839, the Diocesan Convention met in Presbyterian churches because either the local Episcopal church was unusable or had not yet been constructed.

If necessary, Episcopalians would even hold their services in secular buildings. In 1838, Andrew Matthews reported that his Marion congregation held its services in the courthouse. Meeting in a secular building was one thing, but using a church for a secular purpose was something else. In 1847 the vestry of Christ Church, Mobile, proposed holding a concert in the church to raise money, but its rector, Nathaniel Knapp, objected. It is not clear whether Knapp was protesting the use of the church to raise money or for a nonliturgical function or both.[55]

The ecumenical hospitality extended to the Episcopal Church and its clergy is remarkable, especially in light of the fact that the Episcopal Church did not embrace the prevailing revivalist ethos and seemed to resemble the Roman Catholic Church a little too closely. The similarities between the liturgy and polity of the Episcopal Church and the Roman Catholic Church also produced suspicion and misunderstanding. Bishop Cobbs identified a fear that the Episcopal Church was "Romish" as an obstacle to growth, but he seems to have had a good relationship with the clergy and laypeople of other denominations, in spite of the fact that he was sometimes accused of trying to "steal" their members. There is some truth to the charge. At the 1860 Diocesan Convention he reported that he had "received George M. Everhart, late a Methodist minister, as a candidate for Holy Orders."

He was also accused of offering a Methodist woman a cow if she would become an Episcopalian. Cobbs defended himself, saying, "In fact, I would give her two cows. Why should people complain of me because I love them so well that I want them to live with me? The greatest harm I wish to Presbyterians and Methodists is to see them good members of the church." When the daughter of some Baptist friends began reading the bishop's Prayer Book, he took it from her and said, "If you read it you will become an Episcopalian and I cannot requite your parents' kindness by allowing it." But the next time he visited the family, the young woman had acquired her own Prayer Book and eventually the entire family joined the Episcopal Church.[56] The clergy of other denominations appear to have thought well of Cobbs. If his biographer is to be believed, Presbyterian and Methodists ministers and a Roman Catholic priest were with him when he died.[57]

There was some justification for the suspicion that the Episcopal Church was, for some, at least, a halfway house between Protestantism and Roman Catholicism: North Carolina's bishop, Levi Silliman Ives, converted to the Roman Catholic Church in 1852. Prior to Ives's conversion to Roman Catholicism, John Henry Hobart's theology had come to dominate the PECUSA. Hobart's theology was "high church," but prior to the Oxford movement,[58] high churchmanship was more a matter of theology than ritual. As noted in the previous chapter, Hobart and his disciples believed in baptismal regeneration, sacramental grace, and that episcopacy was a divinely instituted polity. The priest Sir Charles Lyell met on the steamboat between Tuscaloosa and Mobile must not have been the only high churchman in the Diocese of Alabama. Three of Alabama's provisional bishops were firmly in the Hobartian camp—Brownell, Otey, and Kemper—and several of its clergy (Stickney and Knapp, in particular) were graduates of New York's General Theological Seminary, which Hobart had founded. That Hobart College bestowed an honorary degree on Bishop Cobbs is a strong indicator of his theological temperature.

Bishop Cobbs Establishes a Theological Climate

Publicly, Cobbs's theological position was that of a moderate high churchman. He articulated his theology most clearly in his 1849 address to the Diocesan Convention. In it he condemned the positions both Anglo-Catholic and Protestant extremists had taken, but he addressed the extreme Anglo-Catholic position first. Cobbs took on catholic extremism first because this was more pressing. John Keble's 1833 Assize Sermon, "National Apostasy," is usually regarded as the beginning of the Oxford movement. The "Tracts of the Times" were published between 1833 and 1841. When Cobbs forcefully condemned those who, "under the pretence of Antiquity and Catholicity" had introduced "various puerilities, in matters connected with the worship and chancel arrangements of the Church," he was referring to American adherents of the Oxford movement. They were, he said,

> a new set of reformers, who, whilst very harsh in denouncing different Protestant bodies as heretics, and schismatics, are yet very tender and apologetic in their remarks in reference to various errors of Romanism, especially the doctrines of Purgatory, Transubstantiation, Auricular Confession, and the Invocation of the Virgin Mary; men who whilst talking about their devotion to the Church, treat with disregard her divinely appointed officers, and who, whilst preaching up obedience, show in their conduct all the willfulness and pride of self, manifested by the most obstinate and wrong headed sectary ... though they may flatter themselves that they are Catholics, they can not justly be called sound churchmen.

At the same time, Cobbs challenged the extreme evangelical or Protestant position, which he characterized as having a "low and defective view ... of the Church, the ministry, and the sacraments." "The consequence of this is that many of her baptized members grow up ignorant of her doctrines, careless of her sanctions, indifferent to her privileges, neglectful of her ordinations; and finally, turning their backs upon their spiritual mother, go off into schism, or heresy, or worldliness." Cobbs may have had in mind his experience at the University of Virginia. Jefferson's deist convictions had led him to found a university in which religion played no official role, and the result, according to Cobbs's biographer, was "a community where religion and its ministers had been regarded with aversion and contempt."[59]

In a personal letter to Tennessee's bishop, James H. Otey, Cobbs expressed an extremely high view of the episcopacy. "The right of governing the church was committed by a divine grant to the Apostles & their Successors," Cobbs wrote. "The truth is—my Dear Bishop—we have carried the lay element ... too far in this country from a morbid jealousy of Bishops." Cobbs was convinced that the church is "a Divine institution, to which it is a Christian duty and a great blessing to belong and from which it is a serious loss, and a fearful sin wantonly to separate." And by "the Church" Cobbs specifically meant those institutions that had maintained the apostolic succession. Although he was convinced that the Roman Catholic Church was in error, he was equally convinced that the other Protestant churches were not "the Church" in the fullest sense. To him it was not "a matter of indifference whether people belong to the One True Catholic and Apostolic Church, or to any Christian organization of human origin." As Bishop Hobart in New York had opposed cooperation with the Bible Society, so Cobbs frowned on "merging of her means and her influence with other associations." Even though Cobbs's theology put him firmly in the high church camp, he maintained close ties with evangelicals, such as Bishop Meade of Virginia, who invited Cobbs to preach at the ordination of the Virginia Theological Seminary's class of 1848.[60]

Church Architecture

The clergy and laypeople of the diocese apparently shared Cobbs's moderate high church theology. One indicator of the theological climate among Alabama Episcopalians is architecture. The earliest Episcopal churches in America (such as Philadelphia's Christ Church) were Georgian Colonial structures, indistinguishable on the outside from Congregational churches. In the original designs the pulpit was squarely in the center with a small communion table beneath it. Sometimes (as one can still see in a few churches, such as St. Peter's, Philadelphia) the communion table was in the back of the church, forcing the congregation to turn completely around on communion Sundays. The Hobartians tended to favor the Gothic Revival churches that put the pulpit to one side and placed the communion table or altar in the center. When congregations were sufficiently affluent, they preferred to build Gothic structures, and many constructed architecturally distinguished buildings. England's Cambridge Camden Society (which spawned the Ecclesiology movement) claimed that Gothic architecture was the ideal form for Anglican worship, theology, and polity.

Well before the Camden Society began to advocate for Gothic architecture, John Henry Hobart was celebrating it. Robert Bruce Mullin writes, "As early as 1812 . . . he praised the power of Gothic architecture in elevating the heart." Preaching at the consecration of St. Stephen's Episcopal Church in Philadelphia, Hobart lauded "the fitness in its architectural arrangements to the end of which it is designed: the worship of that High and Holy Being, to whom it is devoted, with the feelings of awful and reverential, yet lively and cheerful devotion." Architecture served Anglicanism by asserting its claims to having theology, liturgy, and polity that were superior to other denominations. In writing of eighteenth-century Anglican churches, Richard Bushman argues that architecture supported Anglicanism's "ecclesiastical arguments" and was "an instrument of cultural conflict." However, the architectural splendor of Episcopal churches also demonstrated the cultural superiority of those who worshiped there. Bushman quotes a visitor to an American Anglican church in 1781 who observed that "piety is not the only motive that brings the American ladies in crowds to the various places of worship . . . church is the grand theatre where they attend to display their extravagance and finery."[61]

Several of Alabama's early Episcopal churches, including St. Luke's, Jacksonville; St. John's, Forkland; St. Luke's, Cahaba; and St. Andrew's, Gallion, used architect Richard Upjohn's 1852 book, *Upjohn's Rural Architecture: Designs, Work-*

ing Drawings, and Specifications for a Wooden Church, and Other Rural Structures (although Upjohn may have designed St. Andrew's himself), which showed a style known as "carpenter Gothic," because although stone is the ideal medium for Gothic architecture, Upjohn created Gothic plans that could be realized using wood rather than stone. According to Ronald J. Caldwell, Episcopalians "expressed their power in their architecture." Although speaking of St. Luke's, Cahaba, Caldwell's point applies to the social significance of many, if not most, of Alabama's early Episcopal churches. Begun in 1853, Mobile's Trinity Church was designed by Frank Wills and Henry Dudley, enthusiastic disciples of the leading English architect Augustus Pugin. Founder of the New York Ecclesiological Society, Wills did much to promote neo-Gothic architecture in America. Wills and Dudley's work in Mobile created something of a vogue for neo-Gothic churches in Alabama. They went on to design Huntsville's Church of the Nativity and St. John's, Montgomery. Churches with more modest financial resources still managed to build impressive buildings.[62]

Diocesan Schools and Other Institutions

One of Bishop Cobbs's most important legacies was his creation of diocesan institutions. Cobbs not only traveled the diocese tirelessly, he was also indefatigable in establishing diocesan institutions. These fell into two major categories: schools and agencies of the diocese. Alabama's first bishop had begun his career as a schoolteacher and cherished the hope that the Diocese of Alabama would found Episcopal schools for young men and young women, but in this he was mostly frustrated. While serving as rector of Christ Church, Tuscaloosa, Cobbs initiated a "Female School" in 1846, although a year later its principal moved to Columbus, Mississippi, and the school went with him. In 1848, Cobbs tried again and established the Episcopal Female Seminary in Tuscaloosa, and the following year, he also founded The Classical Institute and Mission School of the Diocese of Alabama, but the death of its principal, Charles F. Peake, brought an end to this venture. Undeterred, Cobbs made one more attempt to establish a diocesan school in Tuscaloosa, and in 1850, William Johnson established a school for young women that lasted until 1854 when the contentious vestry of Christ Church, Tuscaloosa, dismissed Johnson. Cobbs continued to speak of his desire to establish schools after he became rector of St. John's, Montgomery, in 1854.[63]

For Cobbs a school for young men would serve two functions. First, it would encourage them to seek ordination, and second, it would then educate them for the priesthood. Anticipating the reasons for founding the University of the South (Sewanee), he also believed that men educated in the South were more likely to remain in the South: "Those educated here, will probably be for the most part, natives of the State, and as such will naturally feel a stronger attachment to the Diocese, and a deeper interest in its welfare, than would those from abroad. They would also have the advantage of a familiar acquaintance with the Institutions and the habits of thought and feeling of the South; which advantage cannot be small, at a time when much distrust and apprehension pervade the public mind, arising out of the diversity of sentiments existing between different portions of the Union."[64] As previously noted, Cobbs was at least as enthusiastic about founding a school for young women. He reasoned "if we wish to have a Samuel, there must be a Hannah to consecrate him to God's service."[65] It is not necessary to psychoanalyze Cobbs to know that this conviction was a direct result of his mother's influence. His Episcopalian mother and her determination to impart her faith to Cobbs made him keenly aware of the influence mothers have over sons. Thus he reasoned that a school for young women would have an enormous impact on the faith of future generations. After his move to Montgomery, Cobbs was successful in founding a school for girls. Under the direction of J. Avery Shepherd, the Diocesan Female Seminary (later Hamner Hall) opened in October 1860 and closed in 1889.

Cobbs's most elaborate scheme for education involved the establishment of a cathedral in Montgomery. Possibly inspired by his visit to England in 1856, Cobbs hoped to give the Diocese of Alabama the first cathedral in the PECUSA. Quoting a letter that no longer exists, Cobbs's son says that his father envisioned a great church that was to have been called "All Souls." It would have been a "free church," open to rich and poor, white and black, without distinction. Following Cobbs's death, at the 1861 convention a committee was formed to look into the feasibility of building "a *Free Church* in memory of the services, zeal, and holy example of our late Right Reverend Father in God." Although Cobbs did not speak of this idea publicly, this proposed memorial sounds enough like Cobbs's idea to suggest that he must have sounded out friends and colleagues with regard to the idea of building a great cathedral. Cobbs's plan for a cathedral was truly visionary and ahead of its time. The cathedral and its close would have seated 1,500 in the nave and another 1,000 in the galleries. In all there would have been nine buildings, including a library and offices for the bishop, a residence for the dean, an infirmary and "house of mercy," a theological seminary, and a home for five deaconesses. Even if Cobbs had not died, the war would have rendered his plan completely impractical. Paradoxically, the one part of his plan that his successor realized, the founding of an order of deaconesses, was probably made possible by the war. Given the urgency of caring for Confederate orphans, Bishop Wilmer's decision to "set apart" women to serve as deaconesses was uncontroversial.[66]

The most successful educational venture in which Cobbs participated was the founding of the University of the South. In 1856, Bishop Polk of Louisiana sent a letter to his fellow southern bishops in which he outlined his plan for a university that would rival Harvard and Yale. Cobbs announced plans for the university at the 1857 Diocesan Convention: "I would also bring to the notice of the Convention the plan for establishing a Southern University, to be conducted under the auspices of the Church. The general outlines of the plan may be found in Bishop Polk's 'Address of the Southern Bishops.'" Cobbs reported that he "attended the meeting of the bishops at Chattanooga" on July 4, 1857, "who assembled for the purpose of consulting about the founding of a University for the South," and that he preached once. He was also present at the "meeting of the Trustees of the Southern University" in Montgomery on November 25 "to decide upon the locality of the contemplated University" at which Sewanee, Tennessee, was chosen as the university's location. There was vigorous debate about the location for the proposed university, and a Huntsville group offered $100,000 and 1,000 acres on top of Monte Sano. The decision to locate the university at Sewanee was made at a meeting at Beersheba Springs, Tennessee, on July 5, 1858. Recognizing that Huntsville would not be the site, Cobbs moved to table a reconsideration of locating the university at Sewanee, saying, "we are fairly beaten, and thoroughly defeated. I give up and surrender. . . . We have done our duty, and the result is against us. Since you [Polk] will not come down from the mountain, I will climb the mountain and join you there."[67]

Cobbs had considerable success in establishing agencies of the diocese. In 1846 the diocese had established a Society for the Relief of Disabled Clergy and the Widows and Orphans of Deceased Clergy. Of perhaps even more importance was the establishment of the Diocesan Missionary Society. Although established in 1844 just before Cobbs's election, the bishop became its most enthusiastic supporter. Cobbs constantly urged his clergy and parishes to support missionary outreach. Perhaps the parish that was most committed to outreach by its fund-raising and also by its deeds was Mobile's Christ Church. In 1844 their rector reported that "the Boy's [sic] Missionary Society . . . have contributed $25 for the first year's education of [a] . . . Chinese youth, and they are, also, about to educate in the same way, at the same expense, an Indian boy. The Girl's [sic] Missionary Society . . . have contributed the same amount for the support of an African girl."[68]

Between its organization in 1830 and Cobbs's death in 1861, the Diocese of Alabama had had a resident bishop for just over half its span of existence. The business of building a diocese on the Alabama frontier must have seemed daunting to Bishop Cobbs. When he was consecrated, the Episcopal Church in Alabama consisted of about 450 communicants, eighteen parishes and missions, and about fifteen clergy, but under his leadership, the diocese added new churches and new members rapidly. In 1840 the population of Alabama was approximately 591,000 (free and slave); in 1860, it was close to one million.[69] In 1846, the Diocese of Alabama had 636 communicants and twenty-four parish churches. On the eve of Cobbs's death in 1860, there were thirty-nine churches and 1,683 communicants. The population of the state increased by 78 percent, but the communicant strength of the Episcopal Diocese of Alabama increased by 164 percent. Cobbs, however, must share credit for his accomplishments with his small band of clergy and even more with the nearly 1,700 Episcopal laypeople in the state. Cobbs was faithful, industrious, perhaps even holy, and as his episcopate and life drew to an end, Alabama's first bishop could look back with gratitude and satisfaction, and Alabama's Episcopalians could be thankful for having chosen their first bishop wisely. Although many of Alabama's scattered villages did not yet have an Episcopal church, the influence of Alabama's Episcopalians could be felt everywhere in Alabama. The state was governed under a constitution to which Episcopalians had made significant contributions; Episcopalians had served at every level of government. The state's only university had been launched in a service held in an Episcopal church, and Episcopalians wrote for and edited Alabama newspapers. But before Cobbs died in January 1861, Alabama would risk its future on a catastrophically foolish gamble, and Episcopalians, both lay and ordained, would bless the state's folly.

3

"This worldliness that is rushing upon us like a flood"

Secession and Civil War

Nicholas Hamner Cobbs was strongly opposed to secession. One historian asserts that Cobbs was "the one man of character and influence who in all Alabama had opposed secession in any way, at any time, or for any reason." It is difficult not to believe that his fear of the consequences of secession was behind Cobbs's denunciation of "worldliness" in his jeremiad at the 1859 diocesan convention:

> The spiritual prospects of the Diocese are not flattering:—there is much coldness; there is much worldliness; there is a great deal of worldly conformity. The contributions to charitable objects have fallen very far below the standard of the Gospel; there has been placed upon the Altar of Fashion a great deal that should have been appropriated to the service of the Lord. As a consequence, the blessing of the Lord has not descended upon our Congregations; Confirmations have been few; the additions to the Communion have been few, and we are in great danger of falling into the state of the Laodiceans. . . . There is great and urgent need of self-denial,—for the great evil of the day is worldliness:—is worldly conformity. When a whole country is submerged by a wide wasting inundation, it is too late to talk of dykes and levees.

Cobbs echoed the Book of Revelation, comparing Alabama Episcopalians to the first-century Laodiceans ("because thou art lukewarm, and neither cold nor hot,

I will spue thee out of my mouth"). The Committee on the State of the Church concurred with the bishop. They charged "in many instances the Ball-rooms and the Theatre, divide with the Church the affections of her children" and urged the diocese not to adopt "the drinking usages of society, its immodest amusements, its extravagance of apparel, its avaricious greed, its self-indulgent ease, they emperil [*sic*] the cause of Christ." About a month after the 1859 convention Cobbs wrote to Henry C. Lay complaining in similar words of "this worldliness that is rushing in upon us like a flood." "What is to be done to stay or even to turn it aside?" Cobbs asked. He continued, saying that he was "almost out of heart" and was "tempted to put on a long cassock of cotton [illegible] died [*sic*] black, tied around with a thick rope & to go forth with a long staff mounted with a cross, proclaiming day by day—in the churches—& by the way side— ... In this way the people might be startled for a moment & perchance some might be induced to turn away from the Fiddler . . . & to remember that they had souls to care for." The report of George Cushman, rector of St. Luke's, Cahaba, in the 1861 journal, also echoed Cobb's concerns: "The only encouraging circumstance of the year has been the large attendance upon the daily Lenten service. The Parish has been an [*sic*] loser in numbers and in pecuniary strength. . . . The spiritual weal of the Parish was never at so low an ebb, and, Lord revive Thy work, is the prayer of the faithful."[1]

Even if Cobbs had actually donned his vestments, taken his episcopal staff, and denounced secession in every courthouse square in Alabama, it is overwhelmingly likely that Alabama would have seceded anyway. Only a few members of Cobbs's flock agreed with their chief pastor's opposition to secession. But even at St. John's, Montgomery, where Jefferson Davis and much of the Confederate leadership worshiped, there were differences of opinion. Charles T. Pollard, senior warden of St. John's during the Civil War, noted that "but for the Bishop's wise and serene influence, St John's would probably have been divided." St. John's was not only the church of Unionist congressman Henry W. Hilliard, it was also the church of archsecessionist William Lowndes Yancey.[2]

Alabama Secedes and Bishop Cobbs Dies

In the early hours of November 7, 1860, when Alabamians learned that New York's electoral votes had made Abraham Lincoln the president-elect, Episcopal layman William Hodgson recorded that the people of Montgomery assembled at Estelle Hall to hear two more Episcopalians: N. H. R. Dawson of St. Paul's, Selma, and William L. Yancey. According to Hodgson, Dawson's address was "earnest and thrilling," but it was Yancey whose rhetoric really roused the crowd. In Yancey's opinion, Lincoln and the Republican Party were the real "disunionists," and he urged his listeners to "defend the soil of a State which may be threatened by mercenary bayonets." As Alabama's voters had directed him, Governor Andrew Moore duly summoned a convention, and on January 11, 1861, its delegates voted for secession.[3]

When South Carolina seceded on December 20, 1861, Kate Cumming of St. John's Church, Mobile, recorded that the event was announced by the booming of cannon and that afterward Mobile was "one blaze of light . . . scarcely a window in the whole city . . . was not lit. The noise from the fireworks and the arms was deafening. Speeches were made, processions paraded the streets with banners flying and drums beating, and in fact everything was done to prove that Mobile, at least, approved of what South Carolina had done." John Mitchell, Cobbs's associate at St. John's, Montgomery, shared the general optimism about the prospects of establishing a new Southern nation: "If old Virginia roll wheel into the ranks, now rapidly filling up, I do not think that the Republicans and General Scott, will be fools big enough (however extensive may be their rascality) to attempt to coerce so formidable an array of States. I have had my *private* effusion of tears over the grave of the old Union and now look forward hopefully to the peaceable formation of a *new* one, to include all the Slaveholding States. May God grant it; if he means to correct us, may he do it not in his anger, lest he bring us to *nothing*." Other clergy appraised the situation more realistically. Writing a few months later, Henry C. Lay presciently noted, "I am as disturbed as a man can be at the civil war now opening on us. . . . I am now Southern. . . . But I could weep day and night for the misery before us & the folly that has brought us to it."[4]

At the same time that Alabama was reacting to Lincoln's election and pondering secession, Bishop Cobbs's life was drawing to a close. The bishop had not been well for some time. In 1855 Cobbs was unable to work for two months due to an unidentified illness, and in May of the next year he underwent an operation. At the 1856 Diocesan Convention the Committee on the State of the Church urged him to rest and provided the bishop with the means to take a three-month sabbatical, during which he spent several weeks in England. His last episcopal visitation was to St. Matthew's, Autaugaville, on October 21, 1860. Some time after that he seems to have suffered a severe stroke, after which he was confined to his bed. Later, it would be said that Cobbs had prayed that he would not live to see Alabama secede from the Union, and so at the age of sixty-four, the Diocese of Alabama's first bishop died on January 11, the day the secession convention approved the ordinance of secession. John Mitchell, who followed him as rector of St. John's, was with Cobbs when he died, and wrote of the bishop's death to Henry C. Lay:

I thought I knew how good and holy & heavenly-minded he was before, but I *did not* until I was so much with him during his protracted illness.

He suffered chiefly from nausea & vomiting—how intensely no pen can describe—the nausea almost incessant for eleven weeks . . . and yet not a murmur or other sign of impatience from the beginning to the end. On the contrary, "I thank God for this sickness" was among his most frequent & most fervent exclamations. Nor did he manifest at any time the slightest fear of death. He suffered less the last three days, retained his consciousness up to an hour before he died, & finally "fell asleep" as gently as a child in the arms of its mother.

Kate Cumming observed, "The spirit of the saintly Bishop Cobbs winged its flight to the better land. Many thought he died of grief at the country's woe, and at the perils which surrounded his native State—Virginia." Mitchell was also aware that the diocese had been deprived of Cobbs's leadership precisely when they most needed it: "what a sad, sad time for our country to have lost such a man, and our Church such a Bishop!"[5]

Bishop Cobbs seems to have been universally loved. Writing to William Stickney, a priest in Mobile, Louisa Harrison of the Faunsdale Plantation in Marengo County asked if he had heard of Bishop Cobbs's death: "I suppose you heard of the dear Bishop's illness. Well he has gone home now. He died on the morning of the 11th. Most of the clergy were with him, & Bishop Elliott was expected that day. He had full use of all his faculties, but was so feeble that he lay perfectly still. Mr. Gholson, who was with him, says it was a very affecting scene. I feel as if I had lost a relative in him. But he is far better off than me." In his journal Francis Hanson wrote that Cobbs was "a good man, full of the holy ghost and of faith, and by his influence and labors many were added to the church, for sixteen years he had governed the church in this Diocese. And bore himself with such meekness and humility, that he gained general favour, and his death seems to be lamented as a common calamity. For my own part, I have felt his loss to be a great calamity not only to the church but to myself personally. He was always to me a kind friend and an indulgent Bishop. I was sincerely attached to him."[6] Georgia's Bishop Elliott presided at Cobbs's funeral at St. John's, Montgomery, following which Cobbs was buried in Montgomery's Oakwood cemetery.

For the last eight years of his life, Cobbs served not only as the bishop of Alabama but also as rector of St. John's, Montgomery. From February to April 1861, Montgomery was the capital of the Confederacy, and St. John's was virtually a chapel for the Confederate leadership. Although he was a Baptist at the time, Jefferson Davis, his Episcopalian wife, Varina, and their family occupied pew number 115. Later, when the Confederate administration moved to Richmond, Davis was baptized and confirmed in St. Paul's Church, Richmond. St. John's senior warden during this time, Charles Teed Pollard, wrote that

St. John's seemed to be the very heart of the Confederacy. President Davis and his family, most of the Cabinet members and their families; Staff officers from time to time; all came to St. John's, for all of us knew that this was a time for pray [*sic*] All the young men left in uniform. . . . The church was open for prayer at all times. The vestry and the nearby rectory overflowed with busy women; making gray uniforms, knitting, cooking, and scraping lint for bandages."[7]

J. Avery Shepherd, rector of Hamner Hall Female Seminary, also assisted John Mitchell at St. John's. Ironically, Shepherd not only gave the invocation for the Confederate congress on the morning of Jefferson Davis's inauguration, he was also a member of the Truce Committee that surrendered Montgomery to federal troops.[8]

The fact that Cobbs resided in Montgomery and served as rector of St. John's underscores the close association between the Episcopal Church and the Confederacy. The fact that numerous Confederate civil and military leaders were Episcopalians shows how accurate it was to characterize the Episcopal Church as "the slaveholders' church . . . the church of a class."[9] Episcopalians were overrepresented at the highest levels of Confederate leadership and also disproportionately represented among chaplains to the Confederate army. Generals Robert E. Lee and Ellison Capers (later bishop of South Carolina) were Episcopalians and Bishop Polk of Louisiana "buckled the sword over the gown" and became a lieutenant general in the Confederate army. Lee's chief of artillery, William Nelson Pendleton, was an Episcopal priest, who, after the war, became rector of Grace Church, Lexington, Virginia, the town where Washington and Lee University (formerly Washington College) is located. When Lee became president of Washington College, he also became Pendleton's parishioner. Two Confederate chaplains with strong Alabama ties became bishops following the war: John Beckwith of Trinity, Demopolis, became bishop of Georgia, and Robert Barnwell, who succeeded Beckwith at Demopolis, was elected bishop of Alabama in 1900.

A Rebel Bishop for a Rebel Diocese

In the midst of the whirlwind, the clergy and laymen of the Diocese of Alabama tried and failed to elect a new bishop at the regularly scheduled Diocesan Convention in May. The leading candidate was Henry C. Lay, Missionary Bishop of the Southwest, who had served as rector of Huntsville's Church of the Nativity from 1847 to 1859. Whitaker suggests that Lay was not elected because his fellow clergy felt that "he had assumed the air and authority of a Bishop before his elevation to the Episcopate. . . . Mr. Lay was not popular among the clergy."

However, this is doubtful. At least some of the clergy liked Lay, and some influential priests in the diocese strongly promoted his candidacy. J. M. Banister, Lay's successor in Huntsville, wrote, "Now see here, Lay. I wish you to be Bishop of Alabama.... It would be sad indeed if our next Bishop should be different in character and churchmanship from him of whom, death has bereaved us." Mobile's Joshua Massey wrote, "First, are *you* willing to be a candidate? Many talk of voting for you anyhow; and if you were now a Presbyter I am confident you w[oul]d be elected promptly." Lay was also popular among the lay delegates. The chief objection to choosing Lay to succeed Cobbs was that he was already a bishop. Apparently many clergy felt it was too soon for Lay to move because he had served only about a year and a half as Missionary Bishop of the Southwest. Both Massey and Mitchell refer to this issue. "The question is whether you ought to relinquish y[ou]r. Present work & whether the Ch[urch]. at large w[oul]d justify or condemn you in so doing," wrote Massey. And Mitchell expressed similar thoughts: "many think you w[oul]d not accept & some say you ought not to be even solicited to leave your present post, & therefore they will not vote for you much as they would like to do so if you were not a Bishop already."[10]

Other clergy suggested as successors of Bishop Cobbs included J. M. Banister of Huntsville and Charles T. Quintard of Nashville (subsequently elected second bishop of Tennessee). Both Mitchell and Massey also mentioned a Virginia parish priest from a family strongly associated with the evangelical wing of the Episcopal Church—Richard Hooker Wilmer. "I w[oul]d like to know y[ou]r opinion of one whose name is mentioned as often as any other. I mean our friend Richard Wilmer," asked Joshua Massey in a letter to Lay in March 1861. John Mitchell also noted that Wilmer was under consideration to succeed Cobbs. "These other names are talked up—Dr. Craik, Dr. Morrison, Dr. Pinckney & Dr. Hall of Washington, Dr. R. H. Wilmer, Dr. Curtis of N.C., Dr. Hawks, Quintard, & Banister and perhaps others."[11]

Between the unsuccessful attempt to elect a bishop in May and the Special Convention in September that successfully elected a bishop, Alabama hosted the first convention of the Episcopal Church in the Confederate States of America (CSA). The formation of a new Southern nation raised the question of the relationship between the PECUSA and the southern dioceses. Unlike the Baptists, Methodists, and Presbyterians, Episcopalians spent little time debating slavery. Its bishops, clergy, and laypeople were mostly in favor of it or remained silent if they were opposed. So the Episcopal Church maintained its unity while the other Protestant denominations divided North and South, free and slave.

In a letter dated March 23, 1861, Bishops Polk of Louisiana and Elliott of Georgia (probably the two bishops most in favor of secession) noted that "the rapid march of events and the change which has taken place in our civil relations" raised the question of the relationship between the Episcopal Church in the Confederate States and the church in the United States, and they invited their fellow southern bishops to a meeting in Montgomery in July to "consult upon such matters as may have arisen out of the changes in our civil affairs." Polk believed that the relationship between the Episcopal Church in the CSA and the church in the USA was comparable to that of the church in the newly independent United States to the Church of England. He wrote to the clergy of his diocese: "The State of Louisiana having by a formal ordinance, through her Delegates in Convention assembled, withdrawn herself from all further connection with the United States of America, and constituted herself a separate sovereignty, has by that act removed our Diocese from within the pale of the 'Protestant Episcopal Church in the United States.' We have therefore an independent Diocesan existence."

In his pastoral letter, Polk insisted that he was not advocating schism, saying that he was not motivated by a difference of opinion as to "Christian Doctrine or [c]atholic usage," and that he was calling for "separation, not division, certainly not alienation." Polk's letter and the appeal from Polk and Elliott, however, were issued before Virginia and North Carolina had seceded from the Union, even though they were addressed to the bishops in these states. It is possible that Polk and Elliott were simply anticipating the inevitable secession of these states, but in urging bishops in states still affiliated with the Union to leave the PECUSA, they were, in fact, advocating schism. The delegates to Alabama's Diocesan Convention in May 1861 agreed to send delegates to the meeting Polk and Elliott called for later that year but disagreed with Polk's reasoning. Polk had argued, "the Church must follow nationality." The Alabama delegates, however, adopted a more subtle argument. The constitution of the Diocese of Alabama presupposed that Alabama was a part of the United States; thus secession had rendered the diocesan constitution null and void. Bishops Meade and Johns of Virginia and Bishop Atkinson of North Carolina seem to have felt that Polk and Elliott were acting precipitously. They counseled that the momentous step of separating from the PECUSA and organizing the Episcopal Church in the Confederate states required "as general a representation as possible," so they suggested changing the place of the meeting to Raleigh, Ashville, or Sewanee and requested that it take place a month later. The meeting, however, proceeded as Polk and Elliott had proposed in Montgomery in July. Bishop Atkinson of North Carolina also disagreed, contending that the church could maintain its unity across national boundaries and citing the example of Bishop Boone who planted the Episcopal Church in China but did not establish a separate Chinese Episcopal Church. Polk and Elliott, however, prevailed, and the Confederate dioceses assembled in Montgomery in July 1861.[12]

When Polk and Elliott wrote their letter, Montgomery was a logical place to hold the meeting to organize the Episcopal Church in the Confederate states because it had also hosted the first Confederate Congress. Indeed, by locating the convention to organize the Confederate Episcopal Church in Montgomery, Polk and Elliott were drawing attention to the parallel between political and ecclesiastical secession. Could the southern dioceses fail to follow the example of the southern states and secede from the PECUSA as the states had seceded from the USA?

By the time the southern dioceses met in Montgomery, the Confederate Congress had moved its capital to Richmond, Virginia. Nevertheless, Montgomery was in the heart of secessionist territory. The secessionist impulse was strongest among the planters of the Black Belt—that broad swath of fertile land that stretches across Mississippi, Alabama, and Georgia. This was also the area in which most of Alabama's Episcopalians were located.

Montgomery was not, however, the most agreeable place to be in July. William Howard Russell, *The Times* of London's war correspondent, visiting Montgomery in May 1861, wrote, "Montgomery has little claim to be called a capital. The streets are very hot, unpleasant, and uninteresting. I have rarely seen a more dull, lifeless place."[13] The fear that the convention would be under-attended proved well founded. When the meeting convened the delegates consisted of four bishops (Elliott of Georgia, Green of Mississippi, Rutledge of Florida, and Davis of South Carolina), fourteen clergy, and eleven laymen. After authorizing a committee to prepare a constitution for the Protestant Episcopal Church in the CSA, the meeting adjourned and reconvened in Columbia, South Carolina, in October. The latter meeting was far better attended. The bishops of all the Confederate states were present with the exception of Bishop (now General) Polk.

In addition to preparing the constitution and canons of the Confederate Episcopal Church and modifying the Book of Common Prayer for its use, the Columbia meeting also took up the question of how to provide a bishop for Alabama. The Alabama delegation petitioned the convention "to determine what, if any, provision can be made by this Convention for the consecration of Bishops before the ratification, by the Diocesan Conventions in the confederate States." Alabama's petition was referred to a committee of three bishops, but the convention took no action on the Alabama delegation's question.[14] The members of the committee of bishops were of the opinion that "the Diocese of Alabama [should] proceed under such regulations as have heretofore existed and still exist in the Diocese for the election of a Bishop." Significantly, Richard Hooker Wilmer was one of two clergy deputies representing the Diocese of Virginia at the Columbia meeting. Five of Alabama's delegates to Columbia were also present at the special Diocesan Convention at St. Paul's, Selma, a month later when Wilmer was elected bishop of Alabama.[15]

Wilmer was not an obvious successor to Cobbs. Although both were Virginians, as were many of the clergy of Alabama, Cobbs was decidedly high church in his theology while the Wilmer family was known for its evangelical leaning. Wilmer's father, William H. Wilmer, was the leading evangelical theologian in the Episcopal Church in the early nineteenth century and also a founder of Virginia Theological Seminary. However, writing to Henry Lay, J. A. Massey of Mobile's St. John's parish hinted that Wilmer's theology had become somewhat more high church ("I have seen him very little since his churchmanship took a start upwards") and enigmatically referred to him as an "an old fashioned Evangelical High Churchman."[16] Having failed to elect a bishop at their regularly scheduled May convention, the Diocese of Alabama elected Richard Hooker Wilmer to succeed Bishop Cobbs at a Special Convention on November 12, 1861, at St. Paul's, Selma. He was consecrated at St. Paul's, Richmond, on March 6, 1862.

Born March 15, 1816, Wilmer was a graduate of Yale and the Virginia Theological Seminary. He seems to have been destined for the episcopate. Wilmer was named after Richard Hooker, the Elizabethan priest who was possibly the greatest theologian Anglicanism produced, and his father, William H. Wilmer, who not only helped found Virginia Theological Seminary but also served as the first rector of St. John's, Lafayette Square, in Washington, DC. Even more significantly, the elder Wilmer had first proposed that the new name for "the Church of England in the colonies" be the Protestant Episcopal Church in the United States of America. Alabama's future bishop served rural parishes in Virginia, a North Carolina parish for less than a year, and then in 1858 was asked to organize a new parish just outside of Richmond.[17]

Wilmer was renowned for his wit. In his memoir, *Clerical Errors,* Louis Tucker wrote, "Bishop Wilmer ruled his city and his diocese by epigram. People thought seven times before opposing him, for the sharp lash of his incisive tongue was worse than whips of lightnings. He was perhaps the wittiest person of his day in the whole English-speaking world, for Mark Twain's fame developed later." At a celebration of the centennial of the Diocese of Alabama, Louis Tucker's father, Gardiner, remembered that "one clergyman of the Diocese said that while he loved to have Bishop Wilmer visit his parish, as it was a stimulating blessing, yet it took him six months afterwards to soothe the wounded feelings of several of his parishioners."[18]

An ardent Southerner, Wilmer served for a time as an officer of a "home-guard" unit organized in his community. In his book, *The Recent Past from a Southern Standpoint: Reminiscences of a Grandfather,* Wilmer wrote, "Your father, who is writing these lines, was deeply and passionately involved on the side of his State and section; ready, if his ministerial calling had not forbidden, to have shouldered his musket, and entered the fight. As it was, under a temporary access [*sic*] of passion, he became captain of a home-guard, and drilled daily, while yet rector of a church near Richmond" as "captain and drillmaster of the home-guard raised in his neighborhood." Unlike Bishop Polk, however, Wilmer came to believe that military service was incompatible with a priestly vocation and resigned from his captaincy.[19]

Wilmer was not only convinced of the justice of the South's cause, he also seems to have believed that the South was in some way superior to the North. Many years after the war, Wilmer wrote, "When in these pages I speak of the North and Northern men, I have not in my eye that large body of people whose culture, refinement, and large-hearted generosity challenge my admiration. . . . But I speak of that fanatical, and at times dominant, element, which having waged a destructive war (and for that it becomes me to make no moan), and after having destroyed our wealth, and laid waste our territory, and revolutionized our domestic and political life, persistently aims at our humiliation, still plies us with ignominious epithets, and, to use a vulgar current phrase, 'still waves the bloody shirt.'"[20]

Wilmer was also an apologist for slavery, and not only saw no conflict between slavery and the Christian faith but also regarded the institution of slavery in some sense as benign. "There was something beautiful," Wilmer wrote, in the relationship between slave and slaveholder, "especially in the care of the young and the old," and he lamented its passing. "All gone, or going . . . the faithful old mammy, the decent and comely maid-servant, reverence, obedience, faithful service, and . . . piety—all vanishing into space; and what have we instead? Conflicts of races, animosity and distrust, jealousy of capital, suffrage without sense, religion without morals, service without reverence . . . the old war between oppressive capital and discontented labor." Wilmer insisted that "the slaveholding population of the Southern States were, for the most part, men of standing and culture, imbued oftentimes with a chivalry of spirit which forbade unkindness to the slave who lived under his roof, who ate of his bread, and hearkened unto his voice," and (very significantly) added, "A true Southern man will not be unjust to his dog." Although Wilmer conceded that the "origin" of slavery was "a foul wrong," he believed that God had ultimately "wrought good" out of slavery.[21]

Alabama Episcopalians and Support of the War

The clergy and laypeople of the diocese entered wholeheartedly into the war effort. In spite of Bishop Wilmer's claim that there were too few clergy in Alabama for any to serve as army chaplains ("We have no supernumerary clergy in this diocese," Wilmer reported to the 1864 diocesan convention),[22] at least two priests of the diocese did serve as chaplains. The Reverend Joseph Nicolson of Talladega reported in 1863 that he had "accepted the appointment of Chaplain in the service of the C.S.A." and was "diligently . . . ministering to the well, the sick and dying." John Beckwith, the rector of Trinity Church, Demopolis (and bishop of Georgia after the war), heeded Bishop Wilmer's call to serve as a chaplain, although not without some grumbling. In a letter to his wife, he wrote, "Shot & shell fall pretty thick about these Q[uarte]rs. Sometimes, but so far no one has been hurt. I find as (entre nous) I suspected, that but little work in my profession can be done *here*,—the B[isho]p. to the contrary notwithstanding. I wish he could & would come up here for a little while & try it for himself." Some clergy entered military service not as chaplains but as combatants. Francis Hanson notes in his journal, "The Rev. Thos J. Beard called this morning to take leave of me. He was enlisted as a privet [*sic*] for the war. He has left a church very much attached to him, in order to go as a soldier to defend his country," but the army did not accept Beard. One priest, Charles Alexander Derby, was killed at Sharpsburg while serving as colonel of the 44th Alabama.[23]

One former Alabama priest played a unique role as a prisoner of war. When the war began, former Alabamian Henry C. Lay had been Missionary Bishop of the Southwest only two years and still had strong ties to the state. When Federal forces occupied Fort Smith, Arkansas, where Lay and Eliza, his wife, were living, he sent her to Huntsville. Subsequently, Lay tried to rejoin his wife in Huntsville, although she had fled once more (this time to Richmond) as Federal troops advanced on Huntsville. Upon arriving in Huntsville, the Federals arrested Lay and eleven of Huntsville's leading citizens, most of whom were members of Nativity. General Mitchell agreed to release the prisoners on the condition that they would sign a statement affirming that they "disapprove[d] . . . all unauthorized and illegal war; and . . . believe[d] that citizens who fire upon railway trains, attack the guards of bridges, destroy the telegraph lines and fire from concealment upon pickets deserve and should receive the punishment of death." Lay and his fellow prisoners were unwilling to sign such a document, saying that they could not condemn "to the punishment of death any of our countrymen for acts, the method, motives and circumstances of which are utterly unknown to us." Mitchell then asked Lay and the others to suggest alternative wording, but the prisoners protested that they had been unlawfully arrested and imprisoned. In response, Mitchell had several (including Lay) put in solitary confinement. Lay writes that "we were forbidden to communicate with each other or with citizens: books, dinner trays, even my tobacco bag searched to intercept letters."

Mitchell's harsh tactics had the desired effect; the prisoners sought and received permission to confer about how to reword the general's document and presented him with a document that affirmed that they would "refrain from . . . acts of hostility and annoyance, and [would] discourage our fellow-citizens from them and from all other acts of irregular warfare." They also agreed to "advise all persons that they who commit these acts, rightly forfeit all claim to the protection promised to peaceable citizens, and that no remonstrance can be made when they incur the penalty affixed to such acts by martial law, even to the extremity of capital punishment." The prisoners all signed it and were released on May 15 after a captivity of nearly two weeks. Due to the occupation of Huntsville, Nativity had been closed for several weeks. Lay records that it was only reopened on May 18.

During the Federal occupation of Huntsville, Lay and his wife were devastated by the death of their daughter, Lucy (named after Bishop Cobbs's wife), who succumbed to dysentery on July 5.[24] Lay again found himself separated from Eliza late in 1864 when he was with Confederate troops outside Atlanta. Finding it necessary to cross Federal lines on his way to Huntsville, Lay asked General Sherman for a safe travel pass, a favor Sherman granted. Lay writes that Sherman "graciously received him" and "conversed freely about affairs political & military." Sherman directed that "Bishop Lay may come to Atlanta where the necessary orders papers will be given him to visit the city of Huntsville & return. I will not exact of the Bishop any specific promise, but will presume in his character to respect the war secresy [sic]."[25]

The parish reports during the Civil War show that virtually all of Alabama's parish churches made some contribution to the war effort. The diocesan journal for 1863 notes that St. John's, Montgomery, contributed $220 "for Soldiers wounded in Virginia" and an additional $50 "for [a] miss[ionar]'y to sick and wounded in Virginia." Other contributions included $41 from St. Luke's, Cahaba, for a hospital; a $25 "thank offering" after the Battle of Manasses from Holy Cross, Uniontown; and $25.50 from St. Michael's, Marengo County, for wounded Alabama soldiers in Richmond. At least three churches—St. Paul's, Selma; Christ Church, Tuscaloosa; and Nativity, Huntsville—gave their bells to be recast into weapons for the Confederate army.[26]

The war affected combatants and noncombatants alike. In his journal, Francis Hanson noted that the "unhappy and destructive war . . . has had a very injurious influence on the prosperity of the church. And if it continues much longer God only knows what will become of us. . . . Valuable lives have been lost and much property destroyed and where or how it will end God only knows." As the Confederacy's fortunes waned, hunger became a very real concern. There were bread riots in Mobile in 1863, and in 1864, Episcopal laywoman Louisa Harrison wrote to the Reverend William Stickney that she was in "a besieged City, surrounded on every side by the Enemy" and faced "the gloomy prospect of starvation." Transportation became increasingly difficult as the Confederate infrastructure collapsed and Federal troops penetrated more deeply into the Southern heartland. In his report to the 1865 Diocesan Convention Bishop Wilmer noted that he had "not made the usual number of visitations" and attributed it to his "protracted indisposition during the Fall and Winter" and "to the almost entire interruption of travel during the last few weeks." During the Federal occupation of Huntsville, Nativity's rector, John M. Banister, was banished from the town for refusing (per Bishop Wilmer's instructions) to pray for the US president and could only conduct services by crossing the Tennessee River from occupied Huntsville to unoccupied territory and back again.[27]

Churchwomen and the War

Women as well as men found ways to serve the South's cause. Episcopalian women tended wounded soldiers and cared for children orphaned by the war both as military nurses and as deaconesses. The best known of these women was Mobile's Kate Cumming. By strange coincidence, on the very day Cumming set out on her mission to care for the Confederate wounded she encountered Bishop Wilmer and one of the women (Harriet Irwin) whom Wilmer was soon to "set apart" as a deaconess. "On Tuesday, the 6th I left Montgomery on a steamer for Selma. On the boat I met Bishop Wilmer of Alabama; with him, a highly accomplished lady, Mrs. Irwin, who was on her way to Tuscaloosa, Alabama, to become a deaconess. . . . There are to be church homes for the benefit of the aged and helpless, orphan asylums, and schools, under their supervision. Bishop Wilmer is fortunate in having an excellent lady, Miss Hewitt of Baltimore, as chief deaconess. She is a woman of energy, intelligence, and devout piety." Cumming did not become a deaconess, although she was scarcely less "devout and pious" than the women who did, but she was also responding to a summons to religious duty. After hearing a sermon by Episcopal priest Benjamin Miller, Cumming offered her services to care for the Confederate wounded. "One Sunday morning my folks came from service very much excited. The Rev. Mr. Miller, an old friend of ours, had made an address in the church, calling upon ladies to go to the front and nurse the sick and wounded." Cumming's family emigrated from Edinburgh, Scotland (where she was born in 1835), to Mobile, where they became members of St. John's Episcopal Church. Cumming's family was opposed to her plan, but she won them over, partly by citing the example of Florence Nightingale. "I knew what one woman had done another could." Cumming admits that she "had never been inside of a hospital, and was wholly ignorant of what I should be called upon to do" but went anyway. She left Mobile in April 1862, and served from then until the end of the war, often within earshot of artillery. ("The enemy were so close that, I was told, a shell from their guns could easily have reached us. Not a very pleasing prospect.") She went first to Corinth, Mississippi, where she helped care for soldiers wounded in the Battle of Shiloh. "Words are not in our vocabulary expressive enough to present to the mind the realities of that sad scene. . . . Gray-haired men, men in the pride of manhood, boys in their teens, Confederates and Federals, mutilated in every imaginable way, lying on the floors just as they were taken from the battlefield, and so close together that it was almost impossible to walk without stepping upon them." Cumming and her fellow nurses were spared none of the horrors of war. She writes of seeing limbs amputated and blood seeping across the threshold of the operating room. In addition to her nursing duties, Cumming sometimes acted as an unofficial chaplain: "As we have no chaplain, we have no service. I read the Bible and other books to the men, and they are much pleased to have me do it. I have met with none who have no respect for religion."[28]

More significant than Cumming's solitary example was the order of deaconesses that Bishop Wilmer founded. Cobbs's vision for a cathedral may have partly inspired Wilmer's order of deaconesses, because the cathedral close was to have included a "home for five deaconesses." Other precedents were the deaconesses who were employed in the hospital associated with William Augustus Muhlenberg's parish in New York, and the order of deaconesses founded by Maryland's bishop, William Whittingham, in 1858. On December 20, 1864, at Christ Church, Tuscaloosa, Wilmer "set apart" Rebecca Hewitt, Harriet Irwin, and Jane Williams for service as deaconesses.[29]

According to Rebecca Hewitt's diary, the deaconesses were "set apart" in a service that began with Morning Prayer, after which R. D. Nevius, rector of Christ Church, Tuscaloosa, presented the deaconesses to Bishop Wilmer, saying: "Reverend Father in God, I present unto you these our sisters, who following the example of certain devout women, recorded in the holy Scripture, desire to devote themselves to the relief of the suffering and destitute and have come forward to ask your benediction and the prayers of the congregation, that they may be furthered in their undertaking." Bishop Wilmer then asked them, "Dearly beloved in the Lord . . . have ye duly considered this weighty undertaking and are you prepared with a willing mind to devote yourselves to this office and ministry to the suffering and needy?" And the deaconesses replied, "We have so considered it, and God being our helper, we are prepared to enter upon its duties." After two lengthy collects, the bishop preached a sermon in which he told the deaconesses that God had called them "to no less an office than to be co-workers with him in his work of love to our fallen race. In this work you are associated with the holy men and women of past ages and even with the blessed angels, whose employment and delight it is to minister unto the heirs of salvation. This is indeed a high honor God has conferred upon you, even to accept and assist in that work which the adorable Son of God Himself undertook to accomplish, and which the ever-blessed Spirit is ceaselessly carrying on through the manifold services of angels and men, constituted in a wonderful order." Holy communion followed the sermon.[30]

The women began to work in Mobile even before the bishop set them apart, but the Federal victory in the Battle of Mobile Bay forced them to move to Tuscaloosa where Wilmer had already begun to raise money for an orphanage. In her diary, Rebecca Hewitt records that on November 21, 1864, they began a parish school with ten children, including "Annie (13), Alfred (11), Eli (8), Alonzo (6), children of [illegible] Harris, a most degraded woman of Tuskaloosa. Maddie [illegible] (12) has a father in the army and a respectable mother, [illegible] unable to feed her family." In a letter to William Stickney in August of 1864, the bishop announced an ambitious plan to "raise $50,000 in twenty days. If I can succeed, I can probably purchase an admirable building for a Church Home for Orphans at this place." In 1867 the deaconesses moved back to Mobile where they established the Church Home for Orphans (which became Wilmer Hall). The order of deaconesses thrived after the war, and as Barbara Brandon Schnorrenberg notes, "by the late seventies, there was often a new deaconess set apart every year." However, Schnorrenberg also says that from the 1890s onward fewer and fewer women were drawn to the order, and by 1916 lay administrators replaced the sisters in the management of the Church Home.[31]

Although the order of deaconesses fulfilled part of Cobbs's dream, the Civil War doomed his vision of a grand cathedral for the Diocese of Alabama, although in truth it was never practical. Alabama would not have a cathedral until 1982. Toward the end of the war, however, there was an attempt to build a church in Cobbs's memory. In 1864, the Church of the Holy Comforter, Montgomery—organized by a group of refugees from Pensacola—was admitted to the diocese. The original intention was to call the new congregation the "Memorial Church" in memory of Bishop Cobbs, but John Mitchell, the rector of St. John's, objected, and Bishop Wilmer proposed changing the name to Holy Comforter.[32]

On March 22, 1865, General James H. Wilson crossed the Tennessee River on his way to destroy the Confederate munitions works in Selma. After Union troops destroyed much of the University of Alabama, Wilson attacked Selma on April 22. St. Paul's, Selma, was inadvertently burned when soldiers, pillaging a store next door to the church, ignited a fire that burned both the store and the church. St. Paul's report at the 1865 Diocesan Convention noted, "The Church has suffered greatly by the events of war . . . our Church edifice has been destroyed, with many valuable articles." The following year a fire that was attributed to a "disorderly Federal soldier" also destroyed Trinity Church, Demopolis.[33]

Although God granted Cobbs's prayer not to let him see Alabama secede, nevertheless the Almighty also loosed the flood that Cobbs had feared would burst on Alabama and the South. Unlike Baptists, Methodists, and Presbyterians, the Episcopal Church had not split over the issue of slavery. Indeed, in the South it was the church of slave owners and the Confederate leadership. The fortunes of the Confederate Episcopal Church quickly rose and just as quickly fell with the Confederate government. The "wasting inundation" of the Civil War destroyed (to borrow from Lincoln's Second Inaugural) "all the wealth piled up by the bondsman's . . . unrequited toil" and nearly destroyed the Episcopal Church. Although the Episcopal Church had not divided over slavery, it had indeed divided, North and South, as the Union had divided. Reconstruction of the Union and reunion of the Episcopal Church would not be easily accomplished. Richard Hooker Wilmer, the only bishop elected and consecrated in the Confederate Episcopal Church, would face tests in peace far greater than the ones he faced in war.

4

"How is the South like Lazarus?"

Reconstruction

In 1890, Hilary Abner Herbert, a member of St. Thomas, Greenville, and future US secretary of the navy, described the effect of the Civil War on Alabama with these words:

> It is difficult to convey any proper idea of the wretchedness that prevailed in Alabama at the close of our Civil War. Thousands who were totally unaccustomed to labor found themselves in extreme poverty, and in many cases father, husband, brother or son . . . was sleeping in a soldier's grave. The State had lost of her citizens by the war, including the disabled, 25,227, more than 20 per cent. of those who could now have been counted upon as bread-winners. The credit system had been universal, but now all credit was gone; provision crops had gone to feed both Confederate and Federal armies; plow stock had most of it been destroyed or carried away; negro laborers were demoralized, and flocked into towns and camps around Freedmen's Bureau Agencies; and, to fill the cup to the brim, a severe drought came with its afflictions, so that the crops of corn and small grain throughout the State in 1865 were not more than one-fifth the usual amount.

Physician and former Confederate officer John Allan Wyeth recalled, "the returning soldiers reached home too late to plant a crop; and, as the fields were uncultivated in 1864, the country was destitute of the simplest necessities of life. . . . As the courts had not been reopened, [my father] had little or no law business, but he had many calls for help to which he was sorrowfully unable to respond. In the adjoining counties of Blount and DeKalb the same distressing conditions prevailed, and finally he was told that one or two had died of starvation." Virginia Clay, a member of Huntsville's Nativity Church, whose husband, Clement Comer Clay Jr., had been a senator in both the US and Confederate senates, echoed Wyeth's view of the agricultural situation: "The crops were inconsiderable; scarcely any cotton had been planted, and the appalling cotton tax had already been invented to drain us still further."[1]

Perhaps even more painful than the destruction of their homes and the war's economic devastation was the loss of status that Alabama's ruling elite suffered. Wyeth charged that the Federal forces of occupation had committed the "most monstrous political crime in the records of history. The infamy . . . [was] the effort to hold in subjection to an alien negro race, but a few months before in bondage, the white people of Earth." Virginia Clay shared Wyeth's distress at the enfranchisement and empowerment of former slaves: "the poor, unknowing creatures sought every opportunity to impress the fact of their independence upon all against whom they bore resentment. The women were wont to gather on the sidewalks of the main thoroughfares, forming a line across as they sauntered along, compelling their former masters and mistresses who happened to be approaching to take the street."[2]

Less than a month after Lee surrendered to Grant at Appomattox, the Diocese of Alabama assembled for its annual convention in Greensboro on May 3, 1865. The convention had been scheduled to meet in Mobile, but Bishop Wilmer decided that Mobile's continued occupation by Federal forces (or, as he put it, "the enemy") made it an unsuitable location. However, Mobile and the Black Belt—apart from the attacks on Tuscaloosa and Selma—had suffered far less devastation than the Tennessee Valley in northern Alabama. Wyeth wrote of his return to Guntersville following the war: "As we came west on the train nothing but lonesome-looking chimneys remained of the villages and farm-houses. They were suggestive of tombstones in a graveyard . . . every town in northern Alabama to and including Decatur (except Huntsville, which, being used as headquarters, had been spared)—had been wiped out by the war policy of starvation by fire."[3]

Praying for the President

Bishop Wilmer, who idealized the South's way of life before the war, was devastated by its defeat. Wilmer's fierce loyalty to the South and antipathy to the North led him to direct his clergy to omit the prayer for "all in Civil Authority," arguing that Alabama was under military, not civil authority. This led to a momentous conflict with the military authorities that occupied Alabama after the South's surrender. From its first publication in 1549 the Book of Common Prayer had included prayers for the head of state and other officials. Consequently, English Books of Common Prayer included collects for "the King (or Queen's) Majesty." When the Protestant Episcopal Church in the USA was organized after the American Revolution, the prayer for the sovereign was changed to a prayer for the president. As it became increasingly clear that the South would secede, Bishop Cobbs directed his clergy to omit the prayer for the president in the event of a rupture between North and South.

When Jefferson Davis was elected president of the CSA, the clergy began to pray for him as the Confederate head of state. Bishop Wilmer, foreseeing the possibility that Federal forces might occupy portions of his diocese, counseled his clergy to continue using the prayer for the Confederate president, unless prevented from doing so by force. In that event, the bishop directed his clergy simply to close the church "and the odium and responsibility of suspending the public worship of God will rest where it properly belongs—upon those who make war upon freedom of opinion." Wilmer believed that the Civil War was "not as ordinary wars" but was "a struggle on our part for liberty of thought and speech." A closed church, then, would stand as mute testimony to Wilmer's conviction that the goal of the war was to impose alien values on the South.[4]

With the collapse of the Confederate government came the necessity once again to change the prayer for the state and its officials. Thus Wilmer addressed a pastoral letter to the clergy of Alabama on June 20, 1865. He argued two points: First, that the fall of the Confederacy did not necessarily entail the dissolution of the Episcopal Church in the Confederate states, a point that was to have important consequences for the reunion of the northern and southern branches of the Episcopal Church. It followed from this (as Wilmer further argued) that while the Confederate Episcopal Church still existed, he did not have the authority to amend its Prayer Book: "it is not for me, in my individual capacity to introduce into the Liturgy any other form of words than that which the Church . . . has already established." Second, Wilmer conceded that the "Prayer for the President of the Confederate States" should no longer be used but did not believe that it followed that the prayer for "all in civil authority" should take its place. "When the Civil Authority shall be restored," Wilmer wrote, "it will be eminently proper for the Church to resume the use of that form of prayer."[5]

Anticipating that his pastoral letter would cause difficulties with the military authorities, Wilmer traveled to Mobile where the Department of Alabama was headquartered. In his biography of Wilmer, Walter Whitaker tells us "as Mobile was both the [Military] Department [of Alabama] headquarters and the seat of the Church's greatest strength . . . the storm center would be there." Tennessee's provisional governor, William G. Brownlow, brought Wilmer's pastoral letter to the attention of Major General George H. Thomas, the commander of the Military Division of the Tennessee, which included the Department of Alabama. Like Wilmer, Thomas was a Virginian, and Whitaker tells us that Wilmer had "all through the war, been unsparing of him as a 'renegade.' This characterization of him was not confined to the Bishop of Alabama, but in Wilmer's hands it was especially caustic."[6]

Thomas directed Major General Charles R. Woods to investigate the matter, and Woods sent an officer to Wilmer who demanded to know "when the Bishop intended to use the Prayer for the President of the United States." Wilmer took offense at the way in which he was questioned and refused to give an answer. The officer then suggested that they discuss the issue "as between man and man," and Wilmer agreed. Again, the officer asked the bishop when he would use the prayer for the president, to which Wilmer replied, "When you all get away from here." The officer reported Wilmer's position to General Woods, who then issued "General Orders, No. 38." In his proclamation General Woods characterized Wilmer as having "a factious and disloyal spirit" and as an "unsafe teacher . . . not to be trusted in places of power and influence over public opinion." The general then ordered Alabama's Episcopal churches closed and forbade Wilmer and his clergy "to preach or perform divine service . . . until such a time as said Bishop and clergy show a sincere return to their allegiance to the Government of the United States, and give evidence of a loyal and patriotic spirit by offering to resume the use of the prayer for the President of the United States and all in civil authority, and by taking the amnesty oath prescribed by the President."[7]

The general published his proclamation in the Mobile newspapers but did not send a copy to Wilmer. Wilmer replied in a letter to Woods in which he denied that the military authorities had any jurisdiction over the churches and insisted that his decision not to pray for the US president and others in civil authority was not a sign of disloyalty. Wilmer's letter also inquired if the general would use force to close the churches, and Woods replied that he would do so, if his order were disobeyed. Wilmer then issued a second pastoral letter to the clergy and laity of the diocese. In this second pastoral letter, Wilmer framed the issue thus: "Shall the secular or the ecclesiastical power regulate the worship of the church?" He urged his clergy to "stand up for and to maintain, at whatever cost, the real issue now before us." He also reiterated his loyalty and pointed out that he had taken an Oath of Allegiance as an example to others.

On September 20, 1865, in Mobile's Trinity Church, Bishop Wilmer ordained William Montrose Pettit to the order of deacons. The same day General Woods made good on his promise to close Alabama's Episcopal churches and issued General Orders, No. 38, in which he directed

> that said Richard Wilmer, Bishop of the Protestant Episcopal Church of the Diocese of Alabama, and the Protestant Episcopal clergy of said Diocese be, and they are hereby forbidden to preach or perform divine services, and their places of worship be closed, until such times as said Bishop and clergy show a sincere return to their allegiance to the Government of the United States and all in civil authority, and by taking the amnesty oath prescribed by the President. This prohibition to hold until each individual makes application, through military headquarters for permission to preach and perform divine service and until headquarters grants them permission.

But his orders were widely disobeyed. General Woods's directive had forbidden Episcopal clergy to "preach or perform divine service," but this seems to have been interpreted to mean only that the churches should be closed. If Bishop Wilmer's schedule is any indication, Alabama's Episcopal clergy continued to function in private homes and other venues. According to the bishop's journal, he preached, celebrated the Eucharist, and even married a couple while the military order was in effect. In at least one case, however, the military authorities intervened to prevent a service from taking place in a residence. In a letter dated December 12, 1865, and addressed to the provisional governor of Alabama, Lewis Parsons, Montgomery physician and St. John's vestryman R. F. Michel noted that the principal of Hamner Hall invited the rector of St. John's to hold services there. Michel further noted that Hamner Hall was "the residence of his [the principal's] family and is entirely under his control as if it were his own private property." Yet when the rector and members of his congregation arrived at the school, they were met by a "military official, bringing *verbal orders*" which forbade them to assemble in the school because "it was an invasion of the aforesaid military interdict." Although Michel does not mention the use of force, Charles Teed Pollard, St. John's senior warden from 1844 to 1890, charged that "a detachment" of soldiers "entered the school and with fixed bayonets drove us out."[8]

Bishop Wilmer quickly took action to protest the closure of Alabama's Episcopal churches. Wilmer wrote Bishops Hopkins (at that time the Presiding Bishop of the PECUSA), Clark, and Coxe, apprising them of the situation in Alabama. Wilmer acknowledged that they might disagree with his position on praying for the "President and all in Civil Authority" ("I presume that you would take issue with me"), but argued that the military's violation of the constitutional principle of religious freedom should be of concern to them. Wilmer also acknowledged that anti-Southern feeling in the North might be too strong to permit them to speak out on his behalf: "You have now an opportunity to show to the Church in the Southern States that you are Churchmen, and not Northern Churchmen." In the end, though, the only action the PECUSA took on Wilmer's behalf was to send Bishop McIlvaine of Ohio to Washington to appeal to the government to countermand General Thomas's order, and this was not successful. Next, Wilmer wrote Governor Parsons, who brought Wilmer's case to the attention of President Andrew Johnson. Again, the relief Wilmer sought was not forthcoming. Finally, Wilmer wrote directly to President Johnson. Wilmer stated that Johnson's refusal to consider Governor Parsons's appeal suggested that the general's order was "virtually sustained by the President."[9]

Reuniting North and South

In the midst of the controversy over Wilmer's refusal to allow his clergy to pray for the US president, the bishops and deputies of the Episcopal Church assembled in Philadelphia on the first Wednesday in October 1865 for the triennial General Convention. The rationale for the existence of the Episcopal Church in the Confederate States of America ended with Lee's surrender at Appomattox, and it would seem logical for the southern bishops to return to their places in the House of Bishops when the General Convention convened. Resolving the schism brought on by the war, however, did not proceed smoothly, and for a time it looked as though it might not happen at all. Wilmer's biographer, Walter Whitaker, asserts that "it was well-known that a self-assertive and aggressively patriotic party in the Church of the General Convention had avowed its intention 'to keep the Southern Churchmen for awhile in the cold' and 'to put the rebels upon stools of repentance.'"[10]

John Henry Hopkins, bishop of Vermont and Presiding Bishop of the Episcopal Church (also one of the Episcopal Church's staunchest defenders of slavery) eased the way to reunion by writing a letter to the southern bishops assuring them "of the cordial welcome" they would receive at the General Convention. Hopkins's letter was carefully worded. He noted that the past "may not soon be forgotten," implying that some bishops might have a different position on the reunion of the northern and southern Episcopal churches. The southern bishops were also offered help with travel expenses and "a committee of the Diocese of Pennsylvania gave them a cordial invitation to 'free quarters and kind entertainment' in Philadelphia during the Convention." Others, however, were far more cautious about readmitting the southern dioceses to the PECUSA. The bishop of Delaware, Alfred Lee, believed that "next to the 'leaders of the Conspiracy no class of men have a heavier responsibility' than the clergy." Long Island's bishop,

A. Cleveland Coxe, regarded restoring the southern dioceses to be "lunacy." Phila-delphia's *Episcopal Recorder* went so far as to advocate "hanging the Southern bish-ops and clergy for having sponsored the secession movement" and favored passing a resolution condemning slavery and secession before readmitting the southern dioceses.[11]

The Diocese of New York and its bishop, Horatio Potter, did much to heal the schism between North and South. During its September 1865 convention, the New York diocese voted a resolution that indicated that the southern bishops would be welcome at the General Convention. Furthermore, Charles T. Quin-tard, the bishop-elect of Tennessee and a former Confederate chaplain, was pres-ent at the New York meeting and was warmly received.[12]

Despite the efforts of Hopkins and Potter, not all of the southern bishops were ready to put the past behind them. Paraphrasing *Hamlet*, Bishop Wilmer urged against a too-hasty reconciliation: "The funeral baked meats / [Do] coldly fur-nish forth the marriage tables." Bishops Elliott of Georgia and Davis of South Carolina agreed with Wilmer. Nevertheless, Wilmer professed that he was will-ing to reunite with the PECUSA "provided that no uncatholic concessions were demanded." A priest from Philadelphia warned against "prostrating the Church and her Canons at the feet of the rebellious men who had made no concessions and request." Another obstacle to reunion was the belief many in the North held that the southern bishops were not only schismatics for having organized the Confederate Episcopal Church but also real or potential traitors to the United States.

As for the South, some southern bishops did not regard it as a foregone con-clusion that the southern dioceses should rejoin the PECUSA. The rationale for forming the Confederate Episcopal Church—as Leonidas Polk stated—was that the secession of the Southern states had severed the ties between the southern dioceses and the PECUSA just as surely as the American Revolution had snapped the cord binding the Church of England to its American clergy and laypeople. But now that the Confederacy no longer existed, some southern bishops shifted their position and saw no need to hasten back into the embrace of the PECUSA or even return at all. Bishops Elliott of Georgia, Green of Mississippi, and Wilmer of Alabama now argued that the restoration of the political union need not en-tail a restoration of the ecclesiastical union and that letting political jurisdiction determine an ecclesiastical matter was "Erastian and un-Catholic." In fact, they feared that some of the northern bishops would insist that they repudiate their loyalty to and participation in the Confederacy as a price for reunion. In a letter of August 9, 1865, Mississippi's Bishop Green wrote that he was convinced that "if any one or more of our Bishops shall attend the convention he will receive as many insults on the one hand as kindnesses on the other."[13]

Reunion of the northern and southern churches was eased by the willingness of the northern bishops to forget the recent past and put it quickly behind them; Bishops Lay and Atkinson's decision to attend the General Convention in Philadelphia also helped persuade their fellow southern bishops to rejoin the PECUSA. Although present at the opening of the 1865 General Convention, Bishops Lay and Atkinson would not don episcopal vestments and process with the other bishops. However, after the members of the House of Bishops had entered the church and taken their place, Lay and Atkinson vested and joined their colleagues, but there were two issues that could have derailed efforts at reunion. The first was the issue of Bishop Wilmer's standing in the PECUSA and the second was a proposal to hold a service of thanksgiving for the end of the war.

One of the most critical issues to be resolved before reconciliation could take place was the status of Alabama's bishop. Alone among the southern bishops, Wilmer had been elected and consecrated after the southern dioceses had withdrawn from the PECUSA. There could be no doubt that Wilmer's consecration to the office of bishop was valid. The sacramental requirements for consecration had been met, and if Wilmer was not a bishop, then none of the northern bishops were bishops either. Still, the PECUSA's canonical requirements for consecration to the office of bishop had not been met. Wilmer had received consent for his consecration from a majority of the southern dioceses but had not sought consent from any of the northern dioceses.

Most northern members of the House of Bishops were prepared to acknowledge Wilmer as a duly consecrated bishop, but Alabama's bishop had muddied the water by his belligerent attitude in the matter of praying for the US president. Maryland's Bishop Whittingham proposed that the House of Bishops receive Wilmer and acknowledge his standing as bishop of Alabama, but some of his colleagues balked. Ohio's McIlvaine "charged Wilmer with disloyalty and referred to him as 'that person,'" but the next day McIlvaine apologized. The bishops passed two resolutions: one that proposed acceptance of Wilmer upon receipt of evidence of his valid consecration and public pledge of conformity to the "doctrine, discipline, and worship" of the Episcopal Church, and a second expressing regret for Wilmer's actions since the end of the war.

The House of Deputies was not as welcoming. One deputy wanted Wilmer to pledge his loyalty not only to the PECUSA but also to the United States. In the debate over Wilmer's standing, Alexander H. Vinton, rector of the Church of the Holy Trinity, Philadelphia, a clerical deputy to the 1862 General Convention who had been Wilmer's friend, argued that "all acts of the Southern Church should be considered null and void" until they were endorsed by the General Convention, and he condemned Wilmer's consecration as "irregular, uncanonical, and schismatical," proposing that it be declared "void and of none effect." Wilmer had no quarrel with the requirement that he furnish evidence that he had been properly consecrated a bishop and was willing to make a "declaration of conformity" with the doctrine, discipline, and worship of the Episcopal Church. However, Wilmer did take issue with a statement of "fraternal regret" that was annexed to the legislation permitting the General Convention to receive Wilmer as bishop of Alabama. Wilmer believed the General Convention had no right to censure him for his pastoral letter forbidding the clergy of Alabama to pray for the US president because he had not been a bishop of the PECUSA when he issued the letter, and he also objected to the "regrets" because he was not given an opportunity to respond. In the end, the deputies voted to accept Wilmer upon the same terms to which the bishops had already agreed.[14]

The fight over a national service of thanksgiving that began when Bishop Burgess proposed "that October 12 be set aside for a service of thanksgiving for the preservation of national sovereignty and the abolition of slavery" could also have derailed reconciliation between North and South. The proposal was dropped, then revived, and finally passed. Bishops Lay and Atkinson told their fellow bishops they would be unable to attend such a service and that the resolution would be "'dangerous' in the South." Ultimately, the bishops passed a resolution calling for a service of thanksgiving "for the restoration of Peace in the country and unity in the Church." As with the case of Bishop Wilmer, the House of Deputies debated the matter with considerably more heat than the bishops had. Deputy Horace Binney of Pennsylvania proposed an alternative resolution that called for a service of thanksgiving "for the reestablishment of the national authority over our whole country, and for the removal of that great occasion of national dissension." According to a *New York Times* reporter covering the story, "A dozen delegates jumped up to cry it down, some wanted it withdrawn, others would have it laid on the table. The house was in an uproar, and the tempest raged for some minutes."[15] The House of Deputies concurred with the bishops. Strangely, it was almost two months before Wilmer received word that the PECUSA recognized him officially as the bishop of Alabama. Finally, in New York's Trinity Church on January 31, 1866, Wilmer "made the prescribed Declaration of Conformity, and united with the Presiding Bishop and other bishops and clergy present in the service of Holy Communion."[16]

While the General Convention was meeting in Philadelphia, the final act of Wilmer's presidential prayer drama was playing out. President Andrew Johnson directed General Thomas to withdraw General Orders, No. 38, and about one month before Wilmer made his declaration of conformity, Thomas grudgingly obeyed the president and withdrew his ban on the Episcopal Church in Alabama in General Orders, No. 40, issued on December 22, 1865. Thomas referred to Wilmer as "an individual styling himself Bishop of Alabama" and said that he had forgotten "his mission to preach peace on earth and good will towards men" and promoted "this treasonable course" from "behind the shield of his office." General Orders, No. 40 gives us some insight into Thomas's justification for his violation of the constitutionally guaranteed freedom of worship. He justified closing Alabama's Episcopal churches because Wilmer's "covert and cunning act . . . deprived [him] of the privileges of citizenship, in so far as the right to officiate as a minister of the Gospel." But Thomas stated that "the people of Alabama are honestly endeavoring to restore the civil authority . . . in conformity with the requirements of the Constitution of the United States," and he concluded that Bishop Wilmer's "diabolical schemes" had failed.

Wilmer responded by ordering the clergy to use the prayer for the president, but he claimed that he did so not as a quid pro quo to lift the military ban on Alabama's Episcopal churches. Rather, Wilmer argued that the conditions had been fulfilled for the proper use of the prayer for the president. In his second pastoral letter to the clergy and people of the diocese (September 28, 1865), Wilmer had stated that because Alabama was still a part of the Episcopal Church in the CSA (even though the CSA no longer existed), he was not free to change the liturgy, but "should the 'General Council,' of which the Diocese of Alabama is a component part, order any Prayer in place of that which has ceased of necessity, then, from that time forth, the ordering of the Council would be decisive as the supreme law of the Churches constituting said Council." Wilmer further noted that his position all along had been that Alabama was under *military authority* not *civil authority*, and by the time General Thomas issued General Orders, No. 40, civil authority had been restored: "There has been such a restoration of civil authority as to place over the good people of our commonwealth a Governor and Legislature of their own election."[17]

No other southern bishop followed Wilmer's example. Even though Virginia had suffered far greater devastation than Alabama, Virginia's bishop ordered his clergy to resume praying for the US president as soon as he "received reliable intelligence of the entire failure of the painful and protracted struggle for the independence of the Confederate States, and the reestablishment of the Federal authority." Wilmer's judgment seems to have been deeply biased by his hostility to the North. Even though Wilmer argued that Alabama was not under civil authority, Alabama had been restored to the Union in 1865. Wilmer was correct in arguing that Alabama was under military rule, but it was military rule authorized by a government of which Alabama was a constituent part. Furthermore, Wilmer's argument that he did not have the right to alter the Prayer Book was somewhat hypocritical. Wilmer had authorized special prayers during the war; it would have been a simple matter for Wilmer to frame a prayer for the US president and direct his clergy to use it. Finally, in his history of the Confederate Episcopal

Church, Joseph Cheshire notes that Wilmer ceased to use the prayer for the US president and began to use the prayer for the Confederate president in 1861, even though the Confederate Prayer Book that authorized such a change in the liturgy was not issued until November 1862. "Therefore, when in the summer of 1865, the Bishop of Alabama, by taking the oath of allegiance to the United States, and by recommending his people to do the same, had recognized the restored authority of the United States government, there was exactly the same reason for using the prayer for the President of the United States that there had been for praying for the President of the Confederate States in 1861. He did not think it necessary in 1861 to wait until the Church had legislated for the change of the Prayer Book; there can be no valid reason assigned why in 1863 it was necessary to wait for such a change."[18]

Episcopalians and Alabama's Reconstruction-Era Constitutions

The reconciliation between Alabama and the federal government paralleled that between the PECUSA and the Confederate church. The federal government required the former Confederate states to write new constitutions, and between 1865 and 1875 Alabama wrote three. The 1865 and 1874 constitutional conventions included a disproportionate number of Episcopalians: six out of ninety-one in 1865 and seven out of 101 in 1875. The 1865 constitution neither gave African Americans the right to vote nor included adequate guarantees of their civil rights. In reaction to the refusal to enfranchise and guarantee the civil rights of African Americans, the federal government responded by initiating the so-called radical phase of Reconstruction and called for the former Confederate states to rewrite their constitutions yet again to address the deficiencies of the first postwar constitutions. The Selma *Weekly* wrote of the 1867 Alabama constitutional convention that "fifty odd members are old residents of Alabama; the rest are colored and men from the North. . . . Nearly all the delegates are wholly unknown to our people. With few exceptions none of them have ever before held any position of importance." Episcopalian layman Hilary Herbert noted, "Some of its members were Alabamians, intent on the best government that might be possible; others were natives of the state, with not a thought beyond self; many were negroes, for the most part densely ignorant, and many were northern men who, having failed in life at home, had come South to seek their fortunes in politics."[19]

Although it is impossible to determine how many of the 1867 delegates were Episcopalians, the constitution they produced broke new ground in recognizing the property rights of women and providing for public education. It also borrowed language from the Declaration of Independence to declare that "all men are created equal." When Republican control of the Alabama legislature ended in

November 1874, the victorious Democrats called for yet another constitutional convention. Convened in 1875, the new constitutional convention elected Leroy Pope Walker of Nativity Church, Huntsville, as its chairman. The 1875 convention could not have been more different from the 1867 convention, and the constitution they wrote was a repudiation of the so-called radical constitution of 1868. The 1875 convention made deep cuts in school funding but did not place (nor could it have placed) any serious restrictions on black suffrage. Indeed, the 1875 constitution borrowed heavily from the 1868 document. Contemporary observers termed the 1875 convention the "Bourbon" or "Redeemer" convention, terms that correctly implied that there had been a kind of ruling class in the antebellum South, although the heirs of the planters did not necessarily seek to restore the agrarian values that had prevailed prior to the Civil War. Just as the Episcopal Church had been the preferred denomination of the antebellum ruling class, so it was also the choice of their postwar successors. Prominent "Bourbons" who were also Episcopalians included Hilary Herbert, John Witherspoon DuBose, and Robert McKee.[20]

Bishop Wilmer and the "Lost Cause"

Wilmer was a key figure in the cult of the "Lost Cause" of the Confederacy. In his *The Recent Past from a Southern Standpoint: Reminiscences of a Grandfather,* Wilmer wrote, "I was a slaveholder, and an ardent patriot from the Southern point of view. As such, I have nothing to repent of, and nothing to retract." Other clergy of the Diocese of Alabama also continued to be pro-Southern. Horace Stringfellow, rector of St. John's, Montgomery, from 1870 to 1893, had been rector of St. Paul's, Indianapolis, a church so well known for its Southern sympathies that it was known locally as the Church of the Holy Copperheads, Holy Rebellion, or St. Butternut.[21]

Wilmer and his diocese were also instrumental in the support of a bastion of the Lost Cause—the University of the South (Sewanee). Although Bishops Cobbs, Polk, Elliott, and Otey founded it in 1857, its endowment and first buildings were destroyed during the Civil War. After the war, Tennessee's second bishop, Charles Todd Quintard, refounded Sewanee. From then until well into the twentieth century, Sewanee was closely associated with the Lost Cause. Robert E. Lee was offered (but refused) the position of vice chancellor; William Porcher Dubose, an important American theologian who served as Sewanee's first university chaplain, had been a captain in the Army of Northern Virginia; and Brigadier General Josiah Gorgas became vice chancellor in 1872. For many years a baseball team known as the R. E. Lees, whose uniforms were Confederate gray, was the only organized sports team at Sewanee. A Confederate battle flag hung in the chapel, and

Sarah Elliott (daughter of Georgia's Bishop Stephen Elliott) urged Southerners to "send us others—Flags of our glorious past—to hang where our prayers will hover."[22]

After the war, Bishop Wilmer devoted himself to finding ways to care for the widows and orphans of Confederate soldiers and did not hesitate to ask the South's former enemies for money. On a visit to New York he asked his hosts, "Why is the South like Lazarus? Because she was licked by dogs." Needless to say, some found the bishop's "joke" offensive. One man asked Wilmer why he wanted Yankee money if he regarded them as dogs. "Because, sir," Bishop Wilmer replied, "in the South we believe in the proverb that the hair of the dog is good for the bite."[23] The story indicates how deeply Richard Hooker Wilmer felt about the conflict between North and South. Indeed, he had been prepared to fight and die for the South had he not been a priest or bishop of the church, and there is every reason to believe that Wilmer never changed his views. When the General Convention of 1865 readmitted the southern dioceses unconditionally, a moment passed when it might have been possible to make the southern bishops pause and give thought to the role they had played in perpetuating an institution that treated human beings like property to be bought and sold and also in giving their blessing to a catastrophic fratricidal war. The ease with which the southern dioceses were reintegrated with the PECUSA is in sharp contrast to the exacting conditions the "radical Republicans" wished to establish for the readmission of the Southern states. The radicals sought (although they ultimately failed) to replace the South's former ruling oligarchy with a new and broader body politic. Neither did the PECUSA impose an exacting penance on the southern bishops. While it is impossible to predict precisely how the South and the PECUSA would have been different had this moment been seized, it is beyond question that they would have been very different.

In 1867, Wilmer attended the first Lambeth Conference, a meeting of all bishops in communion with the Archbishop of Canterbury that, since the meeting Wilmer attended, has taken place approximately every ten years (except during the Second World War). While in England, Cambridge University awarded honorary degrees to nineteen American bishops, including Wilmer, on October 11, 1867. Also while in England, Wilmer was asked, "Being a Virginian you are an admirer of George Washington." "O yes," he answered, "We think he was a well meaning old gentleman." A northern bishop said to Wilmer, "But you should hold Washington in reverence." To which Wilmer replied, "He was well meaning enough, but he did Virginia more harm than any man that ever lived." His English host asked, "Why, how?" "Because," Wilmer answered, "he won the fight against England. If it had not been for George Washington we would today be the loyal subjects of a most gracious, virtuous, and Christian queen. But as it is we are the most unwilling subjects of a drunken Tennessee tailor." After Wilmer's death, a writer recalled that the bishop had become weary of hearing the story of the Pilgrims arrival in America, and exclaimed, "I am so tired of hearing about the landing of the Pilgrim Fathers on Plymouth Rock that I heartily wish Plymouth Rock had landed on the Pilgrim Fathers."[24]

A New Relationship with African Americans?

In the aftermath of the Civil War, much changed, but nothing changed more than the relationship between former slaves and former slave owners. Ironically, southern churches were more integrated before the war than after. The South's newly emancipated blacks left not only their former masters' plantations but also their churches. Prior to the Civil War, virtually every Episcopal Church in Alabama had black members. Following the war, blacks who had previously worshiped in Episcopal Churches quickly left to form their own churches, never to return in large numbers to the Episcopal Church. Statistics leave no doubt about the decisiveness of the departure of black people from the Diocese of Alabama. In 1860 Alabama's Episcopal parishes reported that there were ninety-three "colored" communicants, but in 1865 that number had dropped to twenty-seven. "Colored" confirmations dropped from forty-nine to twenty-six, weddings from thirty-three to seventeen, and funerals from thirty-two to nine.[25]

It is not difficult to understand the exodus of African Americans from the Episcopal Church in Alabama. W. E. B. Du Bois wrote that the Episcopal Church "has probably done less for black people than any other aggregation of Christians." Du Bois implied that racial prejudice prevented the Episcopal Church from cultivating black leaders. Citing the decision of Bishop White of Philadelphia to ordain Absalom Jones to the priesthood in 1804, Du Bois said that if White had "consecrated him bishop, to work among his African brethren in this country, the great African Methodist Church to-day would have been Episcopal and in full communion with the church. The church lost that opportunity."[26]

Hoping that they could bring African Americans back into the fold, the PECUSA, like other denominations, created a Freedman's Commission that paralleled the federal government's Freedmen's Bureau. The Episcopal Church's commission also offered practical support, as well as spiritual support, and founded several schools for black people. Although Wilmer objected to the work of the Freedman's Commission, the commission appointed Trinity, Mobile's rector J. A. Massey to the post of honorary district secretary for the Diocese of Alabama, probably because of his work with Good Shepherd, Mobile.[27]

Before the war the Episcopal Church in Alabama's most prominent example of ministry to African Americans was Faunsdale Plantation in Marengo County.

Faunsdale featured a small chapel built especially for the slaves, whom Louisa Harrison Stickney routinely catechized and to whom her husband, William, an Episcopal priest, regularly preached. With emancipation came an entirely new relationship between the Stickneys, on one hand, and their former slaves, on the other. After the war, Stickney prepared labor agreements for his black workers that spelled out the mutual responsibilities and privileges of both sides. Some of these were spiritual or religious in nature. The newly freed servants were expected "at all times to be faithful, honest, sober, obedient, civil & industrious." Stickney promised to "be uniformly kind to my Hird [hired] Servants, and considerate of their temporal and spiritual condition." The servants were also required to attend chapel services. However, after five years of compelling his former slaves to attend chapel, Stickney gave up. Faunsdale's black workers preferred to worship God in their own way. At first Stickney forbade preaching or "professing," along with "conjuring," "tricking," "dealing in spells," and "charms." When a group of Stickney's black employees held their own service, "Stickney stopped the meeting and prayed with the freemen himself, but he apparently did not dismiss any of his workers for their disobedience to his rules."[28]

Most African Americans left the Episcopal Church entirely and found their way to churches that were more welcoming or churches they established themselves. This can be shown both by the previously mentioned statistics indicating the dramatic drop in black baptisms, confirmations, weddings, and funerals following the war, and also by the growth of black churches and even black denominations. Historian Wilson Fallin identifies several reasons for the establishment of separate black churches: "A desire for independence and self-determination . . . the opportunity to worship as they desired, blacks wanted a setting in which they could listen to and react to their own preachers" and the equality that black churches promoted. Fallin draws his conclusions from studying the history of black Baptists, but they are surely applicable to black Episcopalians as well. However, there was an important difference between black Baptists and black Episcopalians: black Baptists could form their own congregations and ordain their own clergy without consulting a bishop, but black Episcopalians could not do these things, and it would be a long time before the white bishops of the Episcopal Church would be ready to consecrate black bishops and give any significant degree of autonomy to black parishes. In 1861 there was only one "colored" parish in the Diocese of Alabama—the Church of the Good Shepherd in Mobile—but many of Alabama's Episcopal churches had black parishioners. After the Civil War, most of the blacks who had been attending Episcopal churches in Alabama left. No new black church was established until the formation of St. Mark's, Birmingham, in 1883. The Civil War shattered the old paradigm of masters catechizing their servants and bringing them to church, but the leaders of the Episcopal Church were slow to realize that only the creation of separate black parishes would bring blacks back to the Episcopal Church in any significant numbers.[29]

In 1866 Wilmer made the first of two important and somewhat lengthy statements about African Americans. In the 1866 statement he correctly pointed out that the Diocese of Alabama had provided for the spiritual needs of African Americans from the very beginning. "This is indeed no new subject of interest to us, for we have always recognized the obligation of the Church to minister unto all persons, without respect to political or social distinctions." He also acknowledged that emancipation had changed things: "there are circumstances of peculiar delicacy connected with any systematic effort which we may make in behalf of the class in question." Furthermore, he rejected what he perceived as interference by the Episcopal Church's Freedman's Commission in his prerogatives as a bishop: "I have taken the ground that I was prepared through instrumentalities of my own selection, to make use of any means which they ('the Commission') might see fit to place in my hands. I see no propriety in departing from the usages of the Church, in accordance with which the Bishop of a Diocese is charged with the selection of the instrumentalities which, in order to work, must work under his supervision." Wilmer then set up a "Committee on the Colored Population," although there is only one recorded report from that committee.

The diocesan journal hints strongly that the commission's report occasioned some kind of controversy: "The Committee on the Colored Population having brought in their amended report, considerable discussion and a general and free expression of opinion ensued thereupon. . . . Immediately after Divine Service, the Convention resumed the discussion of the report on the Colored population, which, after several verbal amendments was adopted." A discussion at a subsequent Diocesan Convention may shed some light on the "considerable discussion" and "free expression" that took place at the 1866 convention. In 1882 an ad hoc committee on "Church Work among the Colored People" began its report by asking the question "Is the Negro a Man; a son of Adam, and therefore a Brother?" The repulsive question indicated an attitude far too common among southern whites. For example, Louis Tucker, rector of Christ Church, Mobile, whose father had also been rector of Christ Church, wrote that his father had been called to Christ Church "because of his good work for negroes." Still, Tucker went on to write, "negroes were nonmoral. They were not immoral. They simply had no morals at all. All little children are nonmoral, too, and so are monkeys and most other animals." On the basis of Acts 1.26 ("[God] hath made of one blood all nations of men for to dwell on all the face of the earth") and a couple of other scriptural references the committee eventually concluded that "Negroes" were human.[30]

The 1866 committee report lacked substance. It acknowledged that "the black man is no longer a bondman or slave. He is a freeman, and is among us everywhere accepted as such, in good faith" and it urged Bishop Wilmer to issue a pastoral letter "setting forth his views of the duty of members of the Church in regard to the intellectual, moral and religious culture of the colored population." But other than that, it said nothing, and Wilmer seems never to have issued the desired pastoral letter.[31]

The next statement on ministry to African Americans was the previously mentioned report in the 1882 *Diocesan Journal.* This statement pointed out that the "vindication" of the Episcopal Church's claim to be a church was its concern "about the present pitiable condition of the African, morally and religiously considered." On the other hand, the committee's report reasoned, "If we are . . . as we are generally supposed to be, the rich folks' sect, then we freely grant that the question has no standing room in this assembly." Yet the committee offered only two practical suggestions: First, "we would suggest, that, where at all practicable, each Parish should organize a Sunday School especially for the colored children," and second, they urged the establishment of a "model parish" for blacks, including a "Church, School House, and Rectory." The committee suggested that such a parish would offer "not only a working model for other similar efforts," but would also be "a light in a dark place; the influence of which would be, not only to elevate those in the Church, but gradually to leaven those on the outside."[32]

Bishop Wilmer had little more to offer. He concurred with the committee that a parish should be established, and he suggested that it be located at a "commercial centre." Wilmer, like Cobbs before him, believed that the Prayer Book could be adapted and made appealing to African Americans. Apparently, both bishops made the mistake of thinking that the characteristic "call and response" pattern of the black church meant that black people had an innate affinity for Anglican verses and responses.[33]

In 1883, seventeen years after Wilmer had first expressed concern for "colored people," he reported to the diocese that he had "purchased a desirable lot of ground" and had "built a Rectory and Church (now used for a Day School and Sunday School also)." Wilmer had also licensed a "colored Layman" to read the office and to "exhort." The school was supervised by "a lady from Virginia." The whole enterprise was under the watchful care of a white priest and parish—the Reverend I. L. Tucker of Christ Church, Mobile. But Wilmer had not established a new black congregation; rather, he was seeking to revitalize a congregation long in existence—the Church of the Good Shepherd, Mobile, first established by Trinity Church, Mobile, in 1854.[34]

Wilmer's most extensive and detailed public statement on African Americans and the Episcopal Church was an address he gave at a conference discussing the relationship between African Americans and the Episcopal Church at

Sewanee in July 1883. The Board of Missions of the Episcopal Church then requested that Wilmer repeat the address at their meeting in Philadelphia in October 1883. William Green, the bishop of Mississippi, had organized the Sewanee conference and invited southern bishops and other interested parties. The Sewanee conference recommended that dioceses establish "special Missionary organizations" for black Episcopalians under the control of the diocesan bishops. Wilmer opposed this plan. His biographer wrote, "He might have favored separation on the ground of incapacity and ignorance . . . but not on that of color . . . he did assert . . . that there were multitudes of white people in some of our States who, in intelligence, education, and manners, were even inferior to that class of colored people who were prepared to enter the communion of this Church. If a separate organization was desired it must be . . . an organization for the ignorant and unintelligent of all colors." Although Wilmer opposed the creation of black missionary districts, he favored the formation of separate black parishes. However, when the Sewanee plan was presented to the General Convention, it was rejected.[35]

Wilmer defended himself and his fellow southern bishops against the charge that they had done little or nothing for black Episcopalians: "For some years the spirit of criticism has busied itself with the supposed and alleged inertness and indifference of Southern Bishops in regard to the colored people. We have no apologies to make." But if other southern bishops had done as little as Wilmer, then the charge was valid. He went on to acknowledge that African Americans had "by toil and sweat, redeemed this southern land from the wilderness; they nursed and tended us in our childhood; and to-day, we are indebted to their industry for whatever great degree of agricultural prosperity we enjoy. They are with us for weal or woe, and it is our bounden duty, no less than our interest, to do all in our power to promote their temporal and spiritual welfare." Wilmer all but says that African Americans were better off before emancipation. "In old times every well-ordered plantation had its one or more homes for the aged—pleasant homes they were for the worn-out laborers—where they finished their course in comfort, tended by the loving care of the old folks at home. All this has passed away." The approach Wilmer recommended to the Board of Missions was exactly the same as the one he followed in Alabama: separate parishes for African Americans that would be under white control. "Alas! They cannot do without our pilotage in their present state."[36]

The Founding of St. Mark's Church and School

Late in Wilmer's long episcopate, a group of black Episcopalians, led by C. V. Auguste, the principal of one of Birmingham's black schools, sought the bishop's permission to establish a parish and school in Birmingham, and in 1892, St. Mark's Church and school were founded. The founding of St. Mark's Church and school was the most important response to the spiritual needs of African Americans by Alabama Episcopalians during Wilmer's tenure. In November 1891, the new church began holding services in a rented room, and within a year they had launched a school for girls in a hall on Avenue A between Nineteenth and Twentieth Streets. An article in the Birmingham *Daily News* on March 29, 1893, announced the opening of the school. James A. Van Hoose, Episcopalian deacon, businessman, and mayor of Birmingham from 1894 to 1896, authored the article, which reported that the principal of the school was "Miss Margaret Kernan, recently of Tuskaloosa, Ala., who comes to the diocese and to this work, from New York City." Van Hoose was a native of Tuscaloosa, a fact that suggests he may have had a hand in recruiting Kernan for the school.

Kernan, a white woman, did not remain at St. Mark's long, and after her departure the faculty became entirely African American. Van Hoose remained involved and interested in St. Mark's until his death in 1936. Still, his initial involvement with the parish and school may have been due as much to political calculation as to piety. When he ran for mayor of Birmingham in 1894, Van Hoose "candidly sought the Negro vote, speaking at large Negro rallies, promising a 'fair and square ballot,' . . . On election day the white voters divided almost evenly, but the Negroes, with thirty-seven percent of the registered votes, went solidly for Van Hoose, who won with sixty-nine percent of the of the total vote."[37]

In his 1896 convention address, Bishop Wilmer praised James Van Hoose for his work at St. Mark's: "with the zeal and energy which characterise the man, he has within a few years, starting from nothing, not only built up a large and growing congregation of colored people, but also erected a commodious brick Church at a cost of about $4,000, and maintained a school for colored children which must be of lasting benefit to many of that race. Further he has established the active co-operation of others and made it possible to establish in Birmingham an industrial school for colored girls." Wilmer praised not the "colored people" themselves by whose initiative St. Mark's had been established but Van Hoose, the white deacon, for his "zeal and energy."

St. Mark's was known as an "industrial school"—that is, it taught "practical" subjects and prepared its students for careers as skilled workers. This model was associated with the educational philosophy of Booker T. Washington, the founder of Alabama's Tuskegee Institute and probably the most influential African American leader in the late nineteenth and early twentieth centuries. The industrial school model may also have played a part in winning support for St. Mark's from Alabama Episcopalians in general and Birmingham industrialists in particular. In her article on St. Mark's, Barbara Brandon Schnorrenberg comments, "the notion of a practical education which would keep working people of any race in their place appealed to the New South industrialists as well as to the wealthy entrepreneurs of the North." But the truth about the curriculum of St. Mark's School was more complicated. In 1917 a US government report found that St. Mark's was teaching not only vocational classes but also English, Latin, mathematics, elementary science, history, civics, and the Bible. St. Mark's School closed in 1940, a victim of the Depression, but its accomplishments were manifold. Furthermore, it was the first religiously affiliated black school in Birmingham, preceding the Methodist-affiliated Miles College (1907) and Birmingham Baptist College (1913). A former pupil and teacher, Frank Davis, commented that St. Mark's was "the best school for Blacks in the state and perhaps in the South. Most of its students went on [to] college and many of its graduates became teachers."[38]

In spite of Wilmer's eloquent statements in favor of black parishes, St. Mark's Church and school were the only black church and school launched during his episcopate. Even Wilmer's statements supporting such parishes were few and far between. His reports to the diocese between 1862 and 1899 have far more to say about the danger of "ritualism" than they do about the importance of reaching out to African Americans. No doubt Wilmer was sincere when he wrote that "there was something beautiful in the relation between the parties—especially in the care of the young and the old. Beautiful and just and benignant was the patriarchal condition in the 'Old Dominion.' All gone, or going—the honest and loving-hearted Uncle Tom, the lovable Eva; fast going—the faithful old mammy, the decent and comely maid-servant, reverence, obedience, faithful service, and Uncle Tom piety." But when "Uncle Tom" and "Eva" left the Episcopal Church after the Civil War, Wilmer seems not to have missed them enough to find ways to bring them back.[39]

Alabama's Clergy in the Late Nineteenth Century

A number of distinguished clergy served Alabama parishes during the period of Reconstruction. In February 1869, Samuel Smith Harris became the rector of St. John's, Montgomery. A former lawyer, he had served in the Confederate Army before Wilmer ordained him in 1869. In 1879 he was consecrated bishop of Michigan, the first native Alabamian to become a bishop.[40] George M. Everhart, rector of St. Peter's, Charlotte, North Carolina, during the war, was rector of Hamner Hall following the Civil War. Jefferson Davis and his party fled to Charlotte following the South's defeat and attended Everhart's church on the Sunday following Lincoln's assassination, when the priest preached a sermon lamenting Lincoln's death. While serving as rector of St. John's, Mobile, Henry Niles Pierce was elected the second bishop of Arkansas, replacing another former Alabama priest, Henry C. Lay. Pierce served as bishop of Arkansas for twenty-nine years, presiding over a period of extraordinary growth in the Diocese of Arkansas and building one of the first cathedrals in the Episcopal Church.

During Reconstruction, Episcopalians, like other Alabamians, sought to care for the wounded, widowed, and orphaned and to rebuild a state devastated by war. The second bishop of Alabama, Richard Hooker Wilmer, proved both a controversial lightning rod and an effective leader. He casuistically defended his directive to the clergy to refrain from praying for the US president and proved a hindrance to the reunion of the northern and southern branches of the Episcopal Church. Wilmer deserves praise for his efforts to raise money and found an order of deaconesses to care for the afflicted, but he also helped to establish and perpetuate the myth of the Lost Cause that misled Southerners about the real nature of the Civil War for generations to come. In the postwar years Alabama's Episcopalians were, if anything, even less responsive to the spiritual needs of African Americans than they had been before the war. African Americans, though, began to take the initiative to care for their own spiritual needs and found a handful of white Alabama Episcopalians to be sympathetic and supportive. The challenges of Reconstruction were enormous; greater but more hopeful challenges awaited Alabama Episcopalians in the age of industrialization about to dawn.

5
The Age of "Dread-Naughts and Sky-Scrapers"

The End of the Nineteenth Century and the Beginning of the Twentieth

"The year 1901 came and the century turned," wrote Episcopalian Hudson Strode. Confirmed in 1913 at Trinity Church, Demopolis, Strode taught English for forty years at the University of Alabama. In his eighties, Strode looked back in his autobiography, *The Eleventh House*, remembering that in 1900 "the south was still poor and the price of cotton low . . . [but] food was abundant and . . . cheap. A dozen eggs cost twelve cents; sirloin steak sold for twenty-four cents a pound." At the age of thirteen, Strode precociously questioned the doctrine of the Trinity as he learned it in confirmation class: "I balked at the doctrine of the Trinity: three Gods in one . . . I accepted the divinity of Christ, but I insisted that he was a man, born to be an example to us, as well as a beloved Son of God. . . . When the bishop came he laid his blessing hands on me as on the other, more submissive ones kneeling at the altar rail."[1]

The Episcopal Church Responds to Industrialization and Urbanization

The most important historical development in Alabama in the waning years of the nineteenth century was its long-delayed industrialization. In 1882, Bishop Wilmer observed, "the Agricultural section of Alabama is in a declining condition, and . . . the larger proportion of our churches are located in that section." Wilmer forecast that there was "much room for hope in the distant future," although he did not expect rapid growth in the "mineral region." Wilmer, however, failed to anticipate how rapidly Alabama would industrialize and what would happen as a result. Not until 1891 did the bishop note that the "sudden and unexampled development of mineral wealth of the State" had caused "much diminution of population in our villages, and a consequent inability of the people to support the ministrations of the Church. Many of our village Churches have been literally drained by the almost magical growth of large centres of population."

Wilmer's description of the "magical growth of large centres of population" could have been lifted from the promotional literature used to sell real estate in and lure workers to Birmingham and other places in Alabama's "mineral region." The president of the Elyton Land Company and Birmingham's second mayor, Colonel James R. Powell ("the Duke of Birmingham"), described Birmingham as "this magic little city of ours" in his second annual report to the stockholders of the Elyton Land Company. As Wilmer had observed, what was magical about Birmingham was its remarkable growth. When it was chartered in 1871, Birmingham's population was about eight hundred, but by February 1873 it had shot up to about four thousand. In addition to rapid population growth, the young city also had "about 250 neat and substantial brick and frame dwellings, six church edifices . . . two public halls, four hotels of from 10 to 30 rooms each, several boarding houses and restaurants, a national bank in successful operation, several manufacturing establishments, and all the other concomitants which go to make up a thriving and prosperous city."[2]

It was also a "magic city" because of its vast natural resources. In 1887 *Harper's Weekly* called Birmingham "the direct offspring of iron and coal, the heart from which new life is coursing through every business artery of Alabama." *Harper's* went on to predict that "in view of [the] southward movement of manufacturing capital and its attendant labor" Birmingham would become the center of "a vast workshop, [and] will have attained that important commercial position and consequent prosperity which its citizens now anticipate with such confidence." The *Harper's* article noted that Birmingham's future prospects were "so brilliant that its values are on a par with those of a city containing several times its population," although *Harper's* admitted that Birmingham at that time contained "few visible evidences of municipal, corporate, or individual affluence." The magazine noted that Birmingham contained "one fine hotel, half a dozen comfortable school-houses, twice as many churches of the ordinary types, and several unpretentious county and municipal buildings." Yet the article concluded with the prediction that "this portion of the New South [would become] the future nucleus of our national strength and glory."[3]

Birmingham quickly established itself as the economic and industrial capital of

Alabama, and in short order had more or less supplanted older towns such as Mobile, Montgomery, and Huntsville. In 1881 Adele DuBose urged Louise Shepard of Faunsdale to visit her in Birmingham, because the "stores are prettier than in Montgomery." Hugh Wilson's experience must have been typical of many young men who came to Birmingham to establish themselves in the world of business. In 1884 Wilson wrote Shepard, saying that he worked half the day at the hotel to pay for his room and board and apprenticed himself at the Exchange Office the rest of the time. Wilson, however, complained that his room was only twenty feet from "where the switch engine is running every five minutes & such blowing & whistling you never heard."[4]

"Magic" of one kind blessed Birmingham with rapid growth, but "magic" of a darker kind cursed the new city with a host of problems associated with industrialization. As with other cities in which the prospect of quick and easy money promoted rapid population growth, the newcomers tended to be young and male. "There were comparatively few girls here," Sallie Harrison Pearson observed, "so girls were at a premium, and each one of us could boast of several beaux. Sometimes we would have four or five invitations to a ball or party, and a girl had to be very un interesting to escape." Along with the rapid influx of young men came violent crime and prostitution. Historian Martha Carolyn Mitchell notes that "'Bad Birmingham' was a national sobriquet and Birmingham was famed for her two M's—minerals and murders!" She estimates that between 1888 and 1908 "there was an average arrest rate of about 30% of the population per year, or three persons out of every ten."[5]

Responses to the problems of industrialization were poorly funded and disorganized. In 1907, Mayor George Ward, commenting on charity appropriations, remarked, "The city of Birmingham probably donates less to work of this nature than any city of similar size in the United States. While we can continue to repudiate such obligations, the duty ever resting on the strong to take care of the helpless is upon us, notwithstanding." Martha Carolyn Mitchell notes that the city's support of the poor was "piteously inadequate." Nevertheless, in 1888, United Charities organized a hospital for the poor, which eventually became Hillman Hospital, the nucleus of the University of Alabama at Birmingham's medical center, and in 1900 the Sisters of Charity, a Roman Catholic order of nuns, organized St. Vincent's Hospital. Furthermore, from the beginning of 1897, the city paid "a Negro city physician" a salary of $10 per month. Established in 1896 the Mercy Home for Girls offered "free maternity wards, care of the chronically ill and the elderly, a home for 'delinquent and defective girls,' and a kindergarten."[6]

Before Birmingham became the industrial and financial dynamo that it was predicted to become, it had to pass through crises that almost extinguished it. In 1873 cholera killed 128 people out of a population of around four thousand, but fear greatly magnified the disease's effect. In the midst of the epidemic Sallie Harrison Pearson wrote of standing in the very heart of Birmingham's commercial district (the corner of Twentieth Street and First Avenue) at 6:00 P.M. and in every direction she saw "no sign of life . . . not even . . . a cat or a dog—everything quiet and not a soul stirring." Then in the fall of 1873 a financial panic closed banks and caused businesses to fail.[7]

Paradoxically, however, "Bad Birmingham" also became known as the "city of churches." One reason for Birmingham's ecclesiastical nickname was the Elyton Land Company's decision to make land available to the major denominations. Birmingham's Baptists, Methodists, Presbyterians, Roman Catholics, and Episcopalians all received lots near the center of the commercial district and churches quickly sprang up, but the lot set aside for the Episcopal Church was then (and still is) even closer to the city's financial, cultural, commercial, and political center than the rest of the denominations' lots. The explanation for the Church of the Advent's favored location is almost certainly due to the fact that at least three of the ten initial stockholders in the Elyton Land Company were Episcopalians— James R. Powell, Benjamin P. Worthington, and William S. Mudd—as were city engineer William P. Barker and George R. Ward, father of Birmingham's future mayor of the same name. The Church of the Advent (later set apart as the diocesan cathedral) occupies the corner of Sixth Avenue and Twentieth Street, and from its steps one can see the entire length and breadth of Birmingham's original city limits. The Church of the Advent grew almost as rapidly and magically as Birmingham. Originally founded as a mission of St. John's in Elyton, the Diocese of Alabama recognized it as a parish only a year after it was founded. In 1870, the Church of the Advent had 112 communicants, but by 1887 that number had almost quadrupled to four hundred. The rector of St. John's, Elyton, Philip A. Fitts, as well as many of its parishioners, left St. John's for the Church of the Advent, which became the church of early Birmingham's leading families.[8]

Soon other Episcopal churches sprang up in the "magic city," including Trinity in the nearby suburb of Bessemer (1887), Grace Church in the Woodlawn neighborhood (1889), St. Mark's (1891), and St. John's in Ensley (1893). In 1887 the Church of the Advent helped to found Birmingham's second Episcopal church when Advent's former minister, James A. Van Hoose, organized a Sunday school in the Birmingham suburb of Highlands, which was incorporated into the city of Birmingham in 1893. In short order, this Sunday school became a parish in its own right—St. Mary's-on-the-Highlands—and was admitted into the Diocese of Alabama in 1888. Like the Church of the Advent, St. Mary's also attracted a congregation that included some of Birmingham's leading citizens.

In a letter written on the occasion of St. Mary's fiftieth anniversary, its first rector, Lysander W. Rose, recalled, "We started out with very few of the accessories of worship, no altar, no altar rail even, no font, no anything in fact but a melodeon and the pulpit was a table with an empty box upturned upon it." On at least one occasion, the new parish had held services in a dance hall. "What with the noise of the [street cars,] the traffic about us in tobacco and confectionaries, the talk of outsiders all through the service and the splashings of swimmers in the natatorium beneath us, it is hardly too much to say that we were not in harmony with our environment."[9]

Diarist Edith Ward London has left a vivid account of her youthful participation in the activities at St. Mary's. Something of a crypto-Anglo-Catholic, London was captivated more by ritual than preaching. "As splendid as our preacher, Mr. Fitzsimmons was, it was not his personality alone that held my attention. It was the picturesque service, full of ceremonial rites, that held me enthralled. The darkened service on Maundy Thursday night, with only the altar candles burning, while Communion was administered. The Three Hours Service on Good Friday. And on Easter Sunday, the inspiring music of the Resurrection." Yet in spite of her love of St. Mary's and enthusiastic participation in church activities, London lost her faith. "As soon as I married and began exchanging serious ideas of life with my husband, and his father; began reading books that made me think, I saw that I could no longer subscribe to the tenets of the church, nor honestly attend it's [sic] services. And though I have faced a surgeon's knife twice, with slight chance of recovery; though I have stood at the bedside of my child and watched him fight against death, I have never felt that I needed the church nor what it had to offer as a consolation."[10]

Not many years after rich natural resources and shrewd boosterism started attracting crowds and capital to Birmingham, a similar combination of men and minerals was the catalyst for the development of Anniston. English industrialist James Noble Sr. established an iron foundry in Reading, Pennsylvania, in 1837, but while visiting the Crystal Palace Exposition in London in 1851, he examined a sample of iron ore from the southeastern United States and was very impressed by its quality. Subsequently, Noble moved his iron foundry to Rome, Georgia. His son, Samuel Noble, visited the area that would become the city of Anniston between 1865 and 1869 and determined that it held plentiful deposits of ore. Following the Civil War, the Nobles and their business partner, Daniel Tyler, launched the Woodstock Iron Company in Woodstock, Alabama. The enterprise attracted workers from the surrounding area and also from Sweden, Scotland, and Poland. Woodstock incorporated as the town of Anniston in 1873, and at the end of the year city council elections were held. Not surprisingly, Samuel Noble and other company officials were elected to one-year terms on the council.[11]

Although Anniston has been called "the model city of the New South," it might be more accurate to describe it as an American version of an English village in which the squire and his family saw to the needs and well-being of the village and its people. The Nobles built an Episcopal church at the heart of Anniston—the small cedar-and-brass gem of Grace Church, which was completed in 1886. An Anglican ethos extended to other parts of Anniston; its principal artery—Quintard Avenue—is named after Charles Todd Quintard, a physician and a Confederate military chaplain, and the second bishop of Tennessee. Grace Church was clearly the "squire's" church. When Daniel Tyler (the Nobles' business partner) died during a trip to New York in 1882, his body was brought back to Anniston for burial in Grace Church, even though the church was not yet finished.

In 1888, Samuel Noble's son, John, realized that the squire's church held little appeal for the workers and approached Bishop Wilmer about the possibility of founding a new church in Anniston. The Nobles were of English origin, and it is likely that John Noble's vision for St. Michael's was informed by English priests who believed that elaborate ritual would attract the urban poor, so St. Michael's was to be a church that would serve the working class and the poor as the Anglo-Catholic "slum priests" of the Church of England were doing in England's heavily industrialized cities. Noble described his vision in a letter to Bishop Wilmer: "we earnestly desire to gather in the working class to the Church, and to do this we want what is called (for want of a better word to express our meaning) a Ritualistic parish." Wilmer seems to have been reluctant to give his permission for an explicitly "ritualist" parish, and Noble renewed his plea to the bishop in a subsequent letter: "We want nothing extreme. I said in my former letter to you that it is called extreme. Again, you say why try to bring in the poor with 'extreme' ritual. It is because I am convinced that nothing else will bring them in and hold them there, and the men who are willing to work among the poor and have the power to control and influence them, are, in almost every case, men who are very careful to have the smallest detail of public worship carried out with reverence and dignity; in other words a Ritualist (so called)."[12] And so, St. Michael's was built.

The Church of St. Michael and All Angels was the Diocese of Alabama's first genuinely Anglo-Catholic parish. John Noble conceived of a church on a grand and costly scale. The tower houses twelve bells that cost $6,000 in 1889, and the altar was carved from a twelve-and-a-half-foot slab of white Italian Carrara marble. All in all, St. Michael's cost John Noble more than $125,000. It was consecrated on September 29, 1890—the Feast of St. Michael and All Angels—with all the pomp and ceremony that could be provided in nineteenth-century Alabama:

At 10 A.M. according to a notice given, the Bishop of the Diocese met the visiting Bishop and Clergy in the Chapel—now used as a S.S. [Sunday school] room—to robe & form in procession. At the same time the choristers met in the choir room for the same purpose and at 10.30 the choir and organist preceded [*sic*] by the Cross bearer entered through the tower marched silently down the centre aisle and formed in open line at the front door. As the procession of Clergy entered headed by Rev. Benj. Dennis of Uniontown as staff bearer followed by Rt. Rev. R. H. Wilmer—bishop of the Diocese, Rt. Rev. C. T. Quintard, Bishop of Tennessee and the visiting clergy 12 in number, the choir closing in and joining the procession followed by the vestry. The Bishop and Clergy repeating the 24th Psalm. . . . When all were in their places Prof. W. Y. Titcomb, a member of the vestry read the request to consecrate and presented the instruments of donation, which the Bp accepted and laid in the altar and proceeded to the Consecration service as set forth in the Prayer Book. Rev. T. F. Gailor again intoned the service—the choir for the first time chanting the Proper Psalms antiphonally. The Sermon, at the request of the Bishop of the diocese, was preached by Rev. R. S. Barrett of Atlanta Ga. The Holy Communion was administered by Rt. Rev. C. T. Quintard Bishop of Tennessee—assisted by the Rev. Mr. Stickney of Faunsdale and the Rev. J. T. Smith who is the pioneer of the church in this place. About 200 communicated. At the close of the service clergy & choir marched to the choir room singing the 190th Hymn. During the Prayer of the Consecration of the Elements the Bells were tapped. The brass Altar Cross—vases & candlesticks were lighted. The choir cross & Communion Service were also used for the first time. St. Michael, St. Gabriel, & St. Raphael were also there in their niches.[13]

It was almost certainly the most elaborate liturgy that had ever taken place in an Episcopal church in Alabama, and one wonders what Bishop Wilmer thought of it.

Noble's vision for St. Michael's, however, was not just about elaborate ritual. He sought to create a church that would minister to people's physical and emotional needs as well as their souls. Plans for the church included a house where a community of deaconesses or sisters would live and an infirmary where they would serve the sick. There were many such needs in Anniston in the late 1880s. A journalist investigating child labor reported that families were living in company-provided cottages with no electricity. She also noted that children as young as four and five years old were doing backbreaking labor in the mills, earning twenty cents a day, and appeared to be years older than their biological ages. The most drastic economic slump, however, took place in the early 1890s. "Stores on Noble Street closed down. Machines rusted. The crime rate rose . . . And 'an atmosphere of gloom' pervaded the entire town."[14]

It was difficult to find a priest acceptable both to the bishop and to John Noble. "The man that takes this parish will have plenty of very hard work to do among a class of people that are not generally sought after, but I believe the parish can be built up into a good strong centre of work but it will take years to do it.—but a 'will to do it will find a way.'" Yet Noble's dream was never satisfactorily realized; Anniston's workers did not flock to St. Michael's as Noble had hoped they would. In a letter to a potential rector, Noble wrote, "The church was built for the working class, but they don't take to it as they should[.] [T]he sects appear to attract them more than the church."[15]

The Wilmer Era Ends

On the twenty-fifth anniversary of his consecration as bishop of Alabama, Bishop Wilmer recorded that he had confirmed 8,134 people, consecrated twenty-four churches, ordained seventeen priests and twenty-nine deacons, and instituted fifteen deaconesses. Interestingly, he listed the deaconesses first.[16] Eighteen parishes founded during Wilmer's episcopate remain active in the Diocese of Alabama in 2012. The most important area of growth in the Diocese of Alabama, however, occurred in the "mineral region." Plainly, Wilmer must have been weary after such an arduous twenty-five years.

The end of Wilmer's episcopate was a time of uncertainty and turmoil. To his credit, Wilmer tried to provide for a stable transition to a new bishop. Finally, in 1888 he was seventy-two years old and suggested for the first time that he might need an assistant bishop to help him carry out his episcopal duties. In 1891 the diocese elected Henry Melville Jackson—the rector of Grace Church, Richmond, but a native of Leesburg, Virginia, Alabama's third bishop from Virginia—to serve as Wilmer's assistant. The canons under which he was elected allowed Jackson to succeed Wilmer upon his retirement or death, but Jackson was forced to resign before he could become diocesan bishop.

Toward the end of his nine years as Wilmer's assistant, Jackson began to suffer mysterious symptoms that he attributed to "gastric catarrh," but others suspected Bishop Jackson of alcohol abuse. At the 1899 diocesan convention at Grace Church, Anniston, the clergy of the diocese confronted Jackson and insisted that he resign. Stewart McQueen prepared a presentment against Jackson that the clergy intended to bring to the Presiding Bishop of the Episcopal Church if he did not step down. The case was strong: McQueen had affidavits from people who claimed they had seen Jackson intoxicated in public on at least two occasions, including Easter Eve. An affidavit from the rector of St. James, Eufaula, charged that the bishop "rarely ever attends Church when at home," and other documents, including a newspaper article, indicated that Jackson had three legal judgments against him for unpaid debts. Most damning was the charge that he had neglected regular episcopal visitations to parishes of the diocese. His second wife, Caroline

Cochran of Eufaula, owned a plantation where the couple entertained guests in a grand manner, and his debts might have been the result of trying to maintain a plantation and a lifestyle appropriate for a plantation owner on the income of a bishop of the Episcopal Church.

Jackson initially resisted the calls for him to resign and published a lengthy defense to the charges made against him, especially the charge of public intoxication. On one occasion he claimed that he had been advised to drink whisky "to stimulate and strengthen me," and on another that an episode of "suppression of urine" and "uraemic poisoning" had been mistaken as drunkenness. The chorus of calls for his resignation only grew louder. The Church of the Advent pressed him to step down and urged other churches to join them. Finally, the House of Bishops sent Bishops Peterkin of West Virginia, Randolph of Southern Virginia, and Capers of South Carolina to ask Jackson to step down, and he yielded, submitting his resignation in December 1899. By May of the next year, Bishop Jackson was dead.[17]

Wilmer called for the election of a new assistant bishop, and on May 8, a Special Convention elected Robert Woodward Barnwell, rector of St. Paul's, Selma. Wilmer died before he could assist in consecrating Barnwell to the office of bishop. Unable to attend the Diocesan Convention in 1900, Wilmer presided in public for the last time at Christ Church on February 25, when he confirmed thirty-four people. His last official action was the baptism of his grandchild, Minnie Wilmer Jones, in his home on May 6. He died on June 14, but his famous wit lasted until the very end. Asked if he thought he was dying, Wilmer replied, "You must remember that I have never passed away, and may not recognize the symptoms."

The funeral took place at Christ Church on June 15. "Throughout the afternoon, the rectors of the Mobile parishes . . . and representatives of the Vestries stood as a guard of honor in the church as a steady line of mourners passed through." Wilmer was known and loved throughout the South, not just in Alabama and by all white Alabamians, not just Episcopalians. On the occasion of his eightieth birthday, the *Atlanta Constitution* wrote, "He is one of the best and most universally loved men in the state, and well deserves to be, and every Christian in Alabama will join The Constitution in wishing him many more years of life and usefulness. . . . His Christian influence has not been confined to his own Church but . . . he has been a worthy example for all of Alabama's Christian workers. He has shown himself intelligent, broad-minded and liberal in his faith, and has at all times discouraged denominational differences and dissensions." Officiating at Wilmer's funeral were Bishops Nelson of Georgia and Thompson of Mississippi. The Rebel bishop was finally laid to rest in Mobile's Magnolia Cemetery, having served longer than any bishop in the history of the Episcopal Church. Five weeks later, Robert Barnwell, the third bishop of Alabama, was consecrated on July 25, in Selma's St. Paul's Church.[18]

Into the Twentieth Century

At the beginning of the twentieth century, Alabama Episcopalians continued to occupy prominent, powerful, and public roles. Two Episcopalians from Alabama would achieve international celebrity early in the twentieth century. Born in 1900 and baptized at Montgomery's Church of the Holy Comforter, Zelda Sayre's name would become practically synonymous with the Jazz Age when she married novelist F. Scott Fitzgerald. Zelda's family had deep roots in Alabama's Confederate past. Her father was Alabama Supreme Court Justice Anthony Dickson Sayre. Justice Sayre's uncle, William Sayre, owned the house that became the first "White House" of the Confederacy. Zelda's maternal grandfather had been a senator in the Confederate senate. However, Zelda's own life sometimes seemed to be a desperate attempt to repudiate middle class respectability. A gifted writer and painter, a number of Zelda's stories and articles were published, as well as one novel (*Save Me the Waltz*, 1932), but despite his greater fame, her husband resented her artistic aspirations. Fitzgerald's drinking and Zelda's mental instability doomed the marriage. The couple never divorced but lived apart after 1934.[19]

Tallulah Bankhead, the hard-drinking, wisecracking star of Hollywood, Broadway, and London's West End, went to services at "the little Episcopal chapel set up in a loft over a seed store" in Jasper, Alabama. Although her father, William Bankhead (speaker of the US House of Representatives from 1936 to 1940) was a Methodist, her mother (who died soon after Tallulah's birth) had been an Episcopalian, and Congressman Bankhead raised his daughter in her mother's faith. On the inside cover of the Bible that had belonged to his wife, the congressman wrote, "As a spiritual source at the end of each exacting day may I recommend to you your little mother's favorite, the 103rd Psalm." Tallulah recalled: "I have never gone to church since I could avoid it without penalty, [but] I have found consolation in: 'He will not always chide: neither will he keep *his anger* for ever. He hath not dealt with us after our sins; nor rewarded us according to our iniquities. . . . For he knoweth our frame; he remembereth that we *are dust*.'"[20]

Another Alabama Episcopalian, Grace Hinds, is not as well known as Zelda Fitzgerald or Tallulah Bankhead, but her marriage in 1917 to Lord Curzon of Kedleston (Viceroy of India from 1899 to 1905 and foreign secretary of Great Britain from 1919 to 1925) made her the Marchioness Curzon of Kedleston. Born and brought up in Decatur, Lady Curzon wrote, "A certain sense of strangeness and discomfort surrounded us there, Republicans in an area of Democrats, Episcopalians in the midst of Methodists. I was conscious of this feeling even as a child." She was also the subject of John Singer Sargent's last oil painting.[21]

The new century also brought new concerns about race. W. E. B. Du Bois wrote, "The problem of the twentieth century is the problem of the color line—the relation of the darker to the lighter races of men in Asia and Africa, in America and the islands of the sea." Apparently, many in Alabama agreed with Du Bois that the "color line" would be the "problem of the twentieth century," and that the relationship between the "darker" and "lighter races" needed to be addressed as the new century dawned. At the start of the twentieth century some Alabama Episcopalians were beginning to advocate equal rights for African Americans, or at least to test the "color line." Others continued to favor white supremacy. The purpose of Alabama's 1901 constitutional convention, as stated by its president, John B. Knox, was "to establish white supremacy in this State."[22] To that end, the convention sought to disenfranchise black men by requiring a literacy test and imposing a poll tax. Ten percent of the 157 delegates to the 1901 constitutional convention were Episcopalians, although less than 1 percent (about 15,000) of Alabama's population was Episcopalian in 1901. None of the Episcopalians at the 1901 convention opposed black disenfranchisement.

A Bishop for the Twentieth Century

Robert Barnwell, who had succeeded Wilmer as bishop of Alabama, died after an episcopate of only two years, the victim of a burst appendix. At a special Diocesan Convention held at St. John's Church, Montgomery (October 8–9, 1903) the Diocese of Alabama elected Charles Minnegerode Beckwith, a Texas priest with Virginia roots (their third from that state), to serve as their bishop.[23] A native of Prince George County, Virginia, Beckwith was the nephew of John Watrous Beckwith, rector of Trinity Church, Demopolis, from 1863 to 1865 and bishop of Georgia from 1868 to 1890. Prior to his election as the fourth bishop of Alabama, Beckwith had served parishes in Georgia and Texas but seems to have found his niche as "General Missionary" in the Diocese of Texas. Even though the Texans thought enough of Beckwith to elect him bishop coadjutor in 1891, Beckwith declined the office in favor of serving as a roving missionary. Beckwith was also a gifted religious educator. Using the Book of Common Prayer as his principal text for religious instruction, Beckwith wrote three books used for religious education in the Episcopal Church.

Beckwith was plainly a man of great energy and began his episcopate with a whirlwind of activity. At the end of his life, even after the diocese had virtually repudiated him and forced him to yield his authority to his bishop coadjutor, Beckwith was remembered as a "a strong and vigorous personality." After the years during which Bishop Wilmer had been enfeebled by age and illness, the Diocese of Alabama needed vigorous and decisive leadership; after the charges of drunkenness, debt, and dereliction of duty made against Bishop Jackson, the diocese needed someone who was above reproach; and after the brief episcopate of Bishop Barnwell, they needed someone who was likely to have a long, healthy life ahead of him. Beckwith, fifty-three years old, rector of several churches, itinerant Episcopalian evangelist, advocate of an innovative approach to religious education, and already elected a bishop elsewhere (even though he had declined the office), must have been an extremely attractive figure to the clergy and delegates who elected him in 1903. Like one of his fellow Episcopalians, President Theodore Roosevelt, Beckwith was a muscular Christian. Using phrases that sounded like Roosevelt, Beckwith declared that "the day of the flint-lock and the ox-cart is past. This is the day of progress—of the smokeless and the horseless and the wireless. It is the day of autos and dread-naughts and sky-scrapers."[24]

Beckwith's first annual report as bishop of Alabama listed more than fourteen areas in which he proposed to work. The first point of his address concerned a diocesan office that he proposed to establish at Birmingham's Church of the Advent. Beckwith was the first bishop of Alabama to propose establishing a diocesan office at the Church of the Advent and to locate his residence in Birmingham. Because of a conflict between Beckwith and the Church of the Advent, however, this plan never came to fruition. Instead of living in Birmingham, Beckwith began his episcopate by living in Anniston, but then he moved to Montgomery in 1911. An avid outdoorsman, he built a fishing camp near Bay Minette in Baldwin County, which he left to the diocese in his will. Today Beckwith Lodge serves as the camp and conference center of the Diocese of the Central Gulf Coast. The conflict between the Church of the Advent and Beckwith was a harbinger. It represented a pattern of behavior that became a grave problem.

Addressing New Social Ills

As Beckwith took up his duties as bishop of Alabama, America's social fabric was being transformed. A nation of farms and villages was becoming one of factories and cities. Industrialization and urbanization brought both bane and blessing. In 1911 the Diocesan Convention heard a litany of ills from the newly created Social Service Commission. They reported on "infant mortality, the birth rate, physical degeneracy, orphanage, illegitimacy, deficient children, accident or child labor." The commission singled out for special consideration child labor, prison reform, and temperance. They proposed making it illegal to employ children younger than fourteen years old, and called for children between seven and fourteen to be required to attend school for a certain period each year. The commission also condemned the convict lease system and attributed "sickness, trouble, sexular [*sic*] immorality, and prostitution" to intemperance. By 1914 the commission noted that a large proportion of Alabama's convicts were black and called for "solving the race question in a spirit of helpfulness to the negro and equal justice to both races." These issues were on the minds of other Alabamians in the early twentieth century. Child labor legislation came before the Alabama legislature in 1902, and in 1905 Alabama's Democratic Party demanded compulsory education and a local option law for the sale of alcoholic beverages. Yet progress was slow, and the convict lease system was not abolished until 1927.[25]

In his first diocesan address Beckwith noted, "the movement of the people is from the smaller communities to the villages; from the villages to the townships, and from the townships to the cities." The bishop went on to say that the diocese would "need ten new men" and identified Gadsden, Woodlawn, and Avondale—towns or neighborhoods that had come into existence as a result of industrialization—as places where there was a need for clergy. Even with Beckwith's vigorous leadership, Alabama's Episcopalians confronted the problems of industrialization and urbanization in piecemeal fashion. However, there were a few Alabama Episcopalians who understood that industrialization and urbanization confronted the church with unprecedented challenges.[26]

Bishop Wilmer ordained James A. Van Hoose to the diaconate but never ordained him to the priesthood, allegedly because of his poor vision. Nevertheless, as explained previously, Van Hoose helped found St. Mary's-on-the-Highlands and in 1894 was elected mayor of Birmingham. Historian Leah Rawls Atkins writes: "Van Hoose . . . claimed to represent the 'best element.' He opposed partisan patronage, proposed establishing a business administration and pledged to close saloons on Sunday and promised to 'prowl around the streets at night' going into 'every nook and crook and hole' to ferret out vice." One of the keys to the success of Van Hoose's campaign was his willingness to seek the support of black voters. Van Hoose was indefatigable, not only assisting in the founding of several churches but also serving as deacon-in-charge of several congregations, including Birmingham's Church of the Advent and Holy Comforter, Gadsden.[27]

Similarly, Edgar Gardner Murphy, rector of the influential and prestigious St. John's Episcopal Church in Montgomery, distinguished himself as an eloquent and ardent advocate in the areas of child labor, education, and race relations. His reputation is well earned in the first two areas but ambiguous in the third. Born near Fort Smith, Arkansas, in 1869, Murphy matriculated at the University of the South in 1885, where he was deeply influenced by theologian William Porcher Dubose. After further study at the General Theological Seminary in New York City, Murphy returned to the South and took up his first charge at Christ Church,

Laredo, Texas. Following his time in Laredo, Murphy served churches in Ohio and New York before being called to St. John's, Montgomery, in 1898.[28]

During his time in Montgomery, Murphy's career as a reformer really got under way. Murphy's greatest passion and his most significant accomplishments were in the area of child labor reform. Murphy personally visited factories to compile statistics and anecdotes for his campaign against the employment of children. Observing a girl of seven who had lost three fingers in an industrial accident, Murphy asked the factory foreman what had happened. He replied, "the children are so careless." Murphy commented, "My God! Hasn't a child seven years of age, got a right to be careless?" After years of work, Murphy was largely responsible for legislation that the Alabama legislature passed in 1907 prohibiting the employment of children under twelve, limiting work hours for children between twelve and eighteen, and requiring school for children under the age of sixteen.[29]

Murphy resigned from St. John's in November 1901 to become executive secretary of the Southern Education Board. From then until his health forced him to retire, Murphy devoted himself to the cause of improving education in the South. Two years later, Murphy asked Alabama's Bishop Beckwith to release him from his ordination vows. Murphy's close friend, philanthropist Robert C. Ogden, believed that Murphy had left the priesthood in order "to bring his influence to bear without prejudice upon the great mass of the Methodist and Baptist population," but it may also have had something to do with Bishop Beckwith's character. Another friend, Silas McBee, said, "Murphy was unwilling to give up what to him was his life call." Unfortunately, he had "for a bishop a legalist of the first order, and it was plain that all of the power of the Episcopal influence would be used against him if he did this work as a clergyman without tying himself completely to some sort of parochial action and obedience." The goals of the Southern Education Board were to "conduct a campaign of education for free schools for all the people" and to "conduct a Bureau of Information and Advice on Legislation and School Organization." Murphy achieved much in his new position. During the board's first five years, "the Southern states increased their annual appropriations for education by $14,000,000." Ill health finally forced Murphy to step down in 1910.[30]

Murphy's record in the area of race relations is ambiguous. Suddenly and publicly, Murphy became involved in racial problems when a black man was lynched in Laredo while he was serving Christ Church, Laredo, Texas. He became even more aware of and involved in racial matters when he came to St. John's in 1898 and was instrumental in the founding of an African American parish—Montgomery's Church of the Good Shepherd. Concerned with the problem of lynching and with the growing movement across the South to disenfranchise blacks, Murphy organized the Southern Society "to furnish, by means of correspondence, publication, and particularly through public conferences, an organ for the expression of the varied and even antagonistic convictions of representative Southern men" on the race problem. Their first act was to organize the Conference on Race Relations that met in Montgomery in May 1900.

About the time he organized the Southern Society and was planning the conference, Murphy made the acquaintance of Booker T. Washington, who became a lifelong friend. Murphy was in complete agreement with Washington's message of black "self-help" and accommodation to the policies of segregation. Although Murphy intended the conference to offer a balance of opinion between those in favor of civil rights for African Americans and those opposed, it became a platform for virulent racism. Booker T. Washington tried to assist Murphy in planning the conference and suggested several "liberal-minded whites, but Murphy rejected nearly all of them." The result, according to historian Robert J. Norrell, was that Murphy "loaded the program with some of the most vociferous anti-black voices in the South." Murphy described his own position as one of "white supremacy": "the maintenance of white supremacy in Alabama . . . is an end with which I have been in earnest and positive sympathy," although according to Murphy "white supremacy . . . means the supremacy of intelligence, administrative capacity, and public order. It means the perpetuation of those economic and civic conditions upon which the progress of the Negro is itself dependent."

The next year, 1901, when Washington dined at the White House with President Theodore Roosevelt and his family, the white southern press exploded in racist outrage. The Geneva (Alabama) *Reaper* declared, "Poor Roosevelt! He might now just as well sleep with Booker Washington, for the scent of that coon will follow him to the grave, as far as the South is concerned." Even Murphy criticized the black leader: "The average man in the street can see nothing in the incident but a deliberate attempt on the part of the President and yourself to force the issue of inter-marriage and amalgamation!!!!" Historian Ralph E. Luker describes Murphy as "one of segregation's most sophisticated apologists" and characterizes his opinion as "at best . . . benign racism."[31]

While Murphy addressed social problems on the national stage, Carl Henckell was one of the few priests in Alabama seeking to bring the working class into the Episcopal Church. Born in Germany in 1860, Henckell studied at the Medical College of Syracuse University from 1882 to 1883 and became a licensed dentist. In the 1880s, Henckell joined a small colony of German immigrants in the north Alabama town of Cullman. While in Cullman, Henckell was active in St. John's Lutheran Church, but in 1903 the Henckells moved to Birmingham and Dr. Henckell became involved in the Episcopal Church.

Supported by the rector of St. Mary's-on-the-Highlands, Willoughby Newton

Claybrook, Henckell studied for ordination, and Beckwith ordained him both deacon and a priest in 1910. Henckell exercised a different kind of ministry from that of most of Alabama's Episcopal clergy. In an article in the *Alabama Churchman*, Henckell described himself as a missionary and cataloged a ministry that included "visiting hospitals, jails, criminal courts, helping unfortunate girls and finding homes for their children, [and] procuring physicians and food for the underfed and neglected." He shepherded several small missions, eventually becoming rector of Grace Episcopal Church, in Birmingham's Woodlawn neighborhood, in 1918, where he served until his death in 1933. At one time or another, Henckell was in charge of All Saints' Mission on Twenty-Ninth Street; Christ Church, Avondale; Good Shepherd, East Lake; Trinity, West End; Oakman; West Blocton; and Woodlawn. Henckell noted that he was "often called to minister to Church people in Carbon Hill, Corona, Dora, Littleton, Coalburg, and other places."[32]

The church registers of these small churches and missions tell a story quite different from the ones told by similar records at the Church of the Advent and St. Mary's. The members of Henckell's churches were carpenters, mechanics, secretaries, or held similar low- to moderate-income jobs. The fact that most of the churches Henckell served are no longer in existence shows just how unsuccessful the Episcopal Church in Alabama was in ministering to this economic group. There is no easy way to explain why the church of the affluent and powerful could not also be the church of the working class. In some other parts of the United States (such as Philadelphia, New York, and Boston) working-class parishes thrived, but Alabama's Episcopalians remained overwhelmingly upper class.

Henckell's single most significant accomplishment, and arguably one of the most significant accomplishments of the Episcopal Church in Alabama, was the part he played in founding Birmingham's Children's Hospital. According to the Henckell family history, Children's Hospital was conceived as a result of a conversation between Henckell and Birmingham's city health officer, Dr. James Dedman. "They had been to see a very ill child and had been unable to get him into Hillman Hospital. Dr. Henckell said, 'What we need is a Children's Hospital.' Dr. Dedman replied, 'Tell me more.'" A meeting to organize a hospital for children was held at St. Andrew's rectory and was attended not only by Henckell but also by Raimundo de Ovies, rector of St. Andrew's Church. Initially known as The Holy Innocents Hospital Association, the fledgling hospital soon became too much for the church to manage and it became an independent institution, but Henckell always regretted that the church had relinquished its control.[33]

Henckell family history attributes Carl Henckell's switch to the Episcopal Church at least partly to the influence of J. J. D. "Dad" Hall. Known as the "Billy Sunday of the Episcopal Church," James Jefferson Davis Hall was born in Greenville, Alabama, in 1864. After teaching for several years at the Noble Institute in Anniston, he attended the Virginia Theological Seminary. Influenced by Julia Strudwick Tutwiler, Hall became a prison chaplain in Alabama, then spent the rest of his life doing street ministry in Philadelphia, Boston, and New York. Hall became known as the "bishop of Wall Street" because he and a curate of Trinity Church, Wall Street, held noontime open-air services on the streets of lower Manhattan.[34]

Two major initiatives begun under Beckwith remain important to the Diocese of Alabama today. First, he organized the first college chaplaincy in the diocese. Bishop Barnwell first suggested stationing an Episcopal priest at Auburn with special responsibility for the students in 1900. In 1917 Bishop Beckwith asked, "What are we going to do about Auburn at this Council?" and observed, "every county in the State is represented in the student body." The bishop reasoned that Episcopalians at Auburn were more likely to remain loyal if the church reached out to them with a chaplain and that non-Episcopalians might be attracted to the Episcopal Church. Beckwith also proposed establishing a chaplaincy at Montevallo, but nothing transpired. It proved more difficult to establish an Episcopal chaplaincy at the University of Alabama. The subject was first raised at the 1932 convention and then raised again in 1936, but the chaplaincy at Alabama did not begin until 1942.[35]

Second, H. Lorraine Tracy wrote a letter to the 1919 convention asking the Diocese of Alabama to "take formal action supporting the work as outlined by the Commission on Work among the Deaf in the Province." It pointed out that "the deaf in Birmingham meet at the Church of the Advent." This bore fruit in 1930 when an Alabama clergyman, Robert Capers Fletcher, became "Deaf-Mute Missionary to the Province of Sewanee with headquarters in Birmingham."[36] Fletcher founded St. John's Church for the Deaf in Birmingham in 1935.

The Churches and World War I

Beckwith presided over the Diocese of Alabama during World War I, but the diocesan journals show relatively little concern with that catastrophic conflict. At the 1918 convention Bishop Beckwith spoke of "the terrible conflict now being waged between the powers that would save and the designs that would destroy mankind." He called on the clergy to have "a week-day memorial service, with special prayers to God for the protection of our army and that of our allies." A resolution at the same convention acknowledged that "our country is now at war and is fighting for a righteous and Christian cause" and called for Alabama's Episcopalians to "give special aid and support to raising the $100,000,000.00 War Fund of the American Red Cross." Beckwith also noted that "the army and the ranks of the army have created serious problems which the Church must be prepared to meet. Many of our Clergy have answered the call and are now in active military service."

Because of its proximity to what was then called Camp Sheridan, St. John's, Montgomery, rallied during the Great War. The women of the church not only held open houses on Sunday afternoons, and served in the Red Cross, they also taught literacy classes for poorly educated soldiers. Christ Church, Mobile, also gave significant support to the war effort. According to Louis Tucker, the rector of Christ Church during World War I, although his parish's membership was only "one sixth of one per cent of the population," it did "fifty per cent or more of the local war work, appeals for wounded and orphans and so on, passed through their hands and was headed by one or another of their ladies." Consequently, Tucker entertained "a wounded British officer sent to make good will speeches, a lot of homesick doughboys, an aviator with no face, a dozen torpedoed sailors ... a motley, human masquerade of angels, devils, and poor puzzled sinners, disguised as human beings." One of Christ Church's women, worried about her son who was in military service, "proved a human steam engine in petticoats. In next to no time the parish house was buzzing full of soldiers; and candy pulls, afternoon teas, food and girls kept it packed all the time."[37]

Some of Alabama's clergy may have answered the call to serve as military chaplains, but a parishioner of the Church of the Advent, Mortimer Jordan, was not pleased with the clergy's response to World War I. Responding to a letter that referred to "much war activity at home," Jordan asked his wife if she did not think that the clergy were "getting off rather cheaply" and specifically referred to the Advent's rector, Middleton Barnwell, and prominent Presbyterian pastor, Henry Edmonds, adding that they were "needed in [the] Red Cross & Y.M.C.A." He told his wife that he was "through with preachers for all time."[38]

Bishop Beckwith versus the Diocese of Alabama

Energetic and intelligent as he was, Beckwith was also authoritarian and unbending and came to Alabama trailing a history of confrontation with the parishes he had served. While rector of Christ Church, Houston, he forbade the women of the church to hold a fund-raising performance of *The Pirates of Penzance*. When they went ahead with the performance, Beckwith resigned. From the very beginning of his episcopate, he engaged in an escalating series of conflicts that eventually made it impossible for him to continue to function as the bishop of the diocese. Although Beckwith insisted on rubrical precision that virtually amounted to a kind of "Prayer Book fundamentalism," he held a view of episcopal authority that was not founded in the canons and traditions of the Episcopal Church. Louis Tucker wrote that Beckwith was "a brilliant man but hard to agree with." "We differed about a theory of the Episcopate. He felt that the office of a bishop entitled the holder to be obeyed in everything except where the Church had ruled. In all matters not settled by canon, the Bishop's will was the Church's will and disobedience to the Bishop was disobedience to the Church and God. It is a perfectly tenable position and millions of Christians today hold it; but the Anglican Communion has fought it for a thousand years and the Lambeth Conference, not long before, had ruled against it. Naturally, it repelled me as un-Anglican."[39]

In his first year as bishop of Alabama, Beckwith alienated the Church of the Advent, the largest and wealthiest parish in the diocese. Until Beckwith's arrival, parishes had generally called rectors, and then submitted the rector's name to the bishop for approval. But when the Advent called the Reverend Quincy Ewing of Greenville, Mississippi, Beckwith informed them that they must first ask the bishop's permission before calling a priest. The Advent vestry duly rescinded the call and asked for Beckwith's permission to issue a call. Then Beckwith declared that the Advent vestry could not issue a call because they had fourteen members, rather than the maximum of twelve allowed by diocesan canons. Furthermore, Beckwith believed that Ewing's standing as a priest was compromised because he had presided at the wedding of a divorced person, so he initially refused to consent to the Advent's call. Subsequently, however, the bishop of Mississippi declared himself to be satisfied with Ewing's conduct and Beckwith allowed the Advent to call the Mississippi priest. By that time, the relationship between Beckwith and the Advent vestry was thoroughly poisoned. Beckwith's feud with the Advent's vestry spilled over into his relationship with Ewing. Ewing received a mock Christmas greeting from "Santa Claus" in 1905, in which Santa said, "Bishop Beckwith bade me wish you the merriest kind of Christmas and the happiest possible New Year. He says that your love for him . . . is exceeded only by his love for you."[40]

A November 28, 1911, letter from Beckwith to Randolph Claiborne illustrates Beckwith's tendency to elevate minor matters to major squabbles. While visiting Claiborne's parish, Beckwith had noticed that the congregation joined the priest in saying the General Thanksgiving. Beckwith acknowledged that it was "very beautiful to have the people join in the Thanksgiving" but went on to say that "the Church has never authorized this, and following individual taste would soon destroy the unity of the diocese." He asked Claiborne to discontinue the practice. Beckwith routinely told priests coming to Alabama from other dioceses that "the only standard we have in this Diocese for Church service, Church work, and Church teaching is the Book of Common Prayer. We have no extremes in this Diocese on the one side or the other. The Clergy enjoy all the liberty the Church has permitted and provided for. If you are a Prayer Book Churchman, you would find yourself immediately at home among your brethren here, and with your Bishop. Alabama is no place for a man of extreme views. We have here no 'schools of thought,' and no 'party line'; and the Bishop's effort is to avoid both."[41]

A staunch opponent of Anglo-Catholicism, Beckwith did his utmost to keep high church priests out of Alabama. He wrote to J. J. Orum of Pleasant Hill regarding his son who was attending school at the Holy Cross Monastery at West Point, New York, saying, "that body represents a school of thought that has not my sympathy." In May of 1917, Beckwith wrote to an unidentified fellow bishop, charging that Anglo-Catholics were Roman Catholic "fellow travelers" and subversives: "We are contending here in small ways with the same problem that unsettles the Church in England at the present time. Rome is as far seeing as Germany, and Rome too, for the disseminating of her teachings, had her 'under-ground' warfare. Alabama was long spared the inroad of the ritualist, but Alabama has her trials today." Beckwith went so far as to ask that the Order of Holy Cross not send their magazine to him.[42]

Beckwith's relationship with the diocese, especially with its large urban parishes, went from bad to worse. His obsession with the minutiae of ecclesiastical rules and his aversion to ritualism led to a major controversy with Frederick D. Devall, rector of Montgomery's Church of the Ascension, whom he charged with "disobeying the godly admonition of his bishop." During his visit to the Church of the Ascension, Beckwith had noticed that the choir bowed in reverence to the altar and asked Devall to put a stop to the practice. Devall asked Beckwith to put his request in writing, but in another letter asked the bishop to withdraw his request. Beckwith reiterated his request, but Devall responded with a letter saying that he could not in good conscience obey. In a letter of November 1914, Beckwith accused Devall of not being prepared for his annual visitation: "You received official notice of my visitation two months ahead of the date. You not only failed to make preparation by preparing your class, but you failed to give notice in the Church of your Bishop's coming. In your Ordination vow, you promised to obey the Canons of the Church." In reply, Devall protested his innocence, "Bishop, I can't help but feel that our relations would be so pleasant & cordial if you would credit me with having no ulterior motives in my work."[43]

In a subsequent controversy, Devall allowed laymen vested as acolytes into the chancel during the Sunday liturgy. The point was minor, and Beckwith's anger was out of all proportion to the incident. The ecclesiastical court refused to hear Beckwith's case against Devall, noting that although Devall had violated the bishop's directive against allowing laymen into the chancel during the liturgy, the priest had not violated a canon. Beckwith then refused to issue a letter dismissory to the bishop of Tennessee when Devall moved to a parish in the Diocese of Tennessee, even though the Standing Committee called on the bishop to yield in his battle with Devall. Beckwith's response was to ask the 1916 Diocesan Convention to dissolve the Standing Committee and elect a new one, a step the convention was unwilling to take.[44]

In 1918 Beckwith floated the idea of electing a bishop coadjutor. Many in the diocese, especially those hostile to Beckwith, eagerly seized upon this idea. In 1919 the vestry of St. Paul's, Selma, sent a questionnaire to all the parishes and missions in the diocese to gauge the feelings of the diocese toward Beckwith and to lay the groundwork for forcing his retirement. Among others, the questionnaire asked, "What is the condition of Church life in your parish?" "If unfavorable, what in your judgment is the reason?" "What do you consider to be the state of the Church in the Diocese?" "What do you think is the reason for this?" "Do you think there is any action the Bishop could take to remedy the situation?" and "Do you think the Bishop should resign upon a proper retiring allowance, asking the Council to appoint a successor?"

The degree of hostility the answers revealed was remarkable. St. Michael's, Anniston, was particularly bitter toward Beckwith. They said that their parish life was at "a low ebb," that the state of the diocese was "deplorable," and that the reason was "the attitude of the Bishop." According to an accompanying letter, Beckwith had not allowed Episcopalian chaplains at nearby Fort McClellan to preside at services at St. Michael's while the parish was without a rector. St. John's, Mobile, characterized the diocese as "lamentably . . . disorganized" and blamed the "disposition and actions of the present Bishop." The solution, they believed, was that he "resign and retire from all connection with the affairs of the Diocese." Of the larger parishes, only Nativity, Huntsville, backed Beckwith. In their questionnaire they stated, "This Vestry is with the Bishop." The smaller parishes and missions either did not answer or expressed some support for Beckwith. St. John's, Albany, blamed the situation on "Failure of some of the parishes and priests to cooperate with the Bishop." Barbara Brandon Schnorrenberg insightfully noted, "Beckwith never seemed really comfortable with large wealthy urban parishes; he seems to have particularly disliked the inevitable social aspects of these congregations."[45]

The final straw was Beckwith's feud with Richard Wilkinson, rector of St. John's Church, Montgomery. Wilkinson had invited Rabbi William B. Schwartz from the local synagogue to speak at a New Year's Eve service and to give a lecture titled "The Attitude of the Modern Jew to Jesus." Wilkinson initially sought Beckwith's permission to have the lecture in the church, but Beckwith refused permission. Beckwith never gave any reason for his objection to the rabbi's lecture, and the objection was made all the more mysterious by the fact that Beckwith had noted his happiness at the presence of the rabbi and some of his congregants at the reception following his consecration: "It was a great pleasure to see in the same company Christian people of every name, the Rabbi and members of his flock." Wilkinson went ahead with the lecture in a Sunday school room. In response, the bishop charged Wilkinson with violating his ordination vows, and an ecclesiastical court met in Troy on June 6, 1922, but the members of the court (William G. McDowell, Thomas G. Mundy, and Oscar de Wolf Randolph) found Wilkinson not guilty.[46]

Apparently feeling that Wilkinson's acquittal amounted to a vote of no confidence, Beckwith turned over all diocesan responsibilities to his newly elected bishop coadjutor, William George McDowell Jr., reserving for himself only "the element of authority in the conduct of Diocesan affairs." The convention that elected McDowell took place at St. Paul's, Carlowville, one of the smallest parishes in the diocese. Although St. Paul's had offered to host the next Diocesan Convention, they had no way of knowing that the next convention would be a special meeting to elect a bishop coadjutor (who would, in effect, replace Beckwith immediately). It would seem reasonable that a convention of such importance should be held at a large parish with more resources and better access to railway lines and major roads, and there was precedent for moving Diocesan Conventions even after their locations had been announced. When the *Living Church* and the *Southern Churchman* accused Beckwith of trying to rig the election, he denied the charge, but denied it a bit too strongly, perhaps. He insisted that he selected Carlowville because its isolated location would help the delegates concentrate on their duties. Furthermore, Beckwith also said that he had visited Carlowville to be certain that it was accessible by rail and studied the calendar "in order that the Council might have the benefit of full moon light." Given Beckwith's behavior, it is more than likely that he had hoped that Carlowville's isolated location would give him undue influence over the Special Convention. Following McDowell's election, Bishop Beckwith remained bishop of Alabama in name only until his death on April 18, 1928.[47]

Although the feud between the Diocese of Alabama and its bishop gave the diocese some notoriety in the Episcopal Church nationally, John Gardner Murray, an Alabama priest, brought luster to the Diocese of Alabama's reputation when he became the first elected Presiding Bishop of the Episcopal Church. A well-to-do businessman, Murray had originally studied for the Methodist ministry at Drew Theological Seminary in New Jersey, but he had to leave seminary before graduation when the death of his father left him the sole support of his family. Murray moved to Selma in 1884 where he joined the Episcopal Church. He was ordained to the diaconate in 1893 and made a priest a year later. In 1896 the Church of the Advent called him to be their rector. From the Advent he was called to the Church of St. Michael and All Angels, Baltimore, and then was elected bishop coadjutor of Maryland in 1909. While bishop of Maryland, Murray was elected Presiding

Bishop of the Episcopal Church in 1926 (the first elected Presiding Bishop since the canons of the Episcopal Church were changed in 1919 to provide for an elected chief bishop).[48]

The late nineteenth and early twentieth centuries were times of transition for Alabama's Episcopalians. Agriculture partly gave way to industry; the church of the Bourbons gave way to the church of the Big Mules; and the age of the firm but fatherly Bishop Wilmer gave way to that of the unbending and authoritarian Bishop Beckwith. Priests such as Carl Henckell, Edgar Gardner Murphy, and "Dad" Hall began to meet the challenges of industrialization and urbanization, and Alabama's Episcopalians proved themselves equal to the task of dealing with bishops who underperformed and overmanaged. But the economic and social challenges of the 1920s and 1930s would be the greatest trial that Alabama's Episcopalians had faced since the Civil War.

1. Thomas Church Brownell was bishop of Connecticut from 1824 to 1831 and presided at the first convention of the Episcopal Diocese of Alabama in January 1830.

2. St. John's, Montgomery, was founded in 1834. The building pictured was designed by New York architects Wills and Dudley (who also designed Nativity, Huntsville, and Trinity, Mobile). Confederate president Jefferson Davis and his family worshiped here.

3. St. Luke's, Cahaba, was founded in 1839 and built in a style known as carpenter Gothic. It was based on plans from Richard Upjohn's 1852 book *Upjohn's Rural Architecture: Designs, Working Drawings, and Specifications for a Wooden Church, and Other Rural Structures*. Members of St. Luke's included Congressman William Lowndes Yancey and wealthy merchant Edward Perine.

4. Virginia native Nicholas Hamner Cobbs was the first bishop of the Episcopal Diocese of Alabama. He served as bishop from 1844 until his death in 1861.

5. Richard Hooker Wilmer, the second bishop of Alabama, was the only bishop elected and consecrated in the Confederate Episcopal Church. Elected and consecrated in 1861, Wilmer served until 1900, making him the longest serving of Alabama's bishops.

6. Richard Hooker Wilmer late in life.

7. Students of St. Mark's Normal and Industrial School, the first church school for African Americans in Birmingham. It was founded in 1892 and closed in 1940.

8. Architect Ralph Adams Cram (1863–1942) designed both Montgomery's Church of the Ascension (pictured here; founded 1907) and New York's Cathedral of St. John the Divine. The Church of the Ascension's rector, Thomas Thrasher, facilitated meetings between members of the Montgomery Improvement Association and white city leaders during the Montgomery bus boycott. Photograph courtesy of Libby Weatherly Photography.

9. William George McDowell was bishop coadjutor of Alabama from 1922 to 1928 and bishop of Alabama from 1928 to 1938.

10. Anna Macy and her husband, Dr. R. C. Macy, helped found the Episcopal Church's mission to the Creeks in Atmore. St. Anna's Episcopal Church, Atmore, was named after the biblical prophetess Anna, but the name was also chosen to honor Anna Macy.

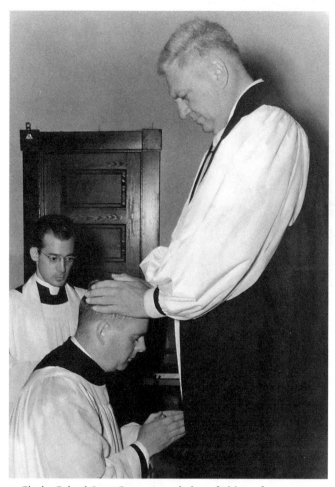

11. Charles Colcock Jones Carpenter was bishop of Alabama from 1938 to 1968. Many older Alabama Episcopalians remember feeling the bishop's large hands on their heads and hearing his deep voice pronounce the words of the rite of confirmation: "May you daily increase more and more in the Holy Ghost."

6
"Great and untried experiments"
From the 1920s to the 1950s

John Temple Graves (1903–1961), a longtime columnist for the *Birmingham News* and a member of the Church of the Advent, recounted his childhood experiences of God in this way:

> My deeper contacts with God were when the sun would set in summer evening glory behind Cox College across the road from our home. . . . I would be looking at God in red, blue, and gold, in seashores of pink ranked shells the clouds would make, in lines of radiance from below the horizon. That was where God was, and he wasn't a white-haired old man. . . . He was a Glory, He was a terrible, eternal, righteous Beauty. He was the Form into which all life was fitted, He was all the things in the world that didn't die. He was something you got lost in and didn't know you were lost. He was yourself all swelled to infinity and dealt around the universe. He was the Impossible that was possible. And most of all He was the winner in a brave battle with the Yankees, the Spaniards, and the Devil.

But Graves was critical of the theology of the social gospel that was making inroads into southern churches in the 1920s: "Whatever else may be said against the religious manner in the South, the churches there may no longer be called 'tools of the mill owners.' There has been much swinging in the other direction, in the

South and elsewhere. The humanitarianism which goes naturally with a worship of God has turned many of God's ministers collectivist. They do not look upon this for what it is, a taking of sides on an economic question in which they are not qualified and by which they impeach their spiritual estate."[1] Despite Graves's criticism of the "collectivist" turn that many clergy were taking, Alabama Episcopalians were becoming more aware of the misery wrought by industrialization, urbanization, and the ups and downs of the economy. At the end of the Great War, Alabamians chose Thomas Kilby, a parishioner of Anniston's Grace Church, as their governor. Kilby addressed a variety of social ills: he increased spending for education, expanded services for the mentally ill, funded and staffed enforcement of child labor laws, and tried but failed to abolish the convict lease system.

Augusta Bening Martin and the House of Happiness

Although the national economy was booming, life was difficult for many Alabamians. According to historian Wayne Flynt, "In 1920, Alabama's per capita income ranked forty-fourth among the forty-eight states. By 1935 the state had dropped to forty-sixth." Flynt points out that the principal industry of Alabama's Appalachian region was tenant farming, because the high mountains and deep valleys of north Alabama made most forms of industry and agriculture simply impossible. Seven of the counties in Alabama's Appalachian region were among the poorest counties in the United States. Hence the isolation and poverty of rural north Alabama made it an obvious field of ministry, and in 1923, the Diocese of Alabama launched one of its most significant and enduring ministries— the House of Happiness, the only large-scale and centrally funded effort of Alabama Episcopalians to reach out to the poor whites of Appalachia. At the 1923 Diocesan Convention, V. G. Lowery, rector of St. Mark's, Troy, urged that the diocese establish an "Industrial School for mountain children," and the Board of Missions responded by convening a committee to look into the need for and feasibility of such a mission. Satisfied that the need was sufficient and the means available, they chose Augusta Bening Martin to head up a mission that would be headquartered in Scottsboro.[2]

The success of the House of Happiness was due almost entirely to Martin's energy, intelligence, and compassion. Born in 1877 and raised in Seale, Alabama, Martin was educated at the Alabama Normal College for Girls in Livingston. Martin's strength of character and decisiveness may have been partly a reflection of her college's president, the remarkable Julia Strudwick Tutwiler. Martin served as a schoolteacher, first in Baldwin County from about 1905 to 1911, and then later in Montgomery. While living in Montgomery, Martin worshiped at St. John's Episcopal Church, and although Edgar Gardner Murphy was rector there only from 1898 to 1901, it is difficult to believe that she was not influenced by his ideals. Martin left teaching to become a deputy state prison inspector, a job that actually had little to do with prisons—her responsibilities had more to do with inspecting mills for child labor abuses. Martin's subsequent career as Alabama's first child labor inspector evolved naturally and directly from her position as deputy prison inspector. The House of Happiness finally brought together most of her interests and gave her the opportunity to employ her many gifts and strengths.[3]

Martin's ability to influence and persuade, as well as her sheer determination, were displayed when Gordon Persons was serving as governor (1951–55). Many years before being elected governor, Martin had taught Persons. When Martin learned that Persons had taken a stand of which she strongly disapproved, she called his office and asked to speak with the governor. The secretary explained that the governor was not available, and Martin demanded that she inform Persons that Augusta Martin wanted to speak to him immediately. Persons not only came to the phone, he also went to Martin's home to discuss the issue. Finally, Persons announced that he had changed his mind.[4]

In today's idiom, Martin's approach to the Appalachian people of north Alabama would be described as "holistic," but she simply called it "soap, soup, and salvation." One of Augusta Martin's first "cases" was that of a sickly little girl named Rose. Martin brought Rose home with her, fed her and nursed her back to health, and gave the child her first bath. Rose, in turn, gave both the mission and Martin new names. Martin became the "Farewell Lady" (i.e., "welfare lady"), and when Rose received her first bath, she exclaimed, "This shore is a happy house!" Thus the mission was christened the House of Happiness.[5]

The reports Martin regularly wrote for the *Alabama Churchman* nearly always contain stories about the doings at the House of Happiness that are poignant or funny or both. One of Martin's first reports in the *Alabama Churchman* is heart-rending. She reported finding a family of five—a mother and four children—in unspeakable conditions: "the family had lived for weeks on roasting ears and a few fish and squirrels. The children slept on piles of grass, covered with sacks and rags. . . . All were emaciated. The children had never tasted cow's milk, had never been to school, had never seen the American flag, had never heard of Christ, and knew God's name only as part of an oath. . . . The court committed the family to our welfare worker [i.e., Martin herself]. House, food, clothing, medicine, and other necessities were provided. The children had their first bath and said their first prayer the evening they were committed to the worker." In one, Martin outlines her daily schedule: "We have only twenty-four hours, and we make the most of them by rising at four and going to bed at any time after ten. We are frequently called out at night to visit the sick."[6]

The House of Happiness regularly received gifts of used clothing from Alabama parishes. In one report Martin noted, "The clothes exchange has wrought wonders in the appearance of our people. At a sacred concert . . . more than two thirds of the audience were wearing clothes from the House of Happiness exchange. The black sunbonnet and the jumper and overalls have almost entirely disappeared from a Sunday gathering." Sometimes the "Scottsboro Hosiery Mill Band" performed for the House of Happiness and its clients; at other times Martin played records on a "graphophone" given by "Miss Hanson of Tuscaloosa." Hearing a recording of violinist Fritz Kreisler, one of Martin's clients commented, "I can almost see that fellow playing his fiddle."[7]

After arriving in Scottsboro in July 1923, Martin quickly became a part of the community. Her initial success came when she investigated charges of truancy in Long Hollow and agreed to teach in the local school for four months. Augusta Martin seems to have had the successful teacher's knack for finding creative solutions to discipline problems. In January 1925, when a male teacher at a rural school had had all the insubordination he could take from his students and resigned abruptly, Martin agreed to take his place for a few months. When her class became restive, Martin regained control of the situation by launching a discussion of World War I. Carrying the theme further, in military fashion Martin lined up her pupils in the playground and drilled them until they were too tired to give her any more trouble in the classroom.[8]

During its first year, the mission occupied a former cowshed and corncrib that measured twelve by twenty-five feet. Martin believed the discomfort she and her helpers endured, however, gave them greater insights into the lives of their neighbors and also gave their neighbors greater respect for them. Then in 1926 the diocese purchased land on which to build a permanent home for the House of Happiness. Martin selected the community of Sauta Bottom (otherwise known as "Hell's Half-Acre") for the new building. When plans were drawn up for a new building for the mission, Martin vetoed the large, comfortable structure that was initially envisioned in favor of a two-room, one-story-and-a-half log cabin. She also insisted on employing members of the community to build it. She reasoned that using community labor and building a house more in keeping with those of her neighbors would enhance her ministry.

One of Martin's most successful ministries was the Happy Hollow School. Soon after moving to Sauta Bottom, Martin became the teacher at the McCutcheon School, a public school that served the Sauta Bottom community. Martin received a salary from the diocese, so she gave her teacher's salary to her assistant, Nettie Barnwell of Memphis (a cousin of Middleton Barnwell, rector of Birmingham's Church of the Advent), who joined Martin in October 1925. In November 1926 Martin asked the Jackson County School Board to consider moving the school to the House of Happiness property, a location that made it more accessible to its students. The board agreed and the school moved to a three-room house already on the mission's land. Soon, the number of students had doubled, and the county was paying the salary of two teachers instead of one. The school library also became a valuable resource for the people of Sauta Bottom. Children educated at the Happy Hollow School often went on to colleges and universities, including Berry College, Auburn University, and the University of Virginia. Adults could also take classes at the school in home economics, farming, and health care. In addition to academic and vocational classes, the school was a community center offering music, games, and square dances.[9]

Martin maintained a firm grasp on the spiritual core of her mission. The House of Happiness staff and other residents gathered for morning and evening prayers every day, and a blessing preceded every meal. On Sundays they worshiped at St. Luke's, Scottsboro. Many of the children she helped were either baptized or confirmed or both. In her report to the Diocesan Convention in 1930, Martin noted that seven children had been baptized and two confirmed.[10]

The Depression almost forced the closing of the House of Happiness. In September 1932 the Faith Fund, which paid Nettie Barnwell's salary, was completely exhausted. At the same time, the school board had no money to pay for teachers at the Happy Hollow School. While the school was closed, Martin continued to offer a Sunday school for children in the neighborhood.[11]

Resourceful, determined, and faithful as Augusta Martin was, no one could indefinitely maintain her punishing workload and schedule. She began to have health problems in the early 1930s. Her physician wrote Bishop McDowell in 1932, giving him a full account of Martin's health. Finally, in the spring of 1933, she collapsed. Physicians diagnosed her with arthritis in her left knee, a kidney infection, hypothyroidism, and pleurisy. While she was unable to work, Nettie Barnwell returned to care for the school and also for Martin. It proved impossible for Martin to recuperate while staying at the mission, and her physician insisted that she leave. Martin returned to her family's home in Seale but hoped and expected that her health would allow her to return to Sauta Bottom. When Bishop McDowell made his annual visitation to the House of Happiness in 1933, Martin went with him. On their return trip, she acknowledged that she would be unable to resume her duties as director of the mission. Her health had improved but not enough. Augusta Martin finally resigned as director of the House of Happiness in September 1935. Following Martin's departure the House of Happiness continued and even seemed to thrive under the direction of a series of Church Army officers.[12] But when a man was fatally shot at one of the mission's Friday night dances in August 1945, the mission went into a downward spiral from which it never recovered, although the diocese continued to support the mission until 1952 when the property was finally sold.[13]

Reaching Out in Other Parts of Alabama

In the late 1920s and early 1930s the Diocese of Alabama also initiated a mission to a group of Creek Indians living near Atmore. In 1929, McDowell asked Edgar Edwards, the priest in Atmore, to look into the condition of some Creeks living nearby. Although most of Alabama's Creeks had been removed to Oklahoma following their defeat at Horseshoe Bend in 1814, a small group remained. By 1929 there were only about five hundred Creeks left. Edwards found them living in a state of extreme poverty, with little access to education, health care, and employment. According to an article in the *Alabama Churchman* in 1930, "Their homes are usually made up of one room and a lean-to. Privacy is impossible, and cleanliness is almost so. Sanitary conditions do not exist. Diseases of poverty and neglect are in evidence everywhere. They have been neglected from a standpoint of education, too. Though native Americans, they cannot go to the white schools and will not go to the colored. Two schools were provided, but one of these has not run for several years 'because it fell down.'" Edwards and McDowell recruited a physician, R. C. Macy, and his wife, Anna, to work with the Indians. Soon the chief of Atmore's Creeks, Alexander Rolin, asked to be baptized. Apparently, both Baptist and Pentecostal ministers refused to baptize Rolin, but Edwards agreed. Rolin's baptism took place on his deathbed (he was over one hundred years old), and other Indians soon sought baptism; Edwards baptized them in a nearby river. Edwards and the Macys began to hold services in the Indian schoolhouse. However, with generous donations of land and materials, a church was built, and St. John's in the Wilderness was opened in January 1932. The death of Dr. Macy in 1931 set back the work, but Anna Macy carried on until 1936. When a second church was built at Perdido Hills, it was given the name of a biblical figure, the prophetess Anna, but that name was also chosen to honor Anna Macy. Not long before his death, McDowell recruited a Church Army sister, Clara Pickrell, to replace Anna Macy.[14]

In 1935 Edward Gamble, the rector of St. Paul's, Selma, from 1903 to 1937, launched a campaign to have the Works Progress Administration (WPA) construct a two-story building for the use of the black population of Selma and Dallas County. The first floor of the building was to include "a large rest room, a colored doctors office, and clinic; a room on either side of the doctors office with beds for men and women who may be sick, to rest. Lavatories for each." The second floor "will have a large assembly hall, offices for county demonstrator, home economics agent and kitchen, and library room."[15]

Gamble was deeply concerned about the well-being of Selma's blacks for two reasons. First, in Jim Crow–era Selma, there were no toilet facilities for black people, except in their own homes (and almost without exception those would have been outhouses). This presented a special problem for black sharecroppers who "came to town" on Saturdays to shop and sell produce they had raised. "There was no provision made by the city for the convenience of the colored people, numbering at times from three to five thousand when they came to town, walking long distances in all weather, then walking all up and down the streets, after they had come, peddling heavy loads upon their heads of farm produce; with no place to rest or to make themselves comfortable." Second, black unemployment was even worse than white unemployment during the Depression, and building the community house would provide some work for at least a few black workers. In a letter to Harry L. Hopkins, the administrator of the WPA, he wrote, "The situation here is most desperate. The state has no relief funds, and the city and county cannot care for but a few of the unemployables. There are white and black men, women and children, able bodied, walking the streets hungry and poorly cladded. These people are not begging for food or clothing but for a chance to work and make an honest living for themselves."[16]

Partly because of bureaucratic red tape, it took years to complete the community house. However, in a letter to Eleanor Roosevelt, Gamble alleged that there was also opposition to the project because of racial prejudice: "The prejudice against doing anything for the negro in this State is terrific, and especially in this section where we have 77.3% negroes. I speak from experience, having been born and reared in the South, and having served my entire forty years as a minister in the South—thirty two years in Selma. The hardship and suffering of the negro is so common that it fails to make the appeal it should; therefore, anything done for them at all seems to be unnecessary, except by the better portion of our people." Prejudice even made it difficult for Gamble to find a location for the facility: "No matter where he tried to put it, there was the strongest objection from those he thought would be most sympathetic." However, in spite of opposition, the city of Selma purchased a lot for the building at a cost of $7,500. Black people supported the building with small donations and offered their labor at reduced rates. Finally, Gamble traveled to Washington and with the support of Governor Bibb Graves (who met him in Washington), the funds were appropriated and the building was completed in late 1939.[17]

The women of the Church of the Advent organized a kindergarten in 1926, and by 1928 sixty children were enrolled in a program that, in addition to classes, furnished them with medical examinations, diphtheria vaccinations, clothes, meals, field trips, and Christmas gifts. Around thirty to thirty-five mothers of the children enrolled in the kindergarten were also involved in a mothers' club. The kindergarten was still in existence in 1940 but appears not to have continued after World War II.[18]

The House of Happiness, the mission to Atmore's Creek Indians, and the

Church of the Advent's kindergarten were examples of a new attitude toward mission and outreach in the Diocese of Alabama. With few exceptions (notably the deaconesses and Wilmer Hall), most outreach initiatives in the nineteenth century had been parochial in scope, but in the 1920s, there was a nearly unprecedented willingness to combine the efforts of the various parishes into diocesan-wide ministries. Furthermore, Edward Gamble's effort to construct a black community center in Selma, although strictly speaking a local project, represented a new attitude toward partnering with the government at the federal, state, and local levels. It is no accident that these efforts occurred after the diocese repudiated Bishop Beckwith. The controversy of the Beckwith years absorbed energy that might otherwise have gone into ministry. Furthermore, William George McDowell, elected bishop coadjutor in 1922, brought a new perspective to the leadership of the diocese.

Alabama's Episcopal Churches and the Depression

Virtually repudiated by the Diocese of Alabama, Bishop Beckwith had agreed to refrain from involvement in the day-to-day affairs of the diocese after the election of a bishop coadjutor, and he did just that for six years. When Beckwith died in 1928, an obituary in the *New York Times* remembered him as a "member of the conservative wing of the Episcopal Church," an opponent of Prayer Book revision, and as the author of several books. Although his successor, William George McDowell, was bishop coadjutor by title, he was the de facto diocesan bishop from his election until he officially became bishop of Alabama in 1928. Alabama's fifth bishop, the fourth Virginian to serve in that office, McDowell had been a military chaplain in World War I, a position he assumed after declining the request of St. John's, Montgomery, to become their rector. Following the war, he went to Auburn in 1919 to represent the National Council of the Episcopal Church as Student Inquirer. McDowell became well known in the Diocese of Alabama as a result of his successful campaign in 1922 to raise funds for a church and parish house in Auburn. McDowell was also an enthusiastic amateur musician. He composed original settings of several Christmas carols, including "While Shepherds Watched Their Flocks by Night," "O Little Town of Bethlehem," and "Sing, O Sing This Blessed Morn," and a setting of the *Gloria* that was sung at the celebration of the centennial of the Diocese of Alabama.[19]

Just a year after Beckwith died and McDowell became diocesan bishop, the stock market crashed, and by 1932 the Great Depression was at its lowest point. Alabama was hit harder than other southern states. Historian Wayne Flynt notes, "Only three Southern states registered an absolute drop in white employment during the decade; Alabama had the dubious distinction of leading the way." In spite of their affluent members, Episcopal churches did not escape the economic malaise that settled upon America. Actually, economic hardship had come to Alabama Episcopalians even before the conventionally accepted beginning of the Great Depression in October 1929. In December 1928, the lead story in the *Alabama Churchman* informed its readers that the diocese faced a "grave emergency" and that the diocese would end the year with a deficit of $10,500, unless the parishes and missions brought their contributions up to date. One of the causes of the crisis, noted the article, was the failure of parishes and missions to pay the salaries of their clergy, which had already brought the deficit up to $4,763.49. The steps proposed to remedy the crisis were drastic and included (among other things) reducing the bishop's salary, reducing the budgets of the Church Home and St. Mark's School, and discontinuing publication of the *Alabama Churchman*.[20]

In September 1932, with the Depression in full force, the vestry of Holy Comforter, Gadsden, acknowledged that they could not meet their financial commitments, including the rector's salary. They subsequently reduced the rector's salary from $2,500 per year to $1,800 and reduced the organist and janitor's salaries by 50 percent. Even though the number of parishioners at St. John's, Ensley, increased from 176 in 1932 to 205 in 1933, the rector's salary was reduced from $900 to $700. In 1932, St. Mary's-on-the-Highlands (one of the largest and wealthiest parishes in Alabama) reduced salaries twice: 10 percent at the beginning of the year and 10 percent in October. Some parishes considered closing or being reduced to mission status. In January 1938, Grace Church in Birmingham's Woodlawn neighborhood considered a number of measures, including "a proposition regarding the possible dissolution of the Corporation." Diocesan institutions also suffered. In June 1931 the Episcopal Church Women at the Church of the Advent received a letter from Bishop McDowell asking for help for the "Mobile Orphanage" (probably Wilmer Hall) because Mobile's Community Chest had reduced their budget by $1,300.[21]

In his July 1932 address to the Democratic National Convention, Episcopalian Franklin Delano Roosevelt promised the country a "new deal for the American people"; he was elected to the presidency that November. Although governor of New York before becoming president, Roosevelt was considered by many an "honorary southerner" because of the time he spent at Warm Springs, Georgia, receiving therapy for the crippling effects of polio. Alabama and the rest of the South enthusiastically supported his bid for the presidency, in spite of the fact that he was a Yankee and a "wet," that is, an opponent of Prohibition. Roosevelt had a vague but sincere faith in God's providence and a firm conviction that he should be "his brother's keeper," so it was not surprising that in 1935 Roosevelt wrote letters to thousands of Protestant, Roman Catholic, and Jewish clergy, seeking information about conditions in their communities and asking their opinions with regard to his administration's programs. In fact, Roosevelt may have been more concerned to have the clergy's support for (or at least dampen their opposition to) his bid for a second term, but FDR's complicated mind was perfectly capable of maintaining both motives simultaneously.[22]

Only a handful of Alabama's Episcopal clergy replied to FDR's letter, but most of those who did viewed the president and his programs more or less favorably. Some shared very detailed information with Roosevelt. Richard A. Kirchhoffer, rector of Mobile's Christ Church, had served as president of the Community Chest, chairman of the Juvenile Court Commission of Mobile County, and a member of the board of directors of the Family Welfare Bureau, among other community activities. Kirchhoffer pleaded with FDR to do more for laid-off white-collar workers. "In most cases these workers have been the sole support of their families . . . they are now ineligible for relief . . . and many are in a desperate condition."[23]

Even though he admitted to being a Republican, William A. Thompson, rector of Trinity Church, Florence, echoed Kirchhoffer's concern for white-collar workers: "The gravest criticism of the Act is that the so-called white-collar men are not provided for . . . there are a large number of white-collar men who reach old age without adequate means of support, and thus become . . . a burden on their children." Theodore Evans, rector of Christ Church, Tuscaloosa, was also active in community activities as chairman of the Emergency Relief Committee and said that Tuscaloosa had been spared some of the worst effects of the Depression because of "the money kept in circulation by the large student body at the University." However, one wonders what FDR made of Evans's suggestion that the president participate in drawing up a "modern Ten Commandments so as to get people more conscious of important moral issues."[24]

Charles Alleyn, located in the Tennessee Valley at Sheffield's Grace Church, acknowledged that the TVA-built Wheeler Dam had reduced local unemployment but foresaw a time in the near future when unemployment would return. He urged FDR to place the unemployed on "Small Homesteads" "built along our State and National Highways" "where they may be able to provide most of their own living." Alleyn believed that the "great majority of the people with whom [he] came in contact were in sympathy with [FDR's] Social Security Legislation; Old Age Pensions; aid for Crippled Children; and Un-employment Insurance," but he warned the president of "subtle and vicious" interests who "do not want the Old Order disturbed. They do not want to give up their power." The rector of Montgomery's Church of the Holy Comforter, Edgar M. Parkman, suggested that the government pay men to attend vocational schools.[25]

The most effusive praise came from Richard Wilkinson, rector of St. John's Episcopal Church in Montgomery. He complimented FDR for having "attacked with all the great powers of your mind and heart the problem of the individual, as well as collective need; and you have done it in the spirit, and in the Name of the world's greatest Teacher, Jesus Christ." "Such statesmanship as you have exhibited . . . has never before found expression in practical government since Christ pronounced this basic economic principle for the good of mankind. Before you reach the end of your eighth year, may every nation catch the inspiration of this genuine, practical Christian idealism and become fired by the example of the American government becoming the distributing agency of real human welfare; for everything you have thus far directed has been with due consideration for the rights of all involved, privileged and unprivileged." Wilkinson concluded by saying that it was his "earnest prayer" that Roosevelt be "kept at the helm of this nation" until his "grandest piece of social legislation" had "become a glorious reality as it brings in that crowning day of longed-for security for all our people."[26]

Bishop McDowell, Scottsboro, and a Missing Priest

McDowell exhibited an awareness of national and international issues far greater than that of any previous bishop of Alabama, and his progressive theology ran well beyond the policies of the most forward-thinking politicians in Alabama. In 1927 he endorsed the World Conference on Faith and Order, the precursor of today's World Council of Churches, and he approved of America's participation in the international disarmament conference in 1930 and urged prayers for its success. Although McDowell did not give his blessing to the American Federation of Labor's attempt to organize workers in Alabama, he at least declared neutrality in the AFL's struggle with the National Manufacturers' Association (and this at a time when Birmingham's *Age-Herald* was condemning strikers as Marxists directed by "outside radical leaders").[27]

In analyzing the causes of the Depression, Bishop McDowell condemned the way consumers' "desires are inflamed by clever advertising," and was critical of unfettered capitalism. He saw that a "cause of the present depression is the failure of our moral controls to keep up with our inventive genius. . . . Men become mere pawns in the game of modern business. The old, the weak, the inferior, the unskilled are thrown about at will." Furthermore, at the Lambeth Conference of 1930 McDowell had observed with admiration the way Britain was seeking to "maintain a moral control over a machine age; to think of men before methods; to put human rights before dividends." Fearing perhaps that he had gone too far, McDowell reassured Alabama Episcopalians that his call for a social safety net was not "a socialistic theory but a principle of ethics and of the Gospel." However, in 1935 McDowell praised Roosevelt's New Deal, saying that "great and untried experiments in social welfare" raised "our hopes . . . anew to dream of new heavens and a new earth in which dwelleth righteousness."[28]

On race, however, McDowell, like Edgar Gardner Murphy, was unable to transcend the dilemma of the great majority of white southern liberals. Like Murphy, McDowell was deeply sympathetic to the plight of black people but was also unable to call for the fundamental changes to the South's customs and institutions that would have given them equal rights. McDowell's involvement in the infamous Scottsboro case perfectly illustrates both his concern for justice and the limitations of culture and class that constrained him.

In 1931, two white women, Victoria Price and Ruby Bates, accused nine black men (ranging in age from thirteen to nineteen) of raping them on a Chattanooga to Memphis freight train as it rolled through Alabama's Jackson County. The men were arrested when the train stopped in Scottsboro. At that time merely accusing a black man or men of having sex with a white woman, much less charging them with rape, could easily become a death sentence, either by judicial imposition or by lynch mob. In spite of the fact that there was no physical evidence to support the women's allegation that they had been raped, a grand jury returned indictments against the nine black youths on March 30, 1931. Four trials followed quickly in which all but one of the defendants were found guilty and sentenced to death. Although McDowell could not quite bring himself to cross, much less to challenge, the "color line," he and his friend, Henry Edmonds, pastor of Birmingham's Independent Presbyterian Church, used their influence on behalf of the young men accused of rape in the Scottsboro case.[29]

In May 1932, the US Supreme Court ordered new trials for the Scottsboro defendants on the grounds that their rights to due process had been violated, and the venue for the trials was moved to Decatur. By this time the Scottsboro defendants were being represented by one of America's most skillful criminal defense attorneys, Samuel Leibowitz. Leibowitz was not a Communist, but the International Labor Defense (ILD), a Communist front organization, was paying his fees. Well aware of the Marxist orientation of the ILD, McDowell and Edmonds persuaded prominent Alabama attorney Roderick Beddow to represent the black men, and urged the Scottsboro defendants to replace Leibowitz with Beddow. However, the defendants preferred to have Leibowitz continue defending them. Edmonds wrote, "all our efforts to represent them were in vain. The Communists would not retire and the Negroes were committed and would not change."[30]

McDowell soon had a very different and completely unexpected role to play. Ruby Bates, one of the two women whose allegation of rape had led to the trial and conviction of the Scottsboro boys, made her way to New York, where she seemed to have had an attack of conscience regarding her false testimony against the Scottsboro defendants. Bates went to the home of America's most famous Protestant clergyman—Harry Emerson Fosdick—to make a confession and seek his guidance. "I have just had a pastoral responsibility presented to me which I hope you will not object to sharing with me," Fosdick wrote to Bishop McDowell on March 25, 1933. "Yesterday Ruby Bates . . . came to me, arriving, to the best of my knowledge and belief, alone and of her own free will and accord. She said she wished to present to me a matter of conscience and I, of course, listened to her confession." Fosdick enclosed a copy of Bates's statement along with his letter to McDowell. The gist of Bates's confession was that her allegation of rape against the Scottsboro defendants was false and that her friend, Victoria Price, had coerced her into making the charge. Bates returned to Alabama, and on April 6, 1933, arrived at Bishop McDowell's home. The bishop wrote Fosdick about Bates's arrival and her subsequent departure for Decatur, chaperoned by May Jones, a social worker on the staff of Independent Presbyterian Church. McDowell himself was subpoenaed but (although he did arrive in Decatur) he was never called as a witness and was excused.[31]

Although the story of Bates's recantation and confession to Fosdick is remarkable, it had little impact on the trial. Alabama's attorney general, Thomas Knight, personally prosecuted the case and skillfully undermined Bates's testimony. In a conversation with McDowell, Knight told the bishop that he believed the clergy were "being used for the purpose of creating the appearance of respectability and reliability for this witness, Ruby Bates, although unwittingly on their [the ministers'] part." At first, McDowell seems to have been persuaded by Bates's confession to Fosdick: "As to the truth of her confession, there is much in it that fits in with facts already ascertained by us. It does not account for everything, but it seems reasonably veracious." But after McDowell spoke with Attorney General Knight and visited Decatur himself, the bishop inexplicably changed his mind about Bates. "I feel quite sure," he wrote to Fosdick, "that Ruby Bates was directed to us from where she was being kept awaiting the trial in order that she might have reputable addresses to give by which her movements could be vouched for. Everyone would know that we were not playing anyone's game designedly . . . it would be well for you to be extremely guarded in further dealings with her." Not only had McDowell become suspicious of Bates, he even vouched for the fairness of the trial taking place in Decatur.[32]

The jury in Decatur found Haywood Patterson guilty in spite of the fact that Samuel Leibowitz had used expert medical testimony to demonstrate that there was no physical evidence that she had been raped once, much less nine times, as she had alleged. Following the trial, McDowell observed that "it was impossible to expect an unprejudiced verdict if Mr. Liebowitz [sic] presented the case, because his ILD connections, [and] his previous failures to sense the psychology of the southern juries . . . rendered him a serious handicap." James Edwin Horton Jr., the judge who presided over the Decatur trial, was probably the most heroic figure in the story. Judge Horton set aside the jury's verdict, declared that the prosecution had not proven its case, and ordered a new trial. The judge paid for his integrity at the next election when he ran fourth in a field of four. Although the jury had deliberately overlooked evidence that exonerated the defendants, McDowell vigorously defended them. According to the bishop, one member of the jury was "a vestryman of St. John's Church, Decatur" who was "not at all interested in race prejudice. . . . I understand from those who know them that most of the others were the same kind."[33]

In 1935, McDowell was elected to the board of trustees of Tuskegee Institute, and at Tuskegee he gave his most comprehensive statement on racial issues. In his address, McDowell made many thoughtful observations about the way the relationship between blacks and whites was changing in the South in the early twentieth century. Among other things, McDowell noted that blacks and whites lived largely separate lives: "Because they do not know one another, they no longer trust one another, but stand on their respective rights." McDowell went on to attribute the "separation of the races" to "an inevitable stage in the new self-respect and self-development of the Negro along lines of racial consciousness." Undoubtedly he had in mind Booker T. Washington's philosophy of black self-improvement and self-help that was becoming a thing of the past in the 1930s. The black leaders who were McDowell's contemporaries were beginning to move beyond Washington's philosophy toward a strategy of integration that would lead to the civil rights movement. McDowell went on to say that "poverty and ignorance are still the greatest handicaps to progress that the Negro faces."[34]

The fairest assessment of McDowell may be that he had partly risen above the culture and class in which he was raised but still too often fell back on the assumptions and habits of that culture and class. McDowell went as far as his culture, class, and education would allow him to go, and he went further than many in Alabama were willing or able to go. It took courage for McDowell to work behind the scenes in the Scottsboro case and to condemn "brutality and mass hysteria" in Alabama in the early 1930s. As was so often the case with southerners, cultural biases did not hinder McDowell from having warm personal relationships with African Americans and exerting himself on their behalf. While at Auburn, McDowell helped found St. Andrew's parish in Tuskegee, a black parish attended by faculty, students, and staff of Tuskegee Institute (now Tuskegee University).[35]

In a broader sense, McDowell's compassion was displayed in the way he treated the priest in charge of Mobile's Seamen's Institute who, in 1932, disappeared along with $2,000 of the institute's building fund. The priest had used the money to pay blackmail to a man with whom he had had sex. When an investigation revealed that the money was missing, the priest fled. From Vicksburg, Mississippi, the renegade priest wrote his wife a letter of utter despair. He admitted to her that he had misappropriated church funds but did not explain the circumstances. Rather, he attributed his difficulties to "mental disturbance" without elaborating. He even said that he had taken out additional insurance and had planned to kill himself and make it appear to be an accident. "No one can ever know the hell I am in now," he wrote to his wife, "To you and the children I must be as the dead. I don't know what to tell you to do." And his letter closed simply with "Good bye." The priest also wrote an even more despairing letter to McDowell: "If I could have the *strength* of doing away with myself . . . this would be my last letter." He confessed to theft in his letter to McDowell but not his reason for stealing.[36]

Eventually the fugitive priest found his way to California where he came to his senses. After meeting and talking with a Baptist revivalist, the Alabamian contacted McDowell, who sent him to Perry G. M. Austin, rector of St. Luke's, Long Beach, California. The bishop asked him to request temporary suspension from the ministry and promised to lift the sentence of suspension if the disgraced priest began to pay back the money he had stolen and showed signs of genuine repentance.[37]

McDowell's response was remarkably compassionate. "You need not be afraid of arrest," McDowell wrote the priest on October 18, 1932. "I am anxious only about your immortal soul." He urged the man not to return to Mobile for the time being, but instead, to find work in California and reconcile with his wife and children. "Then begin again as an honest and conscientious layman. Your Church will bring you back to God, who only can save you." In a subsequent letter McDowell assured him that his family would be cared for: "remember I shall look after your family till you are able to care for them."[38]

Eventually, the former Alabama priest found employment with the US Coast and Geodetic Survey in Arizona. As a prerequisite to lifting his suspension from the priesthood, McDowell arranged for a psychiatrist, L. Cody Marsh, to treat him in Tucson. The exchange of letters between Dr. Marsh and Bishop McDowell are remarkable for the insight they give into Bishop McDowell's compassionate and sensitive nature and his relatively progressive attitude toward homosexuality. McDowell wrote Marsh giving him a thorough biography of his Alabama patient, from his family of origin to his breakdown and flight. McDowell was puzzled by the fact that the priest "took to homosexual gratification, when he had been enjoying a normal sex [life] with his wife for many years." McDowell referred to a discussion of homosexuality at the 1930 Lambeth meeting of Anglican bishops, at which "several authorities were quoted as saying that a man who had been guilty of gross homosexual conduct can never be trusted again," but McDowell was prepared to give his former priest another chance if Dr. Marsh assured him that he had "recovered." In reply to McDowell, Marsh reassured him that the priest's behavior probably did not reflect an innate, lifelong orientation. The psychiatrist gave McDowell a thorough account of the former priest's treatment and concluded by writing that "I am of the opinion that [he] is now ready to resume normal married life with his wife." In a separate letter Marsh gave McDowell the go-ahead to lift the priest's suspension: "In my best judgment, he is quite fit to resume his professional life." Walter Mitchell, bishop of the Missionary Diocese of Arizona, was prepared to give the former Alabamian a job. Accordingly, McDowell asked for and received the approval of his fellow bishops to lift the sentence of suspension. The Alabama priest served parishes in Arizona and California until 1947, when he retired from a parish in northern California. Three years later he died of a heart attack at the age of sixty-two.[39]

Alabama's Episcopalian Women Demand to Be Heard

The role of women in American life and especially in the Episcopal Church began to change dramatically in the early twentieth century. During this period women extended and deepened their ministries. The 1919 General Convention gave the women of the Episcopal Church a national role as the Women's Auxiliary to the Domestic and Foreign Missionary Society, but the next year they became the Women's Auxiliary to the Presiding Bishop and the National Council. The Church Service League, an organization for all people involved in social service, gradually withered away.[40]

Although Alabama's legislature voted against it, in 1919 the Nineteenth Amendment to the US Constitution was ratified, giving women the right to vote. In light of the fact that women were often on the front lines of ministry in the Diocese of Alabama, the petition "from certain branches of the woman's auxiliary in the convocation of Mobile" requesting that the diocesan convention "take some action whereby the women of the Church will have equal representation with laymen in all the work of the Diocese of Alabama" seems entirely reasonable. However, because the request was made at the Special Convention to elect William G. McDowell as bishop coadjutor of the diocese, the petition was referred to the Standing Committee, which was to report at the 1923 Diocesan Convention. At the 1923 convention, the Standing Committee failed to report on the women's request, and the convention voted to request that a special committee be formed to look into the matter. Thus the request suffered death at the hands of parliamentary procedure.[41]

Women did not bring up the subject of representation again until 1941. In that year the president of the Diocese of Alabama's Woman's Auxiliary asked, "'Has the time come for the women of the Diocese to have some official representation at the Annual Convention of the Diocese?' The question does not imply the right to sit on vestries, but merely for women to have a legal part in the conduct of the affairs of the Church in the Diocese. . . . For my part, I believe that it would be a generous and just gesture on the part of the men thus to dignify the position of the women." A resolution to allow the president of the Woman's Auxiliary a voice but not a vote in the convention was submitted to the Committee on Constitution and Canons in 1942. The committee judged the proposal unconstitutional but authorized the Executive Council "to elect a representative of the Woman's Auxiliary as a member of that body, when approved by the Convention." At the same convention the Woman's Auxiliary called for the Diocese of Alabama to grant them "the right of representation in the Diocesan Convention" and observed that "practically every Diocese of the Fourth Province as well as in many other sections of the Church women have been granted the right of representation in the Diocesan Convention." In response to the appeal by the Woman's Auxiliary and the finding of the Committee on Constitution and Canons, the president of the Woman's Auxiliary was made a member of the Executive Council.[42]

A commission then studied the policy of other dioceses and found that women could serve as delegates to the Diocesan Convention in only two of sixteen dioceses in the South or Southwest. In twelve, however, the president of the Woman's Auxiliary was an ex officio member of Executive Council. Women served on vestries in only four of the dioceses studied. A resolution was presented in 1943 that would allow women to serve on the Executive Council but would limit them to two places. Another resolution was presented to rescind the action of the previous convention in allowing the president of the Woman's Auxiliary to be a member of the Executive Council, and it carried. Clearly, emotions were running high with regard to the role of women in the councils of the church. However, the 1944 convention took up the issue again and passed legislation allowing the convention to elect women to serve as nonvoting members of the Executive Council, and the first two women were elected in 1945. Not until 1967, however, were women allowed to serve on vestries and as voting delegates to the Diocesan Convention.[43]

The Beginning of the Carpenter Era

In the remarks Bishop McDowell prepared for delivery at the 1938 Diocesan Convention, he noted that in the preceding year he had

> made 115 official visitations to my 106 congregations, and about the same number of unofficial ones. Celebrated Holy Communion 65 times and held 220 other services. Delivered 166 sermons and made 51 addresses – this does not count talks to confirmation classes, Church school, groups and meetings. Attended 121 meetings on Church business, from General Convention to [Young People's Service League]; also met 52 vestries, held 11 congregational meetings, and inspected 31 Church schools, and 4 institutions.

Baptized 6 infants and 3 adults; conducted 6 funerals; married 1 couple; consecrated 1 church; instituted 3 ministers; confirmed 606 persons, the largest number in diocesan history, it is believed. Ordained 4 deacons and set apart 2 deaconesses. Traveled over 30,000 miles; sent over 3,000 letters, half of which were dictated and half written personally by hand; had about 1,800 personal interviews on Church business or personal problems. All this required time for preparation, and the use of judgment involved required much research and careful thinking. Six days in the year I was not on duty; the rest were rather busy.

McDowell's last parish visit was scheduled to take place on March 12, 1938, when he was to meet with the rector and vestry of Mobile's Trinity Episcopal Church. However, by the time McDowell reached the church, he was running a high fever. The bishop was admitted to the Mobile Infirmary, where he was diagnosed with pneumonia. His last act as bishop was to sign a letter to the Standing Committee of the Diocese of Alabama, delegating his authority to them for the period of three weeks, but on March 20, McDowell was dead at the age of fifty-six.[44]

A Special Convention to elect a new bishop was held, and once again tiny St. Paul's, Carlowville, played host, as it had when the Diocesan Convention delegates had met to elect McDowell. The second episcopal election at Carlowville resulted in the selection of the Church of the Advent's rector, Charles Colcock Jones Carpenter, to serve as bishop of Alabama. When he was elected, Carpenter was the youngest bishop in the Episcopal Church. Thirty years later, when he retired, Carpenter would be Alabama's second-longest-serving bishop (surpassed only by Wilmer's thirty-nine years as head of the diocese) and the senior member of the House of Bishops. Carpenter liked to say that his diocese stretched from "the hills of Monte Sano to the shores of Bon Secour," and hundreds of Alabama Episcopalians would forever remember the deep voice and heavy drawl with which he pronounced the words of confirmation—"may you daily increase mo-ah and mo-ah in the Holy Spirit." Others were deeply impressed by the advice he often gave young people: "Remember who you are and what you represent."[45]

Even though he had been rector of Birmingham's Church of the Advent for only two years (1936–38), Carpenter must have been on almost everyone's short list to succeed McDowell. A native of Georgia, Carpenter graduated from Princeton, where his size (six feet four inches tall and 275 pounds) helps explain his success in becoming the Ivy League heavyweight wrestling champion. In 1947, Princeton recognized Carpenter's achievements by awarding him an honorary degree. Other honorary degree recipients that year included actors José Ferrer and Jimmy Stewart, Harvard's distinguished literary scholar F. O. Matthiessen, and New York City park commissioner Robert Moses. After graduating from

Princeton, Carpenter attended the Virginia Theological Seminary, where he was deeply influenced by that school's "low church" ethos. Before coming to Alabama, Carpenter had served parishes in the Diocese of Georgia, including St. John's, Savannah, and had been nominated for bishop of Georgia in 1935. The Diocese of Georgia's Special Convention to elect a bishop adjourned when they failed to elect a bishop after twelve ballots, and Carpenter was not renominated when Georgia's Special Convention reconvened. Instead, the Diocese of Georgia elected Middleton Barnwell, the Missionary Bishop of Idaho. Although not elected bishop of Georgia, Carpenter accepted a call to Birmingham's Church of the Advent, the parish Barnwell had served before he was elected bishop. Furthermore, Carpenter's immediate predecessor at the Advent—Charles Clingman—had left to become bishop of Kentucky. Being rector of the Church of the Advent was a perfect stepping-stone for an able and ambitious young man such as Charles C. J. Carpenter. However, Carpenter was the first, and so far the only, rector of the Advent to be elected bishop of Alabama.[46]

When Carpenter was elected bishop of Alabama, President Roosevelt was trying desperately to combat isolationism and indifference as he watched the countries of Europe drift slowly but steadily toward the second worldwide conflict of the twentieth century. No conscientious priest or bishop could ignore the gathering clouds of war. At his first Diocesan Convention, Carpenter referred to "the frontal attack of paganism against Christianity which we witness with sorrow in many parts of the world" and said that it was "the responsibility of the professed Christian to redouble his efforts as a Soldier in the Church Militant of the Christ." When the United States entered the war following Japan's December 7, 1941, attack on Pearl Harbor, Carpenter condemned war's "utter waste and flagrant brutality," but asserted that there were "conditions worse than war." Bertram Cooper, an assistant priest at the Church of the Advent, served as a navy chaplain, and Richard Sturgis, formerly rector of St. John's, Decatur, served as an army chaplain. The Diocese of Alabama gave a War Cross to each Alabama Episcopalian serving in the armed forces of the United States, and Carpenter wrote twice-monthly letters to Alabamians in military service. In the May 1943, issue of the *Alabama Churchman*, Carpenter referred to "more than 1100 of our Alabama Churchmen [who] have gone forth to fight." An English priest, Michael Coleman, vicar of All Hallows, London, led two preaching missions, one early in the war years and another in 1943. During the latter mission, Coleman spoke to more than ten thousand people, including the Birmingham Brotherhood Association, students at Howard College (now Samford University), Woodlawn High School, and Parker Negro High School. On Saturday afternoons, St. John's, Montgomery, held open houses for British cadets who were stationed at Maxwell Field.[47]

As will be seen in the next chapter, the civil rights movement was the defining experience of Carpenter's episcopacy, and the decisions he made and leadership he exercised from the late 1950s until his retirement in 1968 have forever painted him as a reactionary on racial issues. However, prior to the Supreme Court's *Brown v. Board of Education* decision, Carpenter might have been regarded as a racial moderate. For example, Luther Foster, a member of St. Andrew's, Tuskegee, and president of Tuskegee Institute, represented the Diocese of Alabama as a deputy to the 1955 General Convention of the Episcopal Church in Honolulu, Hawaii. The Diocesan Convention chooses deputies, but it is inconceivable that Foster would have been nominated without Carpenter's approval. It is significant that Foster was selected for the General Convention in Honolulu. The location of the General Convention was changed from Houston to Honolulu when it was learned that Houston did not allow interracial meetings. Foster attended a meeting of the race relations subcommittee of the Commission on Social Reconstruction and wrote that he was "impressed by the fact that the committee approached its work in terms of Christian morality and did not allow itself to be limited in its thinking by existing customs and practices which are sometimes unnatural and illogical."[48]

Bishop McDowell had launched the effort to build an Episcopal church in Tuskegee in 1930, and Carpenter also helped raise money to build a church for St. Andrew's, Tuskegee. In a fund-raising letter, McDowell wrote that he had established St. Andrew's Mission in Tuskegee in 1919, but actually there seems to have been an Episcopal congregation in Tuskegee, connected with Tuskegee Institute, from around 1914. Henry May, the bookkeeper at the institute, brought together a group of Episcopalians and eventually Stewart McQueen, the rector of Ascension, Montgomery, and priest-in-charge of Good Shepherd, Montgomery, presided at a service of holy communion for them once a month. McDowell wrote that with the support of Robert Moton, the president of the institute, $5,000 had been raised to build a church "when the depression temporarily upset our plans." The effort to construct a building for St. Andrew's, Tuskegee, continued under Bishop Carpenter. In December 1939, William Byrd Lee, the priest in charge of both Holy Innocents, Auburn, and St. Andrew's, Tuskegee, wrote asking Carpenter to accompany him to New York and Boston to raise the money still needed for the church. Apparently, World War II also delayed the effort to build the church, and even though Carpenter employed his considerable fund-raising skills, the people of St. Andrew's Mission were still without a church in 1947. Like all colleges and universities, returning servicemen swelled Tuskegee's student body in the years after the war, and the spaces on campus in which St. Andrew's Mission had been meeting became even more crowded. Expressing their frustration, they wrote Carpenter, saying, "we can never tell where we will hold the next service." Construction of the church finally began in 1949.[49]

Carpenter also established a committee to study the problem of recruiting black priests. Speaking at the 1955 Diocesan Convention, Carpenter said: "To my shame I must record the fact that in the 16 years of my Episcopate I have ordained but one Negro clergyman. I do not know where the difficulty lies, but the facts indicate a difficulty which must be discovered and overcome. We are ready and able to give to adequate young Negroes the best possible education. The field is ripe for their service . . . somehow we have failed to stimulate the interest of our best Negro youth." The convention authorized the formation of a committee of "qualified white and Negro communicants to study the problem and make recommendations to the next convention." The committee's report to the 1956 convention pointed out, among other things, that in spite of the fact that blacks made up about one-third of the state's population, there were only four Episcopal congregations in Alabama (three missions—Good Shepherd, Montgomery; St. Mark's, Birmingham; and St. Andrew's, Tuskegee; and one parish—Good Shepherd, Mobile). The committee identified a "chicken and egg" problem: They recognized that it was "urgent and desirable" to work "toward expansion and development of present congregations," and called for the recruitment of two additional black priests to do this. However, they also recognized that younger black men were more likely to consider entering the priesthood as black congregations grew.[50]

There was, however, another story just beneath the surface. William A. Clark, the chairman of the committee and a faculty member at Tuskegee Institute, wrote a confidential letter to Bishop Carpenter in which he noted that the three black priests on the committee—J. Clyde Perry of St. Mark's, Birmingham; John Cole of Good Shepherd, Mobile; and Robert DuBose of Good Shepherd, Montgomery—seemed to be "'trapped' men, embittered, frustrated, and withdrawn from the real potentialities of their fields of service." According to Clark, these priests believed that the catalyst for the formation of the committee was "recent cracks in the walls of segregation," and that the purpose of the committee was really to "perpetuate segregation," presumably by expanding black congregations rather than by opening white congregations to black members. The black clergy believed that segregation was the real reason for the "diminishing influence" of the Episcopal Church in the black community. A subsequent report of the committee in November 1956, was much more frank and identified "segregation in the church, exclusion of Negroes from Camp McDowell, [and] exclusion of Negroes from the Diocesan Youth Convention at Huntsville (1955)" as reasons for the failure of the Episcopal Church to thrive in the black community and to recruit black priests.[51]

Far more significant than either his efforts to raise money for St. Andrew's, Tuskegee, or to study the problem of recruiting black priests was Carpenter's reaction when blacks tried to attend St. Peter's, Talladega. In April 1939, Martha Jane Gibson, a native of Connecticut and member of Christ Church, New Haven, who taught at Talladega College, went to St. Peter's accompanied by some of her students. This incident created the paradigm that Carpenter would follow when dealing with racial incidents for the rest of his life.

In a letter to the bishop, Gibson charged that St. Peter's rector, Robert C. Clingman, had told her that the church was "reserved for the use of white persons only, at all the regular service hours." Gibson stated that Clingman "thus summarily excommunicated these twenty or more Negro communicants." She graciously noted, however, that she liked the priest ("a very pleasing young man") and that she believed that St. Peter's vestry had intimidated him. "I felt very sorry for him, as he was evidently fighting hard to rationalize his conduct as a concern only for the welfare of the parish." Hilda Davis, the dean of women at the college, backed up Gibson, alleging that she and other "Episcopal communicants" at the college had "been denied the privilege of participating in the church services at St. Peter's Church, Talladega." According to Clingman, in November "a dozen of the students came and sat together very discreetly in two back pews on one side. I was frankly delighted to have them and welcome them. . . . The general reaction was bitter among the congregation. I had been in school and worked in the North so long, I'd forgotten the temper of the Southern white."[52]

The priest thought it was unlikely that the vestry would allow him to have a separate "colored" service, but he insisted that he was willing to stand his ground: "forbidding the church to the negro completely is a little more than I can stomach." The point was moot, however, because he believed that "the negroes will not come at all unless they can have absolute equality with the white people," a position Clingman attributed to "Dr. Gibson and the philosophy of the school." Clingman says that he went personally to Gibson, to Dean Davis, and to the president of the college to explain his situation. "I was born and brought up in the South. But somehow along the way I have arrived at a viewpoint absolutely contradictory to that traditional Southern, inbred, caste-conscious attitude."[53]

Carpenter tried to smooth things over with Gibson. He claimed that "the Episcopal Church [was] doing as much as it [could] for the Negro communicant, and I would assure you that the Negro is very much in our hearts . . . we try our best to take care of negro communicants." Carpenter appeared to be groping for a way to justify St. Peter's exclusion of the Talladega College students. "In some parts of the state, due to forces which you probably do not understand, it is not advisable to attempt to mix the two races, and it is not for the good of the Negro that this attempt should be made." Then Carpenter offered another justification for St. Peter's Church's exclusion of Talladega College students: "More and more we are finding it good to have chapels for our college students so that they may worship as a unit." The tone of Carpenter's letter to Gibson was condescending. In effect, he told her that she simply did not understand the "Southern way of life." Carpenter's solution to the problem created by the visit of Gibson's students to

St. Peter's was essentially the one Clingman offered—a separate service for the students at a location other than the church. He even asked if the college could "provide a room which may be used as a chapel . . . at the College."[54]

Clingman's encounter with Gibson and her students was just a preview of things to come. Talladega College students tried to integrate St. Peter's again in 1945. Clingman's successor, Randolph E. Blackford, wrote Carpenter that a "colored" priest, Henry J. C. Bowden, had been appointed chaplain at Tuskegee Veteran's Hospital and that his wife was going to teach at Talladega College. Blackford went to visit Mrs. Bowden and "offered to bring the communion over for her and other Church people at the College, on Sunday morning before my 11 o'clock service." Mrs. Bowden was grateful, but said "that Miss Gibson must be seen." Blackford described Gibson as "the most objectionable Yankee agitator type." Gibson told Blackford that the college's policy "had been for 70 years to fight Jim Crowism" and that he would not be permitted to have a separate service on campus as long as students were barred from St. Peter's.[55]

The battle between St. Peter's and Talladega College continued for years. In 1962 Carpenter wrote to St. Peter's Church's senior warden, Major M. M. DePass, commending the church for diplomatically dealing with a situation when "when certain members of another race came as visitors to the service last Sunday." Carpenter also wrote DePass that "most of the difficulty today arises from people who are not accustomed to the old ways of the South and who want to start new innovations. This is not a time for new innovations, but rather a time for continuing as best we can the long-established ways." In his heart of hearts it seems that Carpenter never really understood what was wrong with "the long-established ways." History, however, was about to present Bishop Carpenter with unprecedented situations in which those "long-established ways" were simply inadequate. Carpenter's reaction to the incidents at St. Peter's reveals a pattern. Publicly he said nothing that could alienate white conservatives, and privately he tried to make small concessions that would satisfy both sides but that really did nothing to change the status quo. He insisted that he was doing as much as possible to change things but seems to have hoped that he would not have to make any uncomfortable or unpleasant alterations to "the long-established ways" that were dear to his heart and to the hearts of most Alabama Episcopalians.[56]

The Religious Vitality of the Post–World War II Era

In spite of his tone deafness to racial matters, Carpenter was practically made-to-order for religious leadership during the 1950s. Under his direction—and aided by the post–World War II "baby boom"—the Diocese of Alabama thrived. During the 1950s, St. Luke's, Mountain Brook; Ascension, Vestavia Hills; and

St. Thomas, Huntsville, were founded as missions but quickly became large parishes. Other churches that had long been missions also achieved parish status, such as St. Andrew's, Tuskegee; and Epiphany, Guntersville, and new missions were founded: Grace, Cullman (1949); St. Alban's, Birmingham (1961); St. Stephen's, Huntsville (1963); and St. Matthias, Tuscaloosa (1961).

One of Carpenter's most significant achievements was the founding of Camp McDowell, an institution aptly termed the "heart of the diocese." In its present location, the Diocese of Alabama's camp and conference center dates to 1948, although the Diocese of Alabama began to have summer camps for young people in 1922. In the wake of World War II, the US government was encouraging churches to "promote home morale." Scott Eppes, vicar of St. Mary's, Jasper, and Randolph Claiborne, rector of Nativity, Huntsville, both of whom had played a part in establishing Camp Mikell in the Diocese of Atlanta, helped search for a location, but it was Eppes who found the land that became Camp McDowell in Winston County, near Jasper. Another priest, Marshall Seifert, learned that Camp McClellan (subsequently Fort McClellan) near Anniston was selling prefabricated housing units previously used as barracks, and the diocese purchased eighteen units and moved them to the site in Winston County. Gradually, parishes and individuals began to build cabins to replace the prefabricated units. Two members of St. Michael's, Anniston, built the first cabin and named it after their parish. Subsequent cabins were constructed by St. Luke's, Birmingham, and the Church of the Advent. With the help of Congressman Carter Manasco, the diocese acquired an additional thirty-two acres of land and built a dam on Clear Creek that helped them create a lake. In 1950, Mrs. Pierce McDonald (whose husband served for many years as rector of Ascension, Montgomery) donated $10,000 to build a chapel but specified that it should resemble her late husband's church, a building designed by Ralph Adams Cram, one of America's most distinguished ecclesiastical architects.

Another important initiative of the Diocese of Alabama in the 1950s was the establishment of St. Martin's in the Pines, a residential facility for senior citizens. In 1954, David Cady Wright, the rector of St. Mary's-on-the-Highlands, said that he was "aghast before the darkness and despair that described the Nursing Homes of Birmingham." At first he considered buying an existing structure and renovating it to serve as a home for the elderly. He found a mansion on Shades Mountain that was being sold for $100,000 but was unable to raise the money to buy it. The next year Wright brought together a group of clergy and laypeople from seven parishes, and they formed the Episcopal Foundation of Jefferson County. They concluded that the Hill-Burton Act of 1946 made it feasible to construct a new facility, and over the next few years they raised $325,000 and expanded their organization until it included all the Episcopal parishes in Jefferson County. Construction of a unit that would accommodate forty residents began in 1958, although Bishop Carpenter officially laid the cornerstone on Palm Sunday, 1959.[57]

Clergy Leadership

As they had in the past, the clergy of the Diocese of Alabama continued to distinguish themselves. Several Alabama priests were elected bishops: James Moss Stoney was rector of Grace Church, Anniston, from 1921 to 1942, when he was elected bishop of the missionary diocese of New Mexico. Stoney set the ambitious goal of confirming one thousand people per year, a goal he never reached but that his successor, Charles James Kinsolving III, realized. Another of Stoney's goals was to establish an archive for his diocese and preserve its records. With the assistance of New Mexico's state historian, Myra Ellen Jenkins, Stoney wrote *Lighting the Candle*, a history of his diocese.[58]

Middleton Barnwell, the nephew of Alabama's third diocesan bishop, Robert Woodward Barnwell, served as rector of the Church of the Advent from 1913 to 1923, then as field secretary of the Episcopal Church for two years before being elected bishop of Idaho in 1925. In 1935, Barnwell was elected bishop coadjutor of Georgia, becoming Georgia's diocesan bishop the next year and serving until 1954. His brother, Carlton, was also an Episcopal priest. The rector of Nativity, Huntsville, Randolph Royall Claiborne Jr., was elected bishop suffragan of Alabama in 1949 and was subsequently elected bishop of Atlanta in 1953. Richard Bland Mitchell was rector of St. Mary's-on-the-Highlands from 1929 to 1938, when he was elected bishop of Arkansas. Although initially opposed to integrating the School of Theology at Sewanee, he supported desegregation in Little Rock. Richard Ainslie Kirchhoffer, rector of Christ Church, Mobile, was elected bishop coadjutor of Indianapolis in 1939 and became diocesan bishop later that year, serving until he retired in 1959.

Although never elected bishop, Raimundo de Ovies, born in Liverpool, England, was rector of St. Andrew's in Birmingham, then served as chaplain of the University of the South in 1927, before being chosen to serve as dean of the Cathedral of St. Philip in Atlanta. De Ovies acquired a national reputation as a pioneer of the pastoral counseling movement and as author of several books. He also presided at the funeral of *Gone with the Wind* author Margaret Mitchell.[59]

The conflicts between Bishop Beckwith and his clergy absorbed energy that might otherwise have been used to comfort and support the poor and needy, so initiatives such as the House of Happiness and the outreach to Atmore's small band of Creek Indians were deferred until the popular and pastoral William McDowell took the helm of the Diocese of Alabama. Unfortunately, the Great Depression forced the diocese and its parishes to cut back, not only on outreach but also on the salaries of clergy and other essential staff. Hundreds of Alabama Episcopalians enlisted in the great struggle against fascism, and the prosperity that followed World War II allowed the diocese to build two of its most successful institutions—Camp McDowell and St. Martin's in the Pines, a comprehensive residential facility for the elderly. McDowell's behind-the-scenes effort to secure effective legal representation for the Scottsboro boys was admirable, but his inability to rise above the prejudices of his class and culture, not to mention Bishop Carpenter's unwillingness to play a constructive role in the attempted integration of St. Peter's, Talladega, foreshadowed greater conflicts to come during the era of civil rights.

7
"The Carpenter of Birmingham must not be allowed to forever deny the Carpenter of Nazareth"

The Civil Rights Era

On Monday, September 16, 1963, local attorney Charles Morgan delivered a powerful jeremiad to Birmingham's Young Men's Business Club:

> Yesterday while Birmingham, which prides itself on the number of its churches, was attending worship services, a bomb went off and an all-white police force moved into action. . . . A police force which has solved no bombings. A police force which many Negroes feel is perpetrating the very evils we decry. And why would Negroes think this? There are no Negro policemen: there are no Negro sheriff's deputies. Few Negroes have served on juries; few have been allowed to vote; few have been allowed to accept responsibility, or granted even a simple part to play in the administration of justice . . . Birmingham is the only city in America where the police chief and the sheriff, in the school crisis, had to call our local ministers together to tell them to do their duty. The ministers of Birmingham who have done so little for Christianity call for prayer at high noon in a city of lawlessness and, in the same breath, speak of our city's "image." Did those ministers visit the families of the Negroes in their hour of travail? Did many of them go to the homes of their brothers and express their regrets in person or pray with the crying relatives? . . . And who is really guilty? Each of us. Each citizen who has not consciously attempted to bring about peaceful com-

pliance with the decisions of the Supreme Court of the United States. . . .
Birmingham is not a dying city. It is dead.

Morgan and his family were members of St. Luke's, Mountain Brook, and he was
one of the few Alabama Episcopalians who spoke out clearly, forthrightly, and
eloquently on the issue of civil rights. Like many others who spoke out, he paid
a price, and although the price he paid was heavy, it was not as heavy as some
others. George Murray, bishop coadjutor of the Diocese of Alabama, had married
Morgan and his wife, Camille, while Murray was chaplain to Episcopal students
at the University of Alabama and the Morgans were students there. The speech
he gave to the Young Men's Business Club marked Morgan as a "troublemaker,"
and after a series of vicious phone calls, crosses burned on his lawn, and threats
against his life and the lives of his wife and son, Morgan left his law practice and
he and his family moved away from Birmingham.[1]

From Complacency to Confrontation

The 1950s had been a decade of exceptional religious vitality during which the
Episcopal Church in Alabama had prospered. Throughout the United States
churches and synagogues—Protestants, Catholics, Jews—added new members
and buildings. Episcopalians in general and the Episcopal Diocese of Alabama
in particular were no exception. However, the 1950s were also marked by complacency and conformity. Historian Mark Noll characterized American Protestantism in the 1950s as "self-indulgent, conformist, and unimaginative. . . . Mainline Protestants, while exerting themselves to build bureaucracies, prepare Sunday
School literature, and provide for a larger clergy, were also busy creating a religion
of the lowest common denominator with less and less that was distinctly Christian." President Dwight Eisenhower embodied a kind of public piety or civic religion and seems to have believed that religion could be reduced to a few simple
principles that were more or less the equivalent of being a good citizen. He once
famously remarked, "Our government has no sense unless it is founded in a deeply
felt religious faith, and I don't care what it is." Bishop Carpenter would hardly
have echoed the president's remark, but even though Carpenter's leadership, plus
fortuitous demographic developments, brought great growth to the Diocese of
Alabama, there was little in it to challenge complacency.[2]

Despite the complacency of the 1950s, however, this was also the decade when
the movement for full and equal rights for African Americans began to gather
momentum. The civil rights movement not only brought economic opportunity
and long-denied human rights to African Americans, it also overturned assumptions, customs, and traditions, especially in the South. But this social dislocation

was payment for a bill that the South's people and their leaders had tried to avoid paying since the end of the Civil War.

Background to the Civil Rights Movement

In 1958, the Episcopal Church elected Arthur Lichtenberger, bishop of Missouri, to serve as Presiding Bishop. Lichtenberger sparked a controversy in the Diocese of Alabama with extemporaneous remarks he made following his institution. According to a January 14, 1959, article in the *Birmingham News*, Lichtenberger had said, "We should move as quickly and quietly as we can into a fully integrated society" and had advocated that the US Congress "permit the use of court injunctions in civil rights cases." Innocuous as they seem now, Lichtenberger's words outraged many Alabama Episcopalians. Attorney Forney Johnston, a member of the Church of the Advent, attacked Lichtenberger's position, asserting that the Presiding Bishop was calling for "interracial access to the home and its every implication and relation, including courtship and marriage," which would lead to "mongrelization." Mobile congressman Frank Boykin, a member of Trinity, Mobile, had Johnston's letter included in the *Congressional Record* and denounced the "persistent and widespread misunderstanding of the friendly relations between the races in the South and the preference of an overwhelming majority of the members of both races of good will . . . for continuance of those relations free from the unwarranted and unwanted pressures and conflicts which have been set in motion." According to Boykin, there had been "splendid progress . . . in educational facilities and in economic opportunity for Negro pupils and adults."[3]

In spite of Boykin's insistence that the relationship between black and white southerners was friendly, the 1950s and early 1960s were especially dangerous times to be black in Alabama. In September 1959, the *New York Times* reported a "revival of Klan strength in Alabama" and cited the flogging of twelve blacks in Pickens County as evidence. There was more truth to Boykin's claim that there had been progress in improving the quality of education in black schools. In 1952, the *New York Times* reported that the salaries of black and white teachers in Alabama were nearly identical. The *Times* also noted that while per pupil expenditure for white students had increased by 171 percent since 1941, per pupil expenditure for black students had increased 530 percent in the same period. However, one of the reasons for the increase in funding for black schools in Alabama and other southern states was to justify the principal of "separate but equal" and prevent school integration. Indeed, when the Supreme Court ordered schools to be integrated, the Alabama legislature briefly considered ending public funding of education rather than support integrated schools.[4]

The *New York Times* also published a series of articles on integration and southern churches in which it noted that the "church conferences and jurisdictional areas" of the Episcopal Church were integrated, even in the South. Although blacks and whites met together for convention and other diocesan events in the Diocese of Alabama, black Episcopalian Yvonne Willie of Birmingham remembers that these events often featured banquets that took place in segregated facilities, forcing black delegates to "find a home or restaurant in the local black community."[5]

Between the Supreme Court's *Brown* decision in 1954 and the assassination of Martin Luther King Jr. in 1968, a great sea change swept over the South. In some Alabama counties where African Americans had been systematically excluded from voting, blacks were elected to office for the first time since Reconstruction, separate black and white restrooms and drinking fountains disappeared, public schools were integrated, police and fire departments began to hire black policemen and firefighters, and businesses began to hire African Americans for jobs only whites had previously held.

Episcopalians played a wide range of roles in the drama of civil rights. Sometimes they were creative and constructive; sometimes they were reactionary and obscurantist. Laypeople, priests, and bishops led protests and opposed protests; they defended the status quo or prophetically denounced institutionalized racism; they worked quietly behind the scenes for change or used their positions to stand in the way of progress; some parishes quietly integrated, while others ejected black worshipers. The Diocese of Alabama was slow to take a stand and when it did speak out its pronouncements were still ambiguous.

Laypeople had more freedom than clergy to play constructive roles in the civil rights movement. Birmingham businessman Lou Willie and his wife, Yvonne, were easily the most prominent black laypeople in the Diocese of Alabama in the 1960s. The fact that Willie had earned his MBA at the University of Michigan and served as comptroller of Alabama's largest black-owned business, Gaston Insurance, gave Willie credibility in the eyes of both the black and white communities. The Willies played a key role in bringing about the integration of Camp McDowell. In 1963 Lou informed William Yon, diocesan Christian education coordinator, that he was interested in attending a Christian education conference at Camp McDowell. Yon, a strong supporter of civil rights, asked Bishop Carpenter what to do, and Carpenter gave his approval for Willie to attend the session at Camp McDowell. Apart from black clergy attending clergy conferences, Willie was probably the first African American to attend an event at the diocesan camp. The next summer, the Willies' son, Lou Willie III, became the first black child to attend a children's camp at Camp McDowell. Previously, black children in the Diocese of Alabama had attended Camp John Hope in Georgia, four or five hours away by car, rather than Camp McDowell, only an hour north of Birmingham.[6]

In contrast with lay leaders, clergy were constrained by their parishes and

Bishop Carpenter. The bishop could and did discipline clergy for taking part in protests or belonging to groups of which he disapproved. But some of Alabama's Episcopal clergy played heroic roles in the civil rights struggle. An outstanding example is Thomas Thrasher, rector of Montgomery's Episcopal Church of the Ascension, who put his career on the line during the Montgomery bus boycott.

Episcopalians and the Montgomery Bus Boycott

In 1947 Thrasher was called to serve as rector of perhaps the most architecturally distinguished church built by Alabama Episcopalians—Montgomery's Episcopal Church of the Ascension (founded in 1910). Designed by Ralph Adams Cram, whose other commissions included New York's Cathedral Church of St. John the Divine, the Ascension is a neo-Gothic jewel in Montgomery's historic and charming Cloverdale neighborhood. Early in his tenure, Thrasher signaled that he would be a different kind of rector by asking the vestry if they would allow the Ascension to host a meeting of the Southern Regional Conference, a fledgling civil rights organization that included both black and white members. The vestry declined Thrasher's request, saying "it would be better if the church were not used for the purpose mentioned." Racial tension also seems to be behind a request that Carpenter relocate or at least reschedule the youth convention scheduled for the Ascension in 1959. Olivia B. Witmer, a member of the Ascension, had written the bishop a letter in 1956 objecting to "mixing with the colored race as we have been at some conventions and conferences."[7]

During the bus boycott (1955–56), Thrasher arranged for members of the Montgomery Improvement Association (the ad hoc organization Dr. Martin Luther King Jr. led that organized the boycott) to meet with city leaders. Thrasher's position on civil rights was unpopular with many at the Ascension. Julian McPhillips, who served as curate under the next rector, Mark Waldo, wrote that "the Ascension membership was not ready for this, nor could they accept it. With a few noticeable exceptions, most of the people turned against Tom." However, the critical turning point occurred in May 1959 when Thrasher administered communion to a black priest—apparently Robert E. DuBose, the vicar of Good Shepherd, Montgomery. In reaction the vestry passed a resolution asserting that the Ascension was a "racially segregated congregation." Thrasher wrote Carpenter claiming that the motion originally proposed to the vestry was that "sentinels" be stationed at the doors to the church "politely but firmly" telling "any Negroes who came where they could find the Church of the Good Shepherd." Lynn Willoughby writes, "From that point onward, the Reverend Mr. Thrasher found his initiatives blocked at every turn." Finally, in 1960 he accepted a call to Chapel of the Cross in Chapel Hill, North Carolina.[8]

The city leader at the heart of the boycott was Montgomery's mayor, W. A.

"Tacky" Gayle, a member and sometime senior warden of the Ascension. Up until the beginning of the bus boycott, Gayle was well regarded in the black community for his willingness to listen to and respond to their concerns. A black women's group, the Women's Political Council, often met with him, and Jo Ann Robinson, the council's president at the time of the boycott, remembers that Gayle would have his secretary call them when issues arose that involved them. She also notes, however, that Gayle was a strict segregationist.[9]

Another white Episcopalian who played a constructive role in the bus boycott was Juliette Morgan, also a member of the Ascension. The daughter of a prominent Montgomery couple, Morgan received a master's degree in English from the University of Alabama in 1935 and stayed on there to teach until 1938. Then she returned to Montgomery where she taught at Lanier High School for a time and finally went to work at the Montgomery Public Library. As early as 1952, Morgan publicly opposed racial discrimination. In a letter to the *Montgomery Advertiser*, she wrote, "Our Lord is against us if we consent to discrimination by color or place of ancestry." From the very beginning of the bus boycott, Morgan was outspoken in her support. In December 1955, she wrote another letter to the newspaper, saying, "I . . . find it hard to work up sympathy for the bus company. I have ridden the buses of Montgomery ever since they have been running . . . and I have heard some bus drivers use the tone and manners of mule drivers in their treatment of Negro passengers." In January 1957, Buford Boone, the editor of the *Tuscaloosa News*, denounced racism in a speech before the Tuscaloosa White Citizens Council, and Morgan wrote him a congratulatory letter: "I had begun to wonder if there were any men in the state—any white men—with any sane evaluation of our situation here in the middle of the twentieth century, with any good will, and most especially any moral courage to express it." Morgan's letter was published in the *States Rights Advocate*, a publication of the White Citizens Council, and the library board responded by dismissing her from her position. A Birmingham psychiatrist began to treat Morgan for anxiety, but the treatment was not effective; she took her own life on July 17, 1957.[10]

Louis Mitchell, Emmet Gribbin, and Julian McPhillips Confront Racism

In 1960, Louis Mitchell came from the Diocese of New York to serve as the assistant at St. Luke's, Mountain Brook. Not long after his arrival, another priest in the diocese invited him to attend an integrated church meeting. Members of Bull Connor's police department raided the meeting, and Mitchell was taken into custody, but attorney Charles Morgan secured his release. On Maundy Thursday in 1963, one of Martin Luther King Jr.'s lieutenants, Andrew Young—whom

Mitchell knew from a conference both had attended—called Mitchell and let him know that a group of blacks planned to attend the Easter Day service at St. Luke's. Mitchell informed Lee Graham, St. Luke's rector, who called a special vestry meeting for Good Friday. When Graham informed the vestry that the parish might have black visitors on Easter, they voted to have the police prevent the blacks from attending. Graham responded by telling the vestry that if anyone was prevented from coming to St. Luke's on Easter, he would stop the service and dismiss the congregation. However, no blacks attempted to visit St. Luke's that Easter. One of St. Luke's former vestry members, A. W. Jones, strongly objected to Mitchell's activities and sent a letter to St. Luke's parishioners that made inflammatory claims about Mitchell. In his letter, Jones said that Mitchell had told members of St. Luke's youth group that "if you were a real christian [*sic*] you would look upon communists just as you would any other persons" and that "communists should be accepted just as anyone else." Jones went on to complain that Mitchell believed in racial integration, entertained black friends in his home, and "had no opposition to the integration of the races in every form and fashion, including inter-marriage." Jones's fear was that Mitchell would try "to persuade any and all of the children of St. Luke's . . . to his way of thinking." Mitchell stayed at St. Luke's through 1963 and then left to take a job with a civil rights organization in Florida.[11]

One unlikely and unsung hero among Carpenter's clergy was the mild-mannered and scholarly Episcopal chaplain to the University of Alabama (UA), Emmet Gribbin. The son of a North Carolina bishop, Gribbin began serving as the Episcopal Church's official representative on the UA campus in 1955 after his predecessor, George M. Murray, had been elected bishop suffragan of the Diocese of Alabama. In the aftermath of the Supreme Court's *Brown* decision, a federal court ordered the desegregation of the University of Alabama and forced the university to register its first black student, Autherine Lucy, on February 1, 1956. Lucy attended classes without incident on Friday, February 3, but on Friday evening students and nonstudents gathered to protest the university's desegregation.

Gribbin tried to play the role of peacemaker during the demonstrations against Lucy's presence on the UA campus. While Lucy attended classes on Monday, February 6, a mob assembled outside the building in which her class was to be held. Gribbin noted that "there was a new element in the membership of the mob this time—a rougher element consisting of people who had no connection with the University and who contributed a stepped-up tempo of viciousness." The mob that gathered on Monday morning began to chant, "Hey, hey, ho, ho, Autherine's gotta go" and "Keep Bama white." The mob booed Oliver Cromwell Carmichael, the university's president, when he appealed for calm. Soon members of the state highway patrol, as well as campus police, were called in because of the gravity of the situation. Around 10:00 A.M., two members of Canterbury Chapel (the Episcopal mission to the university), Sara Healy, dean of women, and Jefferson Bennett, an assistant to President Carmichael, escorted Lucy from the building where she had been attending class. Using Healy's car they took Lucy to her next class. However, the mob pursued them, and according to Gribbin, they pelted the car with eggs and rocks, broke its windows, and tried to overturn it. Gribbin reported that "from this time until late afternoon this area of the campus was in a state of riot or near-riot." He spent the day in the midst of the "riot or near-riot," sometimes addressing groups of "400 or more" and attempting to protect Lucy's driver, black attorney Arthur Shores. At various times Gribbin was "pushed, shoved, [his] arm was grabbed," and he was "kicked in the groin." There is little doubt that Gribbin put himself at substantial risk as he tried to pacify the crowd on the University of Alabama campus.[12]

Gribbin and other members of Canterbury Chapel were also threatened with violence on at least two other occasions. A year after Autherine Lucy matriculated at the university, Canterbury hosted Open Forum, a group organized to discuss racial issues. Seventy robed Klan members picketed Canterbury Chapel on May 9, 1957, while Open Forum was meeting there. The Klansmen "read a statement charging that the Open Forum was a 'University of Alabama Liberal and Communist cell.'" Gribbin observed that at least one of the Klansmen was armed. The Klan picketed Canterbury again in 1961 when the women of Canterbury Chapel planned to attend a meeting at historically black Stillman College in which African students would be participating. Apparently, a member of Canterbury strongly opposed to integration provoked the 1961 incident.[13]

Another priest who took progressive and unpopular positions on civil rights was Julian McPhillips. A successful businessman who had run his family's canned food business in Cullman, he was a convert from the Roman Catholic Church. After McPhillips completed seminary in 1962, Bishop Carpenter asked him to serve as assistant to Mark Waldo at Montgomery's Church of the Ascension. While at the Ascension, he organized Montgomery's first biracial clergy group and also led services at the Church of the Good Shepherd, a black parish. His service at Good Shepherd made him aware that Montgomery had no resources for mentally challenged black children. With assistance from Bishop Murray, McPhillips helped found a facility for black children with mental disabilities and served on its board of directors. After two years at the Ascension, St. Luke's in Mountain Brook called McPhillips to be their rector. His background as a successful businessman made McPhillips appear to be a good fit for the affluent, suburban parish, but (as his wife Eleanor wrote) "none of this group could possibly have known how erroneous, how 'off the mark,' their thinking had been." After only two years at St. Luke's, he left to become Peace Corps director for the eastern region of India.[14]

In one way or another, most of the parishes in the Diocese of Alabama negotiated the rocky and sometimes dangerous path between segregation and integration. A parishioner of Trinity Episcopal Church, Mobile, charged her priest with being a Communist when he supported the integration of Mobile's buses. When the priest asked her to produce evidence for this charge, she brought out a copy of the preceding Sunday's sermon on the topic, "Thou shalt love the Lord thy God with all thy heart, and with all thy soul, and with all thy mind, and . . . thou shalt love thy neighbor as thyself." "That's it," she said, "Don't you know that's communistic!" But a more serious attack came in March 1958, when the KKK burned a cross on his lawn. In 1955 the vestry of Holy Comforter, Gadsden, discussed the "potential problem of colored persons visiting our church." Their rector, John Speaks, suggested allowing the ushers to "use their discretion as to where to seat any such visitors."[15]

The Carpenter of Birmingham

The most enigmatic and controversial figure in the diocese during the heyday of the civil rights movement was Bishop Carpenter, who would surely have echoed Boykin's statement that there had been "splendid progress" in the education and economic opportunities for black Alabamians. Although he became bishop in 1938, Carpenter did not refer to racial issues in his Diocesan Convention addresses until 1955 and then did so only obliquely. On May 17, 1954, the United States Supreme Court had issued its decision in the *Brown v. Board of Education* case. One year later Carpenter told the Diocesan Convention that the *Brown* decision (which he never referred to by name) had created a "very difficult predicament," but he appealed for "charity and forbearance" and asked that people "work together in harmony and good will, seeking earnestly the honest answer."[16] The Committee on Christian Social Relations urged "all Church people . . . to examine their own responsibilities in seeing that this ruling is accepted . . . with consideration and support." They went on to discuss "segregation in the Church wherever it obtains." To varying degrees, segregation was the rule in almost all of Alabama's churches, including the Episcopal Church, and would remain that way for years to come. The challenge to racial segregation in the churches and in the wider culture tested Bishop Carpenter and severely taxed his physical and spiritual resources.[17]

Although he rarely (if ever) spoke about it in public until the late 1950s, race was a constant theme in Carpenter's episcopacy. Not long before the *Brown* decision, Carpenter confronted racial issues when the trustees of the University of the South had to decide whether or not to integrate Sewanee's School of Theology. As a matter of course, bishops of Alabama serve as trustees of the University of the South, and in 1952 neither the college nor the university's school of theology were integrated. Sewanee may have had no explicit policy of segregation, but often in the South, the unwritten rules are sometimes the hardest to change. In October

1951, Province IV of the Episcopal Church (which included the dioceses that controlled Sewanee) recommended that Sewanee's School of Theology accept black students who otherwise would have attended Bishop Payne Divinity School, a black seminary that closed in 1949. The matter came before the Sewanee trustees at their November 1951 meeting, at which time the issue was referred to the committee on theological education and the college faculty. The issue was not raised at the trustees' April 1952 meeting, which was taken up with an attempt to persuade Edward McGrady to stay on as permanent vice-chancellor. Carpenter made his position clear in a letter to elected trustee Newt Campbell of Mobile prior to the June meeting: "It is my purpose if the matter of the admission of Negroes to the Theological Seminary is brought up to move that it be laid on the table. I believe it is the best procedure and a simple majority could stop debate . . . my own feeling is that it would be unfortunate to bring this matter up for much discussion, as I do not see, under the circumstances, Negroes can be brought into the very compact and isolated situation up there on the Mountain." But in June the trustees did discuss the matter and voted against accepting the recommendation from Province IV on the grounds that it would be illegal under Tennessee law to integrate the seminary.[18]

Many southern newspapers commented on the trustees' action—for example: "Sewanee Bars Negro Theologians" (*Nashville Banner*) and "Sewanee Declines Negro Admission" (*Chattanooga Times*). Robert W. Powell wrote Carpenter to protest: "St. Paul made it plain that the great socio-cultural gulfs of his day were not to be allowed to divide the church. If in our day a lot of Episcopalians, weak in the faith will have to have segregated parishes for a few more years, still it does seem that the clergy and seminarians among themselves could act more like mature Christians." Carpenter replied in a letter that set forth what was becoming his standard position on matters related to race: "It was felt that the promotion of interracial relations would not be helped by forcing this issue at the present time but rather would be hurt. We are making tremendous progress, but must consider what will be best for both races in the development of both." Carpenter added a point unique to Sewanee; namely, the fact that that the college, seminary, and prep school were so "closely integrated." In other words, a decision about the School of Theology would affect all the constituent units of the Sewanee community.[19]

In response to the action of the trustees at their June 1952 meeting, eight members of the theology faculty issued a protest and backed it up with a threat to resign en masse. Ironically, one of the eight was Sewanee's chaplain, Richard Hooker Wilmer Jr., whose grandfather had been Alabama's second bishop and an ardent supporter of the Confederate cause. Vice-chancellor McGrady responded to the threatened resignations by asking a committee of trustees to study admitting black students to the School of Theology, but after McGrady forced the resignation of New Testament professor Robert M. Grant, the others went ahead with their threat to resign. In a letter to Bishop Edwin Anderson Penick of North Carolina, Carpenter declared that he thought the protesting faculty members were "absolutely wrong" and accused them of practicing "justification by publicity."[20]

The situation was compounded when McGrady invited James A. Pike, the dean of the Cathedral Church of St. John the Divine in New York (and later bishop of California), to preach the baccalaureate sermon at commencement in 1953 and receive an honorary degree. In response to the faculty resignations, Pike issued a statement turning down the degree and the invitation to preach. Carpenter blasted Pike for his "ungraciousness" in a three-page letter: "Your not accepting this degree and your not preaching the baccalaureate sermon at the University of the South is not a national calamity and did not need the wide-spread publicity you have caused it to be given." He followed up with a letter to McGrady in which he referred to the affair as "Pike's Pique." Finally, the trustees voted to open the School of Theology to all qualified applicants "without regard to race" at their meeting in June 1953. Carpenter's position on integrating Sewanee's School of Theology was the same as his position on integrating St. Peter's, Talladega: We are making progress but must not move too quickly. It was the position he would hold for the rest of his life.[21]

Although the integration of Sewanee's School of Theology played out on a national stage, it was in Montgomery, Birmingham, and a little later, Selma that Carpenter played a role in events that would forever cast him as an opponent of racial progress and would overshadow the accomplishments of his episcopacy.

The March 7, 1960, edition of the *Montgomery Advertiser* featured a front-page article about an attempt by black protestors to march from Dexter Avenue Baptist Church to the Alabama capitol building. According to the article, "Leading the Negro march was the Rev. Robert E. Dubose, Jr. (in black and white robes) pastor of the Good Shepherd Episcopal Church. Standing on his right is the Rev. Ralph D. Abernathy." Above the article a photo stretched from one side of the paper to the other in which DuBose can be seen clearly, vested as an Episcopal priest. The article and photo of DuBose was the catalyst for a storm of letters from angry white Episcopalians to Bishop Carpenter. This letter from F. R. Daugette is fairly typical:

Very few things arouse me and I love our true Southern negro but please let me, confidentially, ask you the following:
1. Why is Dubose participating in this Baptist Church deal (pictured along side this so-called "Rev." Abernathy)?
2. Isn't there something you can do with Dubose to prevent his fur-

ther activity in such events to keep the Episcopal Church's name out of it?

Carpenter received so many letters that he had to compose a form letter to respond to them. The letter was addressed to his "Fellow Communicants":

> You were quite right in feeling as you do that the young Negro should not have worn the priestly vestments on such an occasion. . . . I immediately wrote him telling him that he was in error in this and that he must not wear Church vestments on such occasions. I explained to him that as a citizen he had the right to march if he so desired, but that he must not commit the Church by appearing in vestments. I further advised caution and wisdom on his part and said that I did not feel that this was a time for action such as he had taken.

> Please consider his action as an indiscretion on the part of a young man under great tension, and so do not hold it against him. I feel sure that it will not be repeated. He is doing a good job under most difficult circumstances in building the work of the Church.

Apparently DuBose was arrested in a subsequent protest. Carpenter wrote him a letter on April 7 about his civil rights activities:

> I was sorry to read in the paper yesterday that you had been involved in an incident resulting in arrest. . . . When I talked with you on the phone last Saturday, I reminded you that your doctor told you that you should "coast," and I emphasized the fact that you should do nothing in addition to your routine church work. . . . You have been a sick man, and we want you back in good healthy condition, because we need you in the work of the Church in Alabama. . . . I must insist, for your own good and for your health's sake, that you refrain from any meetings other than your regular routine Church services. . . . Do not eat in public places with white people, and refrain from meetings with white people other than our own Church people in Montgomery.

Either then or later, DuBose's relationship with Carpenter completely broke down and DuBose was forced to seek employment outside the Diocese of Alabama. He became curate at the African Episcopal Church of St. Thomas in Philadelphia and subsequently became the parish's rector.[22]

As his April 1 letter to DuBose indicates, this was not the first time Carpenter had cautioned DuBose about being involved in the civil rights movement. While speaking at New York's St. Thomas Church during Lent, reporters had questioned the bishop about his treatment of the black priest. An Associated Press report stated that Carpenter "had reprimanded a Negro minister for wearing vestments during a recent mass protest." According to the article Carpenter stated, "I advised caution and wise leadership rather than demonstrations in this whole matter of protests." The AP report was printed in the *Birmingham News*, occasioning several white clergy to protest Carpenter's rebuke of DuBose: "We wish respectfully to express our grave concern that a statement by you appeared in the national public press regarding a reprimand of the Rev. Robert DuBose. . . . We deeply regret . . . that the net result is that which was rightly a Godly Admonition became a public issue." Edsel Keith, Emile Joffrion, and Charles McKimmon Jr. had signed the letter. Furthermore, Jim Battles of Birmingham wrote:

> I hope that you were quoted wrongly, but in the event you were not, then, in my personal opinion, your statement was even more inappropriate than the action of the Negro minister involved. . . . This is certainly a time for calm and considered action on the part of all people, white, black or yellow, but it is certainly no time for complete inaction. . . . I most certainly realize that the organized church must be kept intact to accomplish the good that it is doing, but there comes a time when a person can sin by silence. If a minister cannot speak up during these troubled times and if he is completely demobilized from any type of action, then surely we are in for some chaotic times. Shall the arena be left completely clear for political demagogues, communists, and others?[23]

About the same time that Carpenter was dealing with the crisis that DuBose's participation in Montgomery protests provoked, another issue arrived on his doorstep. Members of the Episcopal Church's divisions of Racial Minorities and Christian Citizenship presented a "Background Paper on the Student 'Sit-In' Protest Movement" that effectively gave the church's imprimatur to civil disobedience as a way of promoting civil rights. Carpenter wrote Presiding Bishop Arthur Lichtenberger protesting the fact that the document was given to the press before the bishops, especially those in the South, were notified about it. "As I dictate this my good secretary has just come in to tell me that the radio this morning had an item indicating that the Episcopal Church is endorsing the sit-in demonstrations. . . . My phone hasn't started ringing on this yet, as I have just reached the office, but I imagine I'll have a right busy day trying to explain this thing." Carpenter's main point of contention with the authors of the paper was that civil disobedience was "just another name for lawlessness." He believed that "when the matter of obeying the law if left to individuals to determine, you get only confusion, and we have too much of that already." According to an April 6 article in the *Mobile Press-Register*, Carpenter issued a statement telling Alabama Episcopalians to "ignore" the background paper. This prompted John Morris of the Episcopal Society for Cultural and Racial Unity (ESCRU) to protest Carpenter's statement—the first time, but by no means the last, that Carpenter and ESCRU would be at odds. Carpenter's statement about the background paper also provoked criticism from two of the Diocese of Alabama's most important black leaders. Vernon Jones, rector of St. Andrew's, Tuskegee, and Luther Foster, president of Tuskegee Institute. Jones wrote Carpenter, saying: "On each of the occasions when your statements appeared in the Birmingham News I have been asked: 'What's the Bishop's story this time?', 'Does the Bishop mean that he favors segregation?', 'Why is it always necessary that the Bishop disagree in matters of this kind?' and the like." Foster's letter sharply rebuked the bishop: "I am deeply troubled by the apparent failure of our Church and its most active members and clerical workers, to recognize and deal forthrightly with the great moral question which faces us in our race relations at this time. The tragedy of our negligence will be with us for many decades to come, but I am confident that somehow our churches will take hold before it is too late."[24]

About a year later the Freedom Riders—a group of blacks and whites trying to integrate the interstate bus system—arrived in Birmingham. On May 14, 1961, the police allowed members of the KKK to attack them with baseball bats and lead pipes, and in addition to beating the Freedom Riders viciously, the Klansmen also attacked several bystanders, including at least two reporters. Newspapers around the world carried stories and photographs of the attacks. Evangelist Billy Graham, preparing to leave for a crusade in England, condemned the attacks, called for the prosecution of those responsible, and threw his support to the Freedom Riders' goals: "I think it is deplorable . . . when certain people in any society have been treated as second class citizens." In his June 1961 column in the *Alabama Churchman*, Bishop Carpenter's response was to note that "chivalry" was "at a low ebb," and that "the right to fair fight is not to be denied, but . . . beating a man HELD by other men is dastardly!" Carpenter believed that the Freedom Riders "wanted to create a scene—wanted to make trouble."[25]

In 1961, Carpenter engaged in a somewhat heated exchange of letters with Harvard professor Thomas Pettigrew. Apparently, Pettigrew's article, titled "Racial Tensions," in the September 1961 issue of *Christian Social Relations* (a publication of the Department of Christian Social Relations of the Episcopal Church) touched a nerve. The tone of Carpenter's letters to Pettigrew was uncharacteristically angry. The bishop demanded evidence for Pettigrew's charge that there were Episcopal churches in the Deep South that had refused to seat black worshipers.

"While we are far from integrated, I have never known of a church where 'Negro guests' were not admitted to services." But in fact, Carpenter did know of at least one church that had turned blacks away—St. Peter's, Talladega. Pettigrew replied and sent Carpenter a copy of "Why Have We Failed?," an article he had written about the failure of the Episcopal Church to implement its "pronouncements concerning race relations in America." In it, Pettigrew demolished the position of white "moderates" such as Carpenter. "The moderate's fundamental tenet is that he mans the lonely and unrewarding bastion between two equally dangerous camps of extremists: rabid racists and impatient integrationists.... Of course, this is absurd. To compare bombs and burning crosses with the courts and the ballot box, to compare the violent methods of the Ku Klux Klans and the White Citizens' Councils with the non-violent philosophy of a Martin Luther King clearly reveals that the moderate makes no distinctions whatsoever between different types of challenges to his power."[26]

Martin Luther King Jr.'s 1963 Birmingham campaign emphatically destroyed the position of the white "moderate." King chose Birmingham as the venue for Project C (the "C" was for confrontation) because of its history of violence against African Americans, because Fred Shuttlesworth's Alabama Christian Movement for Human Rights had invited him to Birmingham, and because Birmingham's city government was in turmoil. In March 1963, the people of Birmingham had voted to replace its commission form of government with the more traditional mayor-council form. Although he was a segregationist, mayor-elect Albert Boutwell was also a pragmatist and more likely to be reasonable about the need to negotiate with Birmingham's black community than his opponent in the mayoral race—Public Safety Commissioner Eugene "Bull" Connor. However, Connor, having failed in his bid to become mayor, filed suit to have the election overturned.[27]

Birmingham was sometimes referred to as a "city of churches," but a city of churches must also be a city of pastors. Carpenter was part of a network of Protestant, Roman Catholic, and Jewish clergy who were well acquainted with one another and often cooperated on projects for the well-being of the city. When Governor George C. Wallace declared his intention to defy federal laws requiring the integration of schools and universities, Carpenter and his colleagues issued "An appeal for law and order and common sense": "It is clear that a series of court decisions will soon bring about desegregation of certain schools and colleges in Alabama. Many sincere people oppose this change and are deeply troubled by it. As southerners, we understand this. We nevertheless feel that defiance is neither the right answer nor the solution. And we feel that inflammatory and rebellious statements can lead only to violence, discord, confusion and disgrace for our beloved state." Even though they did not mention Wallace by name their audience understood to whom and about what they were referring. The statement angered many who supported segregation, believing that the clergy had overstepped their bounds. Attorney Maurice Rogers was typical of those who criticized the clergy's statement: "Governor Wallace and his 'radical' kind are actually the last hope that you conformists have to maintain your right to make such uninformed and pusillanimous statements. . . . The truth is your socialist statements have no part in your religion and no basis in your various doctrines."[28]

Learning that King was planning a series of demonstrations during Holy Week, 1963, eight of the religious leaders—including Carpenter and his bishop suffragan George Murray—who had urged Governor Wallace to abide by the federal courts' decisions on school desegregation, issued another statement urging Birmingham's "Negro community" to withdraw its support from King's campaign. The rationale for both statements was the same: members of the clergy were urging people to abide by the laws and work through the courts. In other words, they regarded Wallace's defiance of the courts' desegregation rulings and King's protests against a political and economic structure that systematically excluded African Americans to be morally equivalent. However, the Good Friday statement also noted that "recent public events" created an "opportunity for a new constructive and realistic approach to racial problems." King was arrested on Good Friday, April 12, 1963, and held in Birmingham's city jail for eight days. While there he began to write the civil rights movement's best-known and most important manifesto: "Letter from Birmingham Jail." Although addressed to all of the clergy who had signed the statement opposing demonstrations, King's essay could have been addressed to Bishop Carpenter personally. His prison epistle was a reply to the white ministers' Good Friday statement but would have served equally well as a reply to Carpenter's letter to Martha Jane Gibson of Talladega College in 1939: "the Negro is very much in our hearts, and that we are doing the best we can to solve the problem of his religious education; we try our best to take care of Negro communicants, and gradually work is being developed—not as rapidly as some of us want, but as well as we are able with our rather limited facilities." King eloquently dismissed Carpenter's arguments with unassailable logic. Using words that echoed Pettigrew's article, King delivered a devastating blow to the white "moderate" "who paternalistically feels that he can set the time-table for another man's freedom; who lives by the myth of time and who constantly advises the Negro to wait until a 'more convenient season.' Shallow understanding from people of good will is more frustrating than absolute misunderstanding from people of ill will. Lukewarm acceptance is much more bewildering than outright rejection. . . . For years now I have heard the word 'Wait!' It rings in the ear of every Negro with piercing familiarity. This 'wait' has almost always meant 'never.'" Birmingham's white leadership reached an agreement with King and his allies one week after his arrest.

It included the end of separate black and white water fountains and restrooms, the integration of lunch counters, and a commitment to hire black salesclerks. It also established a "committee on Racial Problems and Employment" to "carry out a program of upgrading and improving employment opportunities with the Negro citizens of the Birmingham community." Bishop Carpenter was selected to lead the committee.[29]

Carpenter left no record of what he thought and felt before, during, and after the Birmingham campaign. King's "Letter from Birmingham Jail" had demolished the argument against slow, gradual progress that moderates had been using for decades, and the apparent success of his Birmingham campaign made a powerful case for his strategy of nonviolent resistance and revealed the potential for violence behind segregation. However, one could argue that real change only came after four little girls were killed in the Sixteenth Street Baptist Church bombing. Another major factor in the passage of the 1964 federal civil rights legislation was President Kennedy's assassination in November 1963, which President Johnson used as leverage to convince Congress to enact his civil rights legislation as a way of honoring Kennedy's memory. Bishop Murray served as a trustee of a fund created to aid the families of the deceased children and other victims of the bombing. With one exception, there is no record of any of the clergy of the diocese, including its bishops, making a public statement about the church bombing. However, Thomas Smythe, editor of the *Alabama Churchman*, vigorously condemned the bombing and the silence of Alabama Episcopalians in the October 1963 issue: "In the months and years gone by the Episcopal Church in this Diocese has been rather quiet on the subject of race relations.... Three weeks ago the blast that rocked a Birmingham church and killed children enlightened Alabama to a moment of truth ... we Episcopalians with our recorded indecision helped create the atmosphere for the lunatic fringes on both sides of the matter."[30]

The confrontation and carnage in Birmingham may also have played a role in motivating the Episcopal Church to change its canons at its 1964 General Convention in St. Louis. Here the church passed Canon 16, Sec. 4: "Every communicant or baptized member of this Church shall be entitled to equal rights and status in any Parish or Mission thereof. He shall not be excluded from the worship or Sacraments of the Church, nor from parochial membership, because of race, color, or ethnic origin."[31]

Bishop Carpenter and the March from Selma to Montgomery

There was to be one more indirect confrontation between Carpenter and King— the Selma march—but Selma was a much greater trial for the bishop because it put Carpenter into a nearly impossible position, caught between his fellow bishops on one hand and Alabama Episcopalians on the other. Striking down the laws that upheld segregation was a fragile victory at best unless black people could vote. After the 1964 presidential election, King and his colleagues began to focus their attention on obstacles to black voter registration in Alabama and Mississippi. Nowhere in the United States was the disparity between blacks as a percentage of the population and black voter registration greater than in the Black Belt of Alabama and Mississippi. Blessed with exceptionally rich, dark soil (which was also the source of the region's nickname), this had been the epicenter of slavery in the antebellum South. Following the Civil War some counties of the Black Belt had four or five times as many African Americans as whites, although in places only a few dozen blacks were registered to vote. Early in their struggle to register black voters, King and his colleagues began to focus on Selma, the county seat of Dallas County. In 1963, 55 percent of the population of Dallas County was black, but blacks accounted for only 2.3 percent of the registered voters.[32]

The tactics King and the Southern Christian Leadership Conference (SLC) had used with great success in Birmingham were likely to work well in Selma: They could reasonably expect the overreaction of local authorities to focus national and international attention on the systematic violations of the rights of black voters. Historian J. Mills Thornton describes Selma before the civil rights movement as Alabama's "most inflexibly and fervently segregationist" town. Alabama's first White Citizens' Council was organized there in 1954, and its purpose was to "maintain complete segregation of the races" and to "make it difficult, if not impossible, for any Negro who advocates de-segregation to find and hold a job, get credit or renew a mortgage." Judge James Hare, an archsegregationist and a member of St. Paul's Episcopal Church in Selma, "had issued an injunction banning all gatherings in the wake of local efforts to desegregate public accommodations after the Civil Rights Act became law." King and his lieutenants planned to launch their Selma campaign at a mass meeting on January 2, 1965. Beginning on January 18, a series of demonstrations followed the mass meeting and went on for two months, culminating in the Selma-to-Montgomery march for voting rights on March 7.[33]

The marchers gathered at Brown Chapel AME Church on the morning of March 7, 1965, and proceeded from there to the Edmund Pettus Bridge that spanned the Alabama River. As they descended the east side of the steep bridge, Dallas County sheriff Jim Clark warned them that they were "an unlawful assembly," but the marchers refused to turn back. A few minutes later Alabama state troopers and Dallas County deputies, on foot and on horseback, waded into the crowd of marchers. The law enforcement officials viciously beat the marchers with nightsticks and fired tear gas into the throng, forcing them to fall back to Brown Chapel. At least fifty-seven people were injured, and fourteen were hospitalized.

The scene was filmed by television news crews and photographed by journalists. That evening ABC interrupted its broadcast of *Judgment at Nuremberg*, a film about the trial of Nazi leaders following World War II, to broadcast scenes of Alabama law enforcement officials violently attacking peaceful demonstrators. One week following the attack on the demonstrators in Selma, Julian McPhillips condemned the violence in a powerful sermon at St. Luke's, Birmingham:

> We still have much further to go in removing the evils or the effects of our lack of love of both God and neighbor. A dramatic illustration of this has been seen in the events of the last week in Selma. Last Monday night we witnessed on television State Troopers clubbing unarmed Negroes. In Christian conscience, do you think it is necessary to strike unarmed non-resisting people with clubs or whips to move them back? Later a 38 year old minister, the father of 4 children was clubbed to death by white persons. All this because Negro citizens express their indignation at not being able to exercise their constitutional right to vote. Why have people suffered this past week? I'll tell you why—because we who call ourselves Christians have not loved our neighbors as we have loved ourselves.[34]

In response to the Bloody Sunday march, King announced a second Selma-to-Montgomery march for Tuesday and issued a summons: "I call . . . on clergy of all faiths, representatives of every part of the country, to join me for a ministers' march to Montgomery. . . . In this way all America will testify to the fact that the struggle in Selma is for the survival of democracy everywhere in our land." In spite of federal judge Frank Johnson's order forbidding the march, King led the marchers across the Edmund Pettus Bridge, paused for prayers on its eastern side, and then returned to Brown Chapel.[35]

Although he took a dim view of the marchers in general and King in particular, *Selma Times Journal* editor and member of St. Paul's Episcopal Church Roswell Falkenberry was a rare voice of reason and genuine moderation during the Selma campaign. He regarded the March 7 march as "stupidity," but he also condemned the state troopers' violent response, saying that there was "no logical reasoning behind the display of force employed by state troopers and members of the mounted units who participated in dispersing the demonstrators." When Unitarian minister James Reeb was attacked as he left a Selma restaurant and died a few days later in a Birmingham hospital, Falkenberry condemned Reeb's murder as a "savage act of brutality" and called on Selma's ministers "to include memorial prayers for Mr. Reeb during their services."[36]

St. Paul's Episcopal Church in Selma is a church with deep roots in Alabama's past. Founded in 1843, the church was burned in the Battle of Selma. St. Paul's parishioners were proud of their heritage as heirs of the Black Belt's antebellum planters. In an article titled "Pew 62," C. C. Grayson wrote of his experience as a St. Paul's parishioner: "Directly in front of my pew is the Baptismal Font which was placed in the church by Captain Dan Partridge in memory of his wife. . . . Bishop Wilmer, I think, was the most beloved man I ever knew. At the last stages of the Civil War the good bishop was ordered by the Federal general in command to cease using the prayer for the president of the Confederate States or he would be compelled to put him in prison. . . . Bishop Wilmer ignored the threat and continued praying for Jeff Davis until the end."

The Bloody Sunday march and the throngs of demonstrators from all over the country who gathered in Selma in March 1965 created an unprecedented situation for the people of St. Paul's and their rector, T. Frank Matthews. A long-established way of life came under national and international scrutiny, and a system of segregation and discrimination that had been in place for a century began to crumble and fall. Struggling to maintain the only order they had ever known, St. Paul's ushers turned black worshipers away from their doors twice—March 14 and 21—not appreciating the irony of the stained glass window in their nave inscribed with the words of Jesus: "Come unto me, all ye that labor." The irony was compounded further by the fact that the whole situation might have been avoided if the Diocesan Convention in January 1964 had not tabled a resolution that would have declared the parishes of the dioceses open to all people without regard to race.[37]

Carpenter urged Episcopalians to refrain from taking part in "the demonstrations that are causing much ill-will and unnecessary unhappiness in our state." To him the march was a "costly public nuisance" that he attributed to "the childish instinct to parade" and said that it could "serve no good purpose." Carpenter was especially dismayed by the participation of leaders of his own church. Acting in collaboration with the National Council of Churches, John B. Hines, Presiding Bishop of the Episcopal Church (Carpenter participated in Hines's consecration as bishop coadjutor of Texas and the two remained close friends), declared the Selma march a "recognized ecumenical activity," a move that allowed Episcopal clergy to participate in the Selma march and attendant events without Carpenter's permission. On Monday, March 11, Hines notified Carpenter and Murray that Arthur Walmsley, a member of the national staff of the Episcopal Church, would be coming to Selma. Ultimately, more than five hundred Episcopalian clergy, including Hines, came to Selma.[38]

Not only was Carpenter irate because his church had given its blessing and money to clergy and employees who came to march in Selma, he was also disappointed by the National Council of Churches (NCC). Carpenter had consistently defended that organization against the charges of many Alabama Episcopalians who believed the NCC had mixed religion and politics, was too liberal, and might even be Communist-influenced. In 1962 the Diocesan Convention had voted to ask the bishop of Alabama to launch an investigation of the NCC, but the committee that investigated the NCC found more to commend than to criticize. Carpenter's principal complaint against the senior leadership of the Episcopal Church was that they had authorized and funded what he seems to have regarded as a kind of "invasion" of his diocese without his permission. In a March 15 letter from Carpenter to Hines, the Alabama bishop asked the Presiding Bishop by what authority the NCC was urging people to join the Selma march. "I had understood," Carpenter went on, "that the National Council of Churches would not take this sort of action unless there was some consideration given by the main group in that body." Carpenter reiterated his standard position on civil rights: "I think we were making a little progress until the recent foolish . . . action by the National Council of Churches."[39]

Most disturbing, though, was Carpenter's inability to grasp that there was any justification at all for the Selma demonstrations, and his main concern (expressed in the letter to Hines about the NCC's participation in the demonstrations) was that "the poor people of that city are being rubbed raw by the continual persecution." An undated memo prepared by Presiding Bishop John Hines for the Executive Council of the Episcopal Church carefully outlined the sequence of events between Bloody Sunday and the second and third Selma marches. He noted that "the Presiding Bishop had advised the Alabama bishops of the expected participation of Episcopalians in the Selma march" and that they had "counseled against such participation." Also, as Carpenter had feared, the Episcopal Church had paid the expenses of three priests attending the march in an official capacity (Arthur Walmsley, Alison Stivers, and Tolley Caution).[40]

Kilmer Myers, bishop suffragan of Michigan (later elected to succeed James Pike as bishop of California), was a particular thorn in Carpenter's side. In a telegram dated March 18, Myers requested permission to celebrate the Eucharist in St. Paul's on March 20 for Episcopalians participating in the demonstrations. Without waiting for a reply from Carpenter, Myers sent a follow-up telegram to Wilson Baker, Selma's director of public safety, announcing that "clergy and laity from Alabama and elsewhere" would join him at St. Paul's on Saturday, March 20, at 1:30 P.M. It is difficult to imagine that Myers did not know that his request was not only impossible given the attitudes of the rector and people of St. Paul's but also that the two telegrams would raise the temperature of Carpenter's anger from simmer to high boil. Carpenter did everything in his power to prevent Myers from achieving his goal. Carpenter fired a telegram back to Myers immediately: "Your action in announcing service at St. Paul's Church without any consultation with bishop or vestry entirely out of order, and I am amazed at your presumption. This service will not be held by you." In a subsequent letter, Carpenter reminded Myers that "it is not customary for a Bishop to plan to conduct services of worship . . . in another Bishop's diocese without first consulting with that Bishop." Carpenter also reiterated his belief that the march was a "great piece of folly" and that the people of Selma "have paid a tremendous price for any lack of right doing which may be attributed to them, and it is wrong, I think, to keep pounding them. They are raw already with the constant vilification and disturbance put upon them." Carpenter also wrote to Myers's superior, Stanley M. Emrich, the bishop of Michigan, complaining of Myers's "cavalier disregard for any of the amenities which normally prevail in Episcopal relations" and urged Emrich to "give him some work to do which will keep him busy up there in Detroit and keep him out of Alabama." But Myers defied Carpenter, came to Selma, and did celebrate the Eucharist (although not in St. Paul's) on March 20. Following Myers's "guerilla mass" in the streets of Selma, Carpenter wrote him an irate letter: "Your crude and rude action in this matter makes me doubt the sincerity of your motives in coming to Selma where you did damage to the life and work of the Church, particularly at a time when we are trying to work through a very difficult situation. . . . Before you come down this way again I hope that you will learn some manners and come to help and not to hinder."[41]

Attending Myers's unauthorized Eucharist were Louis and Yvonne Willie of St. Mark's, Birmingham, and Louis's brother, Charles Willie, a member of the Department of Sociology and Anthropology at Syracuse University. The Willies, their son, Lou Willie III, and Bruce Wirtz, the rector of St. Andrew's, Birmingham, and priest-in-charge of St. Mark's, Birmingham, brought the communion vessels from St. Mark's. Still hoping to celebrate at the altar in St. Paul's, Myers; Richard Millard, bishop suffragan of California; Charles Willie; Louis and Yvonne Willie; and a crowd of about two hundred would-be worshipers set out from Brown Chapel for the short walk to St. Paul's. Only about a block from Brown Chapel, however, Selma's public safety commissioner, Wilson Baker, ordered them to stop. There, on the sidewalk, Bishop Millard led the Penitential Office, a liturgy used for the formal confession of sin. The ancient words of the liturgy seemed especially apt for the occasion: "O God, whose nature and property is ever to have mercy and to forgive; Receive our humble petitions; and though we be tied and bound with the chain of our sins, yet let the pitifulness of thy great mercy loose us." Returning to Brown Chapel they borrowed a table and Bishop Myers celebrated the Eucharist on the sidewalk. Gathered around the table they sang "In Christ there is no east or west" and "Were you there when they crucified my Lord," adding a new verse to the old spiritual: "Could you tell whether He was black or white?" Professor Willie pondered, "I have often wondered about the power of prayer. Saturday there was tangible evidence. The public became joyful and the police jittery."[42]

Carpenter's characterization of the march as a "nuisance" may have played a role in St. Paul's decision to turn away black worshipers during the voting rights demonstrations. After black worshipers were refused entry on March 14, Malcolm E. Peabody Jr. wrote a letter of protest on behalf of ESCRU, alleging that a group of nineteen (mostly Episcopal priests) had gone to St. Paul's. There the ushers had told them that only white laypeople and clergy would be admitted. Furthermore, Peabody said that they had been told that "demonstrators" would not be admitted, which (presumably) excluded all of them. Peabody reminded Carpenter of Canon 16, Sec. 4, which mandated that the church open its doors to all worshipers, regardless of race. Peabody also alleged that Frank Matthews, the rector of St. Paul's, had told the visitors that he saw nothing wrong with segregated worship. Accompanying the demonstrators was a reporter for the *Houston Chronicle*, who reported that Matthews had "not been able to see the evils in a separated system of worship." When asked if he believed that "Christ and Christianity" were breaking down the "walls between men," Matthews agreed but said that he could not tell his congregation this because he would no longer be able to preach to them. In spite of Peabody's letter, St. Paul's turned away another group of black and white worshipers on March 21.[43]

St. Paul's vestry met on March 22, and under pressure from Bishop Carpenter agreed to abide by the canons of the Episcopal Church that required them to admit all Episcopalians, regardless of race, to their services. Matthews announced the vestry's action in two letters to his parishioners—one on March 23 and a subsequent letter on the twenty-fifth to clarify and amplify the first. In his March 25 letter, Matthews noted that although the decision had not been unanimous, the vestry had voted to comply with the canons of the church. The consequences of failing to do so, he explained, would be that St. Paul's would no longer be a part of the Episcopal Church. Matthews also complimented his parishioners on being "'Big people' who love your church with a 'big love.'" A note from Carpenter accompanied Matthews's letter, in which the bishop commended the vestry and rector for their "fine action" and said that he knew the people of St. Paul's "in their usual spirit of wisdom and loyalty" would support the rector and vestry. Presiding Bishop Hines warmly thanked Carpenter for using his influence to persuade St. Paul's vestry to comply with the canons of the Episcopal Church and admit black worshipers.[44]

The third, final, and ultimately successful march that made it all the way to Montgomery was scheduled for Sunday, March 21. Arm in arm, leading the march were Martin Luther King Jr.; his lieutenant, Ralph Abernathy; an unidentified nun; and two eminent rabbis: the great scholar Abraham Joshua Heschel and Maurice Eisendrath, president of the Union of American Hebrew Congregations. The marchers arrived in Montgomery on Wednesday, March 24, and King gave one of his most powerful speeches from the steps of the capitol building where Jefferson Davis had been sworn in as Confederate president 104 years earlier. "There never was a moment in American history more honorable and more inspiring than the pilgrimage of clergymen and laymen of every race and faith, pouring into Selma to face danger at the side of its embattled Negroes," King proclaimed. "How long will justice be crucified and truth buried?" King asked. "How long? *Not* long! Because the arc of the moral universe is *long*, but it bends toward justice."[45]

The Martyrdom of Jonathan Daniels

Episcopalian Jonathan Myrick Daniels, a student at the Episcopal Theological Seminary in Cambridge, Massachusetts, defied Carpenter and came to Selma in spite of the Alabama bishop's disapproval. A native of Keene, New Hampshire, Daniels had been a member of the Congregational Church until his senior year in high school when he was confirmed in the Episcopal Church. After graduating from the Virginia Military Institute in 1961, Daniels spent a year as a graduate student in English literature at Harvard before deciding to seek ordination in the Episcopal Church. Initially, Daniels argued that Bishop Carpenter had the right to demand that Episcopalians stay away from demonstrations in Alabama, but his views changed after Dr. King's plea to clergy of all faiths to come to Selma. Finally, during a service of Evening Prayer, Daniels felt himself called to go to Selma: "as usual I was singing the Magnificat with the special love and reverence I have always for Mary's glad song: 'He hath showed strength with his arm.' As the lovely hymn of the God-bearer continued, I found myself peculiarly alert, suddenly straining toward the decisive, luminous, spirit-filled 'moment.' . . . Then it came. 'He hath put down the mighty from their seat, and hath exalted the humble and meek. He hath filled the hungry with good things.' I knew then that I must go to Selma."[46]

Daniels and several other seminarians made it to Selma in time for the abortive march on Tuesday, March 9. He was also a member of the group that was turned away from St. Paul's on Sunday, March 14. After a brief return to Cambridge, Daniels and fellow seminarian Judith Upham returned to Selma under the auspices of ESCRU. While living with black families in Selma, Daniels helped blacks register to vote in both Dallas County and also later in neighboring Lowndes County. He also helped blacks by gathering information about social services in Selma and Dallas County and writing a pamphlet about how to access such services.

Another of Daniels's concerns was building bridges between St. Paul's and Selma's black community. Frank Matthews and St. Paul's vestry had agreed to comply with the canons of the Episcopal Church, but their agreement contained a sizeable loophole. The vestry minutes recording the resolution to comply with the canons also noted "the ushers shall be under their canonical duty to 'maintain order and decorum during the time of public worship.'" Consequently, when Daniels brought an interracial group to the early service on Easter day, they were seated at the back of the church with six pews between them and the rest of the congregation. In a letter to Carpenter, Daniels also said that an usher had "insisted that we not bring any negroes to the festal celebration at eleven," and that he and the blacks with him had "repeatedly been the objects of obscene remarks and insults by some of the congregation." Carpenter replied to his letter on April 23, but the only point of Daniels's letter that concerned him was the allegation that members of St. Paul's had used obscene language: "This is very strong language, and I cannot imagine the good people of St. Paul's Church, Selma, using obscene language in your presence. Please tell me by immediate mail just what these obscene remarks were. I would like to have the exact wording so that I may look further into this situation." Daniels and Upham gave Carpenter a personal account of their experience in a meeting with him in Birmingham on April 27. Unsatisfied with Carpenter's response to their concerns, Daniels, Upham, and other members of ESCRU picketed Carpenter House on April 30. ESCRU also issued a statement alleging that Carpenter had "sanctioned a 'devious maneuver' to segregate worshippers at Communion services. 'The Carpenter of Birmingham,' they declared, 'must not be allowed to forever deny the Carpenter of Nazareth.'" Daniels continued to worship at St. Paul's, and Matthews eventually prevailed upon the ushers to discontinue segregated seating.[47]

Some of St. Paul's parishioners were hostile to Daniels and the blacks who accompanied him, but that was not the whole story. Although they may have disagreed with him about the civil rights movement, several of St. Paul's parishioners were gracious and kind. Daniels recorded that he had cordial conversations with attorney Harry Gamble and his wife, Kate, as well as Miller Childers, another attorney. Daniels also got to know Roswell Falkenberry, the moderate editor of the *Selma Times*, and even Frank Matthews was personally friendly to Daniels.[48]

On August 1, Matthews wrote Carpenter about the progress that St. Paul's had made in overcoming segregation and noted that Daniels and a young black woman had attended the 11:00 A.M. service without incident. In his reply, Carpenter said, "If he is hanging around causing trouble, I think I will just have to write to his Bishop and tell him to take him on back to Seminary." In hindsight, Carpenter's words have a slightly ominous ring, because Daniels's activism was about to prove as fatal for him as the activism of Jimmy Lee Jackson, James Reeb, and Viola Liuzzo had proved for them.[49]

On August 13—one day after Carpenter's letter to Matthews—Daniels and several other demonstrators were arrested during a demonstration in Fort Deposit in Lowndes County and taken to the jail in Hayneville. Finally released on August 20, Daniels and Catholic priest Richard Morrisroe, accompanied by two young black women, Joyce Bailey and Ruby Sales, walked from the jail to the nearby Cash Store. In front of the store they encountered Tom Coleman, an employee of the state highway department. Coleman had heard a rumor to the effect that after their release from jail, the civil rights workers were going to create a disturbance. Armed with a pistol and shotgun, Coleman had gone to the Cash Store. When Daniels and his companions approached the store, Coleman shouted, "Get off this property, or I'll blow your goddamn heads off, you sons of bitches." Daniels pushed Ruby Sales out of the way, and Coleman fired his shotgun at the seminarian, killing him instantly. As Morrisroe grabbed Joyce Bailey's hand and fled, Coleman fired at the priest, hitting him in the lower right side of his back.[50]

Charles H. Douglass, rector of St. John's, Montgomery, heard about Daniels's death on the six o'clock news, although Daniels was erroneously identified as an Episcopal priest from New Haven, Connecticut. After learning Daniels's correct identity from his Virginia Military Institute ring, he called Bishop Carpenter at home that evening. Douglass also contacted the president of the Standing Committee of the Diocese of New Hampshire. Through him, Douglass contacted the priest in Keene and Daniels's mother, Constance. Ms. Daniels requested that Douglass collect her son's belongings and send them to her. Daniels's body was returned to New Hampshire via a circuitous route. ESCRU's John Morris had Daniels's body flown to Washington, DC, on a friend's private plane; in Washington he rented a plane to take Daniels's remains as far as Boston where inclement weather forced them to land. Finally, the journey to Keene was completed in a hearse.[51]

In death as in life, Daniels was controversial. The Saturday, August 21, edition of the *Birmingham News* featured an enormous banner headline: "Civil Rights Worker Slain; Priest Shot at Hayneville." Services commemorating Daniels were held in Washington, Chicago, Atlanta, Boston, and St. Louis. Charles F. Hall, the bishop of New Hampshire, spoke at a memorial service for Daniels at Selma's Brown Chapel AME Church on August 27, a service that also featured remarks by John B. Coburn, dean of the Episcopal Theological Seminary (ETS). Frank Matthews and his parishioners were conspicuously absent from the service at Brown Chapel, although on the Sunday following Daniels's death, Matthews said prayers for him at St. Paul's and Dean Coburn from ETS spoke. In a letter to Carpenter, Matthews said that he had decided not to have a memorial service for Daniels at St. Paul's "because of the uncertain and unsettled conditions and because of the distinct possibility of violence."[52]

The situation was exacerbated when *The Witness*, a socially progressive journal of the Episcopal Church, reported that although there had not been a service for Daniels, there *had* been a service for KKK lawyer Matt Murphy, which robed

Klansmen had attended. (Murphy had been killed in an auto accident the same day as Daniels's murder.) But the truth was more complicated. Murphy, identified in the *Birmingham News'* article about his death as the "Imperial Klonsel of the Ku Klux Klan," had successfully defended the Klan members accused of murdering Viola Liuzzo. Formerly a member of Birmingham's St. Mary's-on-the-Highlands, he had become a Baptist. A scribbled note on Bishop Murray's personal notepaper says that Murphy was "a black sheep in [a] wonderful family." Murray informed William Spofford, the editor of *The Witness*, that Murphy's family—members of St. Mary's-on-the-Highlands—had asked its rector, David Cady Wright, to conduct Murphy's funeral. Wright did conduct the funeral, Murray said, but in a funeral home, not a church, and no robed Klansmen were present. Spofford partially apologized for some of the inaccuracies in his article in *The Witness*, but eventually produced a *New York Times* article from which he had drawn his facts.[53]

Other than an anemic statement Carpenter made (by telegram) when asked for one by *The Living Church* ("Daniels' death deplorable. Another incident in the current wave of lawlessness sweeping our country."), Alabama's Episcopal bishops maintained public silence about Daniels's death. In contrast, Matthews's remarks to *The Living Church* were warm and appreciative and seemed to express genuine remorse about Daniels's death: "Episcopalians in Selma were shocked by the tragic slaying of Jonathan Daniels. . . . Since March he has been a frequent attendant at St. Paul's, and I had many pleasant conversations with him in my study. His deep sincerity and unfailing dedication to his job, as well as his pleasing personality and intellectual competence were immediately evident. The Episcopal Church has lost a capable candidate for Holy Orders and a potential leader in the field of theological education."[54]

From the first, Richmond Flowers, Alabama's attorney general, feared that it would be impossible to try the case fairly in Lowndes County, and his fears were confirmed when the grand jury indicted Tom Coleman for first-degree manslaughter, even though he had been charged initially with first-degree murder. Concerned that the prosecutor was either incompetent or biased in Coleman's favor or both, Flowers took charge of the case. Flowers and his deputy, Joe Gantt, sought first a delay until Father Morrisroe was well enough to testify. When the judge denied this, they tried to have the charge of first-degree manslaughter dismissed so that they could seek an indictment of first-degree murder. Again, the judge refused their request. When Gantt refused to continue with the trial, the judge replaced him with the original prosecutor. The trial began on Monday, September 27, and concluded three days later. Coleman's lawyers argued that he had acted in self-defense and produced witnesses who claimed to have seen Daniels and Morrisroe holding weapons. As Attorney General Flowers had feared, the white men who made up the jury found Coleman not guilty.

There was widespread outrage at Coleman's acquittal. The *Nashville Tennes-*

sean commented, "Alabama has succeeded again in telling the world that those who come to that state to promote equal justice for all citizens do so at the risk of their lives." According to the *Louisville Courier-Journal*, "Nothing in the whole proceeding was more shameful than the appearance of local clergymen [as character witnesses for Coleman] who gave absolution to the affair, fatally qualifying one of the commandments." Presiding Bishop John Hines said, "It is simply inconceivable to intimate acquaintances of both young men that Jonathan Daniels flashed a knife or that Father Morrisroe was armed. . . . The studied care with which the defense assassinated the character of a man already dead rightfully angers fair-minded men everywhere. Fortunately, Jonathan Daniels's character survives such despicable action."[55]

The outcry against the verdict was swift and vehement everywhere, except at the headquarters of the Diocese of Alabama. Alabama's bishops issued a weak and ambiguous statement. The bishops were "disturbed to have heard all too many church members condoning the slaying or beating of civil rights workers." The word "disturbed" hardly seems adequate under such circumstances. Furthermore, if Carpenter and Murray had "heard . . . church members condoning the slaying or beating of civil rights workers," then as chief pastors of the Diocese of Alabama, were they not under a sacred obligation to denounce such threats of violence and murder in an emphatic and public manner? Yet, there is no record that they did so. A major concern of Carpenter and Murray's statement was that the people of Alabama would lose "further freedoms for the governing of our own affairs because of the widespread impression that there is a failure in the administration of justice within our State." In a letter to George Murray, Frederick M. Morris, the rector of St. Thomas Church on New York's Fifth Avenue, noted, "your statement referring to a 'widespread impression' concerning injustice in Alabama aggravated the situation. It is not a matter of 'an impression' but rather of facts, we believe." John Krum of New York's Church of the Ascension expanded on Morris's observation: "What is not said—and surely needs to be said—is that the conduct of the trial so clearly did not conform to the standards of a fair trial. The refusal of a postponement until the wounded Roman Catholic priest was able to testify was so obviously unjust and unfair that it is difficult to see how your statement could fail to refer to it . . . the reaction here in New York to the Alabama bishops' statement troubles us deeply."[56]

The Alabama bishops' statement concluded: "We . . . call upon all Christian people in Alabama to get on their knees and pray earnestly that the whole process of indictment and trial in the case of Jonathan Daniels shall in no wise be interpreted as a license to kill or injure those with whom we disagree or whose behavior we disapprove and that the importance of the Christian doctrine of the infinite worth of human life shall not be diminished in the minds of our people." Surely there were many things the bishops should have urged Alabama's Episcopalians to "get on their knees and pray" about, such as their silence in the face of violence and injustice or their complicity in the systematic denial of the civil rights of African Americans. And perhaps Carpenter should have been as adamant in reminding his people of "the infinite worth of human life" as he had been in urging King not to demonstrate or in frantically trying to keep Episcopalians from marching in Selma.

One of the most vigorous and passionate responses to Coleman's acquittal was a sermon that Julian McPhillips, the rector of St. Luke's, Mountain Brook, preached. The Sunday after the trial McPhillips preached on the sixth commandment: "Thou shalt do no murder." "It seems that in some places in this state of ours there are people who believe there must be an appendage to this commandment. 'Thou shalt do no murder'—except against one who is crazy enough or committed enough to be involved in Civil Rights." Unlike his bishops, McPhillips did not hesitate to call the Coleman trial a "miscarriage of justice." McPhillips made the connection that Carpenter and Murray had failed to make between Daniels's murder and the killings of Jimmy Lee Jackson, James Reeb, and Viola Liuzzo. "These cases fit into a pattern . . . which is becoming all too clear . . . in which murder is acceptable—that it is not punishable by law—as long as it is Civil Rights Workers who are murdered."[57]

In the aftermath of Daniels's murder and Coleman's acquittal, the reputation of Alabama and especially the Episcopal Church in Alabama were at a low ebb. Bishop Murray helped to repair the damage by accepting an invitation to speak at Daniels's seminary—Episcopal Theological Seminary—in Cambridge, Massachusetts. Dean Coburn invited Murray to visit the seminary in the fall of 1965, and his visit seems to have been a great success. In a thank-you note afterward, Coburn wrote, "That was an exhausting visit for you . . . but certainly one of the most worthwhile visits anybody has ever made to this School . . . there was some measure of disagreement with your position but . . . it is all the healthy type of disagreement which can result in the furtherance of the work of the Church and the strengthening of the ties that bind members of the Church together. It is also true that your visit has helped modify in some fashion many of the points of view of the students." A group of students wrote Murray, "It was good for some of us to realize the tremendous gap between the world of thoughts and ideas and their implementation. Your honest, faithful and patient commitment to Christian dialogue is very heart-warming." All the letters expressed respect for Murray and appreciation for his willingness to enter the "lion's den." But some also questioned the position he and Carpenter had taken. One student read between the lines of their statement at the end of the Coleman trial: "while this statement is undoubtedly true, it is not a peculiarly Christian reaction to these tragic events.

I would have hoped that the Church in Alabama might have found more Christian grounds for objecting to murder and lack of justice." While in Cambridge, Murray also spoke to Harvard students studying with the well-known psychologist Erik Erikson.[58]

Daniels had come to Selma to march and demonstrate but had stayed to assist African Americans in Dallas and Lowndes Counties in negotiating the voter registration process. He had also begun to build bridges between the black community and the wide range of social agencies that were already there or had come into existence because of LBJ's "war on poverty." During the demonstrations and marches in 1965, the various religious groups that had come to Selma began to explore ways to create a permanent presence there to demonstrate their ongoing concern and to continue the process of voter registration and provide assistance to the poor. They created an organization, the Selma Interreligious Project, and chose an Episcopal priest who was originally from Alabama, Francis X. Walter, to direct it. A native Alabamian, Walter had grown up in Mobile, attended Spring Hill College, and completed his seminary training at General Theological Seminary in New York. Upon returning to Alabama, Walter had asked to be assigned to Alabama's oldest black parish—Good Shepherd in Mobile. Carpenter was amenable to the idea, but a business partner of Walter's father was so outraged at the thought that Walter was going to serve a black parish that he threatened to terminate his business relationship with Walter's father. So the young Walter went instead to St. James, Eufaula. In short order, Walter's position on race put him at odds with the people of St. James, but the event that led to his dismissal was his participation in the founding of the Episcopal Society for Cultural and Racial Unity (ESCRU). Carpenter offered to place Walter somewhere else in Alabama on the condition that he sever his ties with ESCRU, a step Walter was unwilling to take. So Carpenter insisted that Walter leave Alabama, and he went to serve an inner-city parish in the Diocese of Newark.[59]

After returning to Alabama, Walter first approached Bishop Murray about the possibility of becoming licensed so that he could function again as a priest in Alabama. "I do want to be licensed in the Diocese and plan to ask Bishop Carpenter for this as soon as I can," but Walter hinted he knew this was unlikely because he not only had a "history" with Carpenter as a civil rights "troublemaker" but had become one of "those people" whom Carpenter told to stay out of Alabama: "I know that in a sense I'm already going against Bishop Carpenter's wishes and I know that you and I have disagreed about the tactics best used in combating racism." Replying the very next day, Carpenter coolly and quickly dashed Walter's hope to be licensed: "I am sorry to have to tell you that knowing how you feel about the Diocese of Alabama . . . and since you will be specifically representing a group of people listed in your letter in whom I have no confidence, I am not able to grant your request to license you to officiate as a Priest of the Church in the Diocese of Alabama."[60]

Bishop Murray replied to Walter with a puzzling letter, stating that he believed that Walter would be "utterly incapable of doing anything about establishing communication between Whites and Negroes" because he had "demonstrated this in the past" and the "intervening time has made you less able rather than more able to do anything at all in that field." He went on to say that the Selma Interreligious Project was a "direct insult to the ministry of all those who are working and have been working in Alabama with a continuing ministry under proper authorization from their churches," but Murray did not say what these "continuing ministries" were. The Diocese of Alabama was not engaged in any ministries that would have overlapped or competed with the work Walter was proposing to do. Frank Matthews received a copy of Murray's letter to Walter and sent the bishop a letter astonishing in its degree of anger at Walter: "You certainly told Francis Walter in no uncertain terms. You have done for me what I want to do but feel like I can't afford to do. If I wrote to him telling him why I thought it unwise for him to come to the Black Belt—and particularly to attempt to do such a job as he outlines in Selma—he and [John] Morris [of ESCRU] would resent my speaking out against them and probably make St. Paul's a target of a spiteful retaliation.... If I antagonize them they'll get vicious and then I may have to call on Tom Coleman to get them off my back." To say the least, Matthews's comment about Tom Coleman plumbed the depths of bad taste.[61]

Walter was already persona non grata before he returned to Alabama, but he further alienated both bishops by comments he made in a letter published in the *Bulletin* of the General Theological Seminary (GTS) in their Spring 1966 issue. Walter was replying to a letter by Emmet Gribbin. Gribbin had sent an open letter to a GTS alumnus, Malcolm McDowell, who had marched in Selma. Gribbin complimented McDowell for displaying "concern for racial problems in Alabama and the South" but urged him to "show a continuing concern and come and live with these problems and the people who are both part of the problem and part of the solution." Walter replied in the next issue of the *Bulletin* by pointing out that it would be difficult or impossible for a priest who had marched in Selma to get a job in Alabama. "A priest from 'outside' if suspect or not well known must undergo not only a session with the vestry on the subject but also a little exam given by the Bishops . . . I believe that it is rare for a priest to be accepted in Alabama who has ever rocked the racial boat elsewhere." Walter's letter shed a harsh light on racial attitudes in the Diocese of Alabama: "Episcopal parochial schools in Alabama are segregated preserves for whites scared of segregation. State schools and Roman Catholic schools announced desegregation long ago. The diocesan orphanage in Mobile is segregated. There has been no new missionary work among

Negroes (save on college campuses) since 1900. Missions are started in Alabama for the wealthy." Walter's letter prompted Murray to accuse him of lying, but everything he said was accurate.[62]

Evaluating Bishop Carpenter

Outside of Alabama there was almost-universal criticism for Bishop Carpenter. Within Alabama opinions ran the gamut from those on the right who thought the bishop was too liberal to those on the left who thought he was too conservative with the great majority in the middle who warmly supported him and praised him for his opposition to the Selma march. Frank Yeilding of Birmingham wrote: "Your attitude is the only sensible way to look at the distressing situation brought about solely by Martin Luther King. There was absolutely no desire on the part of either race in Selma for this condition to be brought about." From Marion came another letter: "My family and I send heartfelt thanks and admiration for your courage in discouraging outside clergy in these parts. We feel the clergy here has lent the movement a sanction and dignity it does not deserve and has baffled well-meaning people more than any other element of the whole unbelievable affair." What is surprising is that there were many in the Diocese of Alabama who believed that Carpenter was moving too slowly on civil rights or simply did not comprehend the situation. "I am shocked that a man of your stature should hold negative views regarding human rights of all citizens of this country," wrote a woman in Birmingham. "I am embarrassed when the church does not take a positive stand on such matters . . . when the lowliest little black child knocks at the pearly gates, St. Peter will tell him 'go to the back door, boy.' This must be true according to the belief implicit in your admonitions to the ministers of your faith."[63]

As one might expect, some of the most forceful criticism came from black Episcopalians. In the aftermath of the Selma march, Vernon Jones, the rector of St. Andrew's, Tuskegee, sharply rebuked Carpenter: "Your public statements on racial problems in the Diocese of Alabama always seem to miss the point entirely." Even Dr. Luther H. Foster, the president of Tuskegee Institute and a lay deputy to the General Convention in Honolulu in 1955, who had been on excellent terms with Carpenter, was critical of his bishop. In the aftermath of the Selma march, Foster wrote, taking the blame for having failed to communicate with him as clearly as he should have: "I only wish that I might have been more effective when I was endeavoring to convey to you a sense of urgency and the need to provide a fully democratic setting for all Alabamians. Somehow I have the feeling I have failed at a terribly crucial point of contact with my church; and that my church has failed me."[64]

It would be easy to dismiss Bishop Carpenter as a racist and to sit in judgment of him for his failure to comprehend and act, even though in this he was no different from most white Alabamians. For that matter, he was no different from most other white religious leaders in Alabama. Is it possible to weigh his record with any kind of objectivity? Carpenter had his defenders. In a letter to Bishop Kilmer Myers, Bishop Murray explained that he was "amazed at how good a friend Bishop Carpenter has been to the Negro." Murray went on to say that Carpenter had chaired "an interracial committee in Birmingham, which no one else would touch." He also told Myers that many in Alabama regarded Carpenter as an "integrationist." Furthermore, according to Murray, during "our crisis here in Birmingham, Carpenter House was the *only* place in the City where Negroes and white people could get together for negotiations, and Bishop Carpenter offered it without any hesitation whatsoever." Another strong supporter of Carpenter was Alice Gardner Murphy, a reporter for the *Houston Post* and granddaughter of Edgar Gardner Murphy, who defended Carpenter's record on race relations in a letter to Presiding Bishop John Hines. Like Murray, Murphy mentioned the Alabama bishop's leadership of the interracial committee charged with producing a plan to hire black policemen. In 1949, Carpenter joined other Birmingham religious leaders in denouncing "hooded violence," although interestingly, an article in the *Birmingham News* about the religious leaders' campaign never refers specifically to the Ku Klux Klan or to the fact that its principal targets were African Americans.[65]

Bishop Murray and Alice Gardner Murphy's apologias for Bishop Carpenter leave much unsaid and many questions unanswered. What did Carpenter accomplish for race relations? Historian Jonathan Bass notes that "Carpenter studied ways to improve black educational opportunities and actively recruited blacks to work as priests in Alabama. He sponsored scholarships and helped educate several black priests, but most of these young men found better opportunities outside of the state and the south and never returned." From 1951 to 1954, Carpenter led the Interracial Committee of the Jefferson County Coordinating Council, which included twenty-five white and twenty-five black leaders. One of the responsibilities of Carpenter's committee was to study the city of Birmingham's potential future employment of black policemen, and yet Birmingham was the last major city in Alabama to hire black policemen. One critic of Carpenter's leadership of the interracial committee wrote that he belonged in "the lowest dregs of Christian civilization" and was "betraying the Anglo-Saxon Nordic South." Bishop Murray overheard a phone conversation between Carpenter and a member of the Klan who threatened to ride him out of town on a rail. Carpenter replied, "Well, son, bring one around, and let's try it on for size!" One would like to give Carpenter

166 / Chapter 7

credit for integrating Camp McDowell, but the fact is that the initiative for integration came from Lou Willie and William Yon, a priest on Carpenter's staff, not from Carpenter himself; Carpenter merely yielded to the inevitable.[66]

It would be a bit too easy to absolve Carpenter by saying that he was simply a man of another generation, unable to comprehend the great changes taking place in the relationship between whites and blacks, because others of his generation made the necessary mental and spiritual course corrections demanded by the civil rights movement.[67] One of his closest friends in the House of Bishops, William Scarlett, the bishop of Missouri, was one who understood that it was no longer enough to counsel patience and to work toward a change that never came in a future that was always delayed. "As you find it hard to understand my position," Scarlett wrote Carpenter in July 1960, "so I find it difficult to understand yours. And one covets so deeply enlightened leadership from the Christian Church . . . so deeply. And you have all the elements of such leadership . . . a big frame and a big voice are enormous assets just to start with. . . . And I had hopes." According to Scarlett, "the sight of the great Bishop of Alabama ridden out of his state on a rail because of courageous and enlightened speech, would be one of the greatest events of many years. I still think so: I think you have an opportunity of a hundred years." However, to borrow Bishop Scarlett's language, the tragedy of the Right Reverend Charles Colcock Jones Carpenter and of the Diocese of Alabama during the civil rights struggle was that they had "an opportunity of a hundred years" and failed to seize it.[68]

In the drama of the civil rights movement, Alabama Episcopalians played many roles. Priests such as Thomas Thrasher, Robert DuBose, Louis Mitchell, Emmet Gribbin, Julian McPhillips, and Francis Walter heroically denounced injustice, risked their careers, and sometimes put their lives on the line. Laypeople such as Charles Morgan and Juliette Morgan spoke out and paid a high price (fatal, in Juliette's case). Louis and Yvonne Willie may have risked their lives in traveling to Selma in the company of Bruce Wirtz, a white priest. And Jonathan Daniels, an Episcopalian though not an Alabamian, became a martyr. Most Episcopalians, like most Alabamians, watched the drama play out, went about their daily routines, and were neither heroes nor villains. Bishop Carpenter retired at the end of 1968, having served as bishop of Alabama for thirty years, second only to Wilmer in length of service, and he could be justifiably proud of his leadership.

At the beginning of Carpenter's episcopacy the total baptized membership of the Diocese of Alabama was 19,267, the diocese had thirty-five parishes, and the budget was $38,550. When he retired there were 33,393 baptized members, fifty-three parishes, and the budget was $105,600. In terms of financial strength, membership growth, and the number of new parishes, it was the most impressive record of any bishop of Alabama since Cobbs.[69] Furthermore, Carpenter built one of the Diocese of Alabama's best-loved and most enduring institutions—Camp McDowell. By most standards, Carpenter must be judged an effective and successful bishop. But unlike his friends and colleagues, Bishop William Scarlett in Missouri and Presiding Bishop John Hines (to name only two of the many bishops and priests who managed both to denounce racial injustice and also be effective pastors), Carpenter did not clearly and forcefully address the fear and anger that kept his white communicants from tearing down the walls that separated them from black people and stood between black people and the educational and economic opportunities that white people took for granted. When Carpenter retired, he left not only a heritage of growth but also a legacy of unfinished business in the area of racial reconciliation that the Episcopal Church in Alabama continues to confront.

8
"O thou who changest not . . ."
From 1968 to the Present

Novelist Walker Percy came from a family with strong ties to Alabama's Episcopal churches. At St. John's, Elyton, in 1887, the novelist's grandfather—also named
Walker—married Mary Pratt DeBardeleben, the daughter and granddaughter of
two of the founders of Birmingham's steel industry, Henry DeBardeleben and
Daniel Pratt. Although the novelist's father, LeRoy Percy, joined the Presbyterian
Church when he married in 1915, Walker was an Episcopalian when he converted
to the Roman Catholic Church in 1947. In his novel *Love in the Ruins,* the nar-
rator, a physician named Thomas More, describes his wife, Doris, as "a cheerful
Episcopalian from Virginia [who] became a priestess of the high places." "Beware
of Episcopal women," More says,

> who take up with Ayn Rand and the Buddha and Dr. Rhine formerly of
> Duke University. A certain type of Episcopal girl has a weakness that comes
> on them just past youth. . . . They fall prey to Gnostic pride, commence buy-
> ing antiques, and develop a yearning for esoteric doctrine. . . . Doris began
> talking of going to the Isle of Jersey or New Zealand where she hoped to
> recover herself, learn quiet breathing in a simple place, etcetera etcetera,
> perhaps in the bright shadow of a 'dobe wall or perhaps in a stone cottage
> under a green fell. . . . When she was an ordinary ex-Episcopalian, a good-
> humored Virginia girl with nothing left of her religion, but a fondness for

old brick chapels, St. John o' the Woods, and the superb English of the King James Version, we had common ground.[1]

Percy's description of Doris could be applied to many Episcopalians toward the end of the twentieth century. The love of "old brick chapels" and "the superb English of the King James Version" began to give way to a multitude of new causes and concerns. At the end of the twentieth century and beginning of the twenty-first, Alabama's Episcopalians experienced both loss and gain: many new churches were founded but older churches, wracked by the whirlwinds of controversy gusting through the Episcopal Church, saw longtime members leave or finally fragmented when the center could no longer hold. Episcopalians were members of a liberal denomination in a conservative state. Historically, they were the heirs of the plantation (and slave) owners and the industrialists who had developed the mines, mills, and factories of the "mineral region" in the late nineteenth century. They more or less successfully weathered the civil rights movement, the ordination of women, and Prayer Book revision, but the movement for unconditional acceptance of gays and lesbians in the church proved a bridge too far for some Alabama Episcopalians. Gay rights was the issue that finally shattered the unity of Alabama's Episcopal churches.

A Liberal Church in a Conservative State

While the Episcopal Church moved in a liberal direction, the state of Alabama tacked rightward. The last Democratic presidential candidate Alabamians voted for was Jimmy Carter in 1976. They voted for Republican Ronald Reagan in 1980 and have not supported a Democratic presidential candidate since. In the Reagan landslide of 1980, Alabamians also elected their first Republican US senator since Reconstruction, Jeremiah Denton. Democrat Richard Shelby defeated Denton in 1987, but Shelby switched to the Republican Party in 1994, and at the end of the century Republicans held both of Alabama's US Senate seats. Alabama elected its first Republican governor since Reconstruction, H. Guy Hunt, in 1987, and then the governor's office alternated between Republicans and Democrats until 2011, when Robert J. Bentley, a Republican from Tuscaloosa, succeeded Bob Reilly, also a Republican.

Since the end of World War II, many Alabama Episcopalians had begun to think that the national leadership of the Episcopal Church was becoming unresponsive to their concerns and was going in the wrong direction. The Episcopal Church took official positions on civil rights that were at odds with the status quo in the South, and Bishop Carpenter repeatedly defended the National Council of Churches (of which the Episcopal Church was a critical part) from the charge that it was Communist-influenced. During the civil rights movement and the Vietnam War, the discrepancy between the Episcopal Church and the values of white southerners widened and deepened because of official statements of the Episcopal Church and the unofficial activities of many of its leaders. As previously noted, the Executive Council gave its official endorsement to Dr. King's voting rights march from Selma to Montgomery, and hundreds of Episcopal clergy and laypeople marched (including Presiding Bishop John Hines).

The Special General Convention of 1969, convened to deal at length and in detail with the problems of racial justice, was a major turning point. The Special Convention, which met at the University of Notre Dame in South Bend, Indiana, in August 1969, probably confirmed some of the worst fears of conservative white Episcopalians in Alabama. In the words of historian Gardiner H. Shattuck Jr., the Episcopal Church "seemed to come apart at the seams" during the Special General Convention. The Union of Black Clergy and Laymen (UBCL) seized control of the microphone and the agenda during the first evening meeting. An official of the Black Economic Development Conference, Muhammed Kenyatta, took the microphone from the hands of Presiding Bishop John Hines. Kenyatta and Paul Washington, a black priest from Philadelphia, demanded that the convention set aside its agenda and give immediate consideration to the so-called Black Manifesto, a set of demands drawn up by the National Black Economic Development Conference, which called for white religious institutions to give $500 million as "reparations" for slavery. The Episcopal Church's share of this would have been a mere $60 million. The convention rejected the demand that they adopt the Black Manifesto but ultimately made a controversial appropriation of $200,000 to the National Committee of Black Churchmen to be used for black economic development.

At the Notre Dame convention the Episcopal Church on display was no longer the conservative, white, and male-dominated institution often referred to as "the Republican Party at prayer." Antiwar activists interrupted proceedings by reading aloud the names of soldiers killed in Vietnam; military deserters asked for (and were refused) sanctuary; and during the meeting it was announced that the controversial and erratic James Pike, bishop of California, and his third wife had driven into the Judean wilderness, left their car when it broke down, and were both presumed dead. Diane Pike was rescued, but after an extensive search by Israeli authorities (and after Mrs. Pike had consulted medium Arthur Ford), Pike's body was found only two miles from where his wife had last seen him.

John Krum, rector of New York's Church of the Heavenly Rest, said that the Special General Convention had revealed the Episcopal Church to be "not the comfortable upper middle class version of respectable Christianity [but] the most diverse, motley, widely varied group of human beings that could be imagined."[2]

Comments from Alabama's delegation were mixed: Mark Waldo, rector of Ascension, Montgomery, said that the decision to give $200,000 to the National Committee of Black Churchmen was "a vote for Black racism," and he went on to say "the action can only fuel the fires of much greater and more sophisticated white racism." Most of the Alabama deputies were critical of the Special Convention, but they expressed their views in cautious and temperate ways. Ben Meginnis of Dothan's Nativity parish said that the convention "did better than I thought it would under the circumstances." "The convention offered confrontation in the spirit of love," according to Martin Tilson, rector of St. Luke's, Birmingham. Tilson interpreted the attempt to hijack the agenda as a "toothache that signals that something is wrong and needs diagnosis and treatment." Black businessman Louis Willie of Birmingham, a special nonvoting minority representative, said, "The main issue at Notre Dame was whether or not the church was ready to accord to its black members real decision-making power and trust."[3]

The Episcopal Church continued its liberal course in the 1970s. In 1976 the General Convention, which met in St. Paul, Minnesota, approved two measures that drastically changed the Episcopal Church. The first was the decision to allow women to be ordained to the offices of priest and bishop, and the second was the revision of the Book of Common Prayer. Although opening the priesthood and episcopate to women changed a two-thousand-year-old tradition, it was the revision of the Prayer Book that was to cause more controversy. Marianne Bogel, a hospital chaplain, became the first woman priest in Alabama when Furman Stough ordained her to the priesthood on June 6, 1977, at Huntsville's Church of the Nativity. A few days later on June 11, 1977, George Murray ordained Alabama's second female priest, Evelyn Seymour, at St. James, Fairhope. In the first decade of the twenty-first century, women led some of Alabama's most prominent Episcopal churches, including Anniston's Grace Church (Lee Shafer); All Saints, Homewood (Glenda Curry); and Holy Comforter, Montgomery (Drake Whitelaw). However, the clearest and most visible symbol of the acceptance of women's ordination by the national church membership was the election in 2006 of Nevada's bishop, Katharine Jefferts Schori, as the twenty-sixth Presiding Bishop of the Episcopal Church, the first woman to lead the Episcopal Church, and the first woman to lead a province, making her the functional American equivalent of the Archbishop of Canterbury. Significantly, the runner-up in 2006 was Alabama's bishop, Henry Nutt Parsley Jr.[4]

Unfinished Business from the Time of Bishop Cobbs

The first task of Alabama's Episcopalians in the post-Carpenter era was completion of a project first put forward by Bishop Cobbs: dividing the Diocese of Alabama into smaller and more manageable units. Cobbs proposed that Alabama be divided into three dioceses corresponding to its three largest cities in his day: Huntsville, Montgomery, and Mobile. But in 1970 the dioceses of Alabama and Florida were divided to create the Diocese of the Central Gulf Coast. The new diocese consisted of the lower third of Alabama (from the northern boundaries of Barbour, Pike, Crenshaw, Butler, Wilcox, Clarke and Choctaw Counties) and the panhandle of Florida (from the western boundaries of Jackson, Calhoun, and Gulf Counties). The longer-serving of the bishops of the two founding dioceses, Bishop Juhan of Florida, had the right to become bishop of the new diocese if he so chose, but he declined, and Alabama's Bishop Murray elected to become the first bishop of the Central Gulf Coast. The new diocese had fifty-seven congregations, forty-seven ordained clergy, 17,853 baptized members, and 11,732 communicants. Its first budget was for $299,370.[5]

When Murray became the first bishop of the Diocese of the Central Gulf Coast, the much-needed task of updating the Diocese of Alabama fell to Furman Charles Stough, rector of Florence's Trinity Church, who became Alabama's eighth bishop. Stough guided Alabama's Episcopalians from 1970 to 1988, successfully negotiating women's ordination and Prayer Book revision. In the South in general and in Alabama in particular, style is as important as substance, and even though Stough held liberal opinions on such issues as women's ordination, the death penalty, and Prayer Book revision, his deep Alabama roots and folksy manner helped hold the Diocese of Alabama together.

Stough proved to be a bishop of energy, vision, and, above all, ambition. His accomplishments were manifold, but five stand out: the establishment of a companion diocese relationship with the Diocese of Namibia in South Africa; the building of Episcopal Place, housing for the low-income elderly; the "setting apart" of the Church of the Advent as the diocesan cathedral; the creation of the "Alabama plan" of stewardship; and his run for Presiding Bishop of the Episcopal Church.

After the 1960s, it was essential for the Diocese of Alabama to adopt a more progressive attitude on racial issues. At the very beginning, Stough signaled that he would be more liberal on this issue by choosing a black priest—Vernon Jones, rector of St. Andrew's, Tuskegee—to be a member of the party that presented him for consecration as a bishop. In 1987 Stough also ordained Colenzo Hubbard, the first black priest in the Diocese of Alabama since Bishop Carpenter ordained Robert DuBose in 1953. Even more significant in the area of racial reconciliation was Stough's establishment of a companion diocese relationship with the Diocese of Namibia. Between 1978 and 1988, the Diocese of Alabama contributed more than $400,000 to the Diocese of Namibia. Stough exchanged visits with Bishop James Kauluma of Namibia, and delegations of young people and adults from Alabama also visited Namibia. Namibian students, with support from the Diocese of Alabama, studied at Tuskegee University and Birmingham-Southern College.[6]

Another large project that was launched and completed while Stough was bishop was Episcopal Place I and II, apartment buildings for elderly people with low incomes. Apartments for elderly folks of low and moderate income had been talked about as far back as 1968. An article in the *Birmingham News* on February 29, 1968, titled "Church to Build High Apartments," discussed a $3.2 million proposal by the Church of the Advent to build apartments for the elderly. Evidently, Stough contacted the Department of Housing and Urban Development (HUD) regarding the possibility of receiving federal money to build housing for the elderly, because in February 1975, he received a letter from the Department of Housing and Urban Development in response to his interest in "HUD-assisted housing for the elderly and handicapped." Then Stough brought the idea of building housing for the elderly to the diocesan council in September 1975, the council then endorsed it unanimously. Stough subsequently invited the rectors and senior wardens of Jefferson County parishes to become involved in the project. The US Department of Housing and Urban Development notified Stough in September 1977 that the diocese's application had been accepted and that they would receive a $2.5 million loan for the construction of housing for low-income elderly people. Construction on Episcopal Place began in November 1979.[7]

Furman Stough became well known in the Episcopal Church because of the "Alabama Plan," a program that helped church members understand the spiritual significance of being good stewards of their financial resources and giving a percentage of their income to the church. Throughout the 1970s and '80s, Alabama had the highest level of giving per household in the Episcopal Church. Partly because of the success of the Alabama Plan, Stough was one of four nominees for Presiding Bishop in 1985, but the election went to Stough's close friend, Edmond Browning, bishop of Hawaii. In 1988, Browning tapped Stough to head the Presiding Bishop's Fund (now Episcopal Relief and Development), and the Alabama bishop retired as leader of the Diocese of Alabama and moved to New York for several years.[8]

Another of Bishop Cobbs's dreams deferred was of a cathedral for the Diocese of Alabama. Cobbs had hoped to construct a grand new church to serve as cathedral, but this was financially impossible in the last years before the Civil War and was no more feasible in the late twentieth century. On February 12, 1982, Presiding Bishop John Maury Allin oversaw the "setting apart" of the Cathedral Church of the Advent. The Advent's physical size, its location in the center of Alabama's largest city, its proximity to Carpenter House, and the size and social prominence of its congregation all made its choice as the cathedral almost inevitable.[9]

Building a New Diocese

In a way, George Murray's task may have been somewhat easier than Stough's. Even though the Diocese of the Central Gulf Coast had inherited traditions from both of its parent dioceses, Murray had a unique opportunity to shape a new diocese. A part of the legacy inherited by the Diocese of the Central Gulf Coast was Wilmer Hall, the oldest significant social welfare institution Alabama Episcopalians created. Another part of its heritage was Beckwith Lodge, the hunting and fishing lodge that Bishop Beckwith had bequeathed to the Diocese of Alabama. Murray set to work immediately to expand Wilmer Hall but worked even more enthusiastically to create a diocesan camp at Beckwith Lodge. Created in 1959, Beckwith Lodge was initially used for small group meetings and short-term conferences. In 1971 the Diocese of the Central Gulf Coast declared Beckwith Lodge to be its camp and conference center. In 1973 fifty children attended five summer camps at Beckwith, and the diocese spent $153,000 on property improvements and recreational equipment. By 1994 Beckwith Lodge was hosting 630 campers at eleven sessions, and Bishop Duvall dedicated a new chapel in 1986. Because of her background as a professor of oceanography before becoming a priest, Presiding Bishop Katharine Jefferts Schori showed a special interest in Weeks Bay and the estuary when she visited Beckwith in 2009. By 2010 Beckwith Lodge consisted of eighty-two acres, with eight hundred feet of beach and shoreline, and could accommodate up to two hundred people in a combination of dorms and "motel" rooms.[10]

Charles F. Duvall, rector of the Church of the Advent, Spartanburg, South Carolina, became the second bishop of the Central Gulf Coast in 1981. Under Duvall's leadership the Diocese of the Central Gulf Coast pursued a series of projects and policies somewhat parallel to those of the Diocese of Alabama. While Duvall served as bishop of the Central Gulf Coast, that diocese initiated a companion diocese relationship with the Diocese of Guatemala and successfully completed a $2.5 million capital campaign. Like the Diocese of Alabama, Episcopalians in the Diocese of the Central Gulf Coast were similarly concerned with housing for the elderly. In 1977 they acquired the Ladies' Benevolent Home in Mobile and renovated it to become a forty-one-apartment assisted-living facility. Bishop Duvall dedicated it on November 4, 1998, and renamed it Murray House to honor the first bishop of the Central Gulf Coast. The Diocese of the Central Gulf Coast reached out to other places in the developing world, also establishing a companion diocese relationship with Episcopalians in the Dominican Republic.[11]

In 2001, Philip Duncan, the dean of St. Matthew's Cathedral in Dallas, Texas, became the third bishop of the Diocese of the Central Gulf Coast. A highlight of Duncan's time as bishop occurred in 2003 when the Diocese of the Central

Gulf Coast designated Mobile's Christ Church as its cathedral. Even more than Birmingham's Church of the Advent, there was an inevitability about making the Mobile church a cathedral: It was home to the second oldest Episcopalian congregation in Alabama; it was in Christ Church, Mobile, that the first convention of the diocese was held in 1830; and it was there that Nicholas Hamner Cobbs delivered his first diocesan address in 1845. Thus, the church that might legitimately be termed the "mother church" of the Episcopal Church in Alabama became Alabama's second Episcopalian cathedral.

New Challenges

In June 1988, the Diocese of Alabama elected Robert Oran Miller to serve as the ninth bishop of Alabama. A former United Methodist minister, Miller exemplified the trend of clergy from other traditions entering the Episcopal Church. Miller's episcopacy also coincided with the crest of the first wave of the AIDS pandemic in Alabama. Ever the compassionate pastor, Miller formed a diocesan AIDS taskforce and encouraged parishes to reach out to people infected with and affected by HIV.

Henry Nutt Parsley Jr., rector of Christ Church, Charlotte, North Carolina, was elected bishop coadjutor in 1996 and succeeded Bishop Miller when he retired in 1999. Parsley became the third bishop of Alabama to run unsuccessfully for the office of Presiding Bishop. Parsley's achievements included a successful capital campaign (ACTS 2) that raised just over $6 million; the building of the Chapel of St. Francis at Camp McDowell; and construction of Trinity Commons, a new home for campus ministry to Birmingham area colleges.

In the late twentieth century, Alabama Episcopalians also began to reach out to Alabama's burgeoning Latino population. In 1999 Bishop Parsley invited Onell A. Soto, former bishop of Venezuela, to serve as his assistant and charged him with developing ministries to Latinos. Then in 2000, the diocese hired its first Hispanic missioner, Ernesto Obregon. But even before Bishop Soto and Father Obregon came to Alabama, Christ Church, Albertville, and Grace Church, Birmingham (Woodlawn), had begun developing ministries to the increasing numbers of Latinos living and working in the state.

In 2002 the Diocese of Alabama elected a new bishop suffragan, Mark Handley Andrus, a Virginia priest, but in 2006, Andrus was selected to lead the Diocese of California as its eighth bishop. To replace Andrus, the diocese chose John McKee Sloan, rector of St. Thomas, Huntsville. Presiding Bishop Katharine Jefferts Schori was the principal consecrator at Sloan's ordination to the office of bishop at a service at the Cathedral Church of the Advent.

The Presiding Bishop, whom many Alabama Episcopalians perceived to be considerably more liberal than they, charmed the people of the Diocese of Alabama during her three-day visit and disarmed many skeptics. In addition to Sloan's ordination, she met with the clergy and laypeople at separate events and preached and celebrated the Eucharist at St. John's for the Deaf, as well as at St. Stephen's, Cahaba Heights. During the announcements at Sloan's ordination, the congregation rose and gave Bishop Jefferts Schori at least a thirty-second standing ovation. The last weekend of May 2009, Bishop Jefferts Schori also made an extensive pastoral visit to the Diocese of the Central Gulf Coast, meeting with the campers at Camp Beckwith, the children at Wilmer Hall, and the residents of Murray House. She visited seven churches (including St. Anna's, the parish church built to serve the Creek Indians of Atmore); celebrated the Eucharist twice; dedicated the new parish house at St. Paul's, Daphne, and a Habitat for Humanity house built for refugees from Sudan; and met with civic and ecumenical leaders following Evensong at Christ Church Cathedral. While at Wilmer Hall, dancers from Good Shepherd, Mobile, Alabama's oldest African American parish, entertained her.[13]

The terrorist attacks of September 11, 2001, occurred during the episcopates of Bishops Parsley of Alabama and Duncan of the Central Gulf Coast. At the Diocesan Convention following the attacks, Parsley said, "We must build bridges, not walls. We must be instruments of peace. . . . This is how God is calling us to join with him in 'making all things new' out of the tragedy of September 11." Bishop Duncan of the Diocese of the Central Gulf Coast made similar remarks when his diocese gathered for its convention in February 2012. He told the delegates of a cross fashioned from debris collected at Ground Zero, bearing the Spanish words *Construir de nuevo mi mundo* (Build my world anew). Duncan went on: "There is no going back, there never has been. But there is our moving forward with Christ who embraces us with arms of love."[14]

Gays and Lesbians Seek Full Inclusion in the Episcopal Church

In the late 1980s and 1990s, the movement for the full inclusion of gays and lesbians in the Episcopal Church began to surge. Although the 1930 Lambeth Conference discussed homosexuality in purely negative terms, the tone was very different when the 1978 Lambeth Conference called for "deep and dispassionate study of the question of homosexuality, which would take seriously the teaching of Scripture and the results of scientific and medical research." During these and subsequent years gay and lesbian people were actively working for full acceptance, but dispassionate study would prove difficult.

A major milestone was New York bishop Paul Moore's 1977 ordination of the Episcopal Church's first openly lesbian priest, Ellen Barrett. A subsequent meeting of the House of Bishops in Port St. Lucie, Florida, stopped just short of censuring Bishop Moore for Barrett's ordination. With the Standing Committee's approval, Robert Miller, the ninth bishop of Alabama, began ordaining openly gay but celibate clergy in 1992, and Henry Parsley, the tenth bishop of Alabama continued this practice. In 1994, gay and lesbian Episcopalians organized a chapter of Integrity, the Episcopal Church's gay/lesbian support organization. [15]

A watershed event in this ongoing debate was the acquittal in 1996 of Bishop Walter Righter following his ecclesiastical trial on heresy charges for ordaining a non-celibate gay man. However, two years later gay rights advocates were dealt a setback at the 1998 Lambeth Conference. Alabama's bishop coadjutor, Henry Parsley, served on a subcommittee that prepared a resolution for the conference that affirmed that gays and lesbians were members of the body of Christ and advocated that the churches of the Communion "listen to the experience of homosexual people," but advised against blessing same-sex unions and ordaining those in them. Nevertheless, it called "on all our people to minister pastorally and sensitively to all irrespective of sexual orientation" and condemned "irrational fear of homosexuals." However, on the last morning of the Lambeth Conference, an amendment to the resolution was presented that declared "homosexual practice" to be "incompatible with scripture." Bishops Miller and Parsley voted against the amendment, but when the conference voted in favor of amending the resolution, Miller and Parsley joined the rest of the bishops in voting for the amended resolution.

In 2003, the Diocese of New Hampshire elected Gene Robinson, a partnered gay man, as their bishop, and, amid considerable debate, the General Convention ratified his election. This precipitated a long controversy throughout the Anglican Communion, including the Episcopal Church. New Hampshire's choice of Robinson flew in the face of the Windsor Report, a document produced by a commission chaired by Irish Archbishop Robin Eames in 1994 that had recommended a moratorium on the ordination of partnered gay bishops and the blessing of same-sex couples but did not endorse disciplinary measures against the Episcopal Church. However, by the time of the 2008 Lambeth Conference the furor over gay issues had become considerably less intense, and no controversial resolutions were adopted.

The Diocese of Alabama's Bishop Parsley urged conservatives to remain in the Episcopal Church: "God needs us all and needs us together. . . . In some quarters there is a self-righteous and separatist spirit, which is not only un-Anglican but deadly to the mission of the Church. There are those who, whether in the name of a narrow orthodoxy or Biblical literalism or some other absolute, would separate us from one another. This is not the Spirit's work." Parsley supported the Windsor Report and also chaired the Theology Committee of the House of Bishops, which published several papers on these matters.[16]

In 2012, after years of study and dialogue, the General Convention meeting in Indianapolis approved a provisional rite for the blessing of committed same-sex relationships. General Convention also resolved to honor the diversity of opinions on these matters. Bishop John McKee Sloan, the eleventh bishop of Alabama, voted for the provisional rite, as did Bishop Parsley (who retired in 2011). After the convention Bishop Sloan said that he would not approve its use in the Diocese of Alabama until a period of study and conversation was held in the diocese. In contrast, Bishop Duncan of the Diocese of the Central Gulf Coast voted against the rite but said that he would allow its use on a case-by-case basis.

Not all the leaders of the Episcopal Church in Alabama held conservative views on homosexuality. When Roy Moore, the chief justice of the Alabama Supreme Court, wrote an opinion denying a lesbian mother custody of her three children, he asserted that homosexuality was not only an "inherent evil" but that it was "abhorrent, immoral, detestable, a crime against nature and a violation of the laws of nature and of nature's God." Alabama's bishop suffragan, Marc Andrus, responded by bringing Archbishop Desmond Tutu to the Cathedral Church of the Advent. In his sermon, Tutu said that "all of the peoples of the world are part of God's family . . . rich and poor, *gay and straight*; black, brown, white, and red; Palestinian, Arab, and Jew; people of Iraq, Afghanistan, South Africa, and Israel. 'All are God's people . . . ALL . . . ALL . . . ALL . . . ALL!'"[17]

Alabama's Episcopal Churches React to Change

Even before Robinson's election to the episcopacy, the Episcopal Church's attitude toward homosexuality had been one of the reasons given for the splitting of Christ Church, Mobile. In 1993, Christ Church called Tim Smith to be their rector. A lawyer prior to entering the seminary, Smith was rector of tiny St. Joseph's-on-the-Mountain, Mentone, when called to the venerable Mobile parish. Soon contemporary music replaced traditional hymns, services lasted as long as two hours, worshipers were raising their hands in praise, and Smith began to voice concerns about the liberal theology of the Episcopal Church. On Sunday, October 1, 2000, a majority of those present at a congregational meeting voted to leave the Episcopal Church. Smith said, "The time had come to disassociate ourselves from a denomination that had drifted from its Anglican roots." A few months earlier at the General Convention in Denver, the Episcopal Church had called for clergy to offer pastoral care to gay and lesbian couples as well as to heterosexuals. Smith was especially critical of the Episcopal Church's tolerance of gays and lesbians: "The encouragement of lifestyles that are clearly contrary to holy scripture cannot be pleasing to God. We believe that Christianity should offer forgiveness and healing and not acceptance and toleration of that which God's word deplores." Smith and his congregation joined the Anglican Mission in America, a conservative group receiving episcopal leadership from the Provinces of Southeast Asia and Rwanda. However, when the Diocese of the Central Gulf Coast sued to retain Christ Church, Mobile, the courts ruled in favor of the diocese.[18]

A similar scenario played out at Montgomery's Church of the Ascension. In October 1990, Ascension called a new rector—John Michael Van Dyke of Hilton Head, South Carolina. Van Dyke had already begun moving the parish in a more conservative direction, but (as for many conservatives) New Hampshire's choice of Gene Robinson to be their bishop was the catalyst for drastic action. After the General Convention ratified Robinson's election, Van Dyke called the vote "a daunting turn of events, though not unforeseen." On April 10, 2005, Van Dyke told the congregation of his decision to leave the Episcopal Church. An article about the split in the *Montgomery Advertiser* the next day led many to conclude that the newspaper had been notified in advance of Van Dyke's decision to leave the church. Under the episcopal authority of the Province of Rwanda, Van Dyke and many of Ascension's parishioners started a new parish—Christ Church XP. Ascension, however, not only survived the departure of Van Dyke and his followers but even thrived. The parish celebrated its centennial in 2008 and hosted the Diocesan Convention in 2009. According to Bishop Parsley, "after a difficult time of conflict . . . it has emerged stronger than ever with a new unity and abundant spirit."[19]

Another church, Montgomery's Christ the Redeemer, became so fragmented that it had to close its doors. Christ the Redeemer was formed in 1980 when a group of Episcopalians in Montgomery began to meet together in the city's rapidly growing eastern area, and in 1981, Bishop Stough approved the formation of the new parish. From the very beginning they self-identified as a theologically conservative parish and as a "renewal church" with charismatic tendencies. Christ the Redeemer soon established itself as a strongly charismatic parish where speaking in tongues, "prophecies," "faith healing," and "being slain in the spirit" were commonplace. However, Christ the Redeemer also seems to have been the first predominantly white parish to welcome the leadership of a black priest. In 1990, Vernon Jones, the retired rector of St. Andrew's, Tuskegee, began to help out with services at Christ the Redeemer and served as interim priest in 1994–95 and again in 1999–2000. In 2005, Christ the Redeemer's rector, Doug McCurry, who had become estranged from the Episcopal Church because of what he perceived as doctrinal irregularities and the issue of homosexuality, began a surreptitious campaign to lobby members of the church to leave the diocese. According to Julian McPhillips, "McCurry wasn't just looking after the 'spiritual well-being' of this flock. He was also trying to make sure that his new church . . . would be on solid financial footing." After McCurry and a large number of members left the church,

Christ the Redeemer struggled on until officially being declared dormant by the 2007 convention of the Diocese of Alabama.[20]

St. Luke's, Birmingham, also split, although its division had more to do with a change in priestly leadership than with theology. From 1987 to 2000, John Claypool served as St. Luke's rector. Claypool, identified by *Time* magazine as one of America's best preachers, had had a stellar career as a Southern Baptist but switched to the Episcopal Church after his divorce and remarriage. Anyone would have had a difficult time following Claypool, but his immediate successor, Douglas Richnow, proved to be a particularly ill-equipped choice. St. Luke's was already a diverse group before Claypool's arrival, and his reputation drew many newcomers to the parish. Claypool's charm and eloquence enabled him to hold together people of very different backgrounds and theological opinions, but this was not the case with Richnow. The former senior associate rector of St. John the Divine in Houston, Texas, Richnow had no experience as a rector, and some perceived his management style as abrasive. One parishioner described his attitude as "authoritarian, divisive, and win-lose." Another was alienated by his "'Jerry Falwell sermon' delineating the faults of our country" and an address in which he said, "Christians should not be so tolerant of other religions." On the other hand, another parishioner praised Richnow as a caring pastor and was impressed by his "dynamic and inclusive personality." The differences of opinion and conflicting perceptions of Richnow triggered an escalating series of crises. After less than a year at St. Luke's, Richnow resigned and a large group of St. Luke's members left, many of them forming St. Peter's Anglican Church under the authority of the Anglican Mission in America.[21]

Although it did not split, the Cathedral Church of the Advent veered sharply rightward while Paul F. M. Zahl was its dean from 1995 to 2004. A scholar with impressive credentials, Zahl received his D.Theol. from Germany's University of Tübingen, where he was a student of Jürgen Moltmann, one of the twentieth century's most important theologians. When the General Convention ratified the election of Gene Robinson as bishop of New Hampshire in 2003, Zahl hoisted a black flag of protest above the cathedral. A year later Trinity School for Ministry in Ambridge, Pennsylvania, the most conservative of the Episcopal Church's seminaries, elected Zahl to serve as its dean and president. The cathedral continued its tilt to the right when it called Frank Limehouse, a conservative South Carolina priest, to succeed Zahl as dean.[22]

Lay Leadership in Alabama

Alabama Episcopalians continued to serve in important leadership positions. George Seibels, mayor of Birmingham from 1967 to 1975, was an active member of the Church of the Advent. Champ Lyons, elected to serve on Alabama's Supreme Court in 2000 and reelected in 2006, was a member of Christ Church, Mobile, but left with the exodus Tim Smith led to form a more conservative parish. Alabama's first openly gay elected official, Patricia Todd, and her partner were members of Grace Church, Birmingham (Woodlawn), at the time of her election to the Alabama House of Representatives in 2006.

One of the highest profile lay leaders of the Episcopal Church nationally is Vince Currie of the Diocese of the Central Gulf Coast. A lay delegate to the Primary Convention of the Diocese of the Central Gulf Coast, Currie also served as a member of the diocese's Standing Committee and as diocesan treasurer. On the national level, Currie was a lay deputy to the General Convention of 1976; served in the House of Deputies as chair of the Committee on Program, Budget, and Finance; and then was elected vice president of the House of Deputies. He went on to be elected to the Executive Council of the Episcopal Church, and has served on the board of trustees of the Church Pension Fund. At the beginning of Bishop Charles Duvall's tenure, Currie joined the diocesan staff as administrative assistant to the bishop, a title later changed to diocesan administrator. At the request of Bishop Duncan, he has continued to serve in this office.[23]

In the last quarter of the twentieth century, the Alabama Episcopalian with the highest profile was probably Governor Fob James. Although one of the smallest Protestant groups in the state, Episcopalians served as governors of Alabama for one-fifth of the twentieth century: Charles Henderson from 1915 to 1919; Thomas Erby Kilby from 1919 to 1923; Gordon Persons from 1951 to 1955; and Forrest "Fob" James Jr., from 1979 to 1983 as a Democrat and from 1995 to 1999 as a Republican. All four were successful businessmen, but each left a unique legacy. Henderson was a foe of Prohibition and an advocate of public health and literacy, Kilby unsuccessfully opposed convict leasing but managed to secure improved conditions for prisoners, and Gordon Persons's leadership made Alabama a pioneer in public broadcasting when it became the first state to create an Educational Television Commission. James, however, is the most enigmatic of the four. Elected in 1979, he was, like Henderson, Kilby, and Persons, a successful businessman, but unlike his predecessors James found it difficult to translate the skills that had made him successful in business into those necessary to succeed as an elected official. Even though he could have been reelected, James chose to leave the governor's office in 1983 and return to business. But in 1995, James ran again (this time as a Republican) and was elected to another term as governor of Alabama.[24]

James's career as governor illuminates some of the stresses and strains that affected both the ecclesiastical and civil polity in the late twentieth century. Religion played a significant role in James's two terms as governor. On January 7, 1979, Emanuel Church, Opelika, where James had been a vestry member, held a special prayer service for the governor-elect, and on the morning of his first inauguration Bishop Stough presided at a service of Holy Eucharist at St. John's, Montgomery, with two of James's sons serving as acolytes and other family members reading the scripture lessons. But James and his wife, Bobbie, appeared to be significantly more conservative than most of their fellow Alabama Episcopalians. During his first term, the Alabama legislature passed a bill to encourage voluntary prayer in the public schools. Included in the bill was a prayer written by the governor's son, Fob James III. In his second term, James supported Gadsden judge Roy Moore when a US district judge ordered him to remove a plaque of the Ten Commandments from his courtroom and to cease beginning court with prayer. James also approved a change of policy in Alabama schools, requiring teachers to teach evolution as a theory, not as a fact. Bobbie was a charismatic who spoke in tongues, and the Jameses (especially Bobbie) were sympathetic to the Christian Zionist movement that believed that the establishment of the State of Israel in 1948 was the fulfillment of divine prophecy and heralded the beginning of an apocalyptic scenario that would conclude with the Second Coming. James made several trips to Israel to encourage business ties between Israel and Alabama.[25]

Two Leading Alabama Priests

Many of Alabama's Episcopal clergy made important local, regional, and national contributions. Among the most influential priests in the Episcopal Church in the late twentieth century are two Alabama priests who could not be more different from each other: Mary Adelia McLeod and Charles H. Murphy III. McLeod made history when she became the first woman elected to serve as a diocesan bishop. Prior to ordination, McLeod was involved in a wide range of civic activities as a volunteer, including the Junior League; the Birmingham Music Club; and St. Luke's, Birmingham. Ordained both deacon and priest in 1980, McLeod and her husband, also a priest, served St. Timothy's in Athens. The McLeods went on to serve St. John's in Charleston, West Virginia, an urban parish with extensive ministries to the poor. In 1993, McLeod was elected the ninth bishop of Vermont, the first woman to serve as a diocesan bishop and the third woman to serve as a bishop in the Episcopal Church. While serving as bishop of Vermont, McLeod was a leading advocate of gay rights and testified before Vermont's House and Senate judiciary committees in support of that state's Civil Union Bill. McLeod retired at the beginning of 2001.[26]

In 1975, Bishop Stough ordained Charles H. Murphy III, who was subsequently called as rector of All Saints, Pawleys Island, South Carolina, in 1982. While at All Saints, Murphy felt increasingly alienated from the Episcopal Church because of its liberal theology. In September 1997, Murphy brought together a group of conservative clergy who declared that the Episcopal Church had failed to fulfill the "first promise" of the vows ordained clergy take: to uphold "the doctrine, discipline and worship of Christ."[27] Subsequently, Murphy and John H. Rodgers Jr., former dean of Trinity Episcopal School for Ministry, were ordained bishops. A few months later, Murphy and Rogers organized the Anglican Mission in America (AMiA). Four more bishops were ordained in Denver in June 2001. Murphy, Rodgers, and the other AMiA bishops were given the task of reevangelizing the Episcopal Church and planting new churches. The AMiA repudiated the authority of the Episcopal Church and placed itself under the discipline of Emmanuel Kolini, the Archbishop of Rwanda. Murphy claimed that such an extraordinary breach of Anglican order and tradition was justified because of the Episcopal Church's departure from orthodoxy. By 2005 the AMiA claimed to represent nearly forty parishes and more than five thousand Episcopalians. However, on January 28, 2012, the *Tennessean* reported that the AMiA had broken with the Anglican church of Rwanda and that twenty of the AMiA's 152 congregations had broken away.[28]

Growing through the Changes

In spite of the turmoil in the church and the world, the late twentieth century was also a time of tremendous growth for Alabama's Episcopal churches. Aided by the rapid development of the Alabama and Florida Gulf coasts, the Diocese of the Central Gulf Coast grew by 63 percent in its first thirty years, from about twelve thousand communicants in 1970 to about nineteen thousand in 2000. Starting with fifty-seven congregations in 1970, the Central Gulf Coast had sixty-seven by 2000. And the budget of the new diocese went from almost $300,000 in 1970 to almost $2 million in 2000. Furthermore, since 1970, eighteen congregations have been founded in the Diocese of Alabama, and the Diocese of the Central Gulf Coast has started four congregations in Alabama. It has also been a time of decline for some parishes, and a few have been closed. The parishes that have closed in the Diocese of Alabama are St. Michael's in Birmingham's Center Point neighborhood; St. John's, Ensley; Christ the Redeemer in Montgomery; and Trinity, Union Springs. The Diocese of the Central Gulf Coast has only closed one church in Alabama—St. Mary's, Evergreen.[29]

Since 1970, membership in the Episcopal Church has decreased from just over 3.5 million to just over 2 million. In the same period, the number of Episcopalians in Alabama has increased from approximately 33,200 to approximately 51,200, although the number of Episcopalians as a percentage of the state's population has remained virtually the same. In spite of the fact that Episcopalians in Alabama have defied national trends, it has been a troubled time for the Episcopal Church in Alabama. Large, wealthy, and influential churches in both the Diocese of Alabama and the Diocese of the Central Gulf Coast have divided. However, it has also been a time of building. Both Alabama dioceses have launched ministries to address the needs of low-income elderly people and have reached out to the developing world. The Episcopal Church has dramatically shifted its course, and its membership has decreased alarmingly. Although the overall secularization of North America is responsible for much of this loss, the Episcopal Church's decisions to ordain women, revise the Prayer Book, open the priesthood and episcopate to gays and lesbians, as well as its embrace of a wide array of progressive or liberal causes, are also some of the reasons for the drop in membership.

Alabama Episcopalians have reacted in a variety of ways to the changes in the Episcopal Church. Some of have celebrated the Episcopal Church's change of course, some have resisted it, and some have simply dropped out. Alabama's Episcopal bishops have accepted the ordination of women and Prayer Book revision but have not fully accepted the Episcopal Church's embrace of gays and lesbians. Overall, the bishops who have led Alabama's Episcopal dioceses have advocated loyalty to the Episcopal Church but sought ways to ease the concerns of their more conservative members. The fact that both the Diocese of Alabama and the Diocese of the Central Gulf Coast have grown suggests that the bishops' strategy has been successful. The moderate course it followed in the last quarter of the twentieth century seems to have prepared the Episcopal Church in Alabama to face the challenges of its third century.

Conclusion

"Unto whomsoever much is given, of him shall much be required"

The legacy of the Episcopal Church in Alabama is rich: It has produced distinguished bishops and priests who have served their people and the wider community faithfully and well, and some have acquired national reputations. Alabama Episcopalians claim a proud tradition of eloquent and intelligent preaching, faithful pastoral care, and innumerable works of mercy. Although the members of the Episcopal Church in Alabama have never been more than a small percentage of the state's population, they have been overrepresented at the uppermost levels of Alabama's leadership. Those leaders include Governors John Gayle, Charles Henderson, Thomas Kilby, Gordon Persons, and Fob James; congressmen and senators such as William Lowndes Yancey, Frank Boykin, Hilary Herbert, and Oscar Underwood; educators such as Joab Thomas, Robert Witt, and Hudson Strode; business leaders such as Louis Willie; and artists, actors, writers, and musicians such as Octavia Walton LeVert, Zelda Sayre Fitzgerald, and Tallulah Bankhead.

This book began with the observation that Episcopalians have profoundly shaped Alabama history. The governors, legislators, congressmen, senators, academics, and the like who have belonged to the Episcopal Church seem to offer ample support for that observation. However, if in some sense the Episcopal Church produced Alabama, and if Episcopalians can claim a disproportionate share of Alabama's leaders, then they must also accept a disproportionate share of responsibility for the Alabama they have produced—a state that year after year and in study after study consistently ranks near the bottom of US states in quality-of-life indexes. It would be unfair to place too much blame on Episcopalians for Alabama's problems, but Alabama is the kind of state that favors the people who traditionally occupy the pews of the Episcopal Church: the well-to-do and powerful. In Alabama the burden of taxes falls more heavily on the poor than the affluent. Alabama's poorly funded schools penalize those who cannot afford to live in the wealthy suburbs where schools are well funded or who do not have the means to send their children to private schools.[1]

To whom much is given, much is also expected. What has the Episcopal Church contributed to Alabama? What have Episcopalians done to ameliorate Alabama's ills? Surprisingly, the Episcopal Church in Alabama has produced few significant institutions for the benefit of the wider community. Bishop McDowell recognized this in 1923:

> A distinctive mark of Christ and His Church is that they believe in "doing good," in every way they can, to every person they can. Hospitals, homes, schools, charities in the Name of the Master, are signs of a Church instinct with Christ's spirit of service. But this Diocese has no hospitals, only the Church Home [Wilmer Hall] at Spring Hill, St. Mark's School for Negroes, a few charitable enterprises of guilds and individuals, nearly all of which are allowed to drag out a difficult existence, amid the stolid indifference of the majority of our Church people. Compare and contrast with the institutions and good works of the other Christian communions about us.[2]

In the years since McDowell offered this observation, St. Mark's School has closed. However, the Diocese of Alabama founded St. Martin's in the Pines, a retirement community in Birmingham, as well as Episcopal Place I and II that provide housing for low-income elderly people in Birmingham. The Diocese of the Central Gulf Coast established Murray House, an assisted living facility in Mobile, and continues to maintain and support Wilmer Hall Children's Home in Mobile (although only Wilmer Hall and Episcopal Place could be called social service agencies). In contrast, Alabama's Baptists, Methodists, and Roman Catholics have produced a far more impressive institutional legacy: colleges such as Samford, Judson, the University of Mobile, Birmingham-Southern, Huntingdon, Southern Benedictine (now defunct), and Spring Hill Colleges; resources for health care, such as Baptist Health Systems in Birmingham and Montgomery, Carraway Hospital in Birmingham (also defunct), St. Vincent's Hospital in Birmingham, and Providence Hospital in Mobile; care for orphaned and abused children, such as Baptist Children's Homes in several places in Alabama, United Methodist Children's Home, and Catholic Social Services in several Alabama communities; and facilities for the elderly, such as Benedictine Manor in Cullman. To be fair, Episcopalians founded the University of the South and have continued to support it. Unlike almost every other Episcopalian college or university, Sewanee maintains a close relationship with the Episcopal Church and has a strong sense of its identity as an Episcopalian institution. Also, Episcopalians helped found Children's Hospital of Birmingham, although their association with it was very brief.

The absence of an impressive institutional legacy is another way in which the story of the Episcopal Church in Alabama is the story of the Episcopal Church in the United States writ small. To be sure, the Episcopal Church is the church of many of the signers of the Declaration of Independence, framers of the Constitution, and presidents of the United States. However, it has not been a great engine of social change. For the most part, Episcopalians did not play a constructive role in the greatest social and moral struggle of the nineteenth century—the battle to abolish slavery—and we do not have to look too far to understand why. In his book *The Social Sources of Denominationalism*, theologian H. Richard Niebuhr argues that although denominations insist they are the products of theological convictions, economic and social forces have played a greater role in shaping denominations than doctrine has. According to Niebuhr, the Episcopal Church is "the church of the English middle classes in the East" and "the church of the Southern plantation aristocracy." Just as the Church of England, the spiritual mother of the Episcopal Church, resisted the evangelical awakening associated with White-field and the Wesleys, so its offspring, the Episcopal Church, stayed "aloof from the vivid, popular religion of the frontier." Hence, "in Virginia it lost the border population to the Baptists, Methodists, and Presbyterians." But the Baptists and Methodists (and to a smaller degree the Presbyterians) were the religious groups who not only led the fight against slavery but also profoundly shaped the fabric of American life by building colleges, universities, hospitals and other institutions.[3]

The alliance between the Episcopal Church and the affluent and powerful also helps explain why (in Alabama, at least) the Episcopal Church almost completely failed in its attempt to bring the poor and the lower middle class into the church. Carl Henckell was a self-appointed missionary to the industrial and working-class neighborhoods of Birmingham, and yet, except for Grace Church, in the Wood-lawn area of Birmingham, all the churches he served—Christ Church, Avondale; Good Shepherd, East Lake; Trinity, West End; and others—have disappeared. Although St. Michael's and All Angels, Anniston, was founded as an Anglo-Catholic mission to the working class, it has never really served that purpose. In the late twentieth century, however, at the national level the Episcopal Church has tried to reposition itself as the champion of the poor and the marginalized. Many of its leaders were at the forefront of the civil rights movement and opposed the Vietnam War. Once known as "the Republican Party at prayer," the Episcopal

Church now more often resembles the left wing of the Democratic Party. However, in spite of its recently acquired social activism (some would say because of it), the Episcopal Church has been hemorrhaging members for the past forty years.[4] Once the Episcopal Church provided "chapels of ease" for the plantation owners and the industrialists; more recently, the Episcopal Church has tried to "rebrand" itself as the champion of the downtrodden. However, the heirs of the plantation owners and the industrialists are deserting the Episcopal Church, and the downtrodden are not filling their empty seats. The Episcopal Church may be on the side of the angels in the struggles against racism, sexism, homophobia, war, and capitalism without conscience, but the cost of siding with the angels is often martyrdom. However, there is no reason to think that the Episcopal Church would have thrived if it had not changed the Prayer Book, begun ordaining women, and embraced a more activist social agenda. Whatever the reason, the point is that the traditional constituents of the Episcopal Church (the affluent and powerful) are departing and they are not being replaced.[5]

As previously mentioned, the Episcopal Church in Alabama has never successfully attracted lower-middle-class or working-class people. Time after time, parishes in middle- and working-class neighborhoods have been started and have failed. As long as the Episcopal Church continues to attract the affluent and socially prominent, this does not present too big a problem. However, there are some signs that the well-to-do may be starting to desert the Episcopal Church. Following World War II the GI Bill gave veterans access to higher education that had previously only been available to the well-off. This boosted the finances and the status of many members of Baptist, Methodist, and Pentecostal churches. Some of them became Episcopalians as they rose in the world, but many did not. One disturbing trend is that the percentage of Alabamians with four years of college or more is increasing faster than the number of Episcopalians. Education has traditionally been a hallmark of Episcopalians, but statistics suggest that fewer Alabamians with a college education are joining the Episcopal Church.[6]

The Episcopal Church in Alabama claims a disproportionate share of Alabama's wealthiest, most powerful, and best-educated people, so why has it created so few institutions to serve other Alabamians? Is it reasonable to expect such a small percentage of Alabama's citizens to have created educational and medical facilities for the service of the state?

To understand why the "institutional legacy" of Episcopalians in Alabama is relatively negligible, we must return to the creation of the Diocese of Alabama. Fourteen years elapsed between the organization of the diocese and the election of the first bishop. The reason usually given for this hiatus is that Episcopalians could not raise the money to pay a bishop, but this will not bear close scrutiny. Alabama Episcopalians have not only been powerful, they have also been wealthy.

The 1843 *Diocesan Journal* says that "the cause of religion, as well as the growth of the church, demands that a bishop should be elected and consecrated as soon as the pecuniary condition of the parishes will enable the Diocese to fulfill, in good faith, the promise made to him, of a competent and permanent support." The same year, the convention set the bishop's salary at $2,000 "in connexion [*sic*] with a parochial charge" (i.e., if the bishop would also serve as a parish priest) or $1,200 "independently of such charge." But compared with the $12,000 to $15,000 that the vestry of Christ Church, Mobile, planned to spend on building a church in 1835, the proposed salary of the bishop seems small. Furthermore, the vestry of Christ Church, Mobile, also set its rector's salary at $2,500 and paid its organist $400. In 1829–30, Episcopalians in Huntsville pledged $4,500 to build the Church of the Nativity. St. John's, Montgomery, cost $6,000 to build in 1838; seventeen years later, New York architects Wills and Dudley (who also built Trinity, Mobile, and Nativity, Huntsville) built a new St. John's, twice as big as the old one, for $27,000. Alabama Episcopalians did not lack the financial resources to elect a bishop; either they lacked the will or did not see the necessity. Generally speaking, Alabama's Episcopalians have preferred to build churches rather than colleges or hospitals. They have favored parish outreach projects to those of the diocese and those of the diocese over the denomination. In other words, Alabama Episcopalians maintain control of their financial contributions by funding benevolent projects that are closer to home. Those farther away (or over which they have little control) are less likely to be funded.[7]

Another reason for the failure of Alabama Episcopalians to create much of an institutional legacy is that the very wealth and power they possess is a disincentive to create colleges and hospitals. Episcopalians can afford to send their children to the best universities and pay for first-rate health care, so there is little motivation to create colleges and hospitals. The structure of the Episcopal Church is also not very conducive to institution building. As historian John F. Woolverton notes, "Episcopalians . . . changed radically the inherited ideas about the episcopate by dismantling the medieval, hierarchical pretensions of that office. The church's laity and lower clergy were so successful in their efforts to divide episcopal sovereignty that, as a result, each bishop became the servant, not the lord, of the people within his diocese." In placing clergy, the bishop does little more than "advise and consent." Parishes call a rector, and the bishop routinely gives his blessing to their call. The weakness of the office of bishop means that the authority of the Episcopal Church's traditional constituents—the economic, social, and cultural elite, who are accustomed to giving orders, not taking them—will not be challenged, even in their church. It also means that there is no central authority that can direct and deploy the church's resources for the alleviation of human misery and for the well-being of the wider community.[8]

Finally, the theology of the Episcopal Church may work against the creation of institutions that significantly affect the quality of life. Hobart and his disciples (including Cobbs) believed the bishops of the Episcopal Church were heirs of the apostles and that their church was different in kind and not only in degree from other denominations. Thus Hobart and Cobbs discouraged participation in the evangelical "united front" that sought to encourage Bible reading, reform prisons, promote temperance, and culminated in abolitionism. Later in the nineteenth and twentieth centuries, Anglican theology came to be dominated by incarnationalism. From about the middle of the nineteenth century, Anglican theologians began to reorient their church's teaching away from the traditional Reformed focus on Christ's crucifixion and toward a new emphasis on God's incarnation in Christ as the primary metaphor for Christian theology. Incarnationalism stresses the goodness of the world and human nature rather than its fallenness and sees the incarnation as a reaffirmation of God's blessing on creation in the first chapter of Genesis.

Evangelical Protestants see the world as a dark and dangerous place, a battleground between good and evil. This is a theology that motivates them to "rescue the perishing." Roman Catholic theology sees the world in a similar way. The Episcopal Church, on the other hand, tends to see the world as a good place and God as a genial, grandfatherly figure. In other words, evangelicals and Roman Catholics believe in original sin; Episcopalians believe in "original goodness." If the world is good and God looks upon us with kindly interest, perhaps even winking at our indiscretions, what is there to motivate Episcopalians to engage in a massive rescue effort? Furthermore, a theology of "original goodness" confers a divine blessing on the status quo, not on the struggle to transform it.[9]

Although the Episcopal Church has produced an astonishing number of Alabama's leaders, these leaders have not really set the state's agenda. For the most part, Episcopalians have accommodated themselves to the spirit of the age and followed Alabama's cultural curve. One looks in vain for Episcopalians who spoke out against slavery, although in this they were no different from the rest of Alabama's white Christians. Instead, the chief pastor of Alabama's Episcopalians for most of the nineteenth century, Bishop Wilmer, praised slavery's benevolence and gave his wholehearted support to the South's Lost Cause. When coal and iron industries began to develop in the late nineteenth century, one finds few Episcopalians who addressed the ills of industrialization and urbanization. And when black Alabamians began to insist on equal rights, most of Alabama's Episcopalians remained silent and uninvolved, although exceptions abound.

The story of the Episcopal Church in Alabama is the story of the many who accommodated the culture, but it is no less the story of the brave handful in every generation who sought to build a different Alabama, one that more closely resembled "the city which has foundations, whose builder and maker is God."[10]

Dentist-turned-priest Carl Henckell practiced a ministry of healing and reached out to victims of alcohol and drug abuse, unwed mothers, and children in need of medical treatment. He assisted in the founding of Children's Hospital and tried to build and sustain working-class parishes in Birmingham. Edgar Gardner Murphy spoke out against child labor and won the praise of President Theodore Roosevelt. Augusta Bening Martin, who served poor whites on Sand Mountain in the 1920s and 1930s, was no less a missionary than Emma Jones had been in Shanghai a century earlier. Attorney and Episcopal layman Charles Morgan declared Birmingham "dead" when the Sixteenth Street Baptist Church bombing killed four little girls. When Alabama state troopers beat demonstrators marching for voting rights from Selma to Montgomery, Julian McPhillips rebuked the well-heeled congregation of St. Luke's, Mountain Brook, for not loving their neighbors as themselves, and with the passion of an Old Testament prophet, he denounced the verdict of a jury of white men who acquitted Tom Coleman for the murder of Jonathan Daniels.

If the Episcopal Church in Alabama has not done great things, it has certainly done beautiful things. The choice of Nicholas Hamner Cobbs to be the Diocese of Alabama's first bishop set the Episcopal Church in Alabama on a moderately high church course and created a theological climate favorable to the Gothic Revival movement (also referred to as neo-Gothic) in church architecture. The first and greatest phase of the growth of the Episcopal Church in Alabama coincided with the Gothic Revival, and the choice of New York architects Wills and Dudley (leaders in the Gothic Revival movement) to build the Church of the Nativity in Huntsville, St. John's in Montgomery, and Trinity in Mobile resulted in the creation of three of Alabama's most beautiful and architecturally distinguished churches. The Gothic Revival movement culminated in the work of Ralph Adams Cram, who created the Church of the Ascension in Montgomery, perhaps the "jewel in the crown" of Episcopal churches in Alabama. Furthermore, Alabama Episcopalians have resisted the "cultural curve" in establishing and maintaining dignified and stately worship according to the Book of Common Prayer. Although a theology of exclusion dominates in most of Alabama's churches, the Episcopal Church in Alabama has opened its arms in comprehension and welcome. To those scorched by the fires of revivalism or worn thin by the millstone of fundamentalism, the Episcopal Church in Alabama has been a haven of stately worship, thoughtful preaching, and architectural splendor. These are not small accomplishments.[11]

If the Episcopal Church is to thrive in the twenty-first century, however, it must retain the affluent and educated who have traditionally occupied its pews and at the same time extend its reach to those it has not succeeded in reaching in the past. If it does that, the third century of the Episcopal Church in Alabama will be its greatest.

Appendix A

Episcopal Churches in Alabama in Chronological Order

Year founded	Active*	Inactive	Church name	City	Notes
1828	x		Christ Church	Tuscaloosa	
1828	x		Christ Church	Mobile	Christ Episcopal Church in Mobile was organized in 1828, but it was part of a "union church" of Episcopalians, Methodists, and Presbyterians that dates back to 1822. It was made the cathedral of the Diocese of the Central Gulf Coast in 2005. See chapter 2 for further discussion of Christ Church, Mobile's founding.
1830	x		St. Paul's	Greensboro	
1831		x	Arcola Mission	Arcola, Marengo County	
1834	x		Nativity	Huntsville	
1834		x	St. Andrew's	Gallion	
1834	x		St. John's	Montgomery	
1834	x		St. John's (formerly St. John's-in-the-Prairies)	Forkland	St. John's-in-the-Prairies functioned from 1834 to 1865. The building was given to St. John's, Forkland, in 1878.

Continued on the next page

Year founded	Active*	Inactive	Church name	City	Notes
1834	x		St. Mark's (formerly St. Mark's, Fork of Greene)	Boligee	
1834	x		Trinity	Demopolis	
1836	x		St. Paul's	Selma	
1836	x		Trinity	Florence	
1837		x	Christ Church	Wetumpka	
1838	x		St. James	Eufaula	
1838		x	St. Mary's	Summerville	
1838	x		St. Paul's	Carlowville	
1838		x	St. Peter's	Lowndes County	
1838	x		St. Wilfrid's	Marion	
1838		x	Trinity	Lafayette	
1839	x		St. James	Livingston	
1839		x	St. John's	Tuscumbia	
1839		x	St. Luke's	Cahaba	
1843		x	St. David's	Dallas County	
1844	x		Holy Cross	Uniontown	
1844		x	Holy Cross	Woodville	
1844		x	St. John's in the Wilderness	Oswichee, Russell County	

Year founded	Active*	Inactive	Church name	City	Notes
1844	x		St. Luke's	Jacksonville	
1845		x	Advent	Tuskegee	
1845		x	Grace	Clayton	
1845	x		St. Stephen's	Eutaw	
1845	x		Trinity	Mobile	
1848	x		Holy Trinity	Auburn	
1850		x	St. Cyprian's	Oswichee, Russell County	
1850		x	St. John's	Elyton	
1850	x		St. Paul's	Mobile	
1850	x		St. Peter's	Talladega	
1851		x	St. Mary's	Tallassee	
1852		x	Calvary	Pushmataha	
1852	x		St. Michael's	Faunsdale	
1853	x		St. Alban's	Gainesville	
1853	x		St. John's	Mobile	
1853		x	St. Mary's	Camden	
1854	x		Good Shepherd	Mobile	This is the oldest predominantly black Episcopal church in Alabama.
1857	x		St. Paul's	Lowndesboro	
1858	x		Emmanuel	Opelika	
1858		x	St. James	Claiborne	

Continued on the next page

Year founded	Active*	Inactive	Church name	City	Notes
1859	x		St. Mark's	Prattville	
1859		x	St. Matthew's	Autaugaville	
1859	x		St. Thomas	Greenville	
1860	x		St. Andrew's	Montevallo	
1862		x	Grace	Trinity	
1864	x		Holy Comforter	Montgomery	
1865		x	St. Paul's	Whistler	
1867		x	St. Paul's	Decatur	
1868	x		St. Timothy's	Athens	
1869		x	St. Paul's	Tilden	
1870		x	St. Mary's	Evergreen	
1871		x	Christ Church	Piedmont	
1871		x	St. Andrew's	Hayneville	
1872	x		Advent	Birmingham	The Church of the Advent is Birmingham's oldest church and was Alabama's first cathedral. It was made the cathedral of the Diocese of Alabama in 1982.
1873		x	Trinity	Union Springs	
1876	x		St. Mark's	Troy	
1878	x		St. Peter's	Bon Secour	
1879	x		St. Luke's	Scottsboro	
1881	x		Grace	Anniston	

Year founded	Active*	Inactive	Church name	City	Notes
1886		x	St. Paul's	Coalburg	
1887	x		Grace	Sheffield	
1887	x		St. Mary's-on-the-Highlands	Birmingham	
1887	x		St. Michael and All Angels	Anniston	
1888	x		Holy Comforter	Gadsden	
1888		x	St. Elizabeth's	Letohatchee	
1889	x		Trinity	Bessemer	
1890		x	Christ Church	Avondale, Birmingham	
1890	x		Grace	Woodlawn, Birmingham	
1890	x		St. John's	Decatur	
1891	x		St. Mark's	Birmingham	
1893		x	Christ Church	Bridgeport	
1893		x	Grace	Mobile	
1893	x		Grace	Mt. Meigs	
1893		x	St. Andrew's	Oak Grove	
1893	x		St. James	Monroe County	
1893		x	St. John's	Ensley	
1893		x	St. Luke's	Point Clear	
1895		x	St. Thomas	Citronelle	

Continued on the next page

Year founded	Active*	Inactive	Church name	City	Notes
1895		x	Trinity	Alpine	
1896	x		St. Andrew's	Sylacauga	
1896		x	St. James	Eliska	
1898		x	Black's Chapel	Adamsville	
1898		x	Blossburg Mission	Blossburg	
1898		x	Brookside Mission	Brookside	
1898		x	Cardiff Valley Mission	Cardiff Valley	
1899		x	Lewisburg Mission	Lewisburg	
1900	x		Good Shepherd	Montgomery	
1900	x		Trinity	Atmore	
1902		x	St. Alban's	Loxley	
1902		x	St. Mark's	Barnwell	
1902		x	St. Mary the Virgin	Pell City	
1902		x	St. Paul's Chapel	Magnolia Springs	
1904	x		St. Andrew's	Birmingham	
1905		x	Christ Church	Burnsville	
1905	x		Epiphany	Guntersville	
1905	x		Nativity	Dothan	
1906		x	St. Phillip's	Birmingham	
1907		x	All Saints	Birmingham	
1908	x		Immanuel	Bay Minette	

Year founded	Active*	Inactive	Church name	City	Notes
1909	x		All Saints	Mobile	
1909	x		Ascension	Montgomery	
1909		x	St. Mary's	Pinedale	
1910		x	Trinity	West End, Birmingham	
1911		x	St. John the Evangelist	Robertsdale	
1911		x	St. Mark's	Toulminville	
1912	x		St. Andrew's	Tuskegee	
1912		x	St. Paul's	Irvington	
1913		x	Trinity	Clanton	
1914		x	Berlin Mission	Berlin, Dallas County	
1915		x	Good Shepherd	Birmingham	
1917	x		Trinity	Alpine	
1919		x	St. Mark's	Oakman	
1920	x		St. James	Fairhope	
1922		x	Resurrection	Anniston	
1922	x		St. John's	Monroeville	
1922	x		St. Mary's	Jasper	
1922	x		St. Stephen's	Glennville	
1924	x		St. Paul's	Foley	

Continued on the next page

Year founded	Active*	Inactive	Church name	City	Notes
1926		x	Redeemer	Anniston	
1926	x		St. Paul's	Daphne	
1929	x		All Saints	Homewood	
1929	x		Christ Church	Fairfield	
1929	x		St. Anna's	Atmore	
1929		x	St. John's	Atmore	
1929		x	St. Peter's	Decatur	
1930		x	St. Luke's in the Pines	Mobile	
1935	x		St. John's for the Deaf	Birmingham	
1936		x	Incarnation	Mobile	
1937		x	Epiphany	Anniston	
1942	x		Holy Cross	Trussville	
1946	x		Trinity	Wetumpka	
1946	x		St. James	Alexander City	
1947		x	St. Mary's	Andalusia	
1948	x		St. Mark's for the Deaf	Mobile	St. Mark's, Toulminville, became St. Mark's for the Deaf.
1949	x		Grace	Cullman	
1949	x		St. Luke's	Birmingham	
1949	x		St. Mary's	Childersburg	
1949		x	St. Michael's	Chickasaw	
1950		x	St. Stephen's	Brewton	

Year founded	Active*	Inactive	Church name	City	Notes
1951	x		Canterbury Chapel	Tuscaloosa	
1952		x	Epiphany	Enterprise	
1952		x	St. Peter's	Jackson	
1953	x		St. Michael's and All Angels	Millbrook	
1953	x		Ascension	Vestavia Hills	
1954		x	Holy Cross	Huntsville	Merged with St. Christopher's in 1976 to form a new parish.
1954	x		St. Matthew's in-the-Pines	Seale	
1954		x	St. Barnabas	Roanoke	
1955		x	Resurrection	Phenix City	
1955	x		St. Phillip's	Fort Payne	
1955		x	St. Michael's	Birmingham	
1956		x	St. Andrew's	Mobile	
1957	x		All Saints	Montgomery	
1957	x		St. Dunstan's	Auburn	
1957		x	St. Michael's	Ozark	
1958	x		St. Thomas	Huntsville	
1959		x	St. Luke's	Mobile	
1960		x	St. Matthew's	Mobile	
1961	x		St. Alban's	Hoover	

Continued on the next page

Year founded	Active*	Inactive	Church name	City	Notes
1961		x	St. Christopher's	Huntsville	Merged with Holy Cross in 1976 to form a new parish.
1961	x		St. Matthias	Tuscaloosa	
1962	x		St. Bartholomew's	Florence	
1963	x		St. Stephen's	Huntsville	
1964		x	St. Mary's-by-the-Sea	Coden	
1969		x	Transfiguration	Birmingham	
1971	x		St. Joseph's-on-the-Mountain	Mentone	
1972	x		Resurrection	Rainbow City	
1975	x		St. Simon	Pell City	
1975		x	St. Mary's	Dadeville	
1976	x		Holy Cross/St. Christopher's	Huntsville	
1978	x		Christ Church	Albertville	
1979	x		St. Francis	Dauphin Island	
1980	x		Messiah	Heflin	
1980		x	Christ the Redeemer	Montgomery	
1980	x		Epiphany	Leeds	
1980	x		St. Francis	Indian Springs	
1981	x		Redeemer	Mobile	
1984	x		Holy Spirit	Gulf Shores	
1984		x	St. Peter's	Dallas County	

Year founded	Active*	Inactive	Church name	City	Notes
1985	x		St. Barnabas	Hartselle	
1985	x		St. Francis	Dauphin Island	
1988		x	All Souls	Gardendale	
1995	x		Holy Apostles	Hoover	
2000	x		St. Columba's	Huntsville	
2002	x		Advent	Lillian	
2002	x		Holy Spirit	Alabaster	
2008	x		Epiphany	Tallassee	
2009	x		St. Catherine's	Chelsea	
2009	x		St. Dismas	Atmore	Mission station serving inmates at Fountain Correctional Center.

Information for this table was derived from the WPA *Inventory of the Church Archives of Alabama* (1939); the *2010 Directory of the Diocese of Alabama*; the Journal of the Diocese of the Central Gulf Coast; and information supplied by the Rev. S. Albert Kennington, Secretary of the Diocese of the Central Gulf Coast. This appendix omits several small missions that were not included in the WPA inventory. Where the dates given in the WPA *Inventory* conflict with either the Diocese of Alabama's directory or Father Kennington's information, I have chosen to rely on the directory and Father Kennington.

*"Active" means that services were still conducted at that church as of 2012.

Appendix B

Bishops of the Diocese of Alabama and the Diocese of the Central Gulf Coast

Bishops of Alabama

Diocesan Bishops	Years
Nicholas Hamner Cobbs	1844–61
Richard Hooker Wilmer	1861–1900
Robert Woodward Barnwell	1900–1902
Charles Minnegerode Beckwith	1902–28
William George McDowell	1928–38
Charles Colcock Jones Carpenter	1938–68
George Mosley Murray	1969–70
Furman Charles Stough	1970–89
Robert Oran Miller	1989–99
Henry Nutt Parsley Jr.	1999–2011
John McKee Sloan	2012–
Bishops Coadjutor	
William George McDowell	1922–28
George M. Murray	1959–68
Henry Nutt Parsley Jr.	1996–98
Bishops Suffragan	
Henry Melville Jackson*	1891–99
Randolph Royall Claiborne	1949–53
George M. Murray	1953–59
Robert Oran Miller	1986–88
Marc Handley Andrus	2002–6
John McKee Sloan	2008–11

Bishops of the Central Gulf Coast

Diocesan Bishops	Years
George M. Murray	1971–81
Charles Farmer Duvall	1981–2001
Phillip Menzie Duncan II	2001–

*Jackson's title was actually "assistant bishop," not "bishop suffragan." The offices of bishop suffragan and bishop coadjutor were created later.

Appendix C

Membership of the Episcopal Church and US Population at Ten-Year Intervals from 1830 to 2010

	1830*	1840	1850	1860	1870
US pop.	12,867,000	17,069,500	23,347,884	31,442,960	38,555,983
Communicants TEC**	30,939	55,427	79,987	146,600	220,000
Communicants as % of US pop.	0.24%	0.32%	0.34%	0.46%	0.57%

	1880	1890	1900	1910	1920
US pop.	50,152,866	62,480,540	76,295,220	92,284,139	105,710,620
Communicants TEC	344,789	409,149	714,575	886,942	1,096,895
Communicants as % of US pop.	0.68%	0.65%	0.93%	0.96%	1.03%

	1930	1940***	1950	1960	1970
US pop.	122,729,615	132,122,446	152,271,417	180,671,158	205,052,174
Communicants TEC	1,287,431	1,489,384	1,651,426	2,123,110	2,238,538
Communicants as % of US pop.	1.04%	1.12%	1.08%	1.17%	1.09%

	1980	1990	2000	2010
US pop.	227,224,681	249,438,712	281,421,906	308,745,538
Communicants TEC	2,018,870	1,698,240	1,857,843	1,624,025
Communicants as % of US pop.	0.88%	0.68%	0.66%	0.52%

*US population and communicants of TEC figures for 1830 through 1930 are from *The Living Church Annual* (Milwaukee, WI: Morehouse Publishing, 1931).

**TEC=the Episcopal Church.

***US population figures for 1940 through 2010 are from the US Census. In 1953 *The Living Church Annual* was renamed *The Episcopal Church Annual*, but it continued to report the membership statistics of TEC.

Appendix D

Episcopal Church Membership and Population of Alabama from 1830 to 2010

	1830	1840	1850	1860	1870	1880	1890	1900
Communicants	***	***	718	1,761	2,634	3,458	5,777	7,295
Baptized members	***	***	**	**	**	**	**	12,880
State population	309,527	590,756	771,623	964,201	996,992	1,262,505	1,513,401	1,828,697
Baptized members as % of Ala pop.								0.70
Communicants as % of Ala pop.				0.18	0.26	0.27	0.38	0.39

	1910	1920	1930	1940	1950	1960	1970
Communicants	9,292	9,491	10,540	11,599	13,208	18,843	22,592
Baptized members	13,879	11,697	14,838	16,911	18,824	29,093	33,405
State population	2,138,093	2,348,174	2,646,848	2,832,961	3,061,743	3,266,740	3,444,165
Baptized members as % of Ala pop.	0.64	0.49	0.56	0.59	0.61	0.89	0.9
Communicants as % of Ala pop.	0.43	0.4	0.39	0.4	0.43	0.57	0.65

	1980	1990	2000	2010
Communicants Dio Ala	16,872	20,810	27,238	28,897

Continued on the next page

	1980	1990	2000	2010
Communicants				
Dio CGC*	14,038	15,176	17,975	15,264
Baptized members				
Dio Ala	22,859	26,713	31,877	32,406
Baptized members				
Dio CGC*	20,062	19,747	20,775	19,349
Total communicants	30,910	35,986	45,213	44,161
Total baptized members	42,921	46,460	52,652	51,755
State population	3,893,888	4,040,587	4,447,100	4,779,736
Baptized members as % of Ala pop.	1.1	1.1	1.1	1
Communicants as % of Ala pop.	0.79	0.86	1.01	0.92

*Only includes figures from Central Gulf Coast parishes that are in Alabama.
**Number of baptized not available.
***No statistics available for these years.

Appendix E

Percentage of Alabamians Twenty-Five Years Old and Older with Four or More Years of Postsecondary Education from 1950 to 2010

	1950	1960	1970	1980	1990	2000	2010
# of Alabamians with at least 4 yrs of college*	56,840	95,131	103,018	151,761	258,231	359,402	447,402
Alabama population*	3,061,743	3,266,740	3,444,165	3,893,888	4,040,587	4,447,100	4,779,736
Episcopalian communicants**	13,208	18,843	22,592	30,910	35,986	45,213	44,161
Episcopalian communicants as a % of Alabamians with at least 4 yrs of college	23.20	19.80	21.93	20.36	13.93	12.58	9.87

*Figures from the US Census.
**Figures from parochial reports.

Abbreviations Used in Notes

AEC   Archives of the Episcopal Church
AEH   Anglican and Episcopal History
BPL   Birmingham Public Library
HMPEC   Historical Magazine of the Protestant Episcopal Church
Owen   Thomas McAdory and Marie Bankhead Owen, *History of Alabama and Dictionary of Alabama Biography* (Chicago: S. J. Clarke Publishing, 1921)
SHC   Southern Historical Collection, Wilson Library, University of North Carolina–Chapel Hill

For convenience, the journals of diocesan conventions are referred to as "Diocesan Convention (YEAR)."

Notes

Acknowledgments

1. Robert G. Chapman, *Our Church* (Tuscaloosa: Robert G. Chapman, 1995).

Introduction

1. The four governors were Charles Henderson (governor from 1915 to 1919), Thomas E. Kilby (1919–23), Gordon Persons (1951–55), and Forrest "Fob" James Jr. (1979–83 and 1995–99). For most of the twentieth century Alabama governors were limited to one term. Each of Alabama's twentieth-century Episcopalian governors served a single term, except for James, who served one term as a Democrat, then after retiring from politics returned to serve one more term as a Republican.

2. Although the Mobile and Tuscaloosa churches were founded only two weeks apart, the Mobile church originated from a Protestant "union" church founded in 1822 and made up of Episcopalians, Methodists, Presbyterians.

3. Not until the Diocese of Alabama elected its first bishop in 1844 did the process of reporting parochial statistics become standardized. Statistics are missing or incomplete for the years between 1830 and 1844. However, where statistics are available, they show that the number of Episcopalians in Alabama in the early nineteenth century was miniscule. For example, in 1831, Christ Church, Tuscaloosa, reported twenty-one baptisms (including ten adults) and a total of thirty-one communicants. In 1836, Christ Church, Mobile, reported sixteen baptisms and seventy-five communicants. The population of Alabama was 309,527 in 1830 and grew to 590,756 in 1840. For George W. Owen, see Owen, IV/1308–1309; for Garrow, see Owen, III/640; for Lipscomb, see Owen, IV/1865; and for Gayle, see Samuel L. Webb and Margaret E. Armbrester, *Alabama Governors: A Political History of the State* (Tuscaloosa: University of Alabama Press, 2001), 31–34.

4. Greenough White, *A Saint of the Southern Church: Memoir of the Right Reverend*

Nicholas Hamner Cobbs (New York: Thomas Whittaker, 1900), 98. "The Church of England in the South was controlled by planters and . . . they were not interested in 'theological disputation or mystical contemplation.' Instead they wanted 'a decent orderly religion which would remind everybody of his position, his duties, and his limitations.'" S. Charles Bolton, *Southern Anglicanism: The Church of England in Colonial South Carolina* (Westport, CT: Greenwood Press, 1982), 13.

5. For Bibb Graves's coinage of the term "Big Mules," see Wayne Flynt, "David Bibb Graves (1927–31, 1935–39)," in "Encyclopedia of Alabama," http://www.encyclopediaofalabama.org/face/Article.jsp?id=h–1565. See chapter 5 for the churches that were founded during Alabama's period of industrialization and flourished in its industrial centers.

6. Kit Konolige and Frederica Konolige, *The Power of Their Glory: America's Ruling Class, the Episcopalians* (New York: Wyden Books, 1978), 386. In *Episcopal Vision/American Reality: High Church Theology and Social Thought in Evangelical America* (New Haven, CT: Yale University Press, 1986), Robert Bruce Mullin writes that "throughout the first half of the nineteenth century the backbone of Episcopal Church membership was primarily the upper-middle-class professional and business community" (35).

7. The three bishops of Alabama who were nominated for Presiding Bishop are William George McDowell, Furman Charles Stough, and Henry Nutt Parsley Jr. John Gardner Murray was ordained to the priesthood in Alabama and served churches in Selma and Birmingham, but he was the bishop of Maryland when he was elected to the office of Presiding Bishop.

Chapter 1

1. It was Sir John Seeley who stated that the British Empire was acquired in a fit of absent-mindedness: "We seem, as it were, to have conquered and peopled half the world in a fit of absence of mind." See Sir John Seeley, *The Expansion of England* (1883; Boston: Little, Brown, 1922).

2. For Mobile's French and British past, see Michael V. R. Thomason, ed., *Mobile: The New History of Alabama's First City* (Tuscaloosa: University of Alabama Press, 2001), 3–63. For the information about Hart's salary, see Peter J. Hamilton, *Colonial Mobile*, ed. Charles G. Summersell (University: University of Alabama Press, 1976), 264. Hamilton is also the source of information about Hart's successor, William Gordon. According to Frederick Lewis Weis (*The Colonial Clergy of Virginia, North Carolina, and South Carolina* [Baltimore: Genealogical Publishing, 1976], 79), Hart became rector of St. John's Parish, Berkeley, South Carolina. For the story about Hart and the Native American chief, see Walter C. Whitaker, *History of the Protestant Episcopal Church in Alabama, 1763–1891* (Birmingham, AL: Roberts and Sons, 1898), 12–13.

3. King's Chapel's story illustrates what could happen in the absence of episcopal leadership. In 1782, unable to find a priest to lead them, the people of King's Chapel invited James Freeman, a recent Harvard graduate, to serve as their lay minister. Freeman did not object to the use of the Book of Common Prayer (1662) but suggested that it be purged of Trinitarian language. Thus, King's Chapel became one of America's first Unitarian churches, although it continued to use its doctrinally altered Prayer Book (and still does so).

4. David Holmes, *A Brief History of the Episcopal Church* (Harrisburg, PA: Trinity Press International, 1993), 30.

5. John F. Woolverton, *Colonial Anglicanism in North America* (Detroit: Wayne State University Press, 1984), 28–29.

6. Carl Bridenbaugh quotes Mayhew in *Mitre and Sceptre: Transatlantic Faiths, Ideas, Personalities, and Politics, 1689–1775* (New York: Oxford University Press, 1962), 241.

7. See Nancy L. Rhoden, *Revolutionary Anglicanism: The Colonial Church of England Clergy during the American Revolution* (New York: New York University Press, 1999), 7, and Holmes, *Brief History*, 49.

8. The name was abbreviated as PECUSA at first and then ECUSA when the word "Protestant" was dropped in 1967.

9. My description of Hobart's theology is dependent on Robert Bruce Mullin's chapter "Finding a Voice, Defining a Space: John Henry Hobart and the Americanization of Anglicanism," in *One Lord, One Faith, One Baptism: Studies in Christian Ecclesiality and Ecumenism in Honor of J. Robert Wright*, ed. Marsha L. Dutton and Patrick Terrell Gray (Grand Rapids, MI: Eerdmans Publishing, 2006), 129–43, and his book *Episcopal Vision/American Reality: High Church Theology and Social Thought in Evangelical America* (New Haven, CT: Yale University Press, 1986), 60–96.

10. Mullin, *Episcopal Vision*, 42, 50–59

11. Charles Pettit McIlvaine, *Some Thoughts on Regeneration*, 12. Quoted in Diana Butler Bass, *Standing against the Whirlwind: Evangelical Episcopalians in Nineteenth-Century America* (New York: Oxford University Press, 1996), 193.

12. John F. Woolverton writes, "Virginia lacked that communal sense of obligation, competency, and the desire for hard work which characterized Massachusetts Bay." The Anglican colonies of the Chesapeake region were characterized by a "high demand for labor and high mortality rates." Their populations were "disproportionately male, young, single, immigrant, and mobile. The process of family formation was slow. Social institutions were weak, authority was tenuous, and individualism was strong." In contrast, Puritan New England was characterized by "communal impulses . . . rapid community and family development . . . elaborate kinship networks, and visible and authoritative leaders," and they "quickly developed vigorous social institutions, including many schools, and deeply rooted populations." *Colonial Anglicanism in North America*, 57. Jack P. Greene also deals with regional differences in American culture in his book *Pursuits of Happiness: The Social Development of Early Modern British Colonies and the Formation of American Culture* (Chapel Hill: University of North Carolina Press, 1988).

13. For the formation of the Domestic and Foreign Missionary Society, see Robert E. Holzhammer, "The Formation of the Domestic and Foreign Missionary Society," HMPEC 40, no. 3 (1971): 257–72; and Holzhammer, "The Domestic and Foreign Missionary Society: The Period of Expansion and Development," HMPEC 40, no. 4 (1971): 367–97; also see Lawrence Brown, "1835 and All That: Domestic and Foreign Missionary Society and the Missionary Spirit," HMPEC 40, no. 4 (1971): 399–405.

14. Mark Noll, *A History of Christianity in the United States and Canada* (Grand Rapids, MI: Eerdmans Publishing, 1992), 166–70; David Brown to DFMS, 1854, AEC; Richard Cobbs to DFMS, April 4, 1854, AEC; William A. Stickney to the DFMS, May 1, 1848, AEC.

15. John B. Boles, *The Great Revival, 1787–1805* (Lexington: University Press of Kentucky, 1972), 1. Regarding evangelicalism as the religion of the South, Boles also writes, "An evangelical pietism came to characterize southern religion and as such contributed significantly to that perhaps amorphous outlook labeled 'the southern mind'" (183). Richard Rankin, *Ambivalent Churchmen and Evangelical Churchwomen: The Religion of the Episcopal Elite in North Carolina, 1800–1860* (Columbia: University of South Carolina Press, 1993), xii. Rankin cites the estimate that 60 percent of North Carolina's largest planters were Episcopalian from a study by Jane Turner Censor, *North Carolina Planters and Their Children, 1800–1860* (Baton Rouge:

Louisiana State University Press, 1984). For the Episcopal Church's tolerance of fashion and "worldly amusements," see Rankin, *Ambivalent Churchmen and Evangelical Churchwomen*, 6 and 81. It was not only in the South that the Episcopal Church's tolerance of human frailty contrasted favorably with evangelical rigor. Harriet Hanson Robinson (1825–1911) of Lowell, Massachusetts, preferred the Episcopal Church "because their little girls were not afraid of the devil, were allowed to dance, and had so much nicer books in their Sunday-school library." Claudia L. Bushman, *"A Good Poor Man's Wife": Being a Chronicle of Harriet Hanson Robinson and Her Family in Nineteenth-Century New England* (Hanover, NH: University Press of New England, 1981), 54. Harriet E. Amos Doss, *Cotton City: Urban Development in Antebellum Mobile* (Tuscaloosa: University of Alabama Press, 1985), 67.

Chapter 2

1. Sir Charles Lyell, *A Second Visit to the United States of North America*, vol. 2 (London: John Murray, 1849), 86–87. Lyell did not explain how it was possible for "an illiterate man" to read the responses.

2. James S. Buckingham, *The Slave States of America*, vol. 2 (London: Fisher, Son, 1842), 482; Wayne Flynt, "Alabama," in *The Encyclopedia of Religion in the South*, ed. Samuel S. Hill (Macon, GA: Mercer University Press, 1984), 11; Randall M. Miller "Roman Catholic Church in the South," in Hill, *Encyclopedia*, 649.

3. *The Spirit of Missions* (July 1838): 206 (*The Spirit of Missions* was the official journal of the Domestic and Foreign Mission Society of the Episcopal Church); Francis Pulszky and Theresa Pulszky, *White, Red, and Black: Sketches of Society in the United States during the Visit of Their Guest*, vol. 3 (London: Trübner, 1853), 6.

4. Lyell, *Second Visit*, 71 and 73; Philip Henry Gosse, *Letters from Alabama, Chiefly Relating to Natural History* (Mountain Brook, AL: Overbrook House, 1983), 153 and 250–51.

5. Buckingham, *Slave States of America*, 289; Pulszky and Pulszky, *White, Red, and Black*, 5–6; Alexander Mackay, *The Western World; or, Travels in the United States in 1846–47: Exhibiting Them in Their Latest Development, Social, Political, and Industrial; Includes a Chapter on California* (London: Richard Bentley, 1849), 280; Buckingham, *Slave States of America*, 482; Anne Newport Royall, *Letters from Alabama, 1817–1822*, biographical introduction and notes by Lucille Griffith (Tuscaloosa: University of Alabama Press, 1969), 118.

6. Mackay, *Western World*, 277; Royall, *Letters from Alabama*, 114–15.

7. Buckingham, *Slave States of America*, 286; Lyell, *Second Visit*, 67.

8. Gosse, *Letters from Alabama*, 250–51; *The Spirit of Missions* (August 1840): 274.

9. Lyell, *Second Visit*, 67; Buckingham, *Slave States of America*, 483–84.

10. Pulszky and Pulszky, *White, Red, and Black*, 4; Gosse, *Letters from Alabama*, 251 and 253.

11. Christ Church, Tuscaloosa, vestry minutes, January 7, 1828. Christ Church's original vestry minutes are in the Hoole Collection at the University of Alabama, and the parish retains a copy of them. The account of the founding of Christ Episcopal Church, Mobile, is in their vestry minutes for February 26, 1828. The original minutes are in Christ Church Cathedral, Mobile, and a microfilm copy is in Special Collections at Samford University (Birmingham, AL). There is some uncertainty about the date of the founding of Christ Church, Mobile. According to Whitaker, in Mobile "in 1822 a few Churchmen had built the first non-Romanist place of worship in the entire district [which had been] wrested from the Spanish nine years before. For three years union services were held in this building, ministers being engaged without

reference to denomination. In 1825 this arrangement ceased, and the Churchmen organized Christ Church parish. A Presbyterian minister, the Rev. Murdoch Murphy, continued to officiate as the parish minister until Mr. Shaw's arrival in December, 1827" (18–19). However, the first volume of Christ Church's parish register includes the following statement: "At a meeting of Sundry Citizens of the City of Mobile on Tuesday night the 26th of February 1828, at the Protestant Church, held pursuant to previous notice, Henry Hitchcock Esquire, was unanimously chosen Chairman and [illegible] Breedin Secretary. The object of the meeting having been stated from the Chair, the following Resolutions were adopted. Resolved – That it is now expedient to establish, and organize a Protestant Episcopal Church in the City of Mobile." So although some services in the "union church" (founded in Mobile in 1822) may have been conducted by an Episcopal priest, the note in Christ Church's parish register seems to establish clearly the fact that Christ Church was founded in 1828. Nevertheless, Christ Church claims 1822 as the date of its founding.

12. William E. Dodd, *The Cotton Kingdom: A Chronicle of the Old South* (New Haven, CT: Yale University Press, 1919), 99. In *Southern Anglicanism: The Church of England in Colonial South Carolina*, S. Charles Bolton amplifies Dodd's comment: "The social values of the Church of England seem to have been carried forward by the Protestant Episcopal Church and incorporated into the regional culture of the South. According to Avery Craven, antebellum southern society was conditioned by a 'rural way of life capped by an English gentleman ideal.' . . . The membership of the Protestant Episcopal Church was small, but it included a disproportionate number of the upper class" (163). For the founding members of Christ Church, Tuscaloosa, see their vestry minutes. For biographical information on their founders, see entries for James M. Davenport in Owen, III/455; William Proctor Gould in Owen, III/685; Henry Minor in Owen, IV/1211; Armand P. Pfister in Owen, IV/1355; and Joel White in Owen, IV/1865. For Thomas Bolling, see G. Ward Hubbs, *Tuscaloosa: Portrait of an Alabama County* (Northridge, CA: Windsor Publications, 1987), 27.

13. For the founding members of Christ Church, Mobile, see Samuel H. Garrow, Owen, III/640; Henry Hitchcock, Owen, III/819; George Owen, Owen, IV/1308; and Abner Lipscomb, Owen, IV/1052. I have previously cited Harriet E. Amos Doss's estimate that almost 61 percent of Mobile's civic leaders were Episcopalians (Amos Doss, *Cotton City*, 67).

14. "The Rector is compelled, very much against his inclination and feelings, to relinquish his labors in that respectable village." *Diocesan Convention* (1832), 4.

15. Ronald J. Caldwell's "A History of Saint Luke's Episcopal Church, Cahaba, Alabama" (unpublished manuscript), 15, deals with both Edward Perine and John Hunter.

16. I have summarized Leah Rawls Atkins's assessment of Yancey from William W. Rogers, Robert D. Ward, Leah R. Atkins, and Wayne Flynt, *Alabama: The History of a Deep South State* (Tuscaloosa: University of Alabama Press, 1994), 152. The quotation about his "indefatigable labors" is from Dwight L. Dumond, *Antislavery Origins of the Civil War in the United States* (Ann Arbor: University of Michigan Press, 1939), 98–99, but is quoted in Rogers et al., *Alabama*, 152. There is some speculation about Yancey's denominational affiliation, but he was married at Christ Episcopal Church, Greenville, South Carolina, and both served on the vestry and according to the Diocesan Convention Journal, also represented St. Luke's, Cahaba, at the Diocesan Convention in 1838. Furthermore, according to the parish records of St. Luke's, Cahaba (on deposit in the archives of the Birmingham Public Library), he was a member of that church's vestry. However, some historians maintain that Yancey was a Presbyterian, because he joined a Presbyterian church when he moved to Wetumpka and was buried from a Presbyterian

church. See John Irvin Selman, "William Lowndes Yancey, Alabama Fire-Eater" (PhD diss., Mississippi State University, 1997).

17. For Jefferson and Varina Davis's association with St. John's, Montgomery, see Mattie Pegues Wood, *The Life of St. John's Parish: A History of St. John's Episcopal Church from 1834 to 1955* (Montgomery, AL: Paragon Press, 1955), 49–51; for Charles Teed Pollard, see Owen, IV/1373; for Albert Gallatin Mabry, see Owen, IV/1142; for the beginning of Nativity, Huntsville, see Frances Roberts, *Sesquicentennial History of Church of the Nativity, Episcopal, 1843–1993, Huntsville, Alabama* (Huntsville, AL: Episcopal Church of the Nativity, 1992), 23; for John Withers Clay, see Owen, III/343.

18. Records of Christ Church, Mobile, vol. 1 (1828–54), 30 and 33. (The records of Christ Church, Mobile, are in their own well-maintained archives. Copies of their records are in Special Collections, Samford University.) Robert Bruce Mullin discusses the relationship between pew rent and the "comparative absence" of the poor from the Episcopal Church in *Episcopal Vision,* 92–93; Henry J. Walker, *Let Us Keep the Feast* (Tallahassee, FL: Sentry Press, 2000) 23; S. Albert Kennington, *From the Day of Small Things* (Mobile, AL: Factor Press, 1996), 9, 11, and 63.

19. *General Convention* (1832), 409; and *Diocesan Convention* (1831), 6–7; Whitaker, *History,* 27.

20. *Diocesan Convention* (1843), 12; Walker, *Let Us Keep the Feast,* 24.

21. The election of a Virginian to serve as Alabama's first bishop set something of a precedent. For nearly a century (1844–1938), with the exception of two years (1900–1902), bishops from Virginia (Cobbs, Wilmer, Beckwith, and McDowell) led the Diocese of Alabama. Even Wilmer's "assistant bishop," Henry Melville Jackson, was born in Virginia. Other than Cobbs's annual reports to the Diocesan Conventions, the principal source of information about his life is Greenough White's *A Saint of the Southern Church.* In his reply to Otey's letter of condolence after the death of his daughter, Cobbs referred to the fact that both he and Otey had "gazed upon" Virginia's Peaks of Otter in childhood and had been "taught by their silent eloquence to look above this cold world & to learn some things of the character of the God & Father of mercy." N. H. Cobbs to J. H. Otey, December, 1852, box 1, folder 5, Otey Papers, SHC.

22. White, *A Saint of the Southern Church,* 18.

23. Ibid., 34.

24. White, *A Saint of the Southern Church,* 65; for the dates and locations of Cobbs's ministry, see ibid., 35–81.

25. *Diocesan Convention* (1845), 11–12; Blake Touchstone, "Planters and Slave Religion in the Deep South," in *Masters and Slaves in the House of the Lord: Race and Religion in the American South, 1740–1870,* ed. John Boles (Lexington: University of Kentucky Press, 1988), 99.

26. *Diocesan Convention* (1845), 13; *Diocesan Convention* (1846), 14.

27. *Diocesan Convention* (1845), 12; White, *A Saint of the Southern Church,* 107.

28. *Diocesan Convention* (1842), 12.

29. *Diocesan Convention* (1846), 14; *Diocesan Convention* (1847), 24. The catechism he refers to was a special catechism for "servants" (i.e., slaves) prepared by Levi Ives, bishop of North Carolina; Alabama Department of Archives and History, Francis Hanson, Diary, 12 (hereafter Hanson, Diary).

30. *Diocesan Convention* (1847), 12.

31. Walker, *Let Us Keep the Feast,* 69. For Perteet's wealth, see Rogers et al., *Alabama,* 111; Kennington, *From the Day of Small Things,* 30. Rogers et al., *Alabama,* 110–11.

32. Parish Register of Christ Church, Mobile (n.p.) on deposit in the archives of Christ

Church, Mobile; *Diocesan Convention* (1847), 26; *Diocesan Convention* (1857), 17; *Diocesan Convention* (1832), 4; *Diocesan Convention* (1831), 10; *Diocesan Convention* (1845), 23–24.

33. Letter from Emma Jones in *The Spirit of Missions* (September 1856): 375–78. See also "First American Woman Missionary to China: A Portrait of Episcopalian Emma G. Jones of Mobile, Alabama" by Thomas G. Oey and J. Barry Vaughn on deposit in the archives of the BPL.

34. The dates of Francis Hanson's service at Demopolis are slightly uncertain. The parish was founded in 1834, and Hanson was serving churches in the vicinity of Demopolis by 1843. However, it appears that on at least two occasions Hanson "withdrew" from Trinity, and for a few years he returned to his native Maryland. But Hanson is not mentioned in connection with Demopolis after 1873.

35. I am indebted to Dr. Thomas Oey of Shaoxing, China, for sharing his research into early Episcopal missionaries to China. My notes on Dr. Oey's research are included in my notes for this book that are on deposit at the BPL archives.

36. Roberts, *Sesquicentennial History of Church of the Nativity*, 31.

37. For a "gentleman of Lafayette County," see *The Spirit of Missions* (July 1838): 206; Walter C. Whitaker gives brief accounts of several of the clergy of the diocese, especially Henry Lay, Henry Pierce, Samuel Smith, and Nathaniel Knapp, in "Personnel of the Clergy," chapter 13 (113–22) in his *History*; Frances Roberts profiles Henry Lay in her history of Nativity, Huntsville; she also refers to Bishop Cobbs as "campus chaplain" at the University of Virginia (Roberts, *Sesquicentennial History of Church of the Nativity*, 21 and 27); Elizabeth Allison (historiographer of the Diocese of Vermont) deals with J. Avery Shepherd in her unpublished paper "The Ministry of the Rev. J. Avery Shepherd in Montgomery, Alabama 1858–1865" (presented at "Opening New Doors: A Symposium on the History of Alabama's Episcopal Church," Birmingham Public Library, February 5–6, 2005); Francis R. Hanson (1807–1873), an Episcopal priest who served parishes in Marengo, Greene, and Hale Counties between 1850 and 1873, relates the story of John Linebaugh's career and death in his journal, which is held by the Alabama Department of Archives and History. Page numbers refer to the typescript copy. Hanson, Diary, 41–43); the first volume of the vestry minutes of Christ Church, Mobile, refer to Connecticut as the home state of Norman Pinney.

38. J. Withers Clay to Henry C. Lay, October 10, 1846, box 1, folder 2, Henry C. Lay Papers, SHC; Nicholas Hamner Cobbs to Henry C. Lay, October 17, 1859, box 1, folder 23, Henry C. Lay Papers, SHC.

39. *Journal of the General Convention of the Protestant Episcopal Church in the United States of America* (1829), 284 (Journals of the General Convention will be cited as *General Convention* [YEAR]); Whitaker, *History*, 18–19; Jackson Kemper's Journal, entry for April 13, 1838; William A. Beardsley, "Bishop Thomas C. Brownell's Journal of His Missionary Tours, 1829 and 1834," HMPEC 7, no. 4 (1938): 316.

40. Leonidas Polk, "Arkansas, Louisiana, Mississippi, and Alabama: From the Right Rev. Leonidas Polk, D.D., Missionary Bishop of Arkansas, and Having Provisional Charge of the Diocese of Louisiana, Mississippi and Alabama," *The Spirit of Missions* 4 (1839): 313.

41. Nicholas Hamner Cobbs to Henry C. Lay (March 22, 1847) in box 1, folder 3, Henry C. Lay Papers, SHC; letter dated March 13, 1854, in Henry C. Lay's letter book and diary for 1854 to 1858, 9, box 4, folder 109, Henry C. Lay Papers, SHC.

42. White, *A Saint of the Southern Church*, 101.

43. J. H. Ticknor to DFMS, October 7, 1851, AEC.

44. Report by W. A. Harris in *The Spirit of Missions* (April 1836): 107.

45. Mackay, *Western World*, 265.

46. Lyell, *Second Visit*, 71.

47. Report from Thomas A. Cook, *The Spirit of Missions* 1, no. 8 (1836): 238.

48. Rogers et al., *Alabama*, 138.

49. J. H. Linebaugh to DFMS, October 7, 1846, AEC.

50. N. H. Cobbs to J. H. Otey, [December?] 17, 1852, box 1, folder 5, J. H. Otey Papers, SHC.

51. *Diocesan Convention* (1837), 9.

52. *Diocesan Convention* (1858), 28.

53. Walker, *Let Us Keep the Feast*, 19.

54. *Diocesan Convention* (1848), 25.

55. William A. Beardsley, D.D., "Bishop Thomas C. Brownell's Journal of His Missionary Tours, 1829 and 1834," HMPEC 7, no. 4 (1938), 316; *Diocesan Journal* (1838), 10; Christ Church, Mobile, records, vol. 1 (1828–54), 242–43; Hanson, Diary, 24; report by W. A. Harris in *The Spirit of Missions* 4, no. 4 (1839): 107; reports from Thomas A. Cook in *The Spirit of Missions* 1, no. 8 (1836): 238, and 2, no. 10 (1837): 299.

56. Wood, *Life of St. John's Parish*, 38.

57. White, *A Saint of the Southern Church*, 118–19 and 173.

58. As its name indicates, the Oxford movement was a theological movement for the reform and renewal of the Church of England led by theologians at Oxford University. The generally accepted date for its start was July 13, 1833, when John Keble, who held the Chair of Poetry at Oxford, preached a sermon titled "National Apostasy."

59. *Diocesan Convention* (1849), 21; White, *A Saint of the Southern Church*, 58.

60. N. H. Cobbs to J. H. Otey (December 17, 1852), box 1, folder 5, Otey Papers, SHC; *Diocesan Convention* (1849), 21.

61. Mullin, "Finding a Voice, Defining a Space," 139–40. Richard Bushman, *The Refinement of America: Persons, Houses, Cities* (New York: Alfred A. Knopf, 1992), 179–80. For a discussion of the spread of Gothic architecture in America, see Jeanne H. Kilde, *When Church Became Theatre: The Transformation of Evangelical Architecture and Worship in Nineteenth-Century America* (Oxford: Oxford University Press, 2002), 68–69.

62. Kennington, *From the Day of Small Things*, 22 and 24; Roberts, *Sesquicentennial History of Church of the Nativity*, 30; Caldwell, "A History of St. Luke's, Cahaba," 15.

63. Walker, *Let Us Keep the Feast*, 31, 33–34; *Diocesan Convention* (1856), 32; and *Diocesan Convention* (1857), 23.

64. *Diocesan Convention* (1849), 11.

65. *Diocesan Convention* (1857), 59.

66. Whitaker, *History*, 143–44; *Diocesan Convention* (1861), 24.

67. *Diocesan Convention* (1857), 23; for the debate about Sewanee's location, see Arthur Ben Chitty, *Reconstruction at Sewanee: The Founding of the University of the South and Its First Administration, 1857–1872* (Sewanee, TN: University Press, 1954), 53; and Samuel Williamson, *Sewanee Sesquicentennial History: The Making of the University of the South* (Sewanee, TN: University Press, 2008), 14.

68. *Diocesan Convention* (1854), 26; for the Society for the Relief of Disabled Clergy, see *Diocesan Convention* (1844), 18.

69. University of Virginia Library Geospatial and Statistical Data Center, http://fisher.lib .virginia.edu/. The 1840 census counted free persons of color; the 1860 census did not, so the 1860 figure does not include Alabama's free persons of color.

Chapter 3

1. The characterization of Cobbs as a Unionist is from Walter L. Fleming, *Civil War and Reconstruction in Alabama* (Spartanburg, SC: Reprint Company, 1978), 57; *Diocesan Convention* (1859), 16–17; for the Committee on the State of the Church, see 23; Revelation 3:16 (KJV); N. H. Cobbs to Henry C. Lay (June 16, 1859), box 1, folder 22, Lay Papers, SHC; for Cushman's report, see *Diocesan Convention* (1861), 31.

2. Pollard's comments are from a typescript copy of his reminiscences in the archives of St. John's Episcopal Church, Montgomery, Alabama. Bishop Cobbs's opposition to secession may help explain why William Lowndes Yancey, who was a member of the vestry at St. Luke's, Cahaba, and also represented that parish at the Diocesan Convention, was buried from the Presbyterian church in Wetumpka. Could it be that Cobbs's opposition to secession alienated Yancey so much that he left the Episcopal Church or at least directed that his funeral not take place in an Episcopal Church?

3. The story of the Estelle Hall meeting is in Joseph Hodgson, *The Cradle of the Confederacy* (1876), excerpted in Malcolm C. McMillan, *The Alabama Confederate Reader* (Tuscaloosa: University of Alabama Press, 1963), 7–12. Hodgson represented St. John's, Montgomery, at the 1867 Diocesan Convention. Dawson represented St. Paul's, Selma, at the 1864 Diocesan Convention and Yancey had twice represented St. Luke's, Cahaba, at the Diocesan Convention and had also served on St. Luke's vestry. Yancey would take center stage once more in the drama of secession. Rumored to have sought the presidency of the Confederacy for himself, the closest Yancey came to it was when he introduced Jefferson Davis to the crowd assembled for his inauguration with the memorable phrase: "The man and the hour have met." Malcolm C. McMillan, *Constitutional Development in Alabama, 1798–1901: A Study in Politics, the Negro, and Sectionalism* (Chapel Hill: University of North Carolina Press, 1955), 12.

4. Kate Cumming, *Gleanings from Southland: Sketches of Life and Manners of the People of the South before, during and after the War of Secession, with Extracts from the Author's Journal and Epitome of the New South* (Birmingham, AL: Roberts and Son, 1895), 20–21; John Mitchell to Henry C. Lay (January 12, 1861), box 1, folder 43, Lay Papers, SHC; Henry C. Lay to Eliza Atkinson Clay (April 19, 1861), box 1, folder 43, Lay Papers, SHC.

5. "Bishop Cobbs submitted to an operation before he left New York and was much benefitted. We have not heard of his arrival in England yet," in a letter from Henry C. Lay to James Hervey Otey (May 1856), in Lay's letter book and diary for 1854–58, box 4, folder 109, Lay Papers, SHC; *Diocesan Convention* (1856), 9 and *Diocesan Convention* (1857), 20; letter from John M. Mitchell to Henry C. Lay, January 12, 1861, box 1, folder 43, Lay Papers, SHC; Cumming, *Gleanings from Southland*, 32. Regarding Cobbs's prayer that he would not live to see Alabama secede, see Whitaker, *History*, 149: "The growing probability and final certainty of national disruption and fratricidal warfare had been to him a great grief, and, although his last official act was to direct the clergy of the diocese to refrain from using the Prayer for the President of the United States so soon as the state and diocese of Alabama were no longer within the limits of the United States, he prayed that he might not live to see this great calamity. His prayer was granted."

6. Louisa Harrison to William Stickney, January 12, 1861, Faunsdale Plantation Papers, BPL; Hanson, Diary, 35–56.

7. Undated typescript of reminiscences of Charles Teed Pollard in the Archives of St. John's Episcopal Church, Montgomery, Alabama.

8. Obituary for J. Avery Shepherd, Middlebury, Vermont, April 15, 1898. Cf. *Journal of the Congress of the Confederate States of America, 1861–1865*, vol. 1 (Washington, DC: Government Printing Office, 1904–5), 62. In her unpublished essay, "The Ministry of the Rev. J. Avery Shepherd in Montgomery, Alabama 1858–1865," Elizabeth E. Allison states: "During the week prior to the surrender, Shepherd spent almost all of his time attempting to persuade his friends and acquaintances to receive the Federal forces with civility. That he was successful is seen in this comment by a member of the general's staff who stayed in Shepherd's home; that nowhere in the entire South had they been received with more courtesy than in Montgomery. On April 12th, the Truce Committee, with Shepherd carrying a white flag which he had made from a piece of white cloth and a whittled stick, met the advancing forces and after some negotiations, surrendered the city. . . . From the beginning of the occupation, Shepherd was given a military escort and the general and his staff were often his guests for both dinner and breakfast."

9. White, *A Saint of the Southern Church*, 98.

10. Whitaker, *History*, 155–56; J. M. Banister to Henry C. Lay, February 1, 1861, Lay Papers, SHC, box 1, folder 43; Massey to Lay, March 12, 1861, box 1, folder 43, Lay Papers, SHC; Massey to Lay, April 11, 1861; and Mitchell to Lay, March 12, 1861, box 1, folder 43, Lay Papers, SHC.

11. Massey to Lay, March 6, 1861, box 1, folder 43, Lay Papers, SHC.

12. *Diocesan Convention* (1861), 3–4; Joseph Blount Cheshire, *The Church in the Confederate States: A History of the Protestant Episcopal Church in the Confederate States* (New York: Longmans, Green, 1912), 14–15, 20; *Proceedings of a Meeting of Bishops, Clergymen, and Laymen, of the Protestant Episcopal Church in the Confederate States, at Montgomery, Alabama, On the 3d, 4th, 5th & 6th of July, 1861* (Montgomery, AL: Barrett, Wimbish, 1861), 27.

13. William Howard Russell, *My Diary, North and South*, ed. Eugene H. Berwanger (New York: Alfred A. Knopf, 1988), 118–19.

14. *Journal of Proceedings of an Adjourned Convention of Bishops, Clergymen and Laymen of the Protestant Episcopal Church in the Confederate States of America, Held in Christ Church, Columbia, South Carolina from Oct. 16th to Oct. 24th, Inclusive in the Year of Our Lord 1861* (Montgomery, AL: *Montgomery Advertiser*, 1861), 24–25.

15. *Confederate Episcopal Church Convention Journal* (1861), 41.

16. Massey to Lay, March 6, 1861, box 1, folder 43, Lay Papers, SHC.

17. See Wilmer's obituary in the *New York Times*, June 5, 1900.

18. Louis Tucker, *Clerical Errors* (New York: Harper and Bothers, 1943), 23. The Gardiner Tucker quotation is from Kennington, *From the Day of Small Things*, 51.

19. Walter C. Whitaker, *Richard Hooker Wilmer, Second Bishop of Alabama: A Biography* (Philadelphia: George W. Jacobs, 1907), 87.

20. Richard Hooker Wilmer, *The Recent Past from a Southern Standpoint: Reminiscences of a Grandfather* (New York: Thomas Whittaker, 1887), 11–12.

21. Wilmer, *Recent Past*, 44, 48–19.

22. "It has been a source of deep regret to me that the Diocese of Alabama has been in a situation to effect so little in the way of ministering directly to the religious necessities of the soldiers in the field. We have no supernumerary Clergy in this Diocese," *Diocesan Convention* (1864), 15.

23. *Diocesan Convention* (1863), 97; Beckwith, [month illegible] 1864, Beckwith Papers, SHC, 1267–Z, folder 1; Caldwell, "A History of St. Luke's, Cahaba"; Hanson, Diary, 37.

24. Henry C. Lay's journal for 1862 and 1863, entries from April 8 to July 6, 1862, Lay Papers, SHC.

25. Henry C. Lay, "Journal of Episcopal Acts," 81–82, box 4, folder 111, Lay Papers, SHC. Cf. Roberts, *Sesquicentennial History of Church of the Nativity*, 43.

26. Vestry minutes, April 18, 1862, Christ Episcopal Church, Tuscaloosa, Alabama; *Diocesan Convention* (1862), 35; and Roberts, *Sesquicentennial History of Church of the Nativity*, 43.

27. Hanson, Diary, 36; letter from Louisa Harrison to William Stickney (March 31, 1864), Faunsdale Plantation Papers, BPL; *Diocesan Convention* (1865), 10; Roberts, *Sesquicentennial History of Church of the Nativity*, 43.

28. Kate Cumming, *Kate: The Journal of a Confederate Nurse,* ed. Richard Barksdale Harwell (Baton Rouge: Louisiana State University Press, 1959), xii, 27, 243–44; Cumming, *Gleanings from Southland,* 45, 62; Cumming, *Kate: The Journal of a Confederate Nurse,* 27.

29. "The Cathedral must be a large building, seating fifteen hundred whites in the body of the church and one thousand negroes in the galleries. About the quadrangle in which the Cathedral should stand were to be nine separate buildings, whose purposes declare the scope of the projected work, viz.: (1) diocesan library and Bishop's office, (2) sexton's house, (3) dean's residence, (4) infirmary and house of mercy, (5) home for five deaconesses, (6) house for theological students, (7) house for high classical school, (8) house for six or eight deacons, (9) steward's house for boarding occupants of last three houses." Whitaker, *History*, 144. For Muhlenberg, see Donald S. Armentrout and Robert B. Slocum, eds., *An Episcopal Dictionary: A User-Friendly Resource for Episcopalians* (New York: Church Publishing, 1999), 461; and for Whittingham, see Barbara Brandon Schnorrenberg, "Set Apart: Alabama Deaconesses, 1864–1915," AEH 63, no. 4 (1994), 468–90; Wilmer Hall manuscript, 2, University of South Alabama Archives.

30. Wilmer Hall manuscript, 7–13, University of South Alabama Archives. A "collect" is a short prayer that gathers together the themes of the day. The Book of Common Prayer provides collects for every Sunday of the church year, as well as for important feast days. In the liturgy of the Holy Eucharist, the collect comes immediately before the first lesson.

31. Wilmer Hall manuscript, 4, University of South Alabama Archives; letter from Richard Hooker Wilmer to William Stickney, August 26, 1864, folder 765.3.7, Faunsdale Plantation Papers, BPL.

32. From a history found in the 1884 parish register of Holy Comforter parish, Church and Synagogue Records, Alabama Department of Archives and History, Box 19, Folder 8. The notes from the 1884 parish register are confusing. They say that the first service of the new congregation was in May 1864. However, the journal for the 1864 Diocesan Convention records that the convention voted to accept Holy Comforter as a parish that year.

33. *Diocesan Convention* (1865), 14, and *Diocesan Convention* (1866), 18.

Chapter 4

1. Hilary A. Herbert, et al., *Why the Solid South? Or, Reconstruction and Its Results* (Baltimore: R. H. Woodward, 1890), 29. Hugh B. Hammett writes, "Hilary Abner Herbert served as a congressman from Alabama from 1877 to 1893 and was secretary of the navy in the second Cleveland administration. . . . He was the editor of and chief contributor to the book *Why the Solid South?*, the leading literary apology for the Bourbon 'redemption' that ushered in the New South at the end of the Reconstruction period. . . . During his three terms in Congress, he served as chairman of the powerful Committee on Naval Affairs of the House of Representatives and became the acknowledged master of naval legislation among the Democrats in

Congress. No man was more intimately connected with the rise of the 'New American Navy' during these years. As a result of his expertise in naval matters, in 1893 Grover Cleveland appointed him secretary of the navy." *Hilary Abner Herbert: A Southerner Returns to the Union* (Philadelphia: American Philosophical Society, 1976), xv–xvi. John Allan Wyeth, *With Sabre and Scalpel: The Autobiography of a Soldier and Surgeon* (New York: Harper and Brothers, 1914), 319; Virginia Clay-Clopton, *A Belle of the Fifties: Memoirs of Mrs. Clay of Alabama, Covering Social and Political Life in Washington and the South, 1853–66* (Tuscaloosa: University of Alabama Press, 1999), 282–83.

2. Wyeth, *With Sabre and Scalpel*, 320; Clay-Clopton, *Belle of the Fifties*, 282–83.

3. Wyeth, *With Sabre and Scalpel*, 313.

4. *Diocesan Convention* (1863), 16.

5. *Diocesan Convention* (1866), Appendix A, 15.

6. Whitaker, *Richard Hooker Wilmer*, 128.

7. Ibid., 125–32.

8. R. F. Michel to Lewis Parsons, December 12, 1865, archives of St. John's, Montgomery. For the Pettis's ordination, see Kennington, *From the Day of Small Things*, 62; for the Hamner Hall incident, see statement by Charles Teed Pollard in St. John's parish archives. No date or page numbers.

9. *Diocesan Convention* (1866), 7 and 9.

10. Whitaker, *Richard Hooker Wilmer*, 152.

11. Cheshire, *Church in the Confederate States*, 203–4; Whitaker, *Richard Hooker Wilmer*, 157; Henry T. Shanks, "The Reunion of the Episcopal Church, 1865," AEH 9, no. 2 (1940): 120–40.

12. See "Episcopal Convention; Proceedings of the Second Day . . . ANNUAL ADDRESS OF THE RIGHT REV. BISHOP POTTER. He Extends the Hand of Love and Sympathy, Aid and Welcome to the Bishops of the South," *New York Times*, September 29, 1865.

13. *Diocesan Convention* (1866), 9; Whitaker, *History*, 159–60; *Diocesan Convention* (1866), 9; Whitaker, *History*, 151–52.

14. For Vinton's remarks and the resolution expressing "fraternal regrets," see Whitaker, *Richard Hooker Wilmer*, 150, 159. See also "The Episcopal Convention; Division of the Diocese of Pennsylvania—Debate on the Case of Dr. Wilmer, Bishop of Alabama," *New York Times*, October 13, 1865.

15. *New York Times*, October 14, 1865.

16. Whitaker, *Richard Hooker Wilmer*, 165–66.

17. *Diocesan Convention* (1866), 13 and 18.

18. Cheshire, *Church in the Confederate States*, 197–98.

19. For the members of the 1865 constitutional convention, see *Journal of the Proceedings of the Convention of the State of Alabama, Held in the City of Montgomery, on Tuesday, September 12, 1865* (Montgomery, AL: Gibson and Whitfield, 1865), 11–12; the Selma *Weekly* comment is in McMillan, *Constitutional Development*, 114; for Hilary Herbert's comment see Herbert, *Why the Solid South?*, 45.

20. For members of the 1875 convention, see *Journal of the Constitutional Convention of the State of Alabama, Assembled in the City of Montgomery, September 6th, 1875* (Montgomery, AL: W. W. Screws, 1875), 3–4. Southern historians have written extensively about the appropriateness of the term "Bourbon" when applied to the leadership of the post–Civil War South. See Allen J. Going, *Bourbon Democracy in Alabama, 1874–189* (University: University of Alabama Press, 1951); James Tice Moore, "Redeemers Reconsidered: Change and Continuity in

the Democratic South, 1870–1900," *Journal of Southern History* 44, no. 3 (1978): 357–78; and "Bourbons" and "Redeemers" in *The Encyclopedia of Southern History* (Baton Rouge: Louisiana State University Press, 1979), 142 and 1042. See Owen, III/511 for John Witherspoon DuBose and IV/1120 for Robert McKee.

21. Wilmer, *Recent Past*, 275. During the Civil War, anti-war or "peace Democrats" were called "Copperheads." Some even wore an image of Liberty cut from copper coins. Some Confederate uniforms were dyed with a dye made from walnut hulls that produced a yellow-brown or butternut color, so Confederate soldiers were sometimes called "butternuts."

22. Charles Reagan Wilson, *Baptized in Blood: The Religion of the Lost Cause, 1865–1920* (Athens: University of Georgia Press, 1980), 148–49, 151. In his *Sewanee Sesquicentennial History: The Making of the University of the South* (Sewanee, TN: University Press, 2008) Samuel R. Williamson Jr. disputes the characterization of Sewanee as "a home of the Lost Cause" but does not specifically address any of the facts that I cite. See chapter 5, "The Lost Cause, Race, and Academic Freedom: The Wiggins Example, 1893–1909."

23. Whitaker, *Richard Hooker Wilmer*, 188–89.

24. For Wilmer's honorary degree, see Cambridge University Archives Book Sigma, 232–33. One of the other bishops who received an honorary doctorate was Henry C. Lay, who had been rector of Nativity, Huntsville, before he became missionary bishop of the southwest. For the story about Plymouth Rock, see Gaillard Hunt, "Story of a Great Southern Bishop," *New York Times*, January 25, 1908.

25. Parochial reports in the Diocesan Journals for 1860 and 1866.

26. W. E. B. Du Bois, *The Negro Church* (Atlanta: Atlanta University Press, 1903), 139 and 142.

27. The minutes of the Freedmen's Commission for October 29, 1875, indicate that Massey was named honorary district secretary for the Diocese of Alabama, but they do not specifically cite his work with Good Shepherd as the reason for his recognition. The minutes of the Freedmen's Commission are on deposit in the Archives of the Episcopal Church.

28. Harriet E. Amos, "Religious Reconstruction in Microcosm at Faunsdale Plantation," *Alabama Review* 42, no. 4 (1989): 243–69.

29. Wilson Fallin, *Uplifting the People: Three Centuries of Black Baptists in Alabama* (Tuscaloosa: University of Alabama Press, 2007), 31. Gardner Shattuck observes that in South Carolina, where there were roughly equal numbers of black and white Episcopalians, the black Episcopalians left the Episcopal churches abruptly "while the African Methodist Episcopal Church, the African Methodist Episcopal Zion Church, and black Baptist churches experienced astounding growth." Gardner Shattuck, *Episcopalians and Race: From Civil War to Civil Rights* (Lexington: University Press of Kentucky, 2000), 8.

30. *Diocesan Convention* (1866), 11–12. The report of the commission is on pp. 27–28. *Diocesan Convention* (1882), 19; Tucker, *Clerical Errors*, 20.

31. *Diocesan Convention* (1866), 27–28.

32. *Diocesan Convention* (1882), 19–21.

33. *Diocesan Convention* (1882), 36–37.

34. Kennington, *From the Day of Small Things*, 30.

35. For a discussion of the debate about black bishops, see David M. Reimers, "Negro Bishops and Diocesan Segregation in the Protestant Episcopal Church: 1870–1954," HMPEC, 31, no. 3 (1962): 231–42. See Shattuck, *Episcopalians and Race*, 13–15, for a more complete account of the Sewanee conference.

36. *Diocesan Convention* (1884), 42; *Diocesan Convention* (1883), 37–38, 30–31.

37. My account of St. Mark's draws heavily on the research of Barbara Brandon Schnorren-berg, who has told this story in great detail in her article "'The Best School for Blacks in the State': St. Mark's Academic and Industrial School, Birmingham, Alabama, 1892–1940," AEH 71, no. 4 (2002), 519–49. Dr. Schnorrenberg graciously allowed me to use the paper on which her article was based, which contains additional information. For Van Hoose's solicitation of the black vote, see Carl V. Harris, *Political Power in Birmingham, 1871–1921* (Knoxville: University of Tennessee Press, 1977), 68.

38. Schnorrenberg paper, "St. Mark's," 9, 31 and 41.

39. Wilmer, *Recent Past*, 44. In his rumination here on characters from *Uncle Tom's Cabin* by Harriet Beecher Stowe, Wilmer may have been thinking of Stowe's black character "Eliza" rather than her white character "Eva."

40. Wood, *Life of St. John's Parish*, 75.

Chapter 5

1. Hudson Strode, *The Eleventh House: Memoirs* (New York: Harcourt, Brace, Jovanovich, 1975), 14 and 25.

2. *Diocesan Convention* (1883), 34–35; *Diocesan Convention* (1891), 48; Marvin Yeomans Whiting, "James R. Powell and 'This Magic Little City of Ours': A Perspective on Local History," in *The Journal of the Birmingham Historical Society: An Anthology Honoring Marvin Yeomans Whiting*, ed. James L. Baggett (Birmingham, AL: Birmingham Public Library and the Birmingham Historical Society, 2000), 1–2.

3. Kirk Munroe, "The Industrial South," *Harper's Weekly* 31, no. 1579 Supplement (1887): 213 and 223.

4. DuBose to Shepard, December 17, 1881, folder 765.15.1; Wilson to Shepard, May 17, 1884, folder 765.15.2, Faunsdale Plantation Papers, BPL.

5. Martha Carolyn Mitchell, "Birmingham: Biography of a City of the New South" (PhD diss., University of Chicago, 1946), 100; Martha Mitchell Bigelow, "Birmingham's Carnival of Crime," *Alabama Review* 3 (April 1950): 123–33.

6. The Ward quotation is in Edward Shannon LaMonte, *Politics and Welfare in Birmingham, 1900–1975* (Tuscaloosa: University of Alabama Press, 1995); Mitchell, "Birmingham," 143, 146–48; for the Mercy Home, see LaMonte, *Politics and Welfare*, 46–47.

7. Sketch of the early history of Birmingham by Sallie Harrison Pearson, folder 314.1.2, Birmingham History, 1868–99, BPL.

8. John Witherspoon DuBose, *Jefferson County and Birmingham, Alabama* (Birmingham, AL: Teeple and Smith Publishers, 1887), 216–17. The Church of the Advent did not become the cathedral of the Diocese of Alabama until 1982, so it would be anachronistic to refer to it as a cathedral before that date.

9. Letter from the Reverend L. W. Rose in file marked "L. W. Rose. 1887–1891" in the archives of St. Mary's-on-the-Highlands, Birmingham, AL. No page numbers.

10. Edith Ward London Diary, vol. 1, 1883–1917, 24, 148, BPL.

11. For Anniston's beginnings, see Grace Hooten Gates, *The Model City of the New South: Anniston, Alabama, 1872–1900* (Huntsville, AL: Stroke Publishers, 1978), 1–80; for further perspective (and background information about one of the pillars of Grace Episcopal Church), see Kevin Stoker, "From Prohibitionist to New Deal Liberal: The Political Evolution of Colonel Harry Mell Ayers of the *Anniston Star*," *Alabama Review* 62, no. 4 (2009), 262–96.

12. John Noble to Wilmer, June 2 and June 15, John Noble Papers, Anniston Public Library, Box 245A.

13. St. Michael and All Angels Church Record Book (1890–1948), 2–3.

14. Gary S. Sprayberry, "'Town among the Trees': Paternalism, Class, and Civil Rights in Anniston, Alabama, 1872 to Present" (PhD diss., University of Alabama, 2003), 40–41.

15. John W. Noble to D. J. Davies, August 21, 1895, letter book, 6, John Noble Papers, Anniston Public Library, Box 245A.

16. *Diocesan Convention* (1887), 42.

17. Bishop Jackson's papers in the archives of the Diocese of Alabama at the Birmingham Public Library include the presentment prepared by Stewart McQueen and the accompanying affidavits, as well as Bishop Jackson's reply to the charges against him. McQueen was rector of Holy Comforter, Montgomery, and the minutes for the August 13, 1899, meeting of his vestry include a copy of a letter the vestry sent to Jackson, saying that "the good of the church in the Diocese requires your resignation as Bishop coadjutor." The letter from the vestry of the Church of the Advent to Jackson dated July 26, 1899, is in the Advent Papers, folder 1300.1.1, Diocese of Alabama archives, BPL. For the announcement of Bishop Jackson's resignation and death, see *Diocesan Convention* (1899), 42–45. Kennington summarized the Jackson affair in *From the Day of Small Things*, 138–39.

18. "Bishop Wilmer Died Yesterday," *Montgomery Advertiser*, June 15, 1900; *Atlanta Constitution*, March 15, 1896, 15; Kennington, *From the Day of Small Things*, 140–41. In a 1908 *New York Times* article about Wilmer, Gaillard Hunt wrote that he was "a truly remarkable man, of splendid personal presence, a scholar who practiced his Latin each day by recording in that language some ordinary event; of great eloquence in the pulpit and a dead shot in the hunting field; an uncompromising adherent of the cause of the South in the civil war and so good a practical economist that through all vicissitudes he was never in debt and never dunned his congregation for his salary; a valiant champion of the independence of Church from State; a noted humorist and wit; a fine horseman, and an expert at billiards." Gaillard Hunt, "Story of a Great Southern Bishop," *New York Times*, January 25, 1908.

19. See "Zelda Sayre Fitzgerald" in the Encyclopedia of Alabama (http://www.encyclopediaofalabama.org/face/Article.jsp?id=h-1120).

20. Tallulah Bankhead, *Tallulah: An Autobiography* (New York: Harper and Brothers, 1952), 48–49.

21. Grace Elvina Trillia Hinds Curzon, Marchioness, *Reminiscences* (New York: Coward-McCann, 1955), 10.

22. *Official Proceedings of the 1901 Constitutional Convention of the State of Alabama, May 21st, 1901 to September 3d, 1901* (Montgomery, AL: Brown Printing, 1901), 8.

23. My account of Beckwith's life and ministry draws heavily on both Barbara Brandon Schnorrenberg's unpublished account of Beckwith's life—"Blessings and Trials: Charles Minnegerode Beckwith, Fourth Bishop of Alabama" (2005)—which is on deposit in the Archives Department of the Birmingham Public Library, and my own account of Beckwith's episcopate in *Our Church*.

24. *Diocesan Convention* (1909), 33. "Muscular Christianity" was a movement in England, Canada, and the United States that encouraged physical exercise and outdoor sports (including camping and hunting) as important components of the Christian life.

25. *Diocesan Convention* (1911), 44, 46–49; *Diocesan Convention* (1914), 80; Rogers et al., *Alabama*, 357, 359, and 423.

26. *Diocesan Convention* (1903), 46.

27. Leah Rawls Atkins, "Feuds, Factions, and Reform: Politics in Early Birmingham," *Alabama Heritage* (Summer 1986): 26. For Van Hoose's service in Gadsden, see "Holy Comforter Church History Recalled on Anniversary," *Gadsden Times*, July 24, 1938.

28. I am indebted to Hugh C. Bailey's *Edgar Gardner Murphy: Gentle Progressive* (Miami: University of Miami Press, 1968) for the details of Murphy's birth, upbringing, education, and career.

29. Edgar Gardner Murphy, "Address to the Society for Ethical Culture," March 20, 1904, in MFS 821, Samford University Special Collections.

30. For Ogden's comment, see Bailey, *Edgar Gardner Murphy*, 160; for McBee, see Ralph Luker, *A Southern Tradition in Theology and Social Criticism, 1830–1930: The Religious Liberalism and Social Conservatism of James Warley Miles, William Porcher Dubose, and Edgar Gardner Murphy* (New York: Edwin Mellen Press, 1984), 342; Bailey, *Edgar Gardner Murphy*, 145, 174 and 182.

31. Bailey, *Edgar Gardner Murphy*, 23–24, 30; for the Montgomery conference, see Robert J. Norrell, *Up from History: The Life of Booker T. Washington* (Cambridge, MA: Belknap Press of Harvard University Press, 2009), 189–92, and for the White House incident, see 245–53; also the letter from Murphy to Washington, October 24, 1901, Booker T. Washington Papers, vol. 6, 272, http://www.historycooperative.org/btw/Vol.6/html/272.html; Ralph E. Luker, "Liberal Theology and Social Conservatism: A Southern Tradition, 1840–1920," *Church History* 50, no. 2 (1981): 200.

32. *Alabama Churchman* 4, no. 3 (1926): 5.

33. Henckell's meeting with Dedman is recounted in an unpublished history of the Henckell family that was in the possession of the late Ms. Frances Henckell. The story of the founding of Children's Hospital is also in the *Year Book of the Children's Hospital (Formerly Called The Holy Innocents' Hospital) of Birmingham* (no date or publisher given) in folder 6.1.2.11, Robert Jemison Jr. Papers, BPL.

34. Sara Palmer, *Dad Hall: "Bishop of Wall Street"* (Chicago: Moody Press, 1954).

35. *Diocesan Convention* (1901), 37; *Diocesan Convention* (1917), 54; *Diocesan Convention* (1918), 49; *Diocesan Convention* (1932), 32; *Diocesan Convention* (1936), 44; *Diocesan Convention* (1943), 40.

36. *Diocesan Convention* (1920), 18–19; *Diocesan Convention* (1930), 37.

37. *Diocesan Convention* (1918), 32 and 4, 44; Wood, *Life of St. John's Parish*, 155–56; Tucker, *Clerical Errors*, 279.

38. From a letter to Jordan's wife, July 7, 1918 ("Somewhere in France"), folder 328.1.1.3.35, Mortimer Jordan letters, BPL.

39. Tucker, *Clerical Errors*, 265.

40. See Schnorrenberg's, "Blessings and Trials," 21–23; also the Church of the Advent vestry minutes for 1903. See "Santa Claus raps his friends here," in George Ward Papers, Scrapbook 5, 1905. The Beckwith-Ewing dispute even made the *New York Times*. See "Dioceses Are at Odds," *New York Times*, October 23, 1903.

41. Beckwith to Randolph Claiborne, November 28, 1911, folder 1046.1.5; Beckwith to the Reverend Jos. E. Williams, December 5, 1913, folder 1046.2.15, Beckwith Papers, BPL.

42. Beckwith to J. J. Orum, March 10 and 20, 1913, folder 1046.2.10; Beckwith to unidentified bishop, May 3, 1917, folder 1046.2.34; Father Hughson of the Order of the Holy Cross to Beckwith, November 5, 1917, folder 1046.3.25, Beckwith Papers, BPL.

43. Beckwith to Devall, March 13, 1913, folder 1046.2.4; Devall to Beckwith, March 26, 1913, folder 1046.2.4; Beckwith to Devall, March 28, 1913, and Devall to Beckwith, April 4, 1913, folder 1046.2.4; Beckwith to Devall, November 17, 1914, folder 1046.2.20; Devall to Beckwith, November 18, 1914, folder 1046.2.20, Beckwith Papers, BPL.

44. *Diocesan Convention* (1916), 28.

45. Questionnaire and letters in the records of St. Paul's, Selma; Schnorrenberg, "Beckwith," 27.

46. *Diocesan Convention* (1903), 62; *Diocesan Convention* (1923), 52–59; the account of Beckwith's feud with Wilkinson is in Wood, *Life of St. John's Parish*. "The Rev. Lewis [*sic*] Tucker, a special correspondent sent by The Churchman from New York, wrote: 'When a real live ecclesiastical trial on the question of discipline suddenly appeared in Alabama the emotions of the general church were like those of a man who has met a mastodon or magatherium in his back yard. The thing was extinct. It had no right to live. Now the last dodo is dead. Let us hope that the last ecclestical [*sic*] trial on discipline or doctrine is chronicaled [*sic*] here.'" Quoted in Wood, *Life of St. John's Parish*, 161.

47. *Diocesan Convention* (1922), 10. The 1863 Diocesan Convention was scheduled for St. Stephen's, Eutaw, but was moved because the Civil War made it impossible to hold the meeting there. However, not only did St. Paul's, Carlowville, host the convention that elected McDowell, they also hosted the convention that elected his successor, Charles C. J. Carpenter, in 1938. *Diocesan Convention* (1923), 55.

48. "Murray's Career Unusual," *New York Times*, October 4, 1929.

Chapter 6

1. John Temple Graves, *The Fighting South* (1943; Tuscaloosa: University of Alabama Press, 1985), 35 and 259.

2. Wayne Flynt, *Poor but Proud: Alabama's Poor Whites* (Tuscaloosa: University of Alabama Press, 1989), 71–72; *Diocesan Convention* (1923), 36; Joan Sue Clemens, "The House of Happiness: An Episcopal Mission in Jackson County, Alabama 1923–1952" (master's thesis, University of Southern Mississippi, 1990), 7–8.

3. For the origins of the House of Happiness and Augusta Martin's life and career prior to becoming director of the mission, see Clemens, "House of Happiness," 7–13.

4. Clemens, "House of Happiness," 14.

5. Campbell Long, *The House of Happiness Story* (Selma, AL: Selma Publishing, 1973), 2.

6. *Alabama Churchman* 1, no. 3 (1923): 8; "A Letter from the House of Happiness," *Alabama Churchman* 4, no. 6 (1926): 9. Copy in folder 241.2.90.13.12, Carpenter Papers, BPL.

7. *Alabama Churchman* 5, no. 8 (1930): 3.

8. Clemens, "House of Happiness," 7–8, 18–19, 30.

9. "A Letter from the House of Happiness," 9; Clemens, "House of Happiness," 43–48.

10. *Diocesan Convention* (1930), 83.

11. Clemens, "House of Happiness," 58.

12. The Church Army is an evangelistic organization for laymen and women that was begun in the Church of England in 1882 and brought to the Episcopal Church USA in 1928.

13. For the account of Martin's meeting with McDowell, see Long, *House of Happiness Story*, 78–79. The Carpenter Papers in the BPL contain letters from M. H. Lynch, MD, about Martin's condition; from McDowell to Martin, urging her to look after her health; and Martin's

letter of resignation to McDowell, folder 241.2.107.13.48, Carpenter Papers, BPL. For the story of the Church Army officers who ran the House of Happiness and its closing, see Clemens, "House of Happiness," 68–125.

14. *Alabama Churchman* (1930); for the background of the Creek Indians near Atmore, see Frank Speck's "Some Notes on the Social and Economic Conditions of the Creek Indians of Alabama in 1941," in *American indígena*. The journal is no longer published, but there is a copy of the article at St. Anna's in Atmore. Rolin's baptism is mentioned in a photo album kept by Edgar Edwards, in folder 241.2.91.13.16, Carpenter Papers, BPL. For the prophetess Anna, see Luke 2:36–38. McDowell to Clara Pickrell, April 23, 1937, folder 241.2.91.13.13, Carpenter Papers, BPL.

15. From an undated document titled "The Colored Community House and Farm Bureau." The original documents are the property of Harry W. Gamble, Esq., of Selma, Alabama, who kindly furnished me with copies of them. The copies are now on deposit in the Department of Archives and Manuscripts at the Birmingham Public Library.

16. Gamble to Harry L. Hopkins, April 15, 1936.

17. Gamble to Eleanor Roosevelt, September 16, 1935. Gamble's contemporary, Rabbi Joseph Gumbiner of Selma's Mishkan Israel congregation, echoed Gamble's concern for African Americans. In an October 25, 1935, letter to FDR, Gumbiner wrote, "Negroes, of course, are disenfranchised, contrary to their constitutional rights. But that is the least of it. In industry they earn from three to ten dollars a week on the theory that a 'n——' can live for almost nothing. He can and does with the result that our section is always poor. In agriculture the people are share croppers or tennant [*sic*] farmers. They work about 150 days in the year on the soil. When the cotton is brought in they are fortunate if they have broken even, that is if they do not owe the 'advancer' more than when they started to make the crop" (box 2, folder 21A, PPF Papers, FDR Library, Hyde Park, New York).

18. On enrollment, see folder 1300.14.12; for services provided to the children, see folders 1300.14.14 and 1300.14.15; for the mothers' club, see folder 1300.14.19, Cathedral Church of the Advent Papers, BPL. There is no indication of where this kindergarten was located.

19. "Bishop C. M. Beckwith of Alabama Is Dead," April 19, 1928, *New York Times*. McDowell to Beckwith, April 13, 1918, folder 1046.3.35, Beckwith Papers, BPL. I found McDowell's compositions in the music library of the Cathedral Church of the Advent.

20. *Alabama Churchman* 6, no. 1 (1928): 1. Flynt also writes, "Although most people think of the Great Depression as a sudden event triggered by the stock market crash of November 1929, it actually was a gradual collapse. As already noted, agriculture entered a depression during the early 1920s and did not fully recover for two decades. Most industries peaked in 1926 or 1927, then began to decline." Rogers et al., *Alabama*, 465.

21. Holy Comforter, Gadsden, vestry minutes, January, 1916, and August, 1933 (Holy Comforter's minutes are in the church office in Gadsden); Grace Episcopal Church, Woodlawn (Birmingham), January 9, 1938, BPL; parochial reports for St. John's, Ensley, folders 1761.14.17, 1761.14.18, and 1761.14.19, BPL; St. Mary's-on-the-Highlands, "Parish Program and Budget for 1933" (St. Mary's-on-the-Highlands' records are in their church archives); the Advent women's groups, June 1, 1931, folder 1300.14.14, Cathedral Church of the Advent records, BPL.

22. For Roosevelt's 1932 convention speech, see the archives of the The Franklin D. Roosevelt Presidential Library and Museum (http://www.fdrlibrary.marist.edu/education/resources /pdfs/demconvention_address.pdf). For Roosevelt's religious faith, see Gary Scott Smith, *Faith and the Presidency: From George Washington to George W. Bush* (Oxford: Oxford University Press, 2006), 219–20: "He experienced a brief crisis of faith after contracting polio, but thereafter he

seemed to maintain a steady belief in God's power, goodness, and love. He frequently spoke about God's providence, saw himself as carrying out God's purposes, and insisted that America would be successful only if its people sought God's guidance and strove to do his will." In *Traitor to His Class: The Privileged Life and Radical Presidency of Franklin Delano Roosevelt* (New York: Anchor Books, 2008), H. W. Brands writes that on the night of his 1932 election FDR said to his son, Jimmy, "After you leave me tonight, Jimmy, I am going to pray. I am going to pray that God will help me, that he will give me the strength and the guidance to do this job and to do it right. I hope you will pray for me, too, Jimmy" (268).

23. Letter from Richard A. Kirchhoffer to FDR, October 5, 1935, PPF #21, Church Matters (Clergy Letters)—Alabama, Franklin D. Roosevelt Presidential Library.

24. Letters from William Thompson to FDR, October 23, 1936, and from Theodore H. Evans to FDR, October 5, 1935, PPF #21, Church Matters (Clergy Letters)—Alabama, Franklin D. Roosevelt Presidential Library.

25. Letters from Charles J. Alleyn to FDR, October 21, 1935, and Edgar M. Parkman to FDR, September 28, 1935, PPF #21, Church Matters (Clergy Letters)—Alabama, Franklin D. Roosevelt Presidential Library.

26. Letter from Richard Wilkinson to FDR, December 20, 1936, PPF #21, Church Matters (Clergy Letters)—Alabama, Franklin D. Roosevelt Presidential Library.

27. *Diocesan Convention* (1927), 39; *Diocesan Convention* (1930), 41. For the *Age-Herald's* opinion of the strike, see Rogers, et al., *Alabama*, 418–19.

28. *Diocesan Convention* (1931), 39–41; *Diocesan Convention* (1935), 39.

29. The basic facts of the "Scottsboro boys" are covered in Dan T. Carter's *Scottsboro: A Tragedy of the American South* (Baton Rouge: Louisiana State University Press, 1969), 3–50. In 1929, Lester Bouyer, a black man accused of assaulting a white woman and killing her companion, had needed fifty National Guardsmen to prevent a crowd from lynching him ("Troops Will Guard Negro in Alabama," *New York Times*, July 23, 1929). McDowell was not unique in his inability to transcend the racial taboos of his class and culture. In the early twentieth century, many of the most prominent Southern Baptist clergy in Alabama held progressive social and theological views but still found ways to justify the marginalization of black people. A. J. Dickinson, pastor of Birmingham's First Baptist Church (who held a PhD from the University of Chicago), declared that he believed in evolution and socialism and advocated public ownership of public transportation and utilities. However, he opposed allowing blacks to attend the Southern Baptist Convention and criticized Booker T. Washington for "instilling 'notions of social equality' in the minds of Tuskegee Institute students." Wayne Flynt, *Alabama Baptists: Southern Baptists in the Heart of Dixie* (Tuscaloosa: University of Alabama Press, 1998), 303.

30. Henry Morris Edmonds, *A Parson's Notebook* (Birmingham, AL: Elizabeth Agee's Bookshelf, 1961), 283.

31. Fosdick to McDowell, March 25, 1933, and McDowell to Fosdick, March 30, 1933, folder 241.20.40, Carpenter Papers, BPL. A signed copy of Bates's statement is in the same folder. Bates testified about her visit to Fosdick, and it is mentioned in the standard books on Scottsboro, but Bates's visit to McDowell is omitted.

32. McDowell to Fosdick, March 30, 1933; April 8, 1933; and April 13, 1933, folder 241.20.40, Carpenter Papers, BPL. Evidently, McDowell had become convinced that the ILD had paid Ruby Bates to change her testimony and that he and Fosdick had been used to give credence to Bates's recantation. "It was quite evident that Ruby Bates and Carter had been taken to New York and carefully schooled by Mr. Brodski of the defense counsel. It was evident that Dr. Fosdick and I were used as two good, disinterested addresses which she could talk about instead

of telling what else she had been doing." McDowell to Clinton Rogers Woodruff, May 10, 1933, folder 241.20.38, Carpenter Papers, BPL.

33. McDowell to Alan Knight Chalmers of the Scottsboro Defense Committee, January 1, 1936, Carpenter Papers, folder 241.20.39; McDowell to Clinton Rogers Woodruff, May 10, 1933, Carpenter Papers, folder 241.20.38.

34. On November 7, 1935, Edmund Burke, secretary of Tuskegee's board, wrote McDowell informing him of his election (folder 241.1.63, Carpenter Papers, BPL).

35. Fund-raising letter from McDowell, May 3, 1935, and Edmund H. Burke, secretary of Tuskegee's board of trustees, to McDowell, Tuskegee Institute, November 7, 1935, folder 1591.1.10, McDowell Papers, BPL.

36. Folders 1591.1.5 and 1591.1.6, McDowell Papers, BPL.

37. Folders 1591.1.5 and 1591.1.9, McDowell Papers, BPL.

38. Folder 1591.1.5, McDowell Papers, BPL.

39. Folders 1591.1.6 and 1591.1.7, McDowell Papers, BPL. The priest's obituary appeared in the *Redwood Journal*, Ukiah, California, July 31, 1950.

40. Barbara Brandon Schnorrenberg explains the evolution of the Women's Auxiliary in "Our Oldest and Best Organization: The Alabama Woman's Auxiliary, 1920–1940," in *Deeper Joy: Lay Women and Vocation in the 20th Century Episcopal Church*, ed. Fredrica Harris Thompsett and Sheryl Kujawa-Holbrook (New York: Church Publishing, 2005), 264–76.

41. *Journal of the Special Council of the Protestant Episcopal Church in the Diocese of Alabama* (1922), 12 and 17; *Diocesan Convention* (1923), 27.

42. *Diocesan Convention* (1941), 63; *Diocesan Convention* (1942), 30 and 32, 67.

43. *Diocesan Convention* (1943), 29, 30, 36; *Diocesan Convention* (1944), 29, and *Diocesan Convention* (1945), 39; *Diocesan Convention* (1967), 80.

44. For McDowell's description of his schedule and duties: *Convention Journal* (1938), 43; for the story of McDowell's illness and death, see Kennington, *From the Day of Small Things*, 225.

45. Charles Colcock Jones Carpenter (hereafter CCJC) was related to the Reverend Charles Colcock Jones (1804–1863), a Presbyterian minister and planter in coastal Georgia, who became known as "the apostle to the Negro slaves" for his work among slaves in antebellum Georgia. Both the Reverend Jones and the Right Reverend Carpenter were educated at Princeton University. Jones was drawn to abolitionism while he was at Princeton but eventually became a champion of slavery. There is considerable irony in the fact that Bishop Carpenter's ancestor wrestled with the issue of slavery. The most comprehensive account of Charles Colcock Jones's life and work is Erskine Clarke's *Dwelling Place: A Plantation Epic* (New Haven, CT: Yale University Press, 2005).

46. The Reverend Douglas Carpenter, Bishop Carpenter's son, has two scrapbooks of the bishop's wrestling memorabilia. Previous rectors of the Church of the Advent who were elected bishop include John Gardner Murray, who was elected bishop coadjutor of Maryland in 1909, succeeded to the role of diocesan bishop the same year, and was elected Presiding Bishop of the Episcopal Church in 1926; Charles Clingman was elected bishop of Kentucky in 1936; and Middleton Barnwell was missionary bishop of Idaho in 1925 and later bishop of Georgia in 1935. Subsequently, Brinkley Morton, the first dean of the Cathedral Church of the Advent was elected bishop of San Diego in 1982. For CCJC's nomination to serve as bishop of Georgia, see the journal of the 113th convention of the Diocese of Georgia (1935), 46–51. The list of honorary degree recipients is in the program for Princeton's 1947 "Alumni Day Convocation" in a scrapbook in Douglas Carpenter's family papers.

47. *Diocesan Convention* (1942), 39, and *Diocesan Convention* (1939), 44. There is a copy of

one of Carpenter's letters to "Alabama Churchmen in the Service" in the September 1943 issue of the *Alabama Churchman*, 8, as well as a photograph of the "service cross." For the figure of 1,100 "churchmen" in service, see the *Alabama Churchman* (May 1943): 3. For the British cadets, see Wood, *Life of St. John's Parish*, 177.

48. Foster issued an extensive statement about his experiences in Honolulu and noted that "the 1955 convention was moved from Houston, Texas to Honolulu, Hawaii, because of the very real possibility that if the convention were held in Houston Christian practice might not prevail as fully as the Church believed was essential." Luther Foster, "The 58th Episcopal Convention as Seen by One Lay Delegate," folder 241.1.65, Carpenter Papers, BPL.

49. A. Henry May, "History [*sic*] Sketch of St. Andrew's Mission, Tuskegee Inst.," October, 1932; William George McDowell, "To the Friends of Tuskegee Institute," May 3, 1935, folder 241.1.63, Carpenter Papers; William Byrd Lee to CCJC, December 4, 1939; "Episcopal Chapel to be Constructed Near Campus," *Campus Digest* (January 29, 1949), folder 241.1.64, Carpenter Papers, BPL.

50. *Diocesan Convention* (1955), 64–65; "Report of the Bishop's Diocesan Committee to Study the Problem of Securing Young Negro Postulants for Holy Orders" (n.d.), 241.2.129.14.32, Carpenter Papers, BPL. A fifth parish—St. Christopher's, Huntsville—was subsequently founded. The one African American whom Carpenter ordained was Robert Earl DuBose Jr.

51. William A. Clark to CCJC, January 13, 1956; committee report (November 1956), folder 241.2.129.14.32, Carpenter Papers, BPL.

52. Martha Jane Gibson to CCJC, April 10, 1939; Hilda Davis to CCJC, April 17, 1939; Clingman to CCJC, April 22, 1939, folder 241.1.122.8, Carpenter Papers, BPL. Clingman's position seems to have been an improvement on that of his predecessor, Marshall Seifert. A couple of years earlier (1937) "perhaps a dozen, students from the College visited the regular 11:00 A.M. Sunday Services at St. Peter's. . . . The negroes evidently interspersed themselves among the white congregation rather indiscriminately, much to the consternation of some of the parishioners." According to Clingman, Seifert "went to the college authorities and asked that the students not return."

53. Clingman to CCJC, April 22, 1939, folder 241.1.122.8, Carpenter Papers, BPL.

54. CCJC to Gibson, April 20, 1939, folder 241.1.122.8.41, Carpenter Papers, BPL.

55. Blackford to CCJC, February 8, 1946, folder 241.1.122.8.41, Carpenter Papers, BPL.

56. CCJC to M. M. DePass, April 26, 1962, folder 241.1.122.8.41, Carpenter Papers, BPL. It is astonishing that Carpenter began to deal with the issue of integrating St. Peter's, Talladega, in 1939, and in 1962 was still refusing to take a firm stand either for or against integration. Apparently the bishop believed that if he just waited long enough, the problem would go away.

57. Taken from materials in the archives of St. Martin's in the Pines, including a personal statement by David Cady Wright. These materials are now on deposit at the archives of the Birmingham Public Library. For the Hill-Burton Act, see "Truman Signs Bill for Billion U.S.-State Hospital Program," *Washington Post*, August 14, 1946, 1.

58. James M. Stoney, *Lighting the Candle* (Santa Fe, NM: Rydal Press, 1961).

59. "Psychiatric Work by Clergy Urged," *New York Times*, October 20, 1955; "Miss Mitchell, 49, Dead of Injuries," *New York Times*, August 17, 1949; "Former Local Cleric Dies in Atlanta," *Birmingham News*, August 31, 1962.

Chapter 7

The title of this chapter comes from a statement made by the Episcopal Society for Cultural and Racial Unity (ESCRU), dated April 29, 1965: "The Carpenter of Birmingham must not be allowed to forever deny the Carpenter of Nazareth" (folder 241.1.119.8.24, Carpenter Papers, BPL).

1. For more on Morgan's speech to the Birmingham's Young Men's Business Club: Charles Morgan Jr., *A Time to Speak* (New York: Holt, Rinehart, and Winston, 1964), 10–14; for the negative community reaction to the speech: Patricia Sullivan, "Charles Morgan Jr.; Lawyer Championed Civil, Voting Rights," *Washington Post*, January 9, 2009.

2. Mark Noll, *A History of Christianity in the United States and Canada* (Grand Rapids, MI: Eerdmans Publishing, 1992), 441. The Eisenhower quotation is from his address at the Freedoms Foundation, Waldorf Astoria Hotel, New York City, December 22, 1952, http://www.eisenhower.archives.gov/all_about_ike/quotes.html#religion.

3. Boykin's statement is in the *Congressional Record*, March 29, 1959, 1. For the article quoting Lichtenberger, see the *Birmingham News*, January 13, 1959, 6. Boykin did not include the name of the letter's author, but Johnston's authorship of the letter is confirmed by the reply that CCJC wrote to him in a letter dated February 25, 1959 (Carpenter Papers, 241.2.5). Johnston implied that his letter had an official imprimatur by saying that he had written "at the request of members of the Standing Committee and Executive Council."

4. "Activity of Klan Rises in Alabama," *New York Times*, September 29, 1959; "Negro Education in South on Rise," *New York Times*, March 16, 1952; and "Alabama Segregation Pushed," *New York Times*, March 24, 1955.

5. "Churches of South Beset by Segregation Dilemma," *New York Times*, July 5, 1959; Yvonne Willie, *My God, It's a Black Man* (unpublished manuscript), 63. I am grateful to Yvonne Willie for permission to use material from her manuscript.

6. Yvonne Willie told me stories of her son's experiences at Camp John Hope and Camp McDowell.

7. Thomas B. Hill Jr., Senior Warden, and Moreland Griffith Smith, Junior Warden, to CCJC, November 17, 1958; and Thomas R. Thrasher to CCJC, November 20, 1958; Olivia B. Witmer to CCJC, April 24, 1956, in 241.7.22, Carpenter Papers, BPL.

8. The Waldo quotation is from Julian and Eleanor McPhillips, *The Drummer's Beat: Our Life and Time: Part I* (1982) (unpublished manuscript), 272; "Excerpt from Minutes of Meeting of the Vestry," July 6, 1959; letter from Thrasher to CCJC, July 25, 1959, in Carpenter Papers, folder 241.7.22. Lynn Willoughby relates the story of the black priest in *The Church of the Ascension: A Resurrection Story* (Montgomery, AL: Donnell Group, 2008), 84–85. Jo Ann Gibson Robinson also writes of Thrasher's role in facilitating meetings between black and white leaders in *The Montgomery Bus Boycott and the Women Who Started It* (Knoxville: University of Tennessee Press, 1987). I am indebted to Brandt Montgomery for identifying DuBose as the black priest who received communion at Ascension in his MDiv thesis.

9. Robinson, *Montgomery Bus Boycott*, 25 and 81.

10. From Sheryl Spradling Summe's "'Alive to the Cause of Justice': Juliette Hampton Morgan and the Montgomery Bus Boycott," in *Stepping Out of the Shadows: Alabama Women, 1819–1990*, ed. Mary Martha Thomas (Tuscaloosa: University of Alabama Press, 1995), 177–90.

11. Louis Mitchell discussed his experiences at St. Luke's with me in a telephone call on June 2, 2011. The notes of our conversation are on deposit in the Birmingham Public Library. A. W. Jones's letter (dated December 5, 1962) was given to me by Charles Morgan's widow, Camille Morgan, and is also on deposit in the BPL.

12. Robert E. Gribbin Jr., "Campus Crisis in Alabama" *Episcopal Church News*, March 18, 1956, 18–19, and "Statement of Rev. R. Emmet Gribbin" in the E. Culpepper Clark Collection, Hoole Special Collections Library, University of Alabama.

13. "Robed Klansmen Picket Forum," *Birmingham Post-Herald*, May 10, 1957; "Open Forum Meeting Undisturbed by KKK," *Tuscaloosa News*, May 14, 1957. The archives of Canterbury Chapel, Tuscaloosa, contain a sermon Gribbin preached on April 23, 1961, in which he mentioned seeing the armed Klansmen. The April 22, 1961, letter from Gribbin to Charles Pointer is also in the Canterbury Chapel archives. See also "Protest Registered," in "Letters to the Editor," *Tuscaloosa News*, April 23, 1961.

14. McPhillips's story is related in Julian and Eleanor McPhillips, *The Drummer's Beat: Our Life and Times* (1982) (unpublished manuscript), part 1.

15. "Thou shalt love the Lord thy God . . .": Deuteronomy 6:5 and Luke 10:27; Kennington, *From the Day of Small Things*, 280; vestry minutes, January 11, 1955, Holy Comforter, Gadsden.

16. In contrast, during the Little Rock school integration crisis, Robert R. Brown, the Episcopal bishop of Arkansas, issued a pastoral letter to be read in all the parishes of his diocese "in which he said the violence at the school shamed the church" and he "castigated its failure to 'exert an adequate Christian leadership.'" Quoted in Michael B. Friedland, *Lift Up Your Voice Like a Trumpet: White Clergy and the Civil Rights and Antiwar Movements, 1954–1973* (Chapel Hill: University of North Carolina Press, 1998), 34. For Carpenter's remarks about the *Brown* decision, see *Diocesan Convention* (1955), 65.

17. There were exceptions to segregation in the churches. In a 1962 letter Carpenter wrote, "For years those of us who are of the old South have recognized the custom of having Negro friends visit from time to time. Frequently they would come as visitors for special services, funerals, marriages, etc., and this is quite in accordance with the old Southern tradition." CCJC to Major M. M. DePass, April 26, 1962, folder 241.1.122.8.41, Carpenter Papers, BPL. But there was a world of difference between attending a funeral or wedding as a guest of a white person and attending a church weekly as one of its members. Carpenter never seems to have had a strong commitment to the integration of schools. In 1961, when St. Luke's Mission in Mobile proposed setting up a school, Carpenter did not urge that St. Luke's school be desegregated until Mobile's public schools were desegregated. "If and when the Mobile schools are desegregated, our school will also be open to applications from negro children which will be considered on an equal basis." CCJC to Lloyd A. Clarke, April 6, 1961, folder 241.1.89.6.49, Carpenter Papers, BPL. For the report of the Committee on Christian Social Relations, see *Diocesan Convention* (1955), 108–9.

18. I have relied on the account of the School of Theology crisis in Williamson, *Sewanee Sesquicentennial History*, 263–76. Letter from CCJC to R. N. Campbell, May 27, 1952, folder 241.2.159.15.32, Carpenter Papers, BPL.

19. Letter from Robert W. Powell to CCJC, July 21, 1952, and letter from CCJC to Powell, August 4, 1952, folder 241.2.159.15.32, Carpenter Papers, BPL.

20. CCJC to Edwin Penick, December 1, 1952, folder 241.2.159.15.33, Carpenter Papers, BPL.

21. CCJC to James Pike, February 19, 1953, and CCJC to Edward McGrady, February 19, 1953, folder 241.2.159.15.33, Carpenter Papers, BPL. For another account of the Sewanee crisis, less sympathetic to the trustees and more critical of McGrady, see Shattuck, *Episcopalians and Race*, 44–50.

22. "City, County, and State Officers Keep Order during Dexter Demonstration," *Montgomery Advertiser*, March 7, 1960; letter from F. R. Daugette to CCJC, March 11, 1960; letter from CCJC to "Fellow Communicants," March 16, 1960; letter from CCJC to Robert Earl DuBose, April 1, 1960, in folder 241.20.35, Carpenter Papers, BPL. Gardner Shattuck says that "Carpenter removed DuBose from both his church positions and forced him to find employ-

236 / Notes to Pages 145–151

ment in a northern diocese instead." Shattuck, *Episcopalians and Race*, 119. Brandt Montgomery says that DuBose went to St. Thomas, Philadelphia. Brandt Montgomery, "Time's Prisoner: The Right Reverend Charles Colcock Jones Carpenter and the Civil Rights Movement in the Episcopal Diocese of Alabama" (MDiv thesis, General Theological Seminary, 2011), 41.

23. "Marching Minister Reprimanded," *Birmingham News*, March 22, 1960; letter from Keith, Joffrion, and McKimmon to CCJC, March 25, 1960; letter from Jim Battles to CCJC, March 25, 1960, in folder 241.20.35, Carpenter Papers, BPL.

24. "Background Paper on the Student 'Sit-In' Protest Movement in the Light of the Church's Authoritative Statements," (March, 1960); letter from CCJC to Arthur Lichtenberger, March 31, 1960; "Bishop Hits Statement," *Mobile Press-Register*, April 1, 1960; "Carpenter's Statement on Sit-In Paper Rapped," *Birmingham News* (no date); letter from Vernon Jones to CCJC, April 29, 1960; letter from Luther Foster to CCJC, April 26, 1960, in folder 241.20.35, Carpenter Papers, BPL.

25. "Graham Deplores Alabama Bus Riot," *New York Times*, May 18, 1961; *Alabama Churchman* (June 1961).

26. "Racial Tensions," *Christian Social Relations* (September 15, 1961); CCJC to Thomas Pettigrew, November 7, 1961, folder 241.20.35, Carpenter Papers, BPL. There is also a copy of Pettigrew's article "Why Have We Failed?" in the same folder.

27. For a detailed account of Birmingham's political turmoil, see J. Mills Thornton, *Dividing Lines: Municipal Politics and the Struggle for Civil Rights in Montgomery, Birmingham, and Selma* (Tuscaloosa: University of Alabama Press, 2002).

28. "An Appeal for Law and Order and Common Sense," Appendix 1 (233–34), in S. Jonathan Bass, *Blessed Are the Peacemakers: Martin Luther King, Jr., Eight White Religious Leaders, and the "Letter from Birmingham Jail"* (Knoxville: University of Tennessee Press, 1996); Maurice Rogers to "The Eleven Self Appointed Leaders," January 16, 1963, folder 241.2.38.10.42, Carpenter Papers, BPL.

29. "The White Ministers' Good Friday Statement" is in Bass, *Blessed Are the Peacemakers*, Appendix 2, 235–36. The Good Friday statement notes that its signers were "among those" who had signed the "Law and order and common sense" statement. David J. Garrow gives an account of King's Birmingham campaign in *Bearing the Cross: Martin Luther King, Jr., and the Southern Christian Leadership Conference* (New York: Vintage Books, 1988), 259. Martin Luther King Jr., "Letter from Birmingham Jail," folder 316.14.23, Birmingham history collection, 1940–80, BPL.

30. George Murray, "Memorandum to Trustees of the 16th Street Baptist Church Memorial Fund," folder 241.21.25, Carpenter Papers, BPL; and the Reverend Thomas B. Smythe Jr., "My Corner," *Alabama Churchman* (October 1963): 12. In the same issue Bishop Carpenter wrote a column about the annual "every member canvass." However, Carpenter's daily calendar indicates that he attended the funeral held at Sixth Avenue Baptist Church on September 18.

31. Shattuck, *Episcopalians and Race*, 146.

32. Statistics from "Negro Gain Slow in Winning Vote," *New York Times*, November 24, 1963.

33. For background to the Selma marches, see Thornton, *Dividing Lines*, 380–499; for the meeting to plan the Selma march, see Garrow, *Bearing the Cross*, 358–59. In *Outside Agitator: Jon Daniels and the Civil Rights Movement in Alabama* (Chapel Hill: University of North Carolina Press, 1993), Charles W. Eagle notes that Judge Hare observed, "Your Negro is a mixture of African types like the Congolite who has a long heel and the blue-gummed Ebo whose I.Q. is about 50 or 55," (48).

34. For the Bloody Sunday march, see Roy Reed, "Alabama Police Use Gas and Clubs to

Rout Negroes," *New York Times*, March 8, 1965; and Taylor Branch, *At Canaan's Edge: America in the King Years, 1965–68* (New York: Simon and Schuster, 2006), 44–57. Julian McPhillips, "Return Ye and Live," a sermon for the second Sunday in Lent, March 14, 1965. McPhillips also said,

> Most of us have no idea of the inner burden that the Negro carries in his heart. We see him as a house servant—not as a person. We love him in our kitchen or as a kindly nurse for our children. . . . Suppose you were well mannered and kind and you had the money to pay for a good meal and imagine how you would feel to be turned away from a restaurant because of one thing only—Your skin was black! Or imagine that you had worked hard and saved and bought yourself a nice shiny automobile and a policeman stopped you and asked for proof that you had not stolen it. The indignity of such! These things happen!

35. Branch, *At Canaan's Edge*, 44–79.

36. Roswell Falkenberry, "Our Considered Opinion," March 9, 1965, and "The Tragedy of the Rev. Reeb," March 14, 1965, *Selma Times Journal*; for an account of Reeb's death, see Garrow, *Bearing the Cross*, 405–7.

37. C. C. Grayson, "Pew 62," from the archives of St. Paul's, Selma. It is only fair to note that at the time of writing several black families worship at St. Paul's regularly and the parish has participated in the annual commemoration of the Selma-to-Montgomery march.

38. For an account of CCJC's participation in Hines's consecration as bishop, see Kenneth Kesselus, *John E. Hines: Granite on Fire* (Austin, TX: Episcopal Seminary of the Southwest, 1995), 130; undated memo from Presiding Bishop Hines to Executive Council, folder 241.2.38.11.15, Carpenter Papers, BPL; Shattuck, *Episcopalians and Race*, 154.

39. "Report of the Committee of the Diocese of Alabama on a Study of the National Council of Churches of Christ in the United States of America" (1962), folder 241.2.38.11.17; CCJC to Hines, March 15, 1965, folder 241.1.119.8.24, Carpenter Papers, BPL.

40. CCJC refers to the people of Selma being "rubbed raw" in a letter to Hines, March 15, 1965, folder 241.1.119.8.24; "Memorandum" to the Executive Council from the Presiding Bishop (n.d.), folder 241.2.38.11.5, Carpenter Papers, BPL. Perhaps as a way of deflecting Carpenter's wrath, Hines noted in his memo that William Marmion, bishop of southwestern Virginia and chairman of the executive council's Department of Christian Social Relations (a former rector of St. Mary's-on-the-Highlands, Birmingham) had attended a rally to support the Selma demonstrations at Washington, DC's Lutheran Church of the Reformation.

41. Telegram from Myers to CCJC, March 18, 1965; telegram from Myers to Wilson Baker, March 18, 1965; telegram from CCJC to Myers, March 18, 1965; letter from CCJC to Myers, March 19, 1965; letter from CCJC to Stanley M. Emrich, March 25, 1965; letter from CCJC to Myers, March 24, 1965, folder 241.2.157.15.28, Carpenter Papers, BPL.

42. Charles V. Willie, "Reflections on a Saturday in Selma," 6–7, folder 241.2.157.15.30, Carpenter Papers, BPL. The Willies and Father Wirtz exposed themselves to danger by driving from Birmingham to Selma early on Saturday morning. In Alabama in 1965, it was still fairly uncommon to see black and white people traveling together in a car, and not long before the Selma march, a member of the KKK had shot and killed Viola Liuzzo, a white civil rights worker from Michigan, while she was driving a car with a young black man as a passenger.

43. Peabody's father was the bishop of central New York and his brother was the governor of Massachusetts. Malcolm Peabody to CCJC, 1965, folder 241.2.157.15.28, Carpenter Papers,

BPL; "Selma Pastor Sees No Evil in Segregated Worship," *Houston Chronicle*, March 11, 1965, folder 241.2.38.11.13, Carpenter Papers, BPL.

44. Letters from Frank Matthews, March 23, 1965, and March 25, 1965, folder 241.1.119.8.24; memo from Carpenter, March 25, 1965, folder 241.2.38.10.50; letter from Hines to CCJC, March 29, 1965, folder 241.21.9, Carpenter Papers, BPL.

45. Branch, *At Canaan's Edge*, 61 and 155–70. The transcript of King's "Our God is Marching On!" speech that is housed at the Martin Luther King Jr. Research and Education Institute at Stanford University actually has: "How long will justice be crucified, and truth bear it?" instead of "truth buried."

46. I have relied on Eagles's *Outside Agitator* for details of Daniels's life and death. For the account of his decision to go to Selma, see 27.

47. Letter from Matthews to St. Paul's parishioners, March 25, 1965, folder 241.2.38.10.50; CCJC to Daniels and Upham, April 23, 1965; "To Whom It May Concern" from Daniels and Upham, May 12, 1965, folder 241.1.119.8.24, Carpenter Papers, BPL. In *Outside Agitator*, Charles Eagles gives a detailed account of Daniels's experiences at St. Paul's on 44–59.

48. Eagles, *Outside Agitator*, 69–71. After Daniels's murder, Matthews wrote Carpenter: "While I agreed with practically nothing Jonathan did nor any of his racial opinions, my contacts with him were all very cordial." Matthew to CCJC, August 24, 1965, folder 241.1.119.8.25, Carpenter Papers, BPL.

49. Matthews to CCJC and George Murray (hereafter GM), August 1, 1965; CCJC to Matthews, August 12, 1965, folder 241.1.119.8.25, Carpenter Papers, BPL.

50. Eagles, *Outside Agitator*, 167–79.

51. Douglass to CCJC, August 26, 1965, folder 241.1.119.8.25, Carpenter Papers, BPL; Eagles, *Outside Agitator*, 182.

52. "Civil Rights Worker Slain," *Birmingham News*, August 21, 1965; Matthews to CCJC, August 24, 1965, folder 241.1.119.8.25, Carpenter Papers, BPL. There is an enigmatic handwritten note in Carpenter's papers on Carpenter's personal notepaper that appears to be the notes CCJC made during his telephone conversation with Charles Douglass the evening of Friday, August 20. It reads: "Jonathan Daniels mentally deranged Negro undertaker [illegible] cursing and asking for trouble act so rude! people talking about his cursing protective custody [illegible] White Chapel [funeral home] wallet gone Jonathan Daniels boys mother in Keene, N.H. John Morris would take body home body in Montgomery Mother wants Charlie Douglass to get personal effects mother wants body shipped home if Morris wants to go with body O.K. Hall on vacation White Chapel in charge Mont. Douglass has talked to mother and local curate Mont. undertaker will send body." Folder 241.1.119.8.25, Carpenter Papers, BPL.

53. "Talking It Over," *The Witness*, September 2, 1965; "Matt Murphy Dies in Auto Accident," *Birmingham News*, August 21, 1965; undated handwritten note on Murray's notepaper, folder 241.2.38.11.11; GM to William Spofford, October 7, 1965, folder 241.1.119.8.26; Spofford to GM, January 27, 1966, folder 241.2.38.11.11, Carpenter Papers, BPL.

54. Undated draft of telegram to *The Living Church*, folder 241.1.119.8.25, Carpenter Papers, BPL.

55. Folder 241.1.119.8.30; statement issued by the Right Reverend John E. Hines, September 28, 1965, folder 241.1.119.8.26, Carpenter Papers, BPL.

56. Statement by CCJC and GM is in *The Bulletin* 1, no. 5 (1965), folder 241.1.119.8.30; Morris to GM, October 25, 1965; and John Krum to GM, October 27, 1965. In reply to Morris, Murray said that he and Carpenter had refrained from speaking more plainly so that they would not "aggravate other judges and courts who are seeking to administer justice fairly in Ala-

bama . . . we have serious failures in the administration of justice here but that does not mean that there is no justice administered here at all." GM to Morris, November 1, 1965. Murray's reply to Krum was weak and unconvincing: "We were not present at the trials and had only the benefit of the newspaper reporting." GM to Krum (November 3, 1965). All letters in folder 241.2.38.11.12, Carpenter Papers, BPL.

57. Julian McPhillips, "Thou Shalt Do No Murder," October 3, 1965. A copy of the sermon was provided by his son and daughter-in-law, Frank and Louise McPhillips.

58. Coburn to GM, November 19, 1959; David W. Robinson and twelve other students to GM, November 18, 1965; Robert Ihloff to GM, November 19, 1965; Thomas J. Cottle to GM, November 1, 1965, folder 241.2.38.11.13, Carpenter Papers, BPL.

59. Information about Walter comes from an interview I conducted with him. A recording of the interview is in the Diocese of Alabama archives at the BPL.

60. Walter to GM, October 4, 1965; CCJC to Walter, October 5, 1965; the people mentioned in Walter's letter in whom Carpenter had "no confidence" were Rabbi Balfour Brickner, Union of American Hebrew Congregations; Dr. Homer Jack, Unitarian Universalist Association; Matthew Ahman, National Catholic Conference for Interracial Justice; Bruce Hanson, National Council of Churches; and John Morris, ESCRU. Folder 241.2.38.10.59, Carpenter Papers, BPL.

61. CCJC to Walter, October 5, 1965; GM to Walter, October 12, 1965; Matthews to GM, October 14, 1965; folder 241.2.38.10.59, Carpenter Papers, BPL.

62. Emmet Gribbin, "Letter from an Alumnus in Alabama," *Bulletin of the General Theological Seminary* (November 1965): 17–18, folder 241.2.38.11.24; Francis X. Walter, "More from Alabama Alumni," folder 241.2.38.11.25. Murray wrote Leland Stark, Walter's bishop in New Jersey, charging that Walter had lied: "Bishop Carpenter and I are accustomed to criticism but deliberate falsehood is more than we can excuse." GM to Leland Stark, April 7, 1966, folder 241.2.11.38.14. For an example of a priest who was discouraged from taking a parish in Alabama because of his views on civil rights, see GM's letter to William Gray of Cedar Falls, Iowa, April 28, 1965, folder 241.2.38.11.7. All letters in Carpenter Papers, BPL.

63. Frank Yeilding to CCJC, March 22, 1965, folder 241.21.12; Mary T. Brown, March 20, 1965, folder 241.21.11; sender's name illegible to CCJC, March 20, 1965, folder 241.21.11, Carpenter Papers, BPL.

64. Vernon Jones to CCJC, March 28, 1965; Luther H. Foster to CCJC, April 1, 1965, folder 241.21.17, Carpenter Papers, BPL.

65. GM to Kilmer Myers, April 30, 1965, folder 241.2.38.11.7; Alice G. Murphy to Hines, April 9, 1965, folder 241.1.38.11.6, Carpenter Papers, BPL. The article about Carpenter's participation in the campaign against "hooded terrorism" is in a scrapbook in the possession of Douglas Carpenter.

66. Jonathan Bass, "Bishop C. C. J. Carpenter: From Segregation to Integration," *Alabama Review* (July 1992): 184–215. In the same article, Bass quotes Carpenter's son, Doug, who said, "That drain 'bothered him a great deal' . . . because [he] believed little leadership existed 'among the black Episcopal community and he wanted there to be.'" Letter from GM to Emmet Gribbin, January 29, 1993, in the possession of Doug Carpenter. For the integration of Camp McDowell, see William Yon, *No Trumpets, No Drums* (unpublished manuscript), 57–58.

67. In nearby Mississippi, future bishop Duncan Gray, the rector of St. Peter's Episcopal Church in Oxford, spoke out clearly, forcefully, and directly, denouncing the University of Mississippi's attempt to prevent integration: "I do not believe that any of us here today could stand in the presence of Jesus of Nazareth, look Him squarely in the eye, and say 'We will not admit

a Negro to the University of Mississippi.' For it was He who said, 'Inasmuch as ye have done it unto one of the least of these my brethren, ye have done it unto me.'" Quoted in Will Campbell, *And Also with You: Duncan Gray and the American Dilemma* (Franklin, TN: Providence House Publishing, 1997), 18.

68. Scarlett to CCJC, July 22, 1960, folder 241.2.155.15.6, Carpenter Papers, BPL.

69. The figures are from the 1938 and 1968 Diocesan Convention Journals, so they reflect the numbers reported those years for the previous year. The total number of congregations (parishes, organized missions, and mission stations) in 1938 was 107. In 1968 the total was 111.

Chapter 8

1. Walker Percy, *Love in the Ruins: The Adventures of a Bad Catholic at a Time Near the End of the World* (New York: Farrar, Straus and Giroux, 1971), 64–65.

2. For the Pike story, see *Time*, September 12, 1969. Shattuck, *Episcopalians and Race*, 187–213; for the Krum quotation, see Shattuck, *Episcopalians and Race*, 194.

3. For an account of the South Bend convention, see *Alabama Churchman* (September 1969); comments from the Alabama delegation are on p. 12.

4. "1rst [*sic*] Woman Episcopal Priest in Alabama to Be Ordained," *Birmingham Post-Herald*, June 6, 1977.

5. Kennington, *From the Day of Small Things*, 312.

6. The relationship with Namibia is detailed in Bishop Stough's uncataloged papers in the archives of the Birmingham Public Library. I have also relied on personal correspondence with the Reverend William Yon.

7. Charles Richardson, "Church to Build High Apartments," *Birmingham News*, February 29, 1968; Jon Will Pitts, area director of HUD, to Stough, February 4, 1975; minutes, Diocesan Council, September 5, 1975; Lawrence B. Simons, assistant secretary of HUD, to Stough, September 23, 1977, in the uncataloged papers of Furman C. Stough, BPL.

8. For the Alabama Plan, see William Yon, *No Trumpets, No Drums* (unpublished manuscript), 80. For Stough's unsuccessful run for Presiding Bishop, see Carol Ann Campbell, "Fascination Drew Him to Church," *Birmingham Post-Herald*, July 27, 1985, and Patsy Place, "Bishop Stough's Nomination Part of 'Firsts' at Episcopal Convention," *Birmingham News*, September 6, 1985. The other nominees for Presiding Bishop were Browning; William Frey, bishop of Colorado; and John Walker, bishop of Washington, DC.

9. Leonard Chambless, "Church of Advent Named Cathedral in Ceremonies," *Birmingham Post-Herald*, February 13, 1982, 1.

10. Information about Beckwith Lodge is drawn from "A Short and Biased History of Beckwith Camp and Conference Center," an unpublished manuscript by the Reverend S. Albert Kennington and is used by his permission.

11. For Murray House, see *Diocesan Convention* (1998) (Central Gulf Coast), 145–46.

12. I say that Christ Church was the "mother church" of the Episcopal Church in Alabama, because although Christ Church, Tuscaloosa, was a few weeks older than Christ Church, Mobile, the Mobile congregation had existed since 1822 as part of a "union" church that included Presbyterians and Methodists.

13. Information about Bishop Jefferts Schori's visit to the Diocese of the Central Gulf Coast provided by the Reverend Albert Kennington. The thirty-second standing ovation at Bishop Sloan's consecration is my own observation.

14. *Diocesan Convention* (Alabama) (2002), 47 and 48, and *Diocesan Convention* (Central Gulf Coast) (2012), 93.

15. "Bishop Moore Ordains a Lesbian as Priest in the Episcopal Church," *New York Times*, January 11, 1977; "Episcopal Bishops Are Divided on Issues Involving Homosexuality," *New York Times*, October 4, 1977; "Absolved in Gay Ordination," *New York Times*, May 19, 1996.

16. "Gay Bishop Wins in Episcopal Vote; Split Threatened," *New York Times*, August 6, 2003; "Episcopalians Approve Rite to Bless Same Sex Unions," *New York Times*, July 10, 2012. For Parsley's comments, see *Diocesan Convention* (2001), 37; *Diocesan Convention* (2005), 27. I am grateful to the Rt. Rev. Henry Nutt Parsley Jr. for reading this section and giving me a first-hand account of some of the events in which he participated.

17. For Justice Moore's opinion, see Kevin Sack, "Judge's Ouster Sought after Antigay Remarks," *New York Times*, February 20, 2002; for Tutu's sermon, see *The Apostle*, May/June 2002, 1 (emphasis added).

18. For the story of the split at Christ Church, see Kristen Campbell, "Christ Church Leaders Consider Split with the Episcopal Church," *Mobile Press-Register*, September 27, 2000, and Campbell, "A House Divided: Why Episcopalians Leave," October 25, 2000; Richard Lake, "Christ Church Splits with Episcopal Church," *Mobile Press-Register*, October 2, 2000.

19. *Alabama Episcopalian*, March/April 2009, 3. For the *Montgomery Advertiser* article about the split, see Julian McPhillips's reference to it in his history of Christ the Redeemer.

20. Julian McPhillips (the oldest son of the Reverend Julian McPhillips, rector of St. Luke's, Birmingham) chronicled the history of Christ the Redeemer in *History of Christ the Redeemer Episcopal Church* (Montgomery, AL: New South Books, 2006). In regard to Christ the Redeemer as a "renewal parish," McPhillips wrote, "Others from local Episcopal churches considered this new church 'crazy,' primarily due to such charismatic flourishes as hand-raising, sharing of prophecies, and/or the occasional speaking or singing in tongues" (16). McPhillips also notes that "in August, 1990, seven representatives from Christ the Redeemer were the only Alabama Episcopalians to attend the 'World Conference on the Holy Spirit and Evangelism,' in Indianapolis, Indiana" (41).

21. See Greg Garrison, "Break-Off Church Joins Anglican Group," *Birmingham News*, November 24, 2002. There are several documents related to the split at St. Luke's that are in the uncataloged material in the archives of the Diocese of Alabama, including the letters cited here.

22. See Greg Garrison, "Local Church Leader Protests Gay Bishop," August 7, 2003; Garrison, "Theologians Spar over Gay Role in Episcopal Church," February 6, 2004; and Garrison, "Zahl Bids Goodbye at Advent," August 1, 2004, all in the *Birmingham News*.

23. I am indebted to the Reverend S. Albert Kennington for information about Vince Currie.

24. For additional information about Henderson, Kilby, Persons, and James, see Samuel L. Webb and Margaret E. Armbrester, eds., *Alabama Governors* (Tuscaloosa: University of Alabama Press, 2001).

25. For James's involvement at Emanuel, Opelika, and the service on the morning of his inauguration, *Alabama Churchman* (January 1979): 1; for James's controversial religious beliefs, see Webb and Armbrester, *Alabama Governors*, 247–48; for the teaching of evolution, see "A Stickler on Correctness" *New York Times*, June 2, 1996; see also Wayne Flynt, *Alabama in the Twentieth Century* (Tuscaloosa: University of Alabama Press, 2004), 150.

26. I am grateful to Bishop McLeod for sharing her memories with me. Nancy M. Neuman has written about McLeod in *A Voice of Our Own: Leading American Women Celebrate*

the Right to Vote (San Francisco: Jossey-Bass, 1996). Prior to McLeod's election to the episcopate, Barbara Harris was elected bishop suffragan of Massachusetts in 1989, and the Diocese of Washington elected Jane Holmes Dixon as their bishop suffragan in 1992.

27. "*The Bishop says to the ordinand* Will you be loyal to the doctrine, discipline, and worship of Christ as this Church has received them?" *Book of Common Prayer* (1976), 526.

28. I have relied on Gardiner H. Shattuck's account of Murphy, All Saints, Pawleys Island, and the formation of the AMiA in his essay, "'The Tradition Club': Culture War, Memory, and the Reinvention of Anglican Identity in the Modern South," in *Religion in the Contemporary South: Changes, Continuities, and Contexts*, ed. Corrie E. Norman and Don S. Armentrout (Knoxville: University of Tennessee Press, 2005), 257–74. Shattuck points out the credibility problem created by the fact that four of the AMiA's eight bishops were not only in a single diocese (South Carolina) but also were members of the staff of All Saints. He also notes the irony of the fact that the AMiA's chief sponsor is an African archbishop, but although there is a large black community in the area around All Saints, the parish has very few black worshipers. An AMiA publication states, "Christianity is no longer a white man's religion" and "has become a religion of the poor, the marginalized, the powerless," but "there is still an extraordinary discontinuity between . . . its stated interest in the faith of downtrodden people in Africa today, and its negligible outreach among the poor in its own community." See also Gustav Niebuhr, "Consecration of Two Splits Anglicans," *New York Times*, March 5, 2000, 26.

29. The new congregations in the Diocese of Alabama are All Saints, Aliceville (1995); Holy Apostles, Hoover (1995); Holy Spirit, Alabaster (2002); Christ Church, Albertville (1978); St. Stephen's, Birmingham (1973); St. Thomas, Birmingham (1991); St. Catherine's, Chelsea (2009); Good Shepherd, Decatur (1995); Resurrection, Gadsden (1971); St. Barnabas, Hartselle (1980); St. Columba's, Huntsville (2000); St. Francis, Indian Springs (1980); Epiphany, Leeds (1980); St. Matthew's, Madison (1991); St. Joseph's-on-the-Mountain, Mentone (1972); Calvary, Oneonta (2002); St. Simon Peter, Pell City (1975); and Epiphany, Tallassee (2008). Christ the Redeemer, Montgomery, began and closed in the last forty years. Congregations begun by the Diocese of the Central Gulf Coast (in Alabama) are St. Dismas, Atmore (2009) (a mission to prisoners at Fountain Correctional Center); St. Francis, Dauphin Island (1979); Advent, Lillian (2002); and Redeemer, Mobile (1981). The only Alabama parish that the Diocese of the Central Gulf Coast has closed is St. Mary's, Evergreen.

Conclusion

The subtitle for the Conclusion is from Luke 12:48 (Authorized Version)

1. See Flynt, *Alabama in the Twentieth Century*, 149, 163–64: "*The Rating Guide to Life in America's 50 States* ranked Alabama in 1994 the third worst state to live in. . . . The nonpartisan Corporation for Enterprise Development regularly assigned grades of D or F to Alabama's economic performance, development capacity, and state policy, and no better than B or C for its business vitality. These scores sometimes ranked the state dead last and always in the bottom 5 or 10 states. . . . At the heart of the problem was education, or lack of it. Alabama consistently ranked among the five bottom states in expenditures on K–12 schools. . . . Throughout the 1990s one industry after another complained about the educational quality of Alabama's workforce."

2. For McDowell's remarks, see *Diocesan Convention* (1923), 46.

3. For example, compared to Baptists, Methodists, Presbyterians, and Roman Catholics, the Episcopal Church, as a denomination, has played little role in promoting higher education in the United States. Baptists have produced Brown, the University of Chicago, the Univer-

sity of Richmond, Wake Forest, and Baylor, among many others; Methodists founded Boston University, Duke, Emory, Vanderbilt, Southern Methodist, and a host of other smaller but exceptionally good colleges; and Presbyterians established or gave significant help to Princeton University, Davidson, and Rhodes, to name a few. Quaker-originated institutions include Bryn Mawr, Cornell, Johns Hopkins, Swarthmore, and Haverford. It would be impossible to list all the Roman Catholic institutions of higher learning here, but they include some of America's most important colleges and universities: Boston College, Notre Dame, Fordham, Catholic University, and Georgetown.

4. I am not arguing that the Episcopal Church is in decline because it has become a champion of social justice. All the "mainline" denominations (i.e., Baptist [American], United Methodist, Presbyterian [PCUSA], Disciples of Christ, United Church of Christ, Reformed Church in America, and Lutheran [ELCA]) have lost large numbers of their members. There are many reasons for this. In *The Churching of America, 1776–2005: Winners and Losers in Our Religious Economy* (New Brunswick, NJ: Rutgers University Press, 2005), authors Roger Finke and Rodney Stark argue that the churches that make the most demands also offer the greatest rewards, and that the mainline churches have gradually "negotiated" away their religious distinctiveness. ("There comes a point, however, when a religious body has become so worldly that its rewards are few and lacking in plausibility. When hell is gone, can heaven's departure be far behind? Here people begin to switch away. Some are recruited by very high-tension movements. Others move into the newest and least secularized mainline firms. Still others abandon all religion" [283].) Even the Southern Baptists have experienced a decline in baptisms. See Greg Warner, "SBC Warned on Veering Further Right," *Christian Century*, July 13, 2004, 10–11. Wade Clark Roof and William McKinney also think that the core beliefs of the mainline churches have become too attenuated but argue that they are losing members not to the conservative churches but to secularism: "Liberal Protestantism's 'competition' is not the conservatives it has *spurned* but the secularists it has *spawned*. . . . If these churches are to reclaim the loyalties of persons lost to this secular-minded constituency, they will need to hold firm to their historic values and to testify to them in as direct and forceful manner as possible." *American Mainline Religion: Its Changing Shape and Future* (New Brunswick, NJ: Rutgers University Press, 1987), 242.

5. This attempt at "rebranding" has produced some high silliness. A former Alabama priest "translated" parts of the Bible and Book of Common Prayer into "hip-hop" (Timothy Holder, *The Hip Hop Prayer Book* [New York: Church Publishing, 2006]), but there is little sign that the "hip-hop community" is thronging to the Episcopal Church.

6. See appendix D.

7. For Christ Church, Mobile, see Parish Register, 15, in the archives of Christ Church, Mobile; for Nativity, Huntsville, see Roberts, *Sesquicentennial History of Church of the Nativity*, 10; for St. John's, Montgomery, see Wood, *Life of St. John's Parish*, 6 and 23–24. Spring Hill College, Alabama's oldest college, a Roman Catholic institution, was founded the same year that the Diocese of Alabama was organized (1830). In 1826, there were only six thousand Roman Catholics in Alabama and Florida combined. For the discussion about the bishop's salary, see *Diocesan Convention* (1843), 12 and 14. The tendency of Episcopalians to prefer parish outreach to that of the diocese, and diocesan outreach to that of the denomination, may also help explain the fact that the educational endeavors most often associated with Episcopalians are private ("day") schools. For the most part, these are controlled at the parish level or controlled by boards that are responsible to a parish to some degree.

8. Woolverton goes on: "From their ranks he had come, to them he owed his exalted po-

244 / Notes to Pages 190–191

sition, and for their sakes he must labor. Henceforth, bishops were responsible first and fore-
most to their diocesan conventions. . . . The laity and the lower clergy were episcopally minded
enough to retain the traditional unitary power of central government in their General Convention. The word of that body became church law, binding on all those who voluntarily chose to
place themselves under its spiritual guidance. Episcopalians were able to do this because they
made sure that their convention remained general, i.e., representative of all orders in the church.
What is more, the laity and the lower clergy were thoroughly and powerfully represented by
voice and vote in a true convention, a meeting of free individuals in which legislation was initiated and then approved or disapproved. Bishops were given a special and 'higher' place where
they alone met to do the church's business, but that business was not theirs alone to perform.
They had to share sovereignty with clerical and lay deputies. Moreover, by a strange American
custom the unitary power of the General Convention was decentralized, placing authority for
month-to-month local church business in the hands of the servant-bishop and those to whom
he owed his election." *Colonial Anglicanism in North America* (Detroit: Wayne State University Press, 1984), 235.

9. The classic statement of late nineteenth- and early twentieth-century Anglican thought
is Arthur Michael Ramsey's *From Gore to Temple: The Development of Anglican Theology between* Lux Mundi *and the Second World War, 1889–1939* (London: Longmans, Green, 1960).
Ramsey remarks, "It is almost a commonplace that a theology of Incarnation prevailed in Anglican divinity from the last decade of the reign of Queen Victoria until well into the new century" (16). Although Hobart did not stress the incarnation, he may have laid the groundwork
for this theological shift in Anglicanism. The uniqueness and apostolic nature of the Episcopal
Church was central to Hobart's thought. "By losing sight of the church, evangelicals had also
lost sight of the power of the incarnation, and with it the belief in a universal humanity that had
been sanctified by Christ's partaking of its nature." Mullin, *Episcopal Vision*, 185. Furthermore,
Hobart certainly exercised a great deal of influence on the founders of the Oxford movement,
and in the context of the Oxford movement the Anglican incarnationalism flourished in the
later nineteenth and early twentieth centuries. For Hobart's influence on the Oxford movement, see Esther de Waal, "John Henry Hobart and the Early Oxford Movement," *Anglican
Theological Review* 65, no. 3 (July 1983): 324–31.

10. Hebrews 11.10 (RSV).

11. In his *Ancient English Ecclesiastical Architecture and Its Principles Applied to the Wants
of the Church at the Present Day* (New York: Stanford and Swords, 1850), Frank Wills believed
there was a "catholicity in Architecture as well as in the Church" that could be "separated from
Popery as well in one as in the other." In other words, he believed in a church architecture that
was *catholic* but not *Roman Catholic*. For Wills, "Christianity laid the broad foundations of its
lengthened aisles, bade arch soar above arch, and all point up to heaven; wrote the incompre-
hensible doctrine of the Trinity on its front, and taught the same awful mystery in every part
of the edifice; bids man when he crosses its threshold humble himself to the dust, and awed
into adoration, prostrate himself before his God." In other words, Wills says, a Christian will
understand that a church "owes its shape as well, as existence, to his creed" (9). Regarding Ralph
Adams Cram, Douglass Shand-Tucci wrote, "[Cram] argued that the Oxford Movement and
the Gothic Revival were each part of the 'same animating impulse,' assertions that laid the theo-
retical ground work of the last phase of the American Gothic Revival, a task Cram did well
enough." *Boston Bohemia, 1881–1900. Ralph Adams Cram: Life and Architecture* (Amherst: University of Massachusetts Press, 1995), 135.

Bibliography

Manuscript Collections

Alabama Department of Archives and History
Hanson, Francis, Diary.
Holy Comforter Episcopal Church, Montgomery, AL. Vestry minutes.

Archives of the Episcopal Church, Austin, TX
Letters from DFMS missionaries.
Minutes of the Freedmen's Commission.

Birmingham Public Library Archives
Allison, Elizabeth. "The Ministry of the Rev. J. Avery Shepherd in Montgomery, Alabama 1858–1865."
Beckwith, Charles Minnegerode, Papers.
Birmingham History.
Caldwell, Ronald. "A History of Saint Luke's Episcopal Church, Cahaba, Alabama." Unpublished manuscript. n.d.
Carpenter, Charles Colcock Jones, Papers.
Church of the Advent, Birmingham, AL. Vestry minutes.
Faunsdale Plantation. Papers.
Grace Episcopal Church (Woodlawn), Birmingham, AL. Vestry minutes.
Jackson, Henry Melville, Papers.
London, Edith Ward, Diary.
McDowell, William George, Papers.
St. John's (Ensley), Birmingham, AL. Vestry minutes.
St. Luke's Episcopal Church, Cahaba, AL. Vestry minutes.
Stough, Furman Charles, Papers.
Ward, George, Papers.

Franklin Delano Roosevelt Presidential Library, Hyde Park, NY
President's Personal Files.

*Southern Historical Collection, Wilson Library, University of North
Carolina–Chapel Hill*
Beckwith, John, Papers.
Lay, Henry C., Papers.
Otey, James Hervey, Papers.

W. S. Hoole Special Collections Library, University of Alabama.
Christ Episcopal Church, Tuscaloosa, AL. Vestry minutes.
Clark, E. Culpepper, Papers.

Special Collections, Samford University
Murphy, Edgar Gardner. "Address to the Society for Ethical Culture." March 20, 1904. MFS 821.

University of South Alabama Archives
Wilmer Hall manuscript

Other Manuscripts
Carpenter, Charles Colcock Jones, Papers. Private collection belonging to the Reverend Douglas Carpenter.
Christ Church Cathedral. Vestry minutes. Archives of Christ Church Cathedral, Mobile, AL.
Episcopal Church of the Nativity. Vestry minutes. Huntsville, AL.
Gamble, Edward, Papers. Private collection belonging to Harry Gamble, Esq. Selma, AL.
Grace Episcopal Church. Vestry minutes. Anniston, AL.
Grayson, C. C. "Pew 62." Archives of St. Paul's Episcopal Church, Selma, AL.
Gribbin, Emmet, Papers. Canterbury Chapel Archives, Tuscaloosa, AL.
History of the Henckell Family. Manuscript in possession of the Henckell family.
Holy Comforter Episcopal Church. Vestry minutes. Gadsden, AL.
Kennington, S. Albert. "A Short and Biased History of Beckwith Camp and Conference Center." Unpublished manuscript in possession of the Reverend S. Albert Kennington.
McPhillips, Julian. "Return Ye and Live" and "Thou Shalt Do No Murder." Sermons by Julian McPhillips in personal collection of Frank and Louise McPhillips, Birmingham, AL.
McPhillips, Julian, and Eleanor McPhillips, *The Drummers' Beat: Our Life and Times*, Unpublished manuscript in personal collection of Frank and Louise McPhillips, Birmingham, AL.
Noble, John, Papers. Anniston (AL) Public Library.
Oey, Thomas, and J. Barry Vaughn. "First American Woman Missionary to China: A Portrait of Emma G. Jones of Mobile, Alabama." Unpublished manuscript in author's possession.
Questionnaire sent to churches of the Diocese of Alabama. Archives of St. Paul's Episcopal Church, Selma, AL.
St. John's Episcopal Church. Charles Teed Pollard's statement. Montgomery, AL.
St. Mary's-on-the-Highlands Episcopal Church. Rector's papers. Birmingham, AL.
St. Michael and All Angels Episcopal Church, Anniston, AL. Church record book (1890–1948).
Willie, Yvonne. "My God, It's a Black Man." Unpublished manuscript.
Yon, William. *No Trumpets, No Drums.* Unpublished manuscript in possession of the Reverend William Yon, Birmingham, AL.

Books

Amos Doss, Harriet E. *Cotton City: Urban Development in Antebellum Mobile.* Tuscaloosa: University of Alabama Press, 1985.

Armentrout, Donald S., and Robert B. Slocum. *An Episcopal Dictionary: A User-Friendly Resource for Episcopalians.* New York: Church Publishing, 1990.

Bailey, Hugh. *Edgar Gardner Murphy: Gentle Progressive.* Miami: University of Miami Press, 1968.

Bankhead, Tallulah. *Tallulah: An Autobiography.* New York: Harper and Brothers, 1952.

Bass, S. Jonathan. *Blessed Are the Peacemakers: Martin Luther King, Jr., Eight White Religious Leaders, and the "Letter from Birmingham Jail."* Knoxville: University of Tennessee Press, 1996.

Boles, John B. *The Great Revival, 1787–1805.* Lexington: University Press of Kentucky, 1972

Bolton, S. Charles. *Southern Anglicanism: The Church of England in Colonial South Carolina.* Westport, CT: Greenwood Press, 1982.

Branch, Taylor. *At Canaan's Edge: America in the King Years, 1965–68.* New York: Simon and Schuster, 2006.

Bridenbaugh, Carl. *Mitre and Sceptre: Transatlantic Faiths, Ideas, Personalities, and Politics.* New York: Oxford University Press, 1962.

Buckingham, James S. *The Slave States of America.* Vol. 2. London: Fisher, Son, 1849.

Bushman, Claudia L. *"A Good Poor Man's Wife": Being a Chronicle of Harriet Hanson Robinson and Her Family in Nineteenth-Century New England.* Hanover, NH: University Press of New England, 1981.

Bushman, Richard. *The Refinement of America: Persons, Houses, Cities.* New York: Alfred A. Knopf, 1992.

Campbell, Will. *And Also with You: Duncan Gray and the American Dilemma.* Franklin, TN: Providence House Publishing, 1997.

Carter, Dan T. *Scottsboro: A Tragedy of the American South.* Baton Rouge: Louisiana State University Press, 1969.

Cheshire, Joseph Blount. *The Church in the Confederate States: A History of the Protestant Episcopal Church in the Confederate States.* New York: Longmans, Green, 1912.

Chitty, Arthur Ben. *Reconstruction at Sewanee: The Founding of the University of the South and Its First Administration, 1857–1872.* Sewanee, TN: University Press, 1954.

Clarke, Erskine. *Dwelling Place: A Plantation Epic.* New Haven, CT: Yale University Press, 2005.

Clay-Clopton, Virginia. *A Belle of the Fifties: Memoirs of Mrs. Clay of Alabama, Covering Social and Political Life in Washington and the South, 1853–66.* Tuscaloosa: University of Alabama Press, 1999.

Cumming, Kate. *Gleanings from Southland: Sketches of Life and Manners of the People of the South before, during, and after the War of Secession, with Extracts from the Author's Journal and Epitome of the New South.* Birmingham, AL: Roberts and Son, 1895.

———. *Kate: The Journal of a Confederate Nurse.* Edited by Richard Barksdale Harwell. Baton Rouge: Louisiana State University Press, 1959.

Curzon, Grace Elvina Trillia Hinds, Marchioness. *Reminiscences.* New York: Coward-McCann, 1955.

Dodd, William. *The Cotton Kingdom: A Chronicle of the Old South.* New Haven, CT: Yale University Press, 1919.

Du Bois, W. E. B. *The Negro Church*. Atlanta: Atlanta University Press, 1903.

DuBose, John Witherspoon. *Jefferson County and Birmingham, Alabama*. Birmingham, AL: Teeple and Smith Publishers, 1887.

Eagles, Charles W. *Outside Agitator: Jon Daniels and the Civil Rights Movement in Alabama*. Chapel Hill: University of North Carolina Press, 1993.

Edmonds, Henry Morris. *A Parson's Notebook*. Birmingham, AL: Elizabeth Agee's Bookshelf, 1961.

Fallin, Wilson. *Uplifting the People: Three Centuries of Black Baptists in Alabama*. Tuscaloosa: University of Alabama Press, 2007.

Finke, Roger, and Rodney Stark. *The Churching of America, 1776–2005: Winners and Losers in Our Religious Economy*. New Brunswick, NJ: Rutgers University Press, 2005.

Flynt, Wayne. "Alabama." In *The Encyclopedia of Religion in the South*, edited by Samuel S. Hill. Macon, GA: Mercer University Press, 1984.

——. *Alabama Baptists: Southern Baptists in the Heart of Dixie*. Tuscaloosa: University of Alabama Press, 1998.

——. *Alabama in the Twentieth Century*. Tuscaloosa: University of Alabama Press, 2004.

——. *Poor but Proud: Alabama's Poor White*. Tuscaloosa: University of Alabama Press, 1989.

Friedland, Michael B. *Lift Up Your Voice Like a Trumpet: White Clergy and the Civil Rights and Antiwar Movements, 1954–1973*. Chapel Hill: University of North Carolina Press, 1998.

Garrow, David J. *Bearing the Cross: Martin Luther King, Jr., and the Southern Christian Leadership Conference*. New York: Vintage Books, 1988.

Gates, Grace Hooten. *The Model City of the New South: Anniston, Alabama, 1872–1900*. Huntsville, AL: Stroke Publishers, 1978.

Going, Allen J. *Bourbon Democracy in Alabama, 1875–1890*. University: University of Alabama Press, 1951.

Gosse, Philip Henry. *Letters from Alabama, Chiefly Relating to Natural History*. Mountain Brook, AL: Overbrook House, 1983.

Graves, John Temple. *The Fighting South*. Tuscaloosa: University of Alabama Press, 1985.

Greene, Jack P. *Pursuits of Happiness: The Social Development of Early Modern British Colonies and the Formation of American Culture*. Chapel Hill: University of North Carolina Press, 1988.

Hamilton, Peter J. *Colonial Mobile*. Edited by Charles Summersell. Tuscaloosa: University of Alabama Press, 1976.

Hammett, Hugh B. *Hilary Abner Herberg: A Southerner Returns to the Union*. Philadelphia: American Philosophical Society, 1976.

Harris, Carl V. *Political Power in Birmingham, 1871–1921*. Knoxville: The University of Tennessee Press, 1977.

Herbert, Hilary A., et al. *Why the Solid South? Or, Reconstruction and Its Results*. Baltimore: R. H. Woodward, 1890.

Holder, Timothy, ed. *The Hip Hop Prayer Book*. New York: Church Publishing, 2006.

Holmes, David. *A Brief History of the Episcopal Church*. Harrisburg, PA: Trinity Press International, 1993.

Journal of the Congress of the Confederate States of America, 1861–1865. Washington, DC: Government Printing Office, 1904–05.

Journal of the Constitutional Convention of the State of Alabama, Assembled in the City of Montgomery, September 6th, 1875. Montgomery, AL: W. W. Screws, 1875.

Journal of the Proceedings of the Convention of the State of Alabama, Held in the City of

Montgomery, on Tuesday, September 12, 1865. Montgomery, AL: Gibson and Whitfield, 1865.

Kennington, S. Albert. *From the Day of Small Things.* Mobile, AL: Factor Press, 1996.

Kesselus, Kenneth. *John E. Hines: Granite on Fire.* Austin, TX: Episcopal Seminary of the Southwest, 1995.

Kilde, Jeanne H. *When Church Became Theatre: The Transformation of Evangelical Architecture and Worship in Nineteenth-Century America.* Oxford: Oxford University Press, 2002.

King, Martin Luther, Jr. *Letter from Birmingham Jail.* Birmingham History Collection, 1940–1980, Birmingham Public Library archives.

Konolige, Kit, and Frederica Konolige. *The Power of Their Glory: America's Ruling Class, the Episcopalians.* New York: Wyden Books, 1978.

LaMonte, Edward Shannon. *Politics and Welfare in Birmingham, 1900–1975.* Tuscaloosa: University of Alabama Press, 1995.

Long, Campbell. *The House of Happiness Story.* Selma, AL: Selma Publishing, 1973.

Luker, Ralph. *A Southern Tradition in Theology and Social Criticism, 1830–1930: The Religious Liberalism and Social Conservatism of James Warley Miles, William Porcher Dubose, and Edgar Gardner Murphy.* New York: Edwin Mellen Press, 1984.

Lyell, Charles, Sir. *A Second Visit to the United States of North America.* Vol. 2. London: John Murray, 1849.

Mackay, Alexander. *The Western World; or, Travels in the United States in 1846–47: Exhibiting Them in Their Latest Development, Social, Political, and Industrial; Includes a Chapter on California.* London: Richard Bentley, 1849.

McMillan, Malcolm C. *The Alabama Confederate Reader.* Tuscaloosa: University of Alabama Press, 1963.

———. *Constitutional Development in Alabama, 1798–1901: A Study in Politics, the Negro, and Sectionalism.* Chapel Hill: University of North Carolina Press, 1955.

McPhillips, Julian. *History of Christ the Redeemer Episcopal Church.* Montgomery, AL: New South Books, 2006.

Miller, Randall M. "Roman Catholic Church in the South." In *Encyclopedia of Religion in the South.* Edited by Samuel S. Hill. Macon, GA: Mercer University Press, 1984.

Morgan, Charles, Jr. *A Time to Speak.* New York: Holt, Rinehart, and Winston, 1964.

Mullin, Robert Bruce. *Episcopal Vision/American Reality: High Church Theology and Social Thought in Evangelical America.* New Haven, CT: Yale University Press, 1986.

———. "Finding a Voice, Defining a Space: John Henry Hobart and the Americanization of Anglicanism." In *One Lord, One Faith, One Baptism: Studies in Christian Ecclesiality and Ecumenism in Honor of J. Robert Wright,* edited by Marsha L. Dutton and Patrick Terrell Gray, 129–43. Grand Rapids, MI: Eerdmans Publishing, 2006.

Neuman, Nancy M. *A Voice of Our Own: Leading American Women Celebrate the Right to Vote.* San Francisco: Jossey-Bass, 1996.

Noll, Mark. *A History of Christianity in the United States and Canada.* Grand Rapids, MI: Eerdmans Publishing, 1992.

Norrell, Robert J. *Up from History: The Life of Booker T. Washington.* Cambridge, MA: Belknap Press of Harvard University Press, 2009.

Official Proceedings of the 1902 Constitutional Convention of the State of Alabama, May 21st, 1901 to September 3d, 1901. Montgomery, AL: Brown Printing, 1901.

Owen, Thomas McAdory, and Marie Bankhead Owen. *History of Alabama and Dictionary of Alabama Biography.* Chicago: S. J. Clarke Publishing, 1921.

Palmer, Sara. *Dad Hall: "Bishop of Wall Street."* Chicago: Moody Press, 1954.

Percy, Walker. *Love in the Ruins: The Adventures of a Bad Catholic at a Time Near the End of the World.* New York: Farrar, Straus and Giroux, 1971.

Proceedings of an Adjourned Meeting of Bishops, Clergymen, and Laymen, of the Protestant Episcopal Church in the Confederate States of America, Held in Christ Church, Columbia, South Carolina from Oct. 16th to Oct. 24th, Inclusive in the Year of Our Lord 1861. Montgomery, AL: *Montgomery Advertiser,* 1861.

Proceedings of a Meeting of Bishops, Clergymen, and Laymen, of the Protestant Episcopal Church in the Confederate States, at Montgomery, Alabama On the 3d, 4th, 5th & 6th of July, 1861. Montgomery, AL: Barrett, Wimbish, 1861.

Pulszky, Francis, and Theresa Pulszky. *White, Red, and Black: Sketches of Society in the United States during the Visit of Their Guest.* Vol. 3. London: Trübner, 1853.

Ramsey, Arthur Michael. *From Gore to Temple: The Development of Anglican Theology between Lux Mundi and the Second World War, 1889–1939.* London: Longmans, Green, 1960.

Rankin, Richard. *Ambivalent Churchmen and Evangelical Churchwomen: The Religion of the Episcopal Elite in North Carolina, 1800–1860.* Columbia: University of South Carolina Press, 1993.

Rhoden, Nancy L. *Revolutionary Anglicanism: The Colonial Church of England Clergy during the American Revolution.* New York: New York University Press, 1999.

Roberts, Frances. *Sesquicentennial History of Church of the Nativity, Episcopal, 1843–1993.* Huntsville, AL: Episcopal Church of the Nativity, 1992.

Robinson, Jo Ann Gibson. *The Montgomery Bus Boycott and the Women Who Started It.* Knoxville: University of Tennessee Press, 1987.

Rogers, William W., Robert D. Ward, Leah R. Atkins, and Wayne Flynt. *Alabama: The History of a Deep South State.* Tuscaloosa: University of Alabama Press, 1994.

Roof, Wade Clark, and William McKinney. *American Mainline Religion: Its Changing Shape and Future.* New Brunswick, NJ: Rutgers University Press, 1987.

Royall, Anne Newport. *Letters from Alabama, 1817–1822.* Biographical introduction and notes by Lucille Griffith. Tuscaloosa: University of Alabama Press, 1969.

Russell, William Howard. *My Diary, North and South.* Edited by Eugene H. Berwanger. New York: Alfred A. Knopf, 1988.

Schnorrenberg, Barbara Brandon. *Grace to Worship... Grace to Serve... Grace to Grow: Grace Episcopal Church, Woodlawn, 1889–2002.* Birmingham: Grace Episcopal Church, 2002.

———. "Our Oldest and Best Organization: The Alabama Woman's Auxiliary, 1920–1940." In *Deeper Joy: Lay Women and Vocation in the 20th Century Episcopal Church,* edited by Frederica Harris Thompsett and Sheryl Kujawa-Holbrook. New York: Church Publishing, 2005.

———. *Things Faithfully Asked and Effectively Obtained: A History of St. Andrew's Parish, Birmingham, Alabama.* Birmingham: St. Andrew's Episcopal Church, 1993.

Shand-Tucci, Douglass. *Boston Bohemia, 1881–1900. Ralph Adams Cram: Life and Architecture.* Amherst: University of Massachusetts Press, 1995.

Shattuck, Gardiner. *Episcopalians and Race: From Civil War to Civil Rights.* Lexington: University Press of Kentucky, 2000.

———. "'The Tradition Club': Culture War, Memory, and the Reinvention of Anglican Identity in the Modern South." In *Religion in the Contemporary South: Changes, Continuities, and Contexts,* edited by Corrie E. Norman and Don S. Armentrout. Knoxville: University of Tennessee Press, 2005.

Smith, Gary Scott. *Faith and the Presidency: From George Washington to George W. Bush.* Oxford: Oxford University Press, 2006.

Stoney, James M. *Lighting the Candle.* Santa Fe, NM: Rydal Press, 1961.

Strode, Hudson. *The Eleventh House: Memoirs.* New York: Harcourt, Brace, Jovanovich, 1975.

Summe, Sheryl Spradling. "'Alive to the Cause of Justice': Juliette Hampton Morgan and the Montgomery Bus Boycott." In *Stepping Out of the Shadows: Alabama Women, 1819–1990,* edited by Mary Martha Thomas. Tuscaloosa: University of Alabama Press, 1995.

Thomason, Michael V. R., ed. *Mobile: The New History of Alabama's First City.* Tuscaloosa: University of Alabama Press, 2001.

Thornton, J. Mills. *Dividing Lines: Municipal Politics and the Struggle for Civil Rights in Montgomery, Birmingham, and Selma.* Tuscaloosa: University of Alabama Press, 2002.

Touchstone, Blake. "Planters and Slave Religion in the Deep South." In *Masters and Slaves in the House of the Lord: Race and Religion in the American South, 1740–1870,* edited by John Boles. Lexington: University Press of Kentucky, 1988.

Tucker, Louis. *Clerical Errors.* New York: Harper and Brothers, 1943.

Walker, Henry J. *Let Us Keep the Feast: The History of Christ Episcopal Church, Tuscaloosa, Alabama, 1828–1998.* Tallahassee, FL: Sentry Press, 2000.

Webb, Samuel L., and Margaret E. Armbrester. *Alabama Governors: A Political History of the State.* Tuscaloosa: University of Alabama Press, 2001.

Weis, Frederick Lewis. *The Colonial Clergy of Virginia, North Carolina, and South Carolina.* Baltimore: Genealogical Publishing, 1976.

Whitaker, Walter C. *History of the Protestant Episcopal Church in Alabama, 1763–1891.* Birmingham, AL: Roberts and Sons, 1898.

———. *Richard Hooker Wilmer, Second Bishop of Alabama: A Biography.* Philadelphia: George W. Jacobs, 1907.

White, Greenough. *A Saint of the Southern Church: Memoir of the Right Reverend Nicholas Hamner Cobbs.* New York: Thomas Whittaker, 1900.

Whiting, Marvin Yeomans. "James R. Powell and 'This Magic Little City of Ours': A Perspective on Local History." In *The Journal of the Birmingham Historical Society: An Anthology Honoring Marvin Yeomans Whiting,* edited by James L. Baggett. Birmingham, AL: Birmingham Public Library and the Birmingham Historical Society, 2000.

Wiener, Jonathan M. "Bourbons." In *The Encyclopedia of Southern History,* edited by David C. Roller and Robert W. Twyman. Baton Rouge: Louisiana State University Press, 1979.

———. "Redeemers." In *The Encyclopedia of Southern History,* edited by David C. Roller and Robert W. Twyman. Baton Rouge: Louisiana State University Press, 1979.

Williamson, Samuel R., Jr.. *Sewanee Sesquicentennial History: The Making of the University of the South.* Sewanee, TN: University Press, 2008.

Willoughby, Lynn. *The Church of the Ascension: A Resurrection Story.* Montgomery, AL: Donnell Group, 2008.

Wills, Frank. *Ancient English Ecclesiastical Architecture and Its Principles Applied to the Wants of the Church at the Present Day.* New York: Stanford and Swords, 1850.

Wilmer, Richard Hooker. *The Recent Past from a Southern Standpoint: Reminiscences of a Grandfather.* New York: Thomas Whittaker, 1887.

Wilson, Charles Reagan. *Baptized in Blood: The Religion of the Lost Cause, 1865–1920.* Athens: University of Georgia Press, 1980.

Wood, Mattie Pegues. *The Life of St. John's Parish: A History of St. John's Episcopal Church from 1834 to 1955.* Montgomery, AL: Paragon Press, 1955.

Woolverton, John F. *Colonial Anglicanism in North America*. Detroit: Wayne State University Press, 1984.

Wyeth, John Allan. *With Sabre and Scalpel: The Autobiography of a Soldier and Surgeon*. New York: Harper and Brothers, 1914.

Journal and Magazine Articles

Atkins, Leah Rawls. "Feuds, Factions, and Reform: Politics in Early Birmingham." *Alabama Heritage* (Summer 1986).

Bass, S. Jonathan. "Bishop C. C. J. Carpenter: From Segregation to Integration." *Alabama Review* 45, no. 3 (1992): 184–215.

Beardsley, William A. "Bishop Thomas C. Brownell's Journal of His Missionary Tours, 1829 and 1834." HMPEC 7, no. 4 (1938): 316–.

Bigelow, Martha Mitchell. "Birmingham's Carnival of Crime." *Alabama Review* (April 1950): 123–33.

Boykin, Frank. "Statement." *Congressional Record*, March 29, 1959.

Brown, Lawrence. "1835 and All That: Domestic and Foreign Missionary Society and the Missionary Spirit." HMPEC 40, no. 4 (1971): 399–405.

Cook, Thomas A. "Report." *The Spirit of Missions* 1, no. 1 (1836): 238.

De Waal, Esther. "John Henry Hobart and the Early Oxford Movement." *Anglican Theological Review* 65, no. 3 (1983): 324–31.

Doss, Harriet E. "Religious Reconstruction in Microcosm at Faunsdale Plantation." *Alabama Review* 42, no. 4 (1989): 243–69.

Harris, W. A. "Report." *The Spirit of Missions* (April 1836): 107.

Holzhammer, Robert E. "The Domestic and Foreign Missionary Society: The Period of Expansion and Development." HMPEC 40, no. 4 (1971): 367–97.

———. "The Formation of the Domestic and Foreign Missionary Society." HMPEC 40, no. 3 (971): 257–72.

Luker, Ralph. "Liberal Theology and Social Conservatism: A Southern Tradition, 1840–1920." *Church History* 50, no. 2 (1981): 193–204.

Moore, James Tice. "Redeemers Reconsidered: Change and Continuity in the Democratic South, 1870–1900." *Journal of Southern History* 44, no. 3 (1978): 357–78.

Munroe, Kirk. "The Industrial South." *Harper's Weekly* 31, no. 1579 Supplement (1887): 213 and 223.

Polk, Leonidas. "Arkansas, Louisiana, Mississippi, and Alabama: From the Right Rev. Leonidas Polk, D.D., Missionary Bishop of Arkansas, and Having Provisional Charge of the Dioceses of Louisiana, Mississippi and Alabama." *The Spirit of Missions* 4 (1839): 306–14.

Reimers, David M. "Negro Bishops and Diocesan Segregation in the Protestant Episcopal Church: 1870–1954. HMPEC 31, no. 3 (1962): 231–42.

Schnorrenberg, Barbara Brandon. "The Best School for Blacks in the State: St. Mark's Academic and Industrial School, Birmingham, Alabama, 1892–1940." AEH 71, no. 4 (2002): 519–49.

———. "Set Apart: Alabama Deaconesses, 1864–1915." AEH 63, no. 4 (1994): 468–90.

Shanks, Henry T. "The Reunion of the Episcopal Church, 1865." *Church History* 9, no. 2 (1940): 120–40.

Stoker, Kevin. "From Prohibitionist to New Deal Liberal: The Political Evolution of Colonel Harry Mell Ayers of the Anniston Star." *Alabama Review* 62, no. 4 (2009): 262–96.

Warner, Greg. "SBC Warned on Veering Further Right." *The Christian Century* 121, no. 4 (2004): 10–11.

Newspaper Articles

NEW YORK TIMES
"Absolved in Gay Ordination." May 19, 1996.
"Activity of Klan Rises in Alabama." September 29, 1959.
"Alabama Police Use Gas and Clubs to Rout Negroes." March 8, 1965.
"Alabama Segregation Pushed." March 24, 1955.
"Bishop C. M. Beckwith of Alabama Is Dead." April 19, 1928.
"Bishop Moore Ordains a Lesbian as Priest in the Episcopal Church." January 11, 1977.
"Consecration of Two Splits Anglicans." March 5, 2000.
"Dioceses Are at Odds." October 23, 1903.
"Episcopal Bishops Are Divided on Issues Involving Homosexuality." October 4, 1977.
"The Episcopal Convention: Division of the Diocese of Pennsylvania." October 13, 1865.
"Episcopal Convention: Proceedings of the Second Day." September 29, 1864.
"Episcopalians Approve Rite to Bless Same Sex Unions." July 10, 2012.
"Gay Bishop Wins in Episcopal Vote; Split Threatened." August 6, 2003.
"Graham Deplores Alabama Bus Riot." May 18, 1961.
Hunt, Gaillard. "Story of a Great Southern Bishop." January 25, 1908.
"Judge's Ouster Sought after Antigay Remarks." February 20, 2002.
"Miss Mitchell, 49, Dead of Injuries." August 17, 1949.
"Negro Education in South on Rise." March 16, 1952.
"Negro Gain Slow in Winning Vote." November 24, 1963.
"Psychiatric Work by Clergy urged." October 20, 1955.
"Troops Will Guard Negro in Alabama." July 23, 1929.

OTHER NEWSPAPERS
"Bishop Stough's Nomination Part of 'Firsts' at Episcopal Convention." *Birmingham News*, September 6, 1985.
"Bishop Wilmer Died Yesterday." *Montgomery Advertiser*, June 15, 1900.
"Break-Off Church Joins Anglican Group." *Birmingham News*, November 24, 2002.
"Carpenter's Statement on Sit-In Paper Rapped." *Mobile Press-Register*, April 1, 1960.
"Christ Church Leaders Consider Split with the Episcopal Church." *Mobile Press-Register*, September 27, 2000.
"Christ Church Splits with Episcopal Church." *Mobile Press-Register*, October 2, 2000.
"Church of Advent Named Cathedral in Ceremonies." *Birmingham Post-Herald*, February 13, 1982.
"City, County, and State Officers Keep Order during Dexter Demonstration." *Montgomery Advertiser*, March 7, 1960.
Falkenberry, Roswell. "Our Considered Opinion." *Selma Times Journal*, March 14, 1965.
"Fascination Drew Him to Church." *Birmingham Post-Herald*, July 27, 1985.
"Holy Comforter Church History Recalled on Anniversary." *Gadsden Times*, July 24, 1938.
"A House Divided: Why Episcopalians Leave." *Mobile Press-Register*, October 25, 2000.
"Local Church Leader Protests Gay Bishop." *Birmingham News*, August 7, 2003.
Obituary for Richard Hooker Wilmer. *Atlanta Constitution*, June 15, 1900.
"Open Forum Meeting Undisturbed by KKK." *Tuscaloosa News*, May 14, 1957.

"Robed Klansmen Picket Forum." *Birmingham Post-Herald*, May 10, 1957.
Sullivan, Patricia. "Charles Morgan Jr.; Lawyer Championed Civil, Voting Rights," *Washington Post*, January 9, 2009.
"Theologians Spar over Gay Role in Episcopal Church." *Birmingham News*, February 6, 2004.
"Zahl Bids Goodbye at Advent." *Birmingham News*, August 1, 2004.

Dissertations

Clemens, Sue. "The House of Happiness: An Episcopal Mission in Jackson County, Alabama, 1923-1952." Master's thesis, University of Southern Mississippi, 1990.
Mitchell, Martha Carolyn. "Birmingham: Biography of a City of the New South." PhD diss., University of Chicago, 1946.
Montgomery, Brandt. "Time's Prisoner: The Right Reverend Charles Colcock Jones Carpenter and the Civil Rights Movement in the Episcopal Diocese of Alabama". Unpub. MDiv thesis. General Theological Seminary, New York, 2012
Selman, John Irvin. "William Lowndes Yancey, Alabama Fire-eater." PhD diss., Mississippi State University, 1997.

Online Resources

"Letter from Edgar Gardner Murphy to Booker T. Washington, Oct. 24, 1901," http://www.historycooperative.org/btw/.

Interviews

McLeod, Mary Adelia. Notes of telephone interview conducted by author on deposit in the BPL Archives.
Walter, Francis. Recording of interview conducted by author on deposit in the BPL Archives.

Other Resources

Alabama Churchman
The Apostle
Journals of the Diocese of Alabama
Journals of the Diocese of the Central Gulf Coast
Journals of the General Convention of the Episcopal Church in the United States of America
The Spirit of Missions

Index